Treaty Series

Treaties and international agreements registered or filed and recorded with the Secretariat of the United Nations

VOLUME 3061

Recueil des Traités

Traités et accords internationaux enregistrés ou classés et inscrits au répertoire au Secrétariat de l'Organisation des Nations Unies

United Nations • Nations Unies
New York, 2023

Print ISBN: 978-92-1-970038-3
e-ISBN: 978-92-1-001305-5
ISSN: 0379-8267
e-ISSN: 2412-1495

TABLE OF CONTENTS

I

Treaties and international agreements registered in August 2015 Nos. 52825 to 52855

TABLE DES MATIÈRES

I

Traités et accords internationaux enregistrés en août 2015
N°s 52825 à 52855

NOTE BY THE SECRETARIAT

Under Article 102 of the Charter of the United Nations, every treaty and every international agreement entered into by any Member of the United Nations after the coming into force of the Charter shall, as soon as possible, be registered with the Secretariat and published by it. Furthermore, no party to a treaty or international agreement subject to registration which has not been registered may invoke that treaty or agreement before any organ of the United Nations. The General Assembly, by resolution 97 (I), established regulations to give effect to Article 102 of the Charter (see text of the regulations, vol. 859, p. VIII; https://treaties.un.org/Pages/Resource.aspx?path=Publication/Regulation/Page1_en.xml).

The terms "treaty" and "international agreement" have not been defined either in the Charter or in the regulations, and the Secretariat follows the principle that it acts in accordance with the position of the Member State submitting an instrument for registration that, so far as that party is concerned, the instrument is a treaty or an international agreement within the meaning of Article 102. Registration of an instrument submitted by a Member State, therefore, does not imply a judgement by the Secretariat on the nature of the instrument, the status of a party or any similar question. It is the understanding of the Secretariat that its acceptance for registration of an instrument does not confer on the instrument the status of a treaty or an international agreement if it does not already have that status, and does not confer upon a party a status which it would not otherwise have.

*

* *

Disclaimer: All authentic texts in the present Series are published as submitted for registration by a party to the instrument. Unless otherwise indicated, the translations of these texts have been made by the Secretariat of the United Nations, for information.

NOTE DU SECRÉTARIAT

Aux termes de l'Article 102 de la Charte des Nations Unies, tout traité ou accord international conclu par un Membre des Nations Unies après l'entrée en vigueur de la Charte sera, le plus tôt possible, enregistré au Secrétariat et publié par lui. De plus, aucune partie à un traité ou accord international qui aurait dû être enregistré mais ne l'a pas été ne pourra invoquer ledit traité ou accord devant un organe de l'Organisation des Nations Unies. Par sa résolution 97 (I), l'Assemblée générale a adopté un règlement destiné à mettre en application l'Article 102 de la Charte (voir texte du règlement, vol. 859, p. IX; https://treaties.un.org/Pages/Resource.aspx?path=Publication/Regulation/Page1_fr.xml).

Les termes « traité » et « accord international » n'ont été définis ni dans la Charte ni dans le règlement, et le Secrétariat a pris comme principe de s'en tenir à la position adoptée à cet égard par l'État Membre qui a présenté l'instrument à l'enregistrement, à savoir que, en ce qui concerne cette partie, l'instrument constitue un traité ou un accord international au sens de l'Article 102. Il s'ensuit que l'enregistrement d'un instrument présenté par un État Membre n'implique, de la part du Secrétariat, aucun jugement sur la nature de l'instrument, le statut d'une partie ou toute autre question similaire. Le Secrétariat considère donc que son acceptation pour enregistrement d'un instrument ne confère pas audit instrument la qualité de traité ou d'accord international si ce dernier ne l'a pas déjà, et qu'il ne confère pas à une partie un statut que, par ailleurs, elle ne posséderait pas.

*

* *

Déni de responsabilité : Tous les textes authentiques du présent Recueil sont publiés tels qu'ils ont été soumis pour enregistrement par l'une des parties à l'instrument. Sauf indication contraire, les traductions de ces textes ont été établies par le Secrétariat de l'Organisation des Nations Unies, à titre d'information.

I

Treaties and international agreements

registered in

August 2015

Nos. 52825 to 52855

Traités et accords internationaux

enregistrés en

août 2015

N°s 52825 à 52855

No. 52825

Germany and Malawi

Agreement between the Government of the Federal Republic of Germany and the Government of the Republic of Malawi concerning Financial Cooperation in 2014. Lilongwe, 17 April 2015

Entry into force: *17 April 2015 by signature, in accordance with article 6*

Authentic texts: *English and German*

Registration with the Secretariat of the United Nations: *Germany, 12 August 2015*

Not published in print, in accordance with article 12(2) of the General Assembly regulations to give effect to Article 102 of the Charter of the United Nations, as amended, and the publication practice of the Secretariat.

Allemagne et Malawi

Accord entre le Gouvernement de la République fédérale d'Allemagne et le Gouvernement de la République du Malawi concernant la coopération financière en 2014. Lilongwe, 17 avril 2015

Entrée en vigueur : *17 avril 2015 par signature, conformément à l'article 6*

Textes authentiques : *anglais et allemand*

Enregistrement auprès du Secrétariat de l'Organisation des Nations Unies : *Allemagne, 12 août 2015*

Non disponible en version imprimée, conformément au paragraphe 2 de l'article 12 du règlement de l'Assemblée générale destiné à mettre en application l'Article 102 de la Charte des Nations Unies, tel qu'amendé, et à la pratique du Secrétariat en matière de publication.

No. 52826

Germany and Kenya

Agreement between the Government of the Federal Republic of Germany and the Government of the Republic of Kenya concerning Financial Cooperation in 2013. Nairobi, 26 February 2015

Entry into force: *26 February 2015 by signature, in accordance with article 6*

Authentic texts: *English and German*

Registration with the Secretariat of the United Nations: *Germany, 12 August 2015*

Not published in print, in accordance with article 12(2) of the General Assembly regulations to give effect to Article 102 of the Charter of the United Nations, as amended, and the publication practice of the Secretariat.

Allemagne et Kenya

Accord entre le Gouvernement de la République fédérale d'Allemagne et le Gouvernement de la République du Kenya concernant la coopération financière en 2013. Nairobi, 26 février 2015

Entrée en vigueur : *26 février 2015 par signature, conformément à l'article 6*

Textes authentiques : *anglais et allemand*

Enregistrement auprès du Secrétariat de l'Organisation des Nations Unies : *Allemagne, 12 août 2015*

Non disponible en version imprimée, conformément au paragraphe 2 de l'article 12 du règlement de l'Assemblée générale destiné à mettre en application l'Article 102 de la Charte des Nations Unies, tel qu'amendé, et à la pratique du Secrétariat en matière de publication.

No. 52827

Germany
and
Rwanda

Agreement between the Government of the Federal Republic of Germany and the Government of the Republic of Rwanda concerning Financial Cooperation in 2014. Kigali, 12 June 2015

Entry into force: *12 June 2015 by signature, in accordance with article 5*

Authentic texts: *English and German*

Registration with the Secretariat of the United Nations: *Germany, 12 August 2015*

Not published in print, in accordance with article 12(2) of the General Assembly regulations to give effect to Article 102 of the Charter of the United Nations, as amended, and the publication practice of the Secretariat.

Allemagne
et
Rwanda

Accord entre le Gouvernement de la République fédérale d'Allemagne et le Gouvernement de la République du Rwanda concernant la coopération financière en 2014. Kigali, 12 juin 2015

Entrée en vigueur : *12 juin 2015 par signature, conformément à l'article 5*

Textes authentiques : *anglais et allemand*

Enregistrement auprès du Secrétariat de l'Organisation des Nations Unies : *Allemagne, 12 août 2015*

Non disponible en version imprimée, conformément au paragraphe 2 de l'article 12 du règlement de l'Assemblée générale destiné à mettre en application l'Article 102 de la Charte des Nations Unies, tel qu'amendé, et à la pratique du Secrétariat en matière de publication.

No. 52828

Germany and Namibia

Agreement between the Government of the Federal Republic of Germany and the Government of the Republic of Namibia concerning Financial Cooperation (Project: Programme for Renewable Energy and Energy Efficiency). Windhoek, 25 June 2015

Entry into force: *25 June 2015 by signature, in accordance with article 4*

Authentic texts: *English and German*

Registration with the Secretariat of the United Nations: *Germany, 12 August 2015*

Not published in print, in accordance with article 12(2) of the General Assembly regulations to give effect to Article 102 of the Charter of the United Nations, as amended, and the publication practice of the Secretariat.

Allemagne et Namibie

Accord entre le Gouvernement de la République fédérale d'Allemagne et le Gouvernement de la République de Namibie concernant la coopération financière (Projet : Programme pour l'énergie renouvelable et l'efficacité énergétique). Windhoek, 25 juin 2015

Entrée en vigueur : *25 juin 2015 par signature, conformément à l'article 4*

Textes authentiques : *anglais et allemand*

Enregistrement auprès du Secrétariat de l'Organisation des Nations Unies : *Allemagne, 12 août 2015*

Non disponible en version imprimée, conformément au paragraphe 2 de l'article 12 du règlement de l'Assemblée générale destiné à mettre en application l'Article 102 de la Charte des Nations Unies, tel qu'amendé, et à la pratique du Secrétariat en matière de publication.

No. 52829

Mexico
and
Cuba

Treaty between the United Mexican States and the Republic of Cuba on extradition. Mexico City, 1 November 2013

Entry into force: *29 April 2015, in accordance with article 23*

Authentic text: *Spanish*

Registration with the Secretariat of the United Nations: *Mexico, 5 August 2015*

Mexique
et
Cuba

Traité d'extradition entre les États-Unis du Mexique et la République de Cuba. Mexico, 1er novembre 2013

Entrée en vigueur : *29 avril 2015, conformément à l'article 23*

Texte authentique : *espagnol*

Enregistrement auprès du Secrétariat de l'Organisation des Nations Unies : *Mexique, 5 août 2015*

[SPANISH TEXT – TEXTE ESPAGNOL]

TRATADO ENTRE LOS ESTADOS UNIDOS MEXICANOS Y LA REPÚBLICA DE CUBA SOBRE EXTRADICIÓN

Los Estados Unidos Mexicanos y la República de Cuba, en adelante denominados "las Partes";

RECONOCIENDO su profundo interés en combatir la delincuencia y la impunidad de sus actores;

ANIMADAS por el deseo de mejorar la eficacia de la cooperación entre ambos países en la prevención y represión del delito;

Han acordado lo siguiente:

ARTÍCULO 1
OBLIGACIÓN DE EXTRADITAR

Las Partes se comprometen a entregarse recíprocamente en extradición, conforme a las disposiciones del presente Tratado, a aquellas personas respecto de las cuales se haya iniciado un proceso penal o sean requeridas para la imposición o ejecución de una sentencia o condena.

ARTÍCULO 2
DELITOS QUE DARÁN LUGAR A LA EXTRADICIÓN

1.- La extradición será procedente cuando la solicitud se refiera a conductas delictivas dolosas o culposas que se encuentren previstas en la legislación nacional de ambas Partes y constituyan un delito sancionado con pena privativa de libertad cuyo término mínimo no sea menor de un (1) año.

2.- Cuando la solicitud de extradición se realice para el cumplimiento de una sentencia firme, el período de la pena privativa de la libertad que le reste por cumplir al reclamado deberá ser de seis (6) meses cuando menos.

3.- Para los efectos del presente Artículo, no importará si la legislación nacional de las Partes denominan a la conducta delictuosa con diferente terminología, siempre que no varíen los hechos que integran los elementos del tipo delictivo.

4.- Si la solicitud de extradición se refiere a dos o más conductas, de las cuales cada una constituya un delito de conformidad con la legislación nacional de ambas Partes, siempre y cuando una de ellas satisfaga las condiciones previstas en los numerales 1, 2 y 3 del presente Artículo, la Parte Requerida podrá conceder la extradición por todas esas conductas.

ARTÍCULO 3
DELITOS FISCALES

La solicitud de extradición será procedente aun cuando se trate de un delito que se refiera a impuestos, aduanas u otra clase de contribuciones de carácter fiscal.

ARTÍCULO 4
CAUSAS PARA DENEGAR UNA EXTRADICIÓN

No se concederá la extradición:

a) si el delito por el cual se solicita es considerado por la Parte Requerida como un delito de carácter/naturaleza politica. Para los efectos de este Tratado, no serán considerados delitos de carácter/naturaleza política y, por tanto, serán extraditables:

1. cualquier delito contra la vida, la integridad física o la libertad de un Jefe de Estado o Gobierno extranjero, o contra miembros de su familia;

2. el genocidio, los crímenes de guerra cometidos contra la paz y la seguridad de la humanidad;

3. los actos de terrorismo, tales como:

i. El atentado contra la vida, la integridad física o la libertad de individuos que tengan derecho a una protección internacional, incluidos los agentes diplomáticos.

ii. La toma de rehenes o el secuestro de personas.

iii. El atentado contra personas o bienes cometidos mediante el empleo de bombas, granadas, cohetes, minas, armas de fuego, explosivos o dispositivos similares.

iv. Los actos de captura ilícita de barcos o aeronaves.

v. Cualquier acto de violencia no incluido entre los anteriores y que esté dirigido contra la vida, la integridad física, o la libertad de las personas, o que viniesen a afectar instituciones.

4. la tentativa en la comisión de delitos previstos en este Artículo o la participación como actor o cómplice de una persona que cometa o intente cometer dichos delitos.

b) si hay motivos fundados para creer que una solicitud de extradición ha sido formulada con el propósito de perseguir o castigar a una persona por su raza, religión, nacionalidad, o creencias políticas;

c) si la conducta por la cual se solicita la extradición es un delito puramente militar;

d) si la persona reclamada ya ha sido juzgada en la Parte Requerida por los mismos hechos que originaron la solicitud de extradición o se le haya otorgado amnistía o indulto por la misma conducta punible en la Parte Requirente o Requerida;

e) si la acción penal o la pena por la cual se pide la extradición ha prescrito conforme a la legislación nacional de la Parte Requirente;

f) si el delito por el cual se solicita es castigado por la Parte Requirente con una pena prohibida por la legislación nacional de la Parte Requerida. Sin embargo, se podrá conceder la extradición con la condición de que la Parte Requirente otorgue a la Parte Requerida las seguridades que estime suficientes de que no se impondrá esa pena o de que, si es impuesta, no será ejecutada;

g) si la persona reclamada hubiera sido condenada o debe ser juzgada en la Parte Requirente por un Tribunal de excepción; y

h) cuando la solicitud de extradición carezca de alguno de los documentos señalados en el Artículo 9 del presente Tratado y no haya sido subsanada dicha omisión.

ARTÍCULO 5
EXTRADICIÓN DE NACIONALES

1.- Ninguna de las Partes está en la obligación de entregar, en virtud del presente Tratado, a sus propios nacionales.

2.- Si la solicitud de extradición es rehusada exclusivamente porque la persona reclamada es un nacional de la Parte Requerida, ésta última deberá someter el caso a sus autoridades competentes para el enjuiciamiento del delito. Para este propósito, la Parte Requerida solicitará a su contraparte las pruebas que acrediten la participación del reclamado en los hechos que se le imputan, pruebas que deberán ser proporcionadas por la Parte Requirente. La Parte Requerida deberá informar a la Parte Requirente sobre la acción tomada con respecto a su solicitud.

ARTÍCULO 6
PRINCIPIO DE ESPECIALIDAD

1.- Una persona extraditada conforme al presente Tratado no será detenida, enjuiciada o sancionada en el territorio de la Parte Requirente por un delito distinto de aquél por el cual se concedió la extradición ni será extraditada por dicha Parte a un tercer Estado a menos que:

a) haya abandonado el territorio de la Parte Requirente después de su extradición y haya regresado voluntariamente a él;

b) no haya abandonado voluntariamente el territorio de la Parte Requirente dentro de los treinta (30) días siguientes a la fecha en que haya estado en libertad de hacerlo; o

c) la Parte Requerida haya dado su consentimiento para que el reclamado sea detenido, enjuiciado o sancionado en el territorio de la Parte Requirente o extraditado a un tercer Estado por un delito distinto de aquél por el cual se concedió la extradición, después de que la Parte Requirente haya presentado por la vía diplomática la solicitud en este sentido, acompañando para tal efecto la orden de aprehensión por el nuevo delito y las disposiciones legales correspondientes, así como los documentos señalados en el Artículo 9 del presente Tratado.

El consentimiento podrá ser otorgado cuando el delito por el que se solicita la extradición origine la obligación de conceder la extradición de conformidad con el presente Tratado.

2.- Estas disposiciones no se aplicarán a delitos cometidos después de la extradición.

3.- Si en el curso del proceso, se cambia la calificación del delito por el cual el reclamado fue extraditado, éste será enjuiciado y sentenciado a condición de que el delito, en su nueva configuración legal:

a) esté fundado en el mismo conjunto de hechos establecidos en la solicitud de extradición y en los documentos presentados en su apoyo; y

b) sea punible con la misma pena máxima que el delito por el cual fue extraditado o con una pena cuyo máximo sea menor.

ARTÍCULO 7
INFORMACIÓN Y DOCUMENTOS COMPLEMENTARIOS

Si la información proporcionada por la Parte Requirente para la tramitación de una solicitud de extradición o los documentos presentados en apoyo de ésta no fueran suficientes para permitir a la Parte Requerida decidir de conformidad con lo dispuesto en el presente Tratado, esta última Parte podrá solicitar que se le proporcione información complementaria o se le presenten los documentos que se omitieron o que fueron deficientes.

ARTÍCULO 8
EXTRADICIÓN SUMARIA

1.- Si el reclamado manifiesta a las autoridades competentes de la Parte Requerida su consentimiento para ser extraditado, dicha Parte deberá conceder su extradición sin mayores trámites y tomará todas las medidas permitidas por sus leyes para expeditar la extradición.

2.- El consentimiento deberá ser libre, expreso y voluntario, debiendo notificarse al requerido acerca de sus derechos y de las consecuencias de su decisión. Una vez resuelta la extradición, el consentimiento es irrevocable.

ARTÍCULO 9
DOCUMENTOS NECESARIOS PARA LA PRESENTACIÓN DE SOLICITUDES DE EXTRADICIÓN

1.- La solicitud de extradición se deberá presentar por la vía diplomática.

2.- La solicitud de extradición deberá contener la expresión del delito por el cual se pide la extradición y será acompañada de:

a) una relación de los hechos imputados;

b) certificación de las disposiciones legales vigentes que fijen los elementos constitutivos del delito;

c) certificación de las disposiciones legales vigentes que determinen la pena correspondiente al delito;

d) certificación de las disposiciones legales vigentes relativas a la prescripción de la acción penal o de la pena;

e) datos y antecedentes personales del reclamado que permitan su identificación y, siempre que sea posible, los conducentes a su localización;

f) copia certificada de la orden de aprehensión o reaprehensión, expedida por las autoridades competentes de la Parte Requirente; y

g) copia certificada de la sentencia firme dictada por las autoridades competentes de la Parte Requirente, en caso que el reclamado haya sido sancionado.

3.- Cuando la solicitud de extradición se refiere a una persona sentenciada, se anexará una certificación de la constancia que indique la parte de la pena que le faltare por cumplir.

4.- Todos los documentos que deban ser presentados por la Parte Requirente, conforme a las disposiciones del presente Tratado, estarán dispensados de todas las formalidades de legalización cuando sean cursados por la vía diplomática.

ARTÍCULO 10
DETENCIÓN PROVISIONAL

1.- En caso de urgencia, la Parte Requirente podrá pedir por vía diplomática, la detención provisional de una persona acusada o sentenciada. El pedimento deberá contener la expresión del delito por el cual se pide la extradición, la descripción del reclamado y de ser posible su paradero, la promesa de formalizar la solicitud de extradición y la manifestación de la existencia de una orden de aprehensión librada por autoridad judicial competente o de una sentencia condenatoria en contra del reclamado.

2.- Al momento de recibir una solicitud de esa naturaleza, la Parte Requerida tomará las medidas necesarias para obtener la aprehensión del reclamado.

3.- Se pondrá fin a la detención provisional, de acuerdo con la legislación de la Parte Requerida, si dentro de un plazo de sesenta (60) días contados a partir de la detención del reclamado, la Parte Requerida no ha recibido la solicitud formal de extradición con los documentos mencionados en el artículo 9 del presente Tratado.

4.- El hecho de que se ponga fin a la detención o prisión provisional en aplicación del numeral 3, no impedirá que se presente posteriormente la petición formal de extradición que cumpla con los requisitos exigidos en el presente Instrumento.

ARTÍCULO 11
SOLICITUDES CONCURRENTES

1.- Si la extradición de la misma persona es solicitada por dos o más Estados, la Parte Requerida deberá determinar a cuál de esos Estados será extraditada la persona, e informará a la Parte Requirente su decisión.

2.- Para determinar a cuál Estado será extraditada la persona, la Parte Requerida tomará en consideración todas las circunstancias relevantes, incluyendo:

a) la gravedad de los delitos, si las solicitudes se refieren a delitos diferentes;

b) el tiempo y lugar de la comisión de cada delito;

c) las fechas respectivas de las solicitudes;

d) la nacionalidad de la persona reclamada;

e) el lugar habitual de residencia del reclamado; y

f) la existencia de Tratados Internacionales en la materia con los otros Estados Requirentes.

ARTÍCULO 12
RESOLUCIÓN Y ENTREGA

1.- La Parte Requerida comunicará por vía diplomática a la Parte Requirente, su decisión respecto de la solicitud de extradición, una vez que ésta ha quedado firme.

2.- En caso de denegación total o parcial de una solicitud de extradición, la Parte Requerida expondrá las razones en que se haya fundado.

3.- Si se concede la extradición, las Partes se pondrán de acuerdo para realizar la entrega del reclamado, que deberá efectuarse dentro de los sesenta (60) días siguientes a la fecha en que la Parte Requirente haya recibido la comunicación a que se refiere el numeral 1 del presente Artículo.

4.- Si el reclamado no ha sido trasladado dentro del plazo señalado, será puesto en libertad y la Parte Requerida podrá posteriormente negarse a extraditarlo por el mismo delito.

5.- Si por caso fortuito o causas de fuerza mayor, la entrega no pudiera llevarse a cabo, ambas Partes establecerán de común acuerdo una nueva fecha de entrega, a la cual resultarán aplicables las disposiciones del numeral 4 del presente Artículo.

6.- Asimismo, podrá fijarse una nueva fecha de entrega cuando, por las condiciones de salud de la persona reclamada, el traslado pudiera poner en peligro su vida o agravar su estado. Para tales efectos, la Parte Requerida presentará a la Parte Requirente un informe médico detallado emitido por un perito en medicina.

ARTÍCULO 13
ENTREGA DIFERIDA

1.- La Parte Requerida podrá, después de acceder a la extradición, diferir la entrega del reclamado cuando existan procedimientos en curso en contra de él o cuando se encuentre cumpliendo una pena en el territorio de la Parte Requerida por un delito distinto de aquél por el que se concedió la extradición; hasta la conclusión del procedimiento o la plena ejecución de la sanción que le haya sido impuesta.

2.- El aplazamiento de la entrega suspenderá el plazo de prescripción en las actuaciones judiciales que tienen lugar en la Parte Requirente, por los hechos objeto de la solicitud de extradición.

ARTÍCULO 14
ENTREGA TEMPORAL

1.- La Parte Requerida podrá, después de haber concedido la extradición y a petición de la Parte Requirente, entregar temporalmente al individuo reclamado que haya recibido una sentencia condenatoria en la Parte Requerida, con el fin de que pueda ser procesado en la Parte Requirente durante la ejecución de la sentencia en la Parte

Requerida. La persona así entregada, deberá permanecer en custodia de la Parte Requirente y ser devuelta a la Parte Requerida al término del proceso correspondiente o del plazo a que se refiere el inciso c) del numeral siguiente.

2.- La solicitud de entrega temporal de la persona reclamada, deberá contener lo siguiente:

a) justificación de la necesidad de llevar a cabo la entrega;

b) manifestación de que la duración del proceso correspondiente no excederá de tres (3) años; y

c) el compromiso de la Parte Requirente, de devolver a la persona reclamada una vez concluido el proceso por el cual se solicite la entrega o transcurridos tres (3) años. En este último caso, la devolución se llevará a cabo aun cuando el proceso en la Parte Requirente no hubiere terminado.

3.- La entrega temporal será procedente cuando el término de la pena privativa de libertad que le falte por cumplir al reclamado en la Parte Requerida sea mayor de tres (3) años.

4.- El tiempo que la persona entregada temporalmente haya permanecido en el territorio de la Parte Requirente, será tomado en cuenta para el cumplimiento de su sentencia en la Parte Requerida.

ARTÍCULO 15
PROCEDIMIENTO

Las solicitudes de extradición que sean presentadas a la Parte Requerida, serán tramitadas de acuerdo a los procedimientos establecidos en la materia y que se encuentran regulados por el derecho de dicha Parte.

ARTÍCULO 16
ENTREGA DE OBJETOS A PETICIÓN DE LA PARTE REQUIRENTE

1.- En la medida en que lo permita la legislación nacional de la Parte Requerida y sin perjuicio de los derechos de terceros, los cuales serán debidamente respetados, los bienes u objetos que sirvieron para la perpetración del delito y los provenientes directa o indirectamente del mismo, o de cualquier manera puedan servir de prueba en el proceso, y que sean encontrados en poder de la persona reclamada en el momento de su detención, serán entregados al concederse la extradición aun cuando la extradición no pueda consumarse por la muerte, desaparición o fuga del acusado.

2.- Cuando existan derechos de la Parte Requerida o de terceros sobre los objetos entregados, se verificará que hayan sido entregados a la Parte Requirente para los efectos de un proceso penal, conforme a las disposiciones de este Artículo, y serán devueltos a la Parte Requerida en los términos que ésta considere y sin costo alguno.

3.- La Parte Requerida podrá retener temporalmente o entregar bajo condición de restitución o devolución los objetos a que se refiere el numeral 1 del presente Artículo y que no se encuentren en poder de la persona reclamada en el momento de su detención, cuando puedan quedar sujetos a una medida de aseguramiento en el territorio de dicha Parte dentro de un proceso penal en curso, previa solicitud de asistencia jurídica.

ARTÍCULO 17
TRÁNSITO

1.- El tránsito por el territorio de una de las Partes de una persona que sea entregada a la otra Parte por un tercer Estado, será permitido mediante la presentación por vía diplomática de una copia certificada de la resolución en la que se concedió la extradición.

2.- Corresponderá a las autoridades del Estado de tránsito la custodia del extraditado mientras permanezca en su territorio.

3.- La Parte Requirente reembolsará al Estado de tránsito, a solicitud de éste, cualquier gasto en que se incurra con tal motivo.

ARTÍCULO 18
GASTOS

Todos los gastos y costos que resulten de una extradición deberán ser cubiertos por la Parte en cuyo territorio se eroguen. Los gastos y costos de traslado del extraditado y aquellos que resulten de un permiso de tránsito correrán a cargo de la Parte Requirente.

ARTÍCULO 19
CONSULTAS Y CONTROVERSIAS

1.- Las Partes celebrarán consultas, en las oportunidades que convengan mutuamente, con el fin de facilitar la aplicación de las disposiciones del presente Tratado.

2.- Las controversias que surjan entre las Partes con motivo de la aplicación, interpretación o cumplimiento de las disposiciones del presente Tratado, serán resueltas de forma amigable mediante negociaciones diplomáticas directas.

ARTÍCULO 20
ÁMBITO TEMPORAL DE APLICACIÓN

El presente Tratado se aplicará a los delitos especificados en su Artículo 2, que hayan sido cometidos antes o después de su entrada en vigor.

ARTÍCULO 21
PROTECCIÓN DE LA INFORMACIÓN

Las Partes se comprometen a garantizar la protección de la información intercambiada en virtud del presente Tratado, de conformidad con lo establecido en su legislación nacional aplicable.

ARTÍCULO 22
RELACIÓN CON OTROS TRATADOS

El presente Tratado no obstará para que las Partes cooperen en materia de extradición de conformidad con otros instrumentos internacionales de los que sean parte.

ARTÍCULO 23
ENTRADA EN VIGOR, ENMIENDAS Y TERMINACIÓN

1.- El presente Tratado entrará en vigor treinta (30) días después de la fecha de recepción de la última notificación en que las Partes se comuniquen por vía diplomática el cumplimiento de los requisitos exigidos por su legislación nacional, y tendrá vigencia indefinida.

2.- A la entrada en vigor del presente Tratado, quedará sin efectos el Tratado de Extradición entre los Estados Unidos Mexicanos y la República de Cuba, suscrito en La Habana, Cuba, el 25 de mayo de 1925.

3.- El presente Tratado podrá ser modificado por mutuo consentimiento de las Partes, formalizado a través de comunicaciones escritas, por la vía diplomática. Dichas modificaciones entrarán en vigor de conformidad con el procedimiento establecido en el numeral 1 del presente Artículo.

4.- Cualquiera de las Partes podrá dar por terminado el presente Tratado, en cualquier momento, mediante notificación escrita, dirigida a la otra Parte, a través de la vía diplomática, en cuyo caso sus efectos cesarán ciento ochenta (180) días después de la fecha de recibo de la notificación correspondiente.

5.- Los procedimientos de extradición pendientes al momento de la terminación del presente Tratado, serán concluidos de conformidad con el mismo.

Firmado en la Ciudad de México, el primero de noviembre de dos mil trece, en dos ejemplares originales en idioma español, siendo ambos textos igualmente auténticos.

POR LOS ESTADOS UNIDOS MEXICANOS	POR LA REPÚBLICA DE CUBA
Jesús Murillo Karam Procurador General de la República	Bruno Rodríguez Parrilla Ministro de Relaciones Exteriores

[TRANSLATION – TRADUCTION]

TREATY BETWEEN THE UNITED MEXICAN STATES AND THE REPUBLIC OF CUBA ON EXTRADITION

The United Mexican States and the Republic of Cuba, hereinafter referred to as "the Parties",

Recognizing their profound interest in combating crime and impunity for its perpetrators,

Desirous of making more effective the cooperation between both countries in the prevention and suppression of crime,

Have agreed as follows:

Article 1. Obligation to extradite

The Parties undertake to extradite to each other, in accordance with the provisions of this Treaty, any person in respect of whom criminal proceedings have been initiated, or any person sought for the imposition or enforcement of a judgment or sentence.

Article 2. Extraditable offences

1. Extradition may be granted for wilful or culpable criminal conduct constituting an offence punishable under the national legislation of both Parties by a custodial sentence of at least one year.

2. When the extradition request relates to a final judgment, the term of the custodial sentence remaining to be served by the person sought shall be at least six months.

3. For the purposes of this article, it shall be immaterial whether or not the national legislation of the Parties designates the offense using different terminology, provided the constituent elements of the offence are the same.

4. If the extradition request relates to two or more offences, each of which constitutes an offence under the national legislation of both Parties, provided one of them satisfies the conditions set forth in paragraphs 1, 2 and 3 of this article, the Requested Party may grant extradition for all such offences.

Article 3. Fiscal offences

An extradition request shall be admissible even in the case of an offence relating to taxes, customs duties or other levies of a fiscal nature.

Article 4. Grounds for denial of extradition

Extradition shall not be granted:

(a) If the offence in respect of which it is requested is regarded by the Requested Party as an offence of a political character/nature. For the purposes of this Treaty, the following shall not be considered offences of a political character/nature and shall therefore be extraditable:

1. Any crime against the life, physical integrity or freedom of a foreign Head of State or Government, or against members of his or her family;
2. Genocide or war crimes committed against the peace and security of humanity;
3. Acts of terrorism, such as:
   (i) Attempts against the life, physical integrity or freedom of internationally protected persons, including diplomatic agents;
   (ii) The taking of hostages or the kidnapping of persons;
   (iii) Attacks against persons or property committed through the use of bombs, grenades, rockets, mines, firearms, explosives or similar devices;
   (iv) The illicit seizure of vessels or aircraft;
   (v) Any act of violence not included above committed against the life, physical integrity or freedom of persons, or that affects institutions.
4. An attempt to commit the offences provided for in this article or participation as a principal or accomplice of a person who commits or attempts to commit such offences.

(b) If there are substantial grounds for believing that an extradition request has been made for the purpose of persecuting or punishing a person on account of his or her race, religion, nationality or political beliefs;

(c) If the conduct in respect of which extradition is requested is an offence of a purely military nature;

(d) If the person sought has already been tried in the Requested Party for the same acts that gave rise to the extradition request, or has been granted amnesty or been pardoned for the same offence in the Requesting or Requested Party;

(e) When the prosecution or the enforcement of the sentence in respect of which extradition is sought has become barred by lapse of time according to the national legislation of the Requesting Party;

(f) If the offence in respect of which extradition is requested by the Requesting Party carries a sentence prohibited by the national legislation of the Requested Party. However, extradition may be granted on the condition that the Requesting Party provide the Requested Party sufficient assurance that the sentence will not be imposed or, if imposed, will not be carried out;

(g) If the person sought has been sentenced or is to be tried in the Requesting Party by a special court; and

(h) If the extradition request is lacking any of the documents listed in article 9 of this Treaty and such lack has not been made good.

Article 5. Extradition of nationals

1. Neither Party is obliged to surrender its own nationals under this Treaty.

2. Should the extradition request be denied solely on the grounds that the person sought is a national of the Requested Party, the latter shall entrust the prosecution of the offence to its own competent authorities. To this end, the Requested Party may ask its counterpart for evidence substantiating the sought person's involvement in the alleged facts. The Requested Party shall inform the Requesting Party of the action taken on its request.

Article 6. Rule of speciality

1. A person extradited under this Treaty may not be detained, tried or sentenced in the territory of the Requesting Party for an offence other than the one in respect of which extradition has been granted, nor be extradited by that Party to a third State, unless:

(a) The person has left the territory of the Requesting Party after his or her extradition and has voluntarily returned to it;

(b) The person has not left the territory of the Requesting Party within 30 days after the date on which he or she was free to do so; or

(c) The Requested Party has given its consent to the sought person's detention, trial or punishment in the territory of the Requesting Party or extradition to a third State for an offence other than the one in respect of which extradition was granted, following the submission by the Requesting Party, through the diplomatic channel, of a request to that effect, together with the arrest warrant for the new offence and the text of the relevant legal provisions, in addition to the documents indicated in article 9 of this Treaty.

Consent may be given when the offence in respect of which extradition is requested entails the obligation to agree to extradite, in accordance with the provisions of this Treaty.

2. These provisions shall not apply to offences committed after extradition.

3. If, during the proceedings, the offence in respect of which the person sought was extradited is reclassified, he or she shall be tried and sentenced, provided the offence, according to its new legal classification:

(a) Is based on the same set of facts established in the extradition request and its supporting documents; and

(b) Is punishable by the same maximum penalty as the offence in respect of which extradition was granted, or a lesser maximum penalty.

Article 7. Additional information and documents

If the information provided by the Requesting Party for the processing of an extradition request or the corresponding supporting documents were not sufficient to enable the Requested Party to reach a decision in accordance with the provisions of this Treaty, the latter Party may ask to be provided with additional information or furnished with documents that were omitted or were inadequate.

Article 8. Summary extradition

1. If the person sought informs the competent authorities of the Requested Party that he or she agrees to be extradited, that Party shall grant extradition without further proceedings and shall take all measures permitted under its laws to expedite the extradition.

2. Consent must be free, explicit and voluntary, and the person requested must be notified of his or her rights and of the implications of his or her decision. Once the extradition is granted, consent is irrevocable.

Article 9. Documents required to file extradition requests

1. The extradition request must be made through the diplomatic channel.

2. The extradition request must state the offence in respect of which extradition is requested and contain:

(a) A statement of the alleged facts;

(b) A certification of the legal provisions in effect describing the elements constituting the offence;

(c) A certification of the legal provisions in effect that determine the sentence corresponding to the offence;

(d) A certification of the legal provisions in effect concerning the extinction of the criminal proceedings or sentence;

(e) Data and personal history establishing the identity and, wherever possible, indicating the location of the person sought;

(f) A certified copy of the arrest warrant or a renewed warrant, issued by the competent authorities of the Requesting Party; and

(g) A certified copy of the final judgment issued by the competent authorities of the Requesting Party, if the person sought has been convicted.

3. Where the extradition request relates to a convicted person, a certified copy of the record indicating what part of the sentence remains to be served shall be attached.

4. All documents to be submitted by the Requesting Party pursuant to this Treaty shall be exempt from all certification requirements when they are transmitted through the diplomatic channel.

Article 10. Provisional arrest

1. In the case of an emergency, the Requesting Party may, through the diplomatic channel, request the provisional arrest of an accused or convicted person. The request must contain a statement of the offence in respect of which extradition is requested, the description of the person sought and, if possible, his or her whereabouts, the commitment to submit an extradition request in due form and confirmation that the person sought is the subject of an arrest warrant issued by the competent judicial authority or has been convicted and sentenced.

2. Upon receipt of such a request, the Requested Party shall take the necessary measures to secure the arrest of the person sought.

3. The person sought shall be released from the provisional arrest, in accordance with the legislation of the Requested Party, if within a period of 60 days after his or her arrest, the Requested Party has not received the formal extradition request accompanied by the documents mentioned in article 9 of this Treaty.

4. The fact that the arrest or provisional detention has been lifted pursuant to paragraph 3 does not preclude the subsequent presentation of a formal extradition request in accordance with the requirements of this Instrument.

Article 11. Concurrent requests

1. If the extradition of the same person is requested by two or more States, the Requested Party shall decide to which State the person is to be extradited and shall so inform the Requesting Party of its decision.

2. In order to determine the State to which the person is to be extradited, the Requested Party shall take account of all relevant circumstances, including:

(a) The seriousness of the offences, if the requests refer to different offences;

(b) The time and place of commission of each offence;

(c) The respective dates of the requests;

(d) The nationality of the person sought;

(e) The usual place of residence of the person sought; and

(f) The existence of international extradition treaties with the other Requesting States.

Article 12. Decision and surrender

1. Once its decision on the extradition request becomes final, the Requested Party shall communicate it to the Requesting Party through the diplomatic channel.

2. In the case of complete or partial denial of an extradition request, the Requested Party shall give the reasons therefor.

3. If extradition is granted, the Parties shall agree on arrangements for the surrender of the person sought, which must take place within 60 days of the date on which the Requesting Party received the communication referred to in paragraph 1 of this article.

4. If the transfer has not taken place within that time limit, the person sought shall be released and the Requested Party may subsequently deny the extradition for the same offence.

5. If circumstances beyond its control prevent the surrender by a Party, the two Parties shall mutually decide upon a new date of surrender, and the provisions of paragraph 4 of this article shall apply.

6. Surrender may also be postponed when, for health reasons, surrender might threaten the life or aggravate the condition of the person sought. In such a case, the Requested Party shall provide the Requesting Party with a detailed medical report issued by a medical expert.

Article 13. Postponed surrender

1. The Requested Party, after granting the extradition, may postpone the surrender of the person sought when that person is being tried for or is serving a sentence in the territory of the Requested Party for a different offence, until the conclusion of the proceeding or the full execution of the sentence imposed.

2. Postponement of the surrender shall suspend the statute of limitations in legal proceedings taking place in the Requesting Party for the acts in respect of which extradition is sought.

Article 14. Temporary surrender

1. The Requested Party may, after granting extradition and at the request of the Requesting Party, temporarily surrender a person sought who has been convicted in the Requested Party to be tried in the Requesting Party while serving a sentence in the Requested Party. The person thus surrendered shall remain in the custody of the Requesting Party and shall be returned to the Requested Party upon conclusion of the relevant proceedings or period referred to in subparagraph (c) of the following paragraph.

2. The request for temporary surrender of the person sought shall contain the following information:

(a) The justification for the surrender;

(b) An assurance that the duration of the proceedings will not exceed three years; and

(c) A commitment by the Requesting Party to return the person sought upon the conclusion of the proceedings or after three years. In the latter case, the person shall be returned even if the proceedings in the Requesting Party have not been completed.

3. Temporary surrender will be appropriate when more than three years remain in the term of the person's custodial sentence.

4. Time spent in the territory of the Requesting Party by the person surrendered temporarily shall be counted as time served in the territory of the Requested Party.

Article 15. Procedure

All extradition requests submitted to the Requested Party shall be handled according to established procedures, as laid down in each Party's laws.

Article 16. Surrender of property at the Requesting Party's request

1. To the extent permitted under the national legislation of the Requested Party, and without prejudice to the rights of third parties, which shall be duly respected, property or items used in the commission of the offence and the direct or indirect proceeds of the offence, or those that may in any way be produced in evidence, and are found in the possession of the person sought at the time of his or her arrest, shall be surrendered upon extradition having been granted, even where extradition cannot proceed because of the death, disappearance or escape of the accused.

2. When the Requested Party or third parties have claims to the items surrendered, it shall be verified that they have been surrendered to the Requesting Party for the purposes of criminal proceedings, in accordance with the provisions of this article, and those items shall be returned to the Requested Party free of charge in the terms specified by the latter.

3. The Requested Party may temporarily retain or surrender on condition of their restitution or return, the items referred to in paragraph 1 of this article which are not in the possession of the person sought at the time of his or her arrest, if they are liable to seizure in the territory of the Requested Party for the purposes of criminal proceedings in progress, upon request for legal assistance.

Article 17. Transit

1. The transit through the territory of one of the Parties of a person who is surrendered to the other Party by a third State shall be granted upon presentation, through the diplomatic channel, of a certified copy of the order granting the extradition.

2. The authorities of the transit State shall be in charge of the custody of the extradited person while that person is in its territory.

3. The Requesting Party shall reimburse the transit State, at its request, for any expenses incurred by the latter in that connection.

Article 18. Costs

All costs and expenses resulting from an extradition shall be borne by the Party in whose territory they are incurred. Costs and travel expenses incurred on account of the extradition, and those resulting from a transit permit, shall be borne by the Requesting Party.

Article 19. Consultations and disputes

1. The Parties shall hold consultations at mutually agreed times, with a view to facilitating the application of the provisions of this Treaty.

2. Any dispute arising between the Parties concerning the application, interpretation or fulfilment of the provisions of this Treaty shall be settled amicably by means of direct diplomatic negotiations.

Article 20. Temporal scope

This Treaty shall apply to the offences specified in article 2, committed either before or after its entry into force.

Article 21. Protection of information

The Parties undertake to guarantee the protection of the information exchanged under this Treaty, in accordance with the applicable provisions of their national legislation.

Article 22. Relationship with other treaties

This Treaty shall not prevent the Parties from cooperating in extradition matters in accordance with other international instruments to which they are party.

Article 23. Entry into force, amendment and termination

1. This Treaty shall enter into force 30 days after the date of receipt of the last of the notifications through which the Parties notify each other, through the diplomatic channel, that the

domestic requirements for its entry into force have been met and shall remain in effect for a period of indefinite duration.

2. Upon entry into force of this Treaty, it shall supersede the Extradition Treaty between the United Mexican States and the Republic of Cuba, signed in Havana, Cuba, on 25 May 1925.

3. This Treaty may be amended by mutual consent of the Parties, formalized by means of written communications, through the diplomatic channel. Those amendments shall enter into force pursuant to the procedure established in paragraph 1 of this article.

4. Either Party may terminate this Treaty, at any time, by means of a written notification to the other Party, through the diplomatic channel, in which case it shall cease to be in force 180 days following receipt of such notification.

5. Any extradition proceedings pending at the time of termination of this Treaty shall be dealt with in accordance therewith.

SIGNED at Mexico City on 1 November 2013, in two originals in the Spanish language, both texts being equally authentic.

For the United Mexican States:
JESÚS MURILLO KARAM
Attorney-General of the Republic

For the Republic of Cuba:
BRUNO RODRÍGUEZ PARRILLA
Minister for Foreign Affairs

[TRANSLATION – TRADUCTION]

TRAITÉ D'EXTRADITION ENTRE LES ÉTATS-UNIS DU MEXIQUE ET LA RÉPUBLIQUE DE CUBA

Les États-Unis du Mexique et la République de Cuba, ci-après dénommés « Parties »,

Reconnaissant leur profond intérêt pour la lutte contre la criminalité et l'impunité de ses acteurs,

Animés par le désir d'accroître l'efficacité de la coopération entre les deux pays en matière de prévention et de répression de la criminalité,

Sont convenus de ce qui suit :

Article premier. Obligation d'extrader

Les Parties s'engagent à extrader l'une vers l'autre, conformément aux dispositions du présent Traité, les personnes à l'égard desquelles une procédure pénale a été engagée ou pour lesquelles le prononcé ou l'exécution d'une peine ou d'une condamnation sont demandés.

Article 2. Infractions donnant lieu à extradition

1. L'extradition est accordée lorsque la demande se rapporte à des comportements criminels intentionnels ou coupables prévus par la législation nationale des deux Parties et constituant une infraction punissable d'une peine de privation de liberté d'au moins un an.

2. Lorsque l'extradition est demandée pour l'exécution d'un jugement définitif, la durée de la peine de privation de liberté restant à purger par la personne réclamée doit être d'au moins six mois.

3. Aux fins du présent article, il importe peu que la législation nationale des Parties désigne l'infraction par des termes différents, à condition que les faits qui constituent les éléments de l'infraction ne changent pas.

4. Si la demande d'extradition se rapporte à deux ou plusieurs actes dont chacun constitue une infraction au regard de la législation nationale des deux Parties, sous réserve que l'une d'entre elles remplisse les conditions énoncées aux paragraphes 1, 2 et 3 du présent article, la Partie requise peut accorder l'extradition pour l'ensemble de ces actes.

Article 3. Infractions fiscales

La demande d'extradition est recevable même si l'infraction a trait aux impôts, aux droits de douane ou à d'autres types de contributions de nature fiscale.

Article 4. Motifs de refus de l'extradition

L'extradition est refusée :

a) Si l'infraction pour laquelle elle est demandée est considérée par la Partie requise comme une infraction de caractère ou de nature politique. Aux fins du présent Traité, les infractions suivantes ne sont pas considérées comme des infractions de caractère ou de nature politique, et donnent donc lieu à extradition :

1. Toute atteinte à la vie, à l'intégrité physique ou à la liberté d'un chef d'État ou de gouvernement étranger, ou des membres de sa famille;
2. Le génocide, les crimes de guerre commis contre la paix et la sécurité de l'humanité;
3. Les actes de terrorisme tels que :
    i. L'attentat à la vie, à l'intégrité physique ou à la liberté de personnes qui ont droit à une protection internationale, y compris les agents diplomatiques;
    ii. La prise d'otages ou l'enlèvements de personnes;
    iii. L'attentat contre des personnes ou des biens commis au moyen de bombes, de grenades, de missiles, de mines, d'armes à feu, d'explosifs ou d'autres dispositifs analogues;
    iv. Les actes de capture illicite de navires ou d'aéronefs;
    v. Tout acte de violence non compris dans ce qui précède et qui est dirigé contre la vie, l'intégrité physique ou la liberté des personnes, ou qui affecterait les institutions;
4. La tentative de commettre les infractions visées au présent article ou la participation en tant qu'acteur ou complice d'une personne qui commet ou tente de commettre ces infractions;

b) S'il existe des motifs sérieux de croire qu'une demande d'extradition a été présentée en vue de poursuivre ou de punir une personne en raison de sa race, de sa religion, de sa nationalité ou de ses opinions politiques;

c) Si l'infraction pour laquelle l'extradition est demandée est une infraction seulement au regard de la loi militaire;

d) Si la personne réclamée a déjà été jugée sur le territoire de la Partie requise pour les mêmes faits que ceux qui ont donné lieu à la demande d'extradition ou a bénéficié d'une amnistie ou d'une grâce pour la même infraction dans la Partie requérante ou la Partie requise;

e) Si les poursuites pénales ou la peine pour laquelle l'extradition est demandée sont prescrites en vertu de la législation nationale de la Partie requérante;

f) Si l'infraction pour laquelle l'extradition est demandée est punie par la Partie requérante d'une peine interdite par la législation nationale de la Partie requise. Toutefois, l'extradition peut être accordée à condition que la Partie requérante donne à la Partie requise des assurances suffisantes à l'effet que la peine ne sera pas prononcée ou, si elle l'est, ne sera pas appliquée;

g) Si la personne réclamée a été condamnée ou doit être jugée dans la Partie requérante par un tribunal spécial; et

h) Si l'un des documents visés à l'article 9 du présent traité manque dans la demande d'extradition et s'il n'a pas été remédié à cette omission.

Article 5. Extradition de ressortissants

1. Aucune Partie n'est tenue, en vertu du présent Traité, de livrer ses propres ressortissants.

2. Si la demande d'extradition est rejetée au seul motif que la personne réclamée est un ressortissant de la Partie requise, cette dernière soumet l'affaire à ses autorités compétentes afin que les poursuites concernant l'infraction soient engagées. À cette fin, la Partie requise demande à la Partie requérante les éléments de preuve qui attestent la participation de la personne aux faits qui lui sont reprochés. La Partie requise informe la Partie requérante de la suite donnée à sa demande.

Article 6. Règle de la spécialité

1. Une personne extradée conformément au présent Traité ne peut être, sur le territoire de la Partie requérante, arrêtée, poursuivie ou punie pour une infraction autre que celle pour laquelle l'extradition a été accordée, ni être extradée par ladite Partie vers un État tiers, sauf :

a) Si la personne a quitté le territoire de la Partie requérante après son extradition et y est revenue de son plein gré;

b) Si la personne n'a pas quitté volontairement le territoire de la Partie requérante dans un délai de 30 jours après la date à laquelle il était libre de le faire; ou

c) Si la Partie requise a consenti à ce que la personne soit arrêtée, poursuivie ou punie sur le territoire de la Partie requérante ou extradée vers un État tiers pour une infraction autre que celle pour laquelle l'extradition a été accordée, après que la Partie requérante a présenté par la voie diplomatique une demande à cet effet, accompagnée du mandat d'arrêt relatif à la nouvelle infraction, des dispositions légales correspondantes ainsi que des documents visés à l'article 9 du présent Traité.

Le consentement peut être donné lorsque l'infraction pour laquelle l'extradition est demandée entraîne l'obligation d'accorder l'extradition conformément au présent Traité.

2. Ces dispositions ne s'appliquent pas aux infractions commises après l'extradition.

3. Si, au cours de la procédure, la qualification de l'infraction pour laquelle la personne réclamée a été extradée est modifiée, cette personne est poursuivie et condamnée, à condition que l'infraction, dans sa nouvelle configuration juridique :

a) Repose sur le même ensemble de faits que ceux établis dans la demande d'extradition et les documents présentés à l'appui de celle-ci; et

b) Soit passible de la même peine maximale que l'infraction pour laquelle la personne réclamée a été extradée ou d'une peine dont la durée maximale est inférieure.

Article 7. Renseignements et documents complémentaires

Si les renseignements fournis par la Partie requérante pour le traitement d'une demande d'extradition ou les documents présentés à l'appui de celle-ci ne sont pas suffisants pour permettre à la Partie requise de prendre une décision conformément aux dispositions du présent Traité, cette dernière peut demander qu'un complément d'information lui soit fourni ou que les documents omis ou manquants lui soient présentés.

Article 8. Extradition simplifiée

1. Si la personne réclamée informe les autorités compétentes de la Partie requise qu'elle consent à être extradée, cette Partie accorde son extradition sans autres formalités et prend toutes les dispositions permises par sa législation pour accélérer l'extradition.

2. Le consentement est libre, exprès et volontaire, et la personne réclamée est informée de ses droits et des conséquences de sa décision. Une fois l'extradition décidée, le consentement est irrévocable.

Article 9. Documents à fournir à l'appui des demandes d'extradition

1. La demande d'extradition est présentée par la voie diplomatique.

2. La demande d'extradition contient la description de l'infraction pour laquelle l'extradition est demandée et s'accompagne :

a) D'un exposé des faits allégués;

b) D'une attestation des dispositions juridiques en vigueur déterminant les éléments constitutifs de l'infraction;

c) D'une attestation des dispositions juridiques en vigueur déterminant la peine prévue pour l'infraction;

d) D'une attestation des dispositions juridiques en vigueur concernant la prescription de l'action pénale ou de la peine;

e) Des données à caractère personnel et des antécédents de la personne réclamée qui permettent de l'identifier et, dans la mesure du possible, de la localiser;

f) D'une copie certifiée conforme du mandat d'arrêt ou de réarrestation délivré par les autorités compétentes de la Partie requérante; et

g) D'une copie certifiée conforme du jugement définitif rendu par les autorités compétentes de la Partie requérante, dans le cas où la personne réclamée a été condamnée.

3. Lorsque la demande d'extradition concerne une personne condamnée, une attestation du procès-verbal indiquant la durée de la peine restant à purger est jointe.

4. Tous les documents qui doivent être présentés par la Partie requérante conformément aux dispositions du présent Traité sont dispensés de toute formalité de légalisation lorsqu'ils sont transmis par la voie diplomatique.

Article 10. Arrestation provisoire

1. En cas d'urgence, la Partie requérante peut demander, par la voie diplomatique, l'arrestation provisoire d'une personne accusée ou condamnée. La demande contient le libellé de l'infraction pour laquelle l'extradition est demandée, la description de la personne réclamée et, si possible, le lieu où elle se trouve, l'engagement de soumettre une demande d'extradition formelle ainsi que l'indication de l'existence d'un mandat d'arrêt délivré par l'autorité judiciaire compétente ou d'un verdict de culpabilité à l'égard de la personne réclamée.

2. Dès réception d'une telle demande, la Partie requise prend les mesures nécessaires pour obtenir l'arrestation de la personne réclamée.

3. Il est mis fin à l'arrestation provisoire, conformément à la législation de la Partie requise, si dans les 60 jours suivant l'arrestation de la personne réclamée, la Partie requise n'a pas reçu la demande officielle d'extradition accompagnée des pièces à l'appui visés à l'article 9 du présent Traité.

4. La remise en liberté d'une personne arrêtée ou en détention provisoire en application du paragraphe 3 ne fait pas obstacle à la présentation ultérieure d'une demande formelle d'extradition conforme aux exigences du présent instrument.

Article 11. Concours de demandes

1. Lorsque des demandes sont reçues de la part de deux ou plusieurs États pour l'extradition de la même personne, la Partie requise décide vers lequel de ces États la personne doit être extradée et notifie la Partie requérante de sa décision.

2. Pour déterminer l'État auquel l'extradition est accordée, la Partie requise tient compte de toutes les circonstances pertinentes, notamment :

a) De la gravité des infractions, si les demandes se rapportent à différentes infractions;

b) Du moment et du lieu où chacune des infractions a été commise;

c) Des dates respectives des demandes;

d) De la nationalité de la personne réclamée;

e) Du lieu de résidence habituelle de la personne réclamée;

f) De l'existence de traités d'extradition internationaux en la matière avec les autres États requérants.

Article 12. Décision et remise

1. La Partie requise communique à la Partie requérante, par la voie diplomatique, sa décision concernant la demande d'extradition, une fois qu'elle est devenue définitive.

2. En cas de rejet total ou partiel d'une demande d'extradition, la Partie requise indique les motifs de sa décision.

3. Si l'extradition est accordée, les Parties conviennent de la remise de la personne réclamée, qui est effectuée dans les 60 jours suivant la date à laquelle la Partie requérante a reçu la communication visée au paragraphe 1 du présent article.

4. Si la personne réclamée n'a pas été transférée dans le délai prévu, elle est remise en liberté et la Partie requise peut ultérieurement refuser d'extrader l'intéressé pour la même infraction.

5. Si, en raison de circonstances imprévisibles ou d'un cas de force majeure, la remise ne peut être effectuée, les deux Parties fixent d'un commun accord une nouvelle date de remise, à laquelle les dispositions du paragraphe 4 du présent article sont applicables.

6. De même, une nouvelle date de remise peut être fixée lorsque, en raison de l'état de santé de la personne réclamée, le transfèrement pourrait mettre sa vie en danger ou aggraver son état.

Dans ce cas, la Partie requise soumet à la Partie requérante un rapport médical détaillé établi par un médecin expert.

Article 13. Remise différée

1. La Partie requise peut, après avoir consenti à l'extradition, différer la remise de la personne réclamée lorsque des poursuites sont en cours à son égard ou lorsqu'elle purge une peine sur le territoire de la Partie requise pour une infraction autre que celle pour laquelle l'extradition a été accordée, jusqu'à la conclusion des poursuites ou l'exécution complète de la peine qui lui a été infligée.

2. Le report de la remise suspend le délai de prescription des poursuites judiciaires en cours dans la Partie requérante pour les faits qui font l'objet de la demande d'extradition.

Article 14. Remise temporaire

1. La Partie requise peut, après avoir accordé l'extradition et à la demande de la Partie requérante, remettre temporairement la personne réclamée qui a fait l'objet d'une condamnation dans la Partie requise, afin qu'elle puisse être poursuivie dans la Partie requérante pendant l'exécution de la peine dans la Partie requise. La personne ainsi remise reste sous la garde de la Partie requérante et est renvoyée à la Partie requise à l'issue de la procédure correspondante ou de la période visée à l'alinéa c) du paragraphe suivant.

2. La demande de remise temporaire de la personne réclamée contient :

a) La justification de la nécessité de procéder à la remise;

b) Une déclaration selon laquelle la durée de la procédure correspondante n'excède pas trois ans; et

c) L'engagement de la Partie requérante à renvoyer la personne réclamée à l'issue de la procédure pour laquelle la remise est demandée ou après une période de trois ans. Dans ce dernier cas, la personne est restituée même si la procédure menée dans la Partie requérante n'est pas terminée.

3. La remise temporaire est recevable lorsque la durée de la peine de privation de liberté que la personne réclamée doit encore purger dans la Partie requise est supérieure à trois ans.

4. Le temps passé par la personne remise à titre temporaire sur le territoire de la Partie requérante est pris en compte pour l'exécution de sa peine dans la Partie requise.

Article 15. Procédure

Les demandes d'extradition adressées à la Partie requise sont traitées conformément aux procédures établies en la matière et régies par le droit de cette Partie.

Article 16. Remise de biens à la demande de la Partie requérante

1. Dans la mesure où la législation nationale de la Partie requise le permet et sans préjudice des droits des tiers, qui seront dûment respectés, les biens ou objets qui ont servi à commettre l'infraction et ceux qui en proviennent directement ou indirectement, ou qui peuvent de quelque

manière que ce soit servir d'éléments de preuve dans le cadre de la procédure, et qui sont trouvés en possession de la personne réclamée au moment de son arrestation, sont remis au moment où l'extradition est accordée, même si l'extradition ne peut être menée à son terme en raison du décès, de la disparition ou de l'évasion de l'inculpé.

2. Lorsque la Partie requise ou des tiers ont des droits sur les objets remis, il est vérifié qu'ils ont été remis à la Partie requérante aux fins d'une procédure pénale, conformément aux dispositions du présent article, et ils sont restitués à la Partie requise dans les conditions que cette dernière jugera appropriées et sans frais.

3. La Partie requise peut retenir temporairement ou remettre sous condition de restitution ou de retour ultérieurs les objets visés au paragraphe 1 du présent article et qui ne se trouvent pas en possession de la personne réclamée au moment de son arrestation, lorsqu'ils peuvent faire l'objet d'une mesure de saisie sur le territoire de cette Partie dans le cadre d'une procédure pénale en cours, sur demande d'entraide judiciaire.

Article 17. Transit

1. Le transit à travers le territoire de l'une des Parties d'une personne qui est remise à l'autre Partie par un État tiers est autorisé sur présentation, par la voie diplomatique, d'une copie certifiée conforme de la décision d'extradition.

2. La garde de la personne extradée incombe aux autorités de l'État de transit tant que ladite personne se trouve sur son territoire.

3. La Partie requérante rembourse à l'État de transit, sur demande de celui-ci, tous les frais engagés à cette fin.

Article 18. Frais

Tous frais et coûts résultant d'une extradition sont à la charge de la Partie sur le territoire de laquelle ils sont engagés. Les frais et coûts de transfèrement de la personne extradée ainsi que ceux résultant d'un permis de transit sont à la charge de la Partie requérante.

Article 19. Consultations et règlement des différends

1. Les Parties se consultent, à des moments convenus d'un commun accord, en vue de faciliter l'application des dispositions du présent Traité.

2. Tout différend entre les Parties concernant l'application, l'interprétation ou l'exécution des dispositions du présent Traité est réglé à l'amiable par la voie de négociations diplomatiques directes.

Article 20. Champ d'application temporel

Le présent Traité s'applique aux infractions visées à l'article 2 qui ont été commises avant ou après son entrée en vigueur.

Article 21. Protection des renseignements

Les Parties s'engagent à protéger les renseignements échangés en vertu du présent Traité, conformément aux dispositions de leur législation nationale applicable.

Article 22. Liens avec d'autres traités

Le présent Traité n'empêche pas les Parties de coopérer en matière d'extradition conformément à d'autres instruments internationaux auxquels elles sont parties.

Article 23. Entrée en vigueur, modifications et dénonciation

1. Le présent Traité entre en vigueur 30 jours après la date de réception de la dernière des notifications par lesquelles les Parties s'informent, par la voie diplomatique, de l'accomplissement des formalités requises par leur législation nationale, et reste en vigueur pour une durée indéterminée.

2. Dès l'entrée en vigueur du présent Traité, le Traité d'extradition entre les États-Unis du Mexique et la République de Cuba, signé à La Havane, Cuba, le 25 mai 1925, cesse de produire ses effets.

3. Le présent Traité peut être modifié par consentement mutuel des Parties, formalisé par des communications écrites adressées par la voie diplomatique. Ces modifications entrent en vigueur conformément à la procédure établie au paragraphe 1 du présent article.

4. Chacune des Parties peut à tout moment dénoncer le présent Traité par notification écrite adressée à l'autre Partie par la voie diplomatique, auquel cas le Traité cesse de produire ses effets 180 jours après la date de réception de ladite notification.

5. Les procédures d'extradition en cours au moment de la dénonciation du présent Traité sont menées à bien conformément au présent Traité.

SIGNÉ à Mexico, le 1er novembre 2013, en double exemplaire en langue espagnole, les deux textes faisant également foi.

Pour les États-Unis du Mexique :
JESÚS MURILLO KARAM
Procureur général de la République

Pour la République de Cuba :
BRUNO RODRÍGUEZ PARRILLA
Ministre des affaires étrangères

No. 52830

Germany and United States of America

Arrangement between the Government of the Federal Republic of Germany and the Government of the United States of America regarding the granting of exemptions and benefits to enterprises charged with providing Troop Care Services to the United States Forces stationed in the Federal Republic of Germany – "Sterling Medical Associates, Inc. (DOCPER-TC-07-36) (VN 110)". Berlin, 29 July 2015

Entry into force: *29 July 2015, in accordance with its provisions*

Authentic texts: *English and German*

Registration with the Secretariat of the United Nations: *Germany, 12 August 2015*

Not published in print, in accordance with article 12(2) of the General Assembly regulations to give effect to Article 102 of the Charter of the United Nations, as amended, and the publication practice of the Secretariat.

Allemagne et États-Unis d'Amérique

Arrangement entre le Gouvernement de la République fédérale d'Allemagne et le Gouvernement des États-Unis d'Amérique relatif à l'octroi d'exemptions et d'allocations aux entreprises chargées de fournir des services de soin aux forces américaines stationnées dans la République fédérale d'Allemagne – « Sterling Medical Associates, Inc. (DOCPER-TC-07-36) (VN 110) ». Berlin, 29 juillet 2015

Entrée en vigueur : *29 juillet 2015, conformément à ses dispositions*

Textes authentiques : *anglais et allemand*

Enregistrement auprès du Secrétariat de l'Organisation des Nations Unies : *Allemagne, 12 août 2015*

Non disponible en version imprimée, conformément au paragraphe 2 de l'article 12 du règlement de l'Assemblée générale destiné à mettre en application l'Article 102 de la Charte des Nations Unies, tel qu'amendé, et à la pratique du Secrétariat en matière de publication.

No. 52831

Germany and Togo

Agreement between the Government of the Federal Republic of Germany and the Government of the Togolese Republic concerning Financial Cooperation 2014. Lomé, 18 June 2015

Entry into force: *18 June 2015 by signature, in accordance with article 6*

Authentic texts: *French and German*

Registration with the Secretariat of the United Nations: *Germany, 12 August 2015*

Not published in print, in accordance with article 12(2) of the General Assembly regulations to give effect to Article 102 of the Charter of the United Nations, as amended, and the publication practice of the Secretariat.

Allemagne et Togo

Accord de coopération financière entre le Gouvernement de la République fédérale d'Allemagne et le Gouvernement de la République togolaise en 2014. Lomé, 18 juin 2015

Entrée en vigueur : *18 juin 2015 par signature, conformément à l'article 6*

Textes authentiques : *français et allemand*

Enregistrement auprès du Secrétariat de l'Organisation des Nations Unies : *Allemagne, 12 août 2015*

Non disponible en version imprimée, conformément au paragraphe 2 de l'article 12 du règlement de l'Assemblée générale destiné à mettre en application l'Article 102 de la Charte des Nations Unies, tel qu'amendé, et à la pratique du Secrétariat en matière de publication.

No. 52832

Germany and United States of America

Arrangement between the Government of the Federal Republic of Germany and the Government of the United States of America regarding the granting of exemptions and benefits to enterprises charged with providing Troop Care Services to the United States Forces stationed in the Federal Republic of Germany – "Science Applications International Corporation (DOCPER-TC-06-07) (VN 106)". Berlin, 25 June 2015

Entry into force: *25 June 2015, in accordance with its provisions*

Authentic texts: *English and German*

Registration with the Secretariat of the United Nations: *Germany, 12 August 2015*

Not published in print, in accordance with article 12(2) of the General Assembly regulations to give effect to Article 102 of the Charter of the United Nations, as amended, and the publication practice of the Secretariat.

Allemagne et États-Unis d'Amérique

Arrangement entre le Gouvernement de la République fédérale d'Allemagne et le Gouvernement des États-Unis d'Amérique relatif à l'octroi d'exemptions et d'allocations aux entreprises chargées de fournir des services de soin aux forces américaines stationnées dans la République fédérale d'Allemagne – « Science Applications International Corporation (DOCPER-TC-06-07) (VN 106) ». Berlin, 25 juin 2015

Entrée en vigueur : *25 juin 2015, conformément à ses dispositions*

Textes authentiques : *anglais et allemand*

Enregistrement auprès du Secrétariat de l'Organisation des Nations Unies : *Allemagne, 12 août 2015*

Non disponible en version imprimée, conformément au paragraphe 2 de l'article 12 du règlement de l'Assemblée générale destiné à mettre en application l'Article 102 de la Charte des Nations Unies, tel qu'amendé, et à la pratique du Secrétariat en matière de publication.

No. 52833

Germany and United States of America

Arrangement between the Government of the Federal Republic of Germany and the Government of the United States of America regarding the granting of exemptions and benefits to enterprises charged with providing Troop Care Services to the United States Forces stationed in the Federal Republic of Germany – "Science Applications International Corporation (DOCPER-TC-06-08) (VN 107)". Berlin, 25 June 2015

Entry into force: *25 June 2015, in accordance with its provisions*

Authentic texts: *English and German*

Registration with the Secretariat of the United Nations: *Germany, 12 August 2015*

Not published in print, in accordance with article 12(2) of the General Assembly regulations to give effect to Article 102 of the Charter of the United Nations, as amended, and the publication practice of the Secretariat.

Allemagne et États-Unis d'Amérique

Arrangement entre le Gouvernement de la République fédérale d'Allemagne et le Gouvernement des États-Unis d'Amérique relatif à l'octroi d'exemptions et d'allocations aux entreprises chargées de fournir des services de soin aux forces américaines stationnées dans la République fédérale d'Allemagne – « Science Applications International Corporation (DOCPER-TC-06-08) (VN 107) ». Berlin, 25 juin 2015

Entrée en vigueur : *25 juin 2015, conformément à ses dispositions*

Textes authentiques : *anglais et allemand*

Enregistrement auprès du Secrétariat de l'Organisation des Nations Unies : *Allemagne, 12 août 2015*

Non disponible en version imprimée, conformément au paragraphe 2 de l'article 12 du règlement de l'Assemblée générale destiné à mettre en application l'Article 102 de la Charte des Nations Unies, tel qu'amendé, et à la pratique du Secrétariat en matière de publication.

No. 52834

Germany and United States of America

Arrangement between the Government of the Federal Republic of Germany and the Government of the United States of America regarding the granting of exemptions and benefits to enterprises charged with providing Troop Care Services to the United States Forces stationed in the Federal Republic of Germany – "Leidos, Inc. (DOCPER-IT-03-07) (VN 258)". Berlin, 25 June 2015

Entry into force: *25 June 2015, in accordance with its provisions*

Authentic texts: *English and German*

Registration with the Secretariat of the United Nations: *Germany, 12 August 2015*

Not published in print, in accordance with article 12(2) of the General Assembly regulations to give effect to Article 102 of the Charter of the United Nations, as amended, and the publication practice of the Secretariat.

Allemagne et États-Unis d'Amérique

Arrangement entre le Gouvernement de la République fédérale d'Allemagne et le Gouvernement des États-Unis d'Amérique relatif à l'octroi d'exemptions et d'allocations aux entreprises chargées de fournir des services de soin aux forces américaines stationnées dans la République fédérale d'Allemagne – « Leidos, Inc. (DOCPER-IT-03-07) (VN 258) ». Berlin, 25 juin 2015

Entrée en vigueur : *25 juin 2015, conformément à ses dispositions*

Textes authentiques : *anglais et allemand*

Enregistrement auprès du Secrétariat de l'Organisation des Nations Unies : *Allemagne, 12 août 2015*

Non disponible en version imprimée, conformément au paragraphe 2 de l'article 12 du règlement de l'Assemblée générale destiné à mettre en application l'Article 102 de la Charte des Nations Unies, tel qu'amendé, et à la pratique du Secrétariat en matière de publication.

No. 52835

Germany and Uganda

Agreement between the Government of the Federal Republic of Germany and the Government of the Republic of Uganda concerning Financial Cooperation in 2013, Part 1. Kampala, 3 December 2014

Entry into force: *3 December 2014 by signature, in accordance with article 5*

Authentic texts: *English and German*

Registration with the Secretariat of the United Nations: *Germany, 12 August 2015*

Not published in print, in accordance with article 12(2) of the General Assembly regulations to give effect to Article 102 of the Charter of the United Nations, as amended, and the publication practice of the Secretariat.

Allemagne et Ouganda

Accord entre le Gouvernement de la République fédérale d'Allemagne et le Gouvernement de la République de l'Ouganda concernant la coopération financière en 2013, Partie 1. Kampala, 3 décembre 2014

Entrée en vigueur : *3 décembre 2014 par signature, conformément à l'article 5*

Textes authentiques : *anglais et allemand*

Enregistrement auprès du Secrétariat de l'Organisation des Nations Unies : *Allemagne, 12 août 2015*

Non disponible en version imprimée, conformément au paragraphe 2 de l'article 12 du règlement de l'Assemblée générale destiné à mettre en application l'Article 102 de la Charte des Nations Unies, tel qu'amendé, et à la pratique du Secrétariat en matière de publication.

No. 52836

Germany
and
Uganda

Agreement between the Government of the Federal Republic of Germany and the Government of the Republic of Uganda concerning Financial Cooperation in 2013, Part 2. Kampala, 18 December 2014

Entry into force: *18 December 2014 by signature, in accordance with article 6*

Authentic texts: *English and German*

Registration with the Secretariat of the United Nations: *Germany, 12 August 2015*

Not published in print, in accordance with article 12(2) of the General Assembly regulations to give effect to Article 102 of the Charter of the United Nations, as amended, and the publication practice of the Secretariat.

Allemagne
et
Ouganda

Accord entre le Gouvernement de la République fédérale d'Allemagne et le Gouvernement de la République de l'Ouganda concernant la coopération financière en 2013, Partie 2. Kampala, 18 décembre 2014

Entrée en vigueur : *18 décembre 2014 par signature, conformément à l'article 6*

Textes authentiques : *anglais et allemand*

Enregistrement auprès du Secrétariat de l'Organisation des Nations Unies : *Allemagne, 12 août 2015*

Non disponible en version imprimée, conformément au paragraphe 2 de l'article 12 du règlement de l'Assemblée générale destiné à mettre en application l'Article 102 de la Charte des Nations Unies, tel qu'amendé, et à la pratique du Secrétariat en matière de publication.

Uganda

Agreement between ... the Government of the Republic of Uganda ... Kampala, 19 December 20..

Entry into force ...

Authentic texts ...

Registration ...

Allemagne

Accord ... de la République ... Kampala, 19 décembre 20..

Entrée en vigueur ...

Textes authentiques ...

Enregistrement ...

No. 52837

Germany and United States of America

Arrangement between the Government of the Federal Republic of Germany and the Government of the United States of America regarding the granting of exemptions and benefits to enterprises charged with providing Troop Care Services to the United States Forces stationed in the Federal Republic of Germany – "General Dynamics Information Technology, Inc. (DOCPER-TC-40-02) (VN 39)". Berlin, 29 July 2015

Entry into force: *29 July 2015, in accordance with its provisions*

Authentic texts: *English and German*

Registration with the Secretariat of the United Nations: *Germany, 12 August 2015*

Not published in print, in accordance with article 12(2) of the General Assembly regulations to give effect to Article 102 of the Charter of the United Nations, as amended, and the publication practice of the Secretariat.

Allemagne et États-Unis d'Amérique

Arrangement entre le Gouvernement de la République fédérale d'Allemagne et le Gouvernement des États-Unis d'Amérique relatif à l'octroi d'exemptions et d'allocations aux entreprises chargées de fournir des services de soin aux forces américaines stationnées dans la République fédérale d'Allemagne – « General Dynamics Information Technology, Inc. (DOCPER-TC-40-02) (VN 39) ». Berlin, 29 juillet 2015

Entrée en vigueur : *29 juillet 2015, conformément à ses dispositions*

Textes authentiques : *anglais et allemand*

Enregistrement auprès du Secrétariat de l'Organisation des Nations Unies : *Allemagne, 12 août 2015*

Non disponible en version imprimée, conformément au paragraphe 2 de l'article 12 du règlement de l'Assemblée générale destiné à mettre en application l'Article 102 de la Charte des Nations Unies, tel qu'amendé, et à la pratique du Secrétariat en matière de publication.

No. 52838

Germany
and
United States of America

Arrangement between the Government of the Federal Republic of Germany and the Government of the United States of America regarding the granting of exemptions and benefits to enterprises charged with providing Troop Care Services to the United States Forces stationed in the Federal Republic of Germany – "Leidos, Inc. (DOCPER-TC-06-08) (VN 552)". Berlin, 25 June 2015

Entry into force: *25 June 2015, in accordance with its provisions*

Authentic texts: *English and German*

Registration with the Secretariat of the United Nations: *Germany, 12 August 2015*

Not published in print, in accordance with article 12(2) of the General Assembly regulations to give effect to Article 102 of the Charter of the United Nations, as amended, and the publication practice of the Secretariat.

Allemagne
et
États-Unis d'Amérique

Arrangement entre le Gouvernement de la République fédérale d'Allemagne et le Gouvernement des États-Unis d'Amérique relatif à l'octroi d'exemptions et d'allocations aux entreprises chargées de fournir des services de soin aux forces américaines stationnées dans la République fédérale d'Allemagne – « Leidos, Inc. (DOCPER-TC-06-08) (VN 552) ». Berlin, 25 juin 2015

Entrée en vigueur : *25 juin 2015, conformément à ses dispositions*

Textes authentiques : *anglais et allemand*

Enregistrement auprès du Secrétariat de l'Organisation des Nations Unies : *Allemagne, 12 août 2015*

Non disponible en version imprimée, conformément au paragraphe 2 de l'article 12 du règlement de l'Assemblée générale destiné à mettre en application l'Article 102 de la Charte des Nations Unies, tel qu'amendé, et à la pratique du Secrétariat en matière de publication.

No. 52839

Germany
and
Ethiopia

Agreement between the Government of the Federal Republic of Germany and the Government of the Federal Democratic Republic of Ethiopia concerning Financial Cooperation in 2014. Addis Ababa, 2 July 2015

Entry into force: *2 July 2015 by signature, in accordance with article 7*

Authentic texts: *English and German*

Registration with the Secretariat of the United Nations: *Germany, 12 August 2015*

Not published in print, in accordance with article 12(2) of the General Assembly regulations to give effect to Article 102 of the Charter of the United Nations, as amended, and the publication practice of the Secretariat.

Allemagne
et
Éthiopie

Accord entre le Gouvernement de la République fédérale d'Allemagne et le Gouvernement de la République fédérale démocratique d'Éthiopie concernant la coopération financière en 2014. Addis-Abeba, 2 juillet 2015

Entrée en vigueur : *2 juillet 2015 par signature, conformément à l'article 7*

Textes authentiques : *anglais et allemand*

Enregistrement auprès du Secrétariat de l'Organisation des Nations Unies : *Allemagne, 12 août 2015*

Non disponible en version imprimée, conformément au paragraphe 2 de l'article 12 du règlement de l'Assemblée générale destiné à mettre en application l'Article 102 de la Charte des Nations Unies, tel qu'amendé, et à la pratique du Secrétariat en matière de publication.

No. 52840

Germany
and
United States of America

Arrangement between the Government of the Federal Republic of Germany and the Government of the United States of America regarding the granting of exemptions and benefits to enterprises charged with providing Troop Care Services to the United States Forces stationed in the Federal Republic of Germany – "Sterling Medical Associates, Inc. (DOCPER-TC-07-35) (VN 105)". Berlin, 29 July 2015

Entry into force: *29 July 2015, in accordance with its provisions*

Authentic texts: *English and German*

Registration with the Secretariat of the United Nations: *Germany, 12 August 2015*

Not published in print, in accordance with article 12(2) of the General Assembly regulations to give effect to Article 102 of the Charter of the United Nations, as amended, and the publication practice of the Secretariat.

Allemagne
et
États-Unis d'Amérique

Arrangement entre le Gouvernement de la République fédérale d'Allemagne et le Gouvernement des États-Unis d'Amérique relatif à l'octroi d'exemptions et d'allocations aux entreprises chargées de fournir des services de soin aux forces américaines stationnées dans la République fédérale d'Allemagne – « Sterling Medical Associates, Inc. (DOCPER-TC-07-35) (VN 105) ». Berlin, 29 juillet 2015

Entrée en vigueur : *29 juillet 2015, conformément à ses dispositions*

Textes authentiques : *anglais et allemand*

Enregistrement auprès du Secrétariat de l'Organisation des Nations Unies : *Allemagne, 12 août 2015*

Non disponible en version imprimée, conformément au paragraphe 2 de l'article 12 du règlement de l'Assemblée générale destiné à mettre en application l'Article 102 de la Charte des Nations Unies, tel qu'amendé, et à la pratique du Secrétariat en matière de publication.

No. 52841

Germany
and
Intergovernmental Authority on Development

Agreement between the Government of the Federal Republic of Germany and the Intergovernmental Authority on Development (IGAD) concerning Financial Cooperation in 2012 and 2013. Djibouti, 2 March 2015

Entry into force: *2 March 2015 by signature, in accordance with article 5*

Authentic texts: *English and German*

Registration with the Secretariat of the United Nations: *Germany, 12 August 2015*

Not published in print, in accordance with article 12(2) of the General Assembly regulations to give effect to Article 102 of the Charter of the United Nations, as amended, and the publication practice of the Secretariat.

Allemagne
et
Autorité intergouvernementale pour le développement

Accord entre le Gouvernement de la République fédérale d'Allemagne et l'Autorité intergouvernementale pour le développement (IGAD) concernant la coopération financière en 2012 et 2013. Djibouti, 2 mars 2015

Entrée en vigueur : *2 mars 2015 par signature, conformément à l'article 5*

Textes authentiques : *anglais et allemand*

Enregistrement auprès du Secrétariat de l'Organisation des Nations Unies : *Allemagne, 12 août 2015*

Non disponible en version imprimée, conformément au paragraphe 2 de l'article 12 du règlement de l'Assemblée générale destiné à mettre en application l'Article 102 de la Charte des Nations Unies, tel qu'amendé, et à la pratique du Secrétariat en matière de publication.

No. 52842

Mexico
and
Cuba

Treaty on mutual judicial assistance in criminal matters between the United Mexican States and the Republic of Cuba. Mexico City, 1 November 2013

Entry into force: *29 April 2015, in accordance with article XXVI*

Authentic text: *Spanish*

Registration with the Secretariat of the United Nations: *Mexico, 5 August 2015*

Mexique
et
Cuba

Traité d'entraide judiciaire en matière pénale entre les États-Unis du Mexique et la République de Cuba. Mexico, 1er novembre 2013

Entrée en vigueur : *29 avril 2015, conformément à l'article XXVI*

Texte authentique : *espagnol*

Enregistrement auprès du Secrétariat de l'Organisation des Nations Unies : *Mexique, 5 août 2015*

[SPANISH TEXT – TEXTE ESPAGNOL]

TRATADO SOBRE ASISTENCIA JURÍDICA MUTUA EN MATERIA PENAL ENTRE LOS ESTADOS UNIDOS MEXICANOS Y LA REPÚBLICA DE CUBA

Los Estados Unidos Mexicanos y la República de Cuba en adelante denominados "las Partes";

INTERESADAS en mejorar y reforzar la colaboración entre los dos países con la intención de reprimir la delincuencia y combatir la impunidad de sus actores;

DESEANDO cooperar más estrechamente con base en los principios de respeto mutuo, soberanía e igualdad;

ANIMADAS por el deseo de fomentar acciones conjuntas de prevención, control y represión del delito en todas sus formas, a través de la coordinación de acciones tendentes a agilizar los mecanismos tradicionales de asistencia jurídica;

CON BASE en el respeto mutuo a la soberanía y a la igualdad entre los Estados;

Han acordado lo siguiente:

ARTÍCULO I
ÁMBITO DE APLICACIÓN

1. Las Partes se prestarán, de conformidad con el presente Tratado, asistencia jurídica mutua en materia penal.

2. La asistencia jurídica se prestará aun cuando las acciones o las omisiones que den lugar a las solicitudes de asistencia jurídica no sean consideradas como delitos por la legislación nacional de la Parte Requerida, excepto en aquellos casos en que dichas solicitudes se presenten para la ejecución de medidas de precaución o precautorias (aseguramiento, embargo, cateo, ocupación o depósito).

3. El presente Tratado se extenderá a las investigaciones y procedimientos penales sobre cualquier delito previsto por la legislación nacional de cualquiera de las Partes.

4. Asimismo, la asistencia jurídica se prestará cuando la solicitud se refiera a delitos relacionados con impuestos, derechos de aduana, control de cambios y otros de naturaleza fiscal.

5. El presente Tratado se aplicará a cualquier solicitud de asistencia jurídica presentada después del inicio de su entrada en vigor, inclusive si las acciones o las omisiones respectivas tuvieron lugar antes de esa fecha.

ARTÍCULO II
AUTORIDADES CENTRALES

1. Para asegurar la debida cooperación entre las Partes en la prestación de la asistencia jurídica objeto del presente Tratado, se designan como Autoridades Centrales, por parte de los Estados Unidos Mexicanos, a la Procuraduría General de la República y por parte de la República de Cuba, al Ministerio de Justicia. Las Partes se notificarán sin demora, por la vía diplomática, cualquier modificación de sus Autoridades Centrales y ámbitos de competencia.

2. Las Autoridades Centrales de las Partes transmitirán y recibirán directamente las solicitudes de asistencia jurídica a que se refiere el presente Tratado y las respuestas a éstas.

3. La Autoridad Central de la Parte Requerida cumplirá las solicitudes de asistencia jurídica en forma expedita o las transmitirá para su ejecución a la autoridad competente, alentando a la misma para el cumplimiento rápido y adecuado de la solicitud de asistencia jurídica de la Parte Requirente.

ARTÍCULO III
ALCANCES DE LA ASISTENCIA JURÍDICA

La asistencia jurídica comprenderá:

1. notificación y entrega de documentos procesales;
2. entrega de documentos, objetos y medios de prueba;
3. intercambio de información;
4. localización e identificación de personas y objetos;

5. recepción de declaraciones y testimonios;

6. realización de peritajes u otras actuaciones procesales establecidas en su legislación nacional, relacionadas con las investigaciones de que se trate;

7. ejecución de medidas de precaución o precautorias sobre activos o bienes, de conformidad con la legislación del país requerido; tales como órdenes de embargo o aseguramiento, cateo, registro, ocupación o depósito de bienes u objetos que sirvieron para la perpetración del delito y los provenientes directa o indirectamente del mismo, así como su devolución y división;

8. citación y traslado de testigos, víctimas y peritos para comparecencia voluntaria ante la autoridad competente de la Parte Requirente;

9. traslado temporal de personas detenidas para comparecer en el territorio de la Parte Requirente en un proceso penal como testigo o víctimas o para otras actuaciones procesales, previamente determinadas en la solicitud de asistencia jurídica;

10. autorización de la presencia de representantes de las autoridades competentes de la Parte Requirente, como observadores durante la ejecución de una solicitud de asistencia jurídica; y

11. cualquier otra forma de asistencia jurídica de conformidad con los fines del presente Tratado, que sea compatible con la legislación nacional de la Parte Requerida.

ARTÍCULO IV
LIMITACIONES EN LA ASISTENCIA JURÍDICA

1. El presente Tratado no faculta a las autoridades de una de las Partes a ejercer, en el territorio de la Otra, funciones cuya competencia esté exclusivamente reservada a las autoridades de esa otra Parte de conformidad con su legislación nacional.

2. Las disposiciones del presente Tratado no otorgan derecho alguno a favor de personas físicas o morales para la obtención, eliminación o exclusión de pruebas solicitadas directa o indirectamente por alguna autoridad o a impedir el cumplimiento de una solicitud de asistencia jurídica.

3. De la misma manera, el presente Tratado no será aplicable:

a) para la detención de personas con fines de extradición, ni para la ejecución de solicitudes de extradición;

b) para la ejecución de sentencias penales, incluido el traslado de personas sentenciadas; o

c) para otorgar asistencia jurídica directa a terceros estados.

ARTÍCULO V
MEDIDAS DE PRECAUCIÓN O PRECAUTORIAS

1. A solicitud por escrito de la Parte Requirente y en caso de que el procedimiento requerido en la solicitud de asistencia jurídica sea admisible, de conformidad con la legislación nacional de la Parte Requerida, ésta podrá ejecutar las medidas de precaución o precautorias correspondientes con el fin de mantener el estado que guarda la situación de hecho y de derecho existente, protegiendo los intereses jurídicos amenazados o de preservar las pruebas al respecto.

2. En casos urgentes, las medidas de precaución o precautorias podrán ser tramitadas desde el anuncio de una solicitud de asistencia jurídica, siempre que se haya proporcionado información suficiente que permita determinar que se han satisfecho las condiciones para solicitar medidas de precaución o precautorias, y serán canceladas si la Parte Requirente no formaliza la solicitud de asistencia jurídica dentro de un plazo razonable.

ARTÍCULO VI
TRÁMITE Y CONTENIDO DE LA SOLICITUD DE ASISTENCIA JURÍDICA

1. La solicitud de asistencia jurídica se formulará por escrito.

2. La Parte Requerida iniciará inmediatamente el trámite de la solicitud de asistencia jurídica al recibirla por fax, correo electrónico u otro medio de comunicación similar, debiendo transmitir la Parte Requirente la solicitud de manera formal dentro de un plazo razonable siguiente a su envío por los medios mencionados.

3. La Parte Requerida informará a la Parte Requirente los resultados de la ejecución de la solicitud de asistencia jurídica después de haberla recibido de manera formal. Sin embargo, si la Parte Requirente manifiesta la urgencia de la asistencia jurídica, la falta de presentación formal de la solicitud de asistencia jurídica, no será obstáculo para que la Parte Requerida notifique los resultados de la misma.

4. La solicitud de asistencia jurídica deberá contener:

a) el nombre de la institución y de la autoridad competente que tiene a su cargo la investigación o el procedimiento penal del que deriva la solicitud;

b) el propósito y la descripción de la misma;

c) la descripción de los hechos materia de investigación o procedimiento penal, la transcripción de las disposiciones legales vigentes que tipifican la conducta como hecho punible y de las que fijan la jurisdicción y, cuando sea necesario, el documento que señale la cuantía del daño causado;

d) el fundamento y descripción de cualquier procedimiento especial que la Parte Requirente desee que se practique al ejecutar la solicitud de asistencia jurídica, siempre y cuando no sea contrario a la legislación nacional de la Parte Requerida;

e) el plazo dentro del cual la Parte Requirente desea que la solicitud de asistencia jurídica sea cumplida, el cual será fijado por las Autoridades Centrales, de conformidad con la legislación nacional de la Parte Requerida;

f) en su caso, la petición para que asistan representantes de las autoridades competentes de la Parte Requirente a la ejecución de la solicitud de asistencia jurídica;

g) la identificación de personas sujetas a investigación o procedimiento penal;

h) el nombre completo o cualquier otro dato como: la fecha de nacimiento, el domicilio, el número de teléfono que permita la identificación y localización de las personas a ser notificadas y su relación con la investigación o proceso judicial en curso;

i) la ubicación o descripción del lugar a catear o inspeccionar;

j) la ubicación y descripción de los bienes o activos a asegurar, ocupar o depositar;

k) las preguntas a ser formuladas en el desahogo del testimonio o en el dictamen pericial; y

l) cualquier otra información que pueda ser de utilidad para la Parte Requerida en el cumplimiento de la solicitud de asistencia jurídica.

5. Si la Parte Requerida considera que la información contenida en la solicitud de asistencia jurídica no es suficiente para efectuarla, podrá solicitar información adicional.

ARTÍCULO VII
DENEGACIÓN O APLAZAMIENTO DE LA SOLICITUD DE ASISTENCIA JURÍDICA

1. La solicitud de asistencia jurídica podrá ser denegada cuando:

a) su cumplimiento pueda causar daño a la seguridad o al orden público de la Parte Requerida;

b) el cumplimiento sea contrario a la legislación nacional de la Parte Requerida o no se ajuste a las disposiciones del presente Tratado o sea contrario a las obligaciones internacionales de la Parte Requerida;

c) la solicitud de asistencia jurídica se refiera a las acciones o a las omisiones por las cuales la persona sujeta a investigación o a proceso penal en la Parte Requirente ya fue sentenciada o absuelta por los mismos hechos en la Parte Requerida o la acción penal haya prescrito;

d) la solicitud de asistencia jurídica se refiera a delitos militares, que no estén contemplados en la legislación penal común;

e) si el delito por el cual se solicita la asistencia jurídica es considerado por la Parte Requerida como un delito de carácter/naturaleza política. Para los efectos de este Tratado, no serán considerados delitos de carácter/naturaleza política y, por tanto, la solicitud de asistencia jurídica será tramitada:

   1. cualquier delito contra la vida, la integridad física o la libertad de un jefe de Estado o Gobierno extranjero, o contra miembros de su familia;

   2. el genocidio, los crímenes de guerra cometidos contra la paz y la seguridad de la humanidad;

   3. los actos de terrorismo, tales como:

      i. El atentado contra la vida, la integridad física o la libertad de individuos que tengan derecho a una protección internacional, incluidos los agentes diplomáticos.

      ii. La toma de rehenes o el secuestro de personas.

      iii. El atentado contra personas o bienes cometidos mediante el empleo de bombas, granadas, cohetes, minas, armas de fuego, explosivos o dispositivos similares.

      iv. Los actos de captura ilícita de barcos o aeronaves.

v. Cualquier acto de violencia no incluido entre los anteriores y que esté dirigido contra la vida, la integridad física, o la libertad de las personas, o que viniesen a afectar instituciones.

4. los delitos cometidos por funcionarios públicos en ejercicio de sus atribuciones o por sujetos activos vinculados o relacionados con servidores públicos; y

5. la tentativa en la comisión de delitos previstos en este Artículo o la participación como actor o cómplice de una persona que cometa o intente cometer dichos delitos.

f) existan motivos fundados por la Parte Requerida para creer que la solicitud de asistencia jurídica se ha formulado con miras a procesar a una persona por razón de su raza, sexo, religión, nacionalidad, origen étnico, pertenencia a un grupo social determinado u opiniones políticas, o que la situación de esa persona pueda resultar perjudicada por cualquiera de esas razones;

g) hubiere posibilidad de que como resultado del procedimiento penal por el cual se solicita la asistencia jurídica, se imponga o ejecute una pena prohibida por la legislación nacional de la Parte Requerida; a menos que la Parte Requirente se comprometa a no aplicarla; y

h) la solicitud de asistencia jurídica no reúna los requerimientos del presente Tratado.

2. El secreto bancario o tributario no podrá ser utilizado como argumento para negar la asistencia jurídica.

3. La Parte Requerida podrá denegar o aplazar el cumplimiento de la solicitud de asistencia jurídica cuando considere que su ejecución puede perjudicar u obstaculizar una investigación o procedimiento judicial en curso en su territorio.

4. Antes de denegar o aplazar la ejecución de una solicitud de asistencia jurídica, la Parte Requerida analizará la posibilidad de que la asistencia jurídica se conceda bajo las condiciones que considere necesarias. Si la Parte Requirente acepta la asistencia jurídica bajo esas condiciones, ésta se desahogará conforme a las mismas.

5. Si la Parte Requerida decide denegar o aplazar la asistencia jurídica, lo informará a la Parte Requirente por medio de su Autoridad Central, expresando los motivos de tal decisión a la brevedad.

ARTÍCULO VIII
VALIDEZ DE LOS DOCUMENTOS

1. Los documentos remitidos en el marco del presente Tratado y certificados por las Autoridades competentes o Centrales de la Parte Remitente se reputarán como auténticos sin necesidad de que medie legalización o formalización alguna.

Sin perjuicio de lo anterior, si en la solicitud se requiere que los documentos tengan una formalidad específica, la Parte Requerida los enviará de esa forma si no lo impide su legislación nacional.

2. Para los efectos del presente Tratado, los documentos que se reconocen como oficiales en el territorio de una de las Partes se reconocen como tales en el territorio de la otra Parte.

ARTÍCULO IX
CONFIDENCIALIDAD Y LIMITACIONES EN EL EMPLEO DE LA INFORMACIÓN

1. La Parte Requerida asegurará la confidencialidad de la recepción de una solicitud de asistencia jurídica, de su contenido y cualquier actuación emprendida conforme a la misma, salvo que su conocimiento sea necesario para ejecutar el requerimiento.

Si para la ejecución de la solicitud de asistencia jurídica fuera necesario contravenir la confidencialidad, la Parte Requerida solicitará la autorización de la Parte Requirente mediante comunicación escrita. Sin dicha autorización, la solicitud de asistencia jurídica no se ejecutará.

2. La Parte Requirente no utilizará ninguna información o prueba obtenida mediante el presente Tratado para fines distintos a los declarados en la solicitud de asistencia jurídica, sin previa autorización de la Parte Requerida.

3. En casos particulares, si la Parte Requirente necesitara divulgar y utilizar, total o parcialmente, la información o prueba para propósitos diferentes a los especificados, solicitará la autorización correspondiente a la Parte Requerida, la que podrá acceder o denegar, total o parcialmente lo solicitado.

4. El uso de cualquier información o prueba que haya sido obtenida de conformidad con el presente Tratado y que tenga el carácter de pública en la Parte Requirente dentro de la investigación o el procedimiento descrito en la solicitud de asistencia jurídica, no estará sujeta a la restricción a que se refiere el numeral anterior.

ARTÍCULO X
EJECUCIÓN DE LA SOLICITUD DE ASISTENCIA JURÍDICA

1. El cumplimiento de la solicitud de asistencia jurídica se llevará a cabo de conformidad con la legislación nacional de la Parte Requerida y de acuerdo con las disposiciones del presente Tratado. La solicitud de asistencia jurídica se ejecutará a la brevedad.

2. La Parte Requerida cumplirá la solicitud de asistencia jurídica de acuerdo con las formas y procedimientos especiales indicados en ella por la Parte Requirente, salvo cuando éstos sean incompatibles con la legislación nacional de la Parte Requerida.

3. La Autoridad Central de la Parte Requerida remitirá oportunamente a la Autoridad Central de la Parte Requirente la información y las pruebas obtenidas como resultado de la ejecución de la solicitud de asistencia jurídica.

4. Cuando no sea posible cumplir con la solicitud de asistencia jurídica, en todo o en parte, la Autoridad Central de la Parte Requerida lo hará saber inmediatamente a la Autoridad Central de la Parte Requirente e informará las razones que impidan su cumplimiento.

ARTÍCULO XI
PRESENCIA DE REPRESENTANTES DE LA PARTE REQUIRENTE EN LA EJECUCIÓN DE LA SOLICITUD DE ASISTENCIA JURÍDICA

1. La Parte Requirente podrá solicitar a la Parte Requerida, la presencia de representantes de sus autoridades competentes, como observadores, en la ejecución de la solicitud de asistencia jurídica, pudiendo requerir que en el desahogo o tramitación de una prueba testimonial o pericial, sus representantes formulen preguntas por medio de la autoridad competente de la Parte Requerida y de acuerdo con la legislación nacional de ambas Partes.

2. La presencia de representantes deberá estar previamente autorizada por la Parte Requerida, misma que informará con antelación a la Parte Requirente sobre la fecha, hora y lugar de la ejecución de la solicitud de asistencia jurídica.

3. La Parte Requirente remitirá la relación de los nombres, cargos y motivo de la presencia de sus representantes así como los cuestionarios a utilizar en el examen del

testigo o perito, con un plazo razonable de anticipación a la fecha de la ejecución de la solicitud de asistencia jurídica.

ARTÍCULO XII
NOTIFICACIÓN Y ENTREGA DE DOCUMENTOS

1. Conforme a la solicitud de asistencia jurídica, la Autoridad Central de la Parte Requerida procederá, en un plazo razonable, a realizar o tramitar la entrega de documentos procesales.

2. El cumplimiento de la solicitud de asistencia jurídica se acreditará por medio de un documento de entrega, fechado y firmado por el destinatario o por medio de una declaración de la autoridad competente de la Parte Requerida constando el hecho, la fecha y la forma de notificación y entrega.

ARTÍCULO XIII
INMUNIDADES Y DERECHOS

1. Si un particular que pueda verse afectado por la ejecución de la solicitud de asistencia jurídica, invoca inmunidad o derecho de conformidad con la legislación nacional de la Parte Requerida, esta invocación será resuelta por la autoridad competente de la Parte Requerida con anterioridad al cumplimiento de la solicitud de asistencia jurídica y comunicada a la Parte Requirente por medio de la Autoridad Central.

2. Si el particular invoca inmunidad o derecho de conformidad con la legislación nacional de la Parte Requirente, tal invocación será informada por medio de las respectivas Autoridades Centrales, a fin de que las autoridades competentes de la Parte Requirente resuelvan al respecto.

ARTÍCULO XIV
OBTENCIÓN DE PRUEBAS EN LA PARTE REQUERIDA

1. La Parte Requerida recabará en su territorio declaraciones de testigos y víctimas, peritajes, documentos, objetos y demás pruebas mencionadas en la solicitud de asistencia jurídica, de conformidad con su legislación nacional y los transmitirá a la Parte Requirente.

2. Previa solicitud de la Parte Requirente, la Autoridad Central de la Parte Requerida le informará a la Autoridad Central de la otra Parte, la fecha, hora y lugar donde se realizará la recepción del testimonio o prueba respectiva.

3. De conformidad con el numeral 1 del presente Artículo, la Parte Requerida entregará a la Parte Requirente las actas de las diligencias, al igual que los documentos, actas, archivos, pruebas u objetos, para los cuales se formuló la solicitud de asistencia jurídica.

4. A efecto de ejecutar la solicitud de asistencia jurídica, la autoridad competente de la Parte Requerida podrá apercibir, mediante citatorio, a la persona cuya presencia se requiera para comparecer y testificar o presentar documentos, archivos u objetos, en las mismas condiciones en que se haría en investigaciones o procedimientos penales en dicha Parte.

5. La Parte Requirente cumplirá toda condición acordada con la Parte Requerida relativa a los documentos u objetos que le entregue, incluyendo la protección de derecho a terceros sobre tales documentos y objetos.

6. A menos que los documentos originales sean expresamente solicitados, se proporcionarán copias certificadas por la Autoridad Central o competente de la Parte Requerida. La Parte Requerida podrá negar la entrega de los documentos originales si éstos fueran necesarios en un procedimiento penal en curso dentro de su territorio.

7. A solicitud de la Parte Requerida, la Parte Requirente devolverá a la brevedad los originales de los documentos y objetos que le hayan sido entregados, de acuerdo con el numeral 1 del presente Artículo.

ARTÍCULO XV
LOCALIZACIÓN E IDENTIFICACIÓN DE PERSONAS Y OBJETOS

A solicitud de la Parte Requirente, las autoridades competentes de la Parte Requerida adoptarán todas las medidas contempladas en su legislación nacional para la localización e identificación de personas y objetos mencionados en la solicitud de asistencia jurídica.

ARTÍCULO XVI
COMPARECENCIA DE PERSONAS EN LA PARTE REQUIRENTE

1. Cuando la Parte Requirente solicite la comparecencia de una persona en calidad de testigo, víctima o perito, que se encuentre en el territorio de la Parte Requerida, para rendir testimonio, peritaje u otras actuaciones procesales en su territorio, la Parte Requerida procederá a su citación y traslado de conformidad con la solicitud de asistencia jurídica formulada.

2. El traslado de la persona sólo podrá realizarse si ésta manifiesta su aceptación por escrito. Asimismo, gozará de las siguientes garantías en la Parte Requirente:

a) no se aplicará medida de apremio o sanción alguna en caso de que no comparezca en la Parte Requirente;

b) no será procesada, detenida o sujeta a cualquier otra restricción de libertad personal en esa Parte por cualquier hecho delictivo cometido previamente a su salida de la Parte Requerida. Sin embargo, será responsable por el contenido de la declaración testimonial o el dictamen pericial que rinda.

   La garantía prevista en este inciso no tendrá aplicación si la persona, estando en libertad para abandonar voluntariamente el territorio de la Parte Requirente, no lo deja en un período de treinta (30) días después de que oficialmente se le haya notificado que ya no se requiere su presencia, o habiendo partido, regresa voluntariamente al territorio de la Parte Requirente; y

c) no estará obligada a declarar en cualquier otro procedimiento diferente al que se refiere la solicitud de asistencia jurídica.

3. La Parte Requerida notificará a la persona a ser trasladada, mediante citatorio, el que deberá contener las garantías a que se refiere el numeral anterior y señalar que los gastos de su traslado corresponderán a la Parte Requirente, de acuerdo con el Artículo XXIII.

4. La Parte Requerida no podrá sancionar a la persona o aplicar medidas de apremio en su contra, en caso de que ésta no comparezca a la citación.

ARTÍCULO XVII
TRASLADO PROVISIONAL DE PERSONAS DETENIDAS

1. Toda persona que se encuentre detenida en la Parte Requerida, independientemente de su nacionalidad, podrá ser trasladada temporalmente a la Parte Requirente, con el consentimiento de la Autoridad Central de la Parte Requerida, para prestar declaración como testigo, víctima o para otras actuaciones procesales mencionadas en la solicitud de asistencia jurídica con la condición de devolver al detenido a la Parte Requerida en el plazo indicado por ésta.

El plazo inicial para el traslado, estadía y regreso de la persona no podrá ser superior a sesenta (60) días. El tiempo de estadía de la persona trasladada podrá ser ampliado por la Autoridad Central de la Parte Requerida, mediante una solicitud fundada de la Autoridad Central de la Parte Requirente.

La forma y condiciones de traslado y el retorno de la persona, se acordarán entre las Autoridades Centrales.

2. Se denegará el traslado:

a) si la persona detenida no consiente en ello por escrito;

b) si su presencia es necesaria para la continuación de un procedimiento penal en curso en el territorio de la Parte Requerida;

c) si el plazo de estadía de la persona en la Parte Requirente puede exceder el término fijado para el cumplimiento de una sentencia privativa de libertad en la Parte Requerida; o

d) si el traslado de la persona al territorio de la Parte Requirente pone en riesgo su seguridad, su salud, o su vida.

3. La Parte Requirente custodiará a la persona trasladada mientras ésta permanezca en su territorio. Si las autoridades de la Parte Requerida levantan la medida restrictiva de libertad de la persona trasladada, la Parte Requirente deberá regresar a la persona trasladada inmediatamente a la Parte Requerida.

4. El tiempo de estadía de la persona trasladada fuera del territorio de la Parte Requerida, se computará para efectos del cumplimiento de la sentencia penal que se le haya dictado en esta última.

5. La persona detenida que no otorgue su consentimiento para comparecer ante la Parte Requirente, no podrá ser sometida a ninguna medida de apremio o sanción por este hecho.

ARTÍCULO XVIII
PROTECCIÓN DE PERSONAS CITADAS O TRASLADADAS A LA PARTE REQUIRENTE

Cuando sea necesario, la Parte Requirente asegurará la protección de las personas citadas o trasladadas a su territorio, de conformidad con los Artículos XVI y XVII del presente Tratado.

ARTÍCULO XIX
AUDIENCIA POR VIDEOCONFERENCIA

1. La Parte Requirente podrá solicitar que la declaración de una persona que se encuentre en territorio de la Parte Requerida, se realice mediante audiencia por videoconferencia.

2. La Parte Requerida consentirá la audiencia por videoconferencia en la medida en que dicho método no resulte contrario a su legislación nacional. Si la Parte Requerida no dispone de los medios técnicos que permitan una videoconferencia, la Parte Requirente podrá ponerlos a su disposición.

3. Las reglas siguientes se aplicarán a la audiencia por videoconferencia:

a) la audiencia será realizada en presencia de una autoridad competente de la Parte Requerida. Esta autoridad también es responsable de la identificación de la persona a la que se toma declaración y del respeto de los principios fundamentales previstos en la legislación nacional de la Parte Requerida. En el caso de que la autoridad de la Parte Requerida estimara que no se respetan los principios fundamentales de su derecho durante la audiencia, adoptará inmediatamente las medidas necesarias para velar porque la audiencia prosiga conforme a su derecho;

b) las autoridades competentes de las Partes convendrán, de ser necesario, las medidas relativas a la protección de la persona a la que se tomará declaración;

c) la audiencia se efectuará directamente por la Parte Requirente o bajo su dirección, de conformidad con su legislación nacional; y

d) al término de la audiencia, la autoridad competente de la Parte Requerida levantará un acta, indicando la fecha, hora y lugar de la misma, la identidad de la persona a la que se tomó declaración, su contenido, así como las identidades y calidades de las demás personas que hayan participado en la audiencia. Este documento será transmitido a la Parte Requirente.

ARTÍCULO XX
CASOS ESPECIALES DE ASISTENCIA

La Parte Requerida presentará en casos especiales, en la medida en que sus autoridades competentes puedan obtenerlos, extractos de expedientes penales y/o documentos u objetos que sean necesarios en una investigación y/o procedimiento penal, salvo aquellos documentos y objetos que contengan la información que constituya secreto de Estado.

ARTÍCULO XXI
TRANSMISIÓN ESPONTÁNEA DE MEDIOS DE PRUEBA Y DE INFORMACIÓN

1. Por conducto de las Autoridades Centrales y dentro de los límites de su legislación nacional, las autoridades competentes de cada Parte podrán, sin que hubiera sido presentada una solicitud de asistencia jurídica en ese sentido, intercambiar información y medios de prueba con respecto a hechos penalmente sancionables cuando estimen que esta transmisión es de naturaleza tal que permitiría a la otra Parte:

a) presentar una solicitud de asistencia jurídica conforme al presente Tratado;

b) iniciar procedimientos penales; o

c) facilitar el desarrollo de una investigación penal en curso.

2. La Parte que proporcione la información podrá, de conformidad con su legislación nacional, sujetar su utilización por la Parte destinataria a determinadas condiciones. La Parte destinataria estará obligada a respetar esas condiciones.

ARTÍCULO XXII
RESTRICCIÓN DEL DOMINIO DE OBJETOS, PRODUCTOS O INSTRUMENTOS DEL DELITO

1. La Parte Requerida, a solicitud de la Parte Requirente, llevará a cabo las diligencias e investigaciones requeridas para averiguar si en su territorio se hallan

objetos, productos o instrumentos de un delito o relacionados con éste y comunicará a la Parte Requirente los resultados de las mismas. Al formular la solicitud, la Parte Requirente comunicará a la Parte Requerida los motivos para considerar que en el territorio de esta última pueden hallarse objetos, ganancias, productos o instrumentos de un delito o relativos a él.

2. Una vez localizadas las ganancias o los productos del delito o los objetos relacionados con éste, de conformidad con el numeral 1 del presente Artículo, la Parte Requerida, a solicitud de la Parte Requirente, adoptará las medidas previstas en su legislación nacional a fin de asegurar los mismos y tomará las medidas necesarias para evitar su transacción, transferencia o enajenación o destrucción.

3. En la medida en que lo permita su legislación nacional y previa solicitud de la Parte Requirente, la Parte Requerida deberá solicitar prioritariamente la restitución a la Parte Requirente de las ganancias y/o productos de los delitos, con miras en particular a indemnizar a las víctimas o restituirlos al propietario legítimo, sin perjuicio de los derechos de terceros de buena fe.

4. La entrega de las ganancias y/o productos del delito se realizará previo acuerdo sobre la compartición de los mismos, de conformidad con la legislación nacional de las Partes. La compartición de las ganancias y/o productos se llevará a cabo a través de un acuerdo entre las Autoridades Centrales, el cual deberá realizarse antes de que cause ejecutoria la resolución que decida sobre la extinción del dominio y entrega de las ganancias y/o productos del delito.

5. La entrega se efectuará en los términos de la legislación nacional de la Parte Requerida y será previa deducción de los gastos propios de su administración y el pago de contribuciones y gravámenes a que estuvieren sujetos.

6. Esta solicitud de asistencia jurídica también incluye a los instrumentos utilizados para cometer el ilícito.

ARTÍCULO XXIII
GASTOS

1. La Parte Requerida asumirá los gastos ordinarios de la ejecución de solicitudes de asistencia jurídica, salvo en los casos siguientes que serán sufragados por la Parte Requirente:

a) gastos relativos al traslado de las personas a su territorio y de regreso, conforme a los Artículos XVI y XVII del presente Tratado y a su estadía en territorio de la Parte Requirente, así como otros gastos personales relacionados con el desahogo de la asistencia jurídica;

b) gastos y honorarios de peritos;

c) gastos relativos a transporte y estadía de los representantes de autoridades competentes de la Parte Requirente durante la ejecución de la solicitud de asistencia jurídica, de conformidad con el Artículo XI, numeral 1, del presente Tratado; y

d) gastos relativos al envío y devolución de objetos trasladados del territorio de la Parte Requerida al territorio de la Parte Requirente.

2. En caso de que la solicitud de asistencia jurídica requiera de gastos cuantiosos o de carácter extraordinario, las Autoridades Centrales se consultarán para determinar las condiciones en que se dará cumplimiento a la solicitud de asistencia jurídica, así como la manera como se sufragarán los gastos.

ARTÍCULO XXIV
OTROS ACUERDOS O INSTRUMENTOS JURÍDICOS

1. Las disposiciones del presente Tratado no afectarán una solicitud de asistencia jurídica más amplia que hubiera sido o fuera convenida entre las Partes en otros acuerdos o instrumentos jurídicos o que resultara de su legislación nacional.

2. Las Partes asegurarán la adopción de todas las medidas necesarias para dar eficacia a las disposiciones del presente Tratado.

ARTÍCULO XXV
CONSULTAS Y SOLUCIÓN DE CONTROVERSIAS

1. Las Autoridades Centrales de las Partes, a propuesta de cualquiera de ellas, celebrarán consultas sobre temas de interpretación o aplicación del presente Tratado en general o sobre una solicitud de asistencia jurídica en específico.

2. Cualquier controversia derivada de la interpretación o aplicación del presente Tratado será resuelta de forma amigable por la vía diplomática.

ARTÍCULO XXVI
ENTRADA EN VIGOR, ENMIENDAS Y TERMINACIÓN

1. El presente Tratado entrará en vigor treinta (30) días después de la fecha de recepción de la última notificación en que las Partes se comuniquen, por escrito y por la vía diplomática, el cumplimiento de los requisitos exigidos por su legislación nacional, y tendrá vigencia indefinida.

2. A la entrada en vigor del presente Tratado, quedará sin efectos el Tratado de Cooperación entre el Gobierno de los Estados Unidos Mexicanos y el Gobierno de la República de Cuba sobre Asistencia Jurídica Mutua en Materia Penal, suscrito en la Ciudad de México el 23 de abril de 1996.

3. El presente Tratado podrá ser modificado por mutuo consentimiento de las Partes, formalizado a través de comunicaciones escritas y por la vía diplomática. Dichas modificaciones entrarán en vigor de conformidad con el procedimiento establecido en el numeral 1 de este Artículo.

4. Cualquiera de las Partes podrá dar por terminado el presente Tratado en cualquier momento, mediante notificación escrita, dirigida a la otra Parte a través de la vía diplomática. La vigencia del Tratado cesará ciento ochenta (180) días después de la fecha de recibo de tal notificación.

5. La terminación del presente Tratado no afectará la conclusión de las solicitudes de asistencia jurídica que se hayan recibido durante su vigencia.

Firmado en la Ciudad de México, el primero de noviembre de dos mil trece, en dos ejemplares originales en idioma español, siendo ambos textos igualmente auténticos.

POR LOS ESTADOS UNIDOS MEXICANOS	POR LA REPÚBLICA DE CUBA
Jesús Murillo Karam Procurador General de la República	Bruno Rodríguez Parrilla Ministro de Relaciones Exteriores

[TRANSLATION – TRADUCTION]

TREATY ON MUTUAL JUDICIAL ASSISTANCE IN CRIMINAL MATTERS BETWEEN THE UNITED MEXICAN STATES AND THE REPUBLIC OF CUBA

The United Mexican States and the Republic of Cuba, hereafter referred to as "the Parties",

Seeking to improve and strengthen cooperation between the two countries in order to suppress crime and combat the impunity of criminals,

Desirous of cooperating more closely on the basis of the principles of mutual respect, sovereignty and equality,

Motivated by the desire to promote joint actions to prevent, control and suppress crime in all its forms, by taking coordinated actions to streamline traditional mechanisms of judicial assistance,

On a basis of mutual respect for sovereignty and equality between the States,

Have agreed as follows:

Article I. Scope of application

1. The Parties shall, in accordance with this Treaty, grant each other mutual judicial assistance in criminal matters.

2. Judicial assistance shall be granted even if the acts or omissions that give rise to requests for judicial assistance are not considered crimes by the national legislation of the Requested Party, except in those cases in which such requests are submitted for the implementation of precautionary or prevention measures (seizure, freeze, search, confiscation or deposit).

3. This Treaty shall apply to criminal investigations and proceedings relating to any crime under the national legislation of either of the Parties.

4. In addition, judicial assistance shall be granted if the request refers to crimes related to taxes, customs duties, exchange control and others of a fiscal nature.

5. This Treaty shall apply to any request for judicial assistance presented after its entry into force, even if the respective actions or omissions occurred before that date.

Article II. Central Authorities

1. In order to ensure appropriate cooperation between the Parties in granting the judicial assistance that is the purpose of this Treaty, the United Mexican States designate as Central Authorities the Office of the Attorney-General of the Republic, and the Republic of Cuba designates the Ministry of Justice. The Parties shall notify each other without delay, through the diplomatic channel, of any change in their Central Authorities and areas of competence.

2. The Central Authorities of the Parties shall transmit and receive directly requests for judicial assistance under this Treaty and the responses thereto.

3. The Central Authority of the Requested Party shall promptly comply with requests for judicial assistance or shall forward them for execution to the competent authority, encouraging it to comply in a swift and proper manner with the Requesting Party's request for judicial assistance.

Article III. Scope of judicial assistance

Judicial assistance shall include:

1. Notification and service of procedural documents;
2. Service of documents, objects and other forms of evidence;
3. Information-sharing;
4. Location and identification of persons and items;
5. Taking of statements and testimony;
6. Conduct of expert examinations or other procedural actions set out in their national legislation related to the investigations in question;
7. Implementation of precautionary or interim measures on assets or property, in accordance with the legislation of the requested country, such as orders for the freezing or seizure, search, confiscation or deposit of goods or objects used in the commission of the crime and the direct or indirect proceeds of the crime, as well as their return and distribution;
8. Summons and transfer of witnesses, victims and experts to appear voluntarily before the competent authority of the Requesting Party;
9. Temporary transfer of detained persons to appear in the territory of the Requesting Party in criminal proceedings as a witness or victim or for other proceedings, who had been previously identified in the request for judicial assistance;
10. Authorizing the presence of representatives of the Requesting Party's competent authorities as observers during the execution of a request for judicial assistance; and
11. Other forms of judicial assistance consistent with the purposes of this Treaty, which are compatible with the national legislation of the Requested Party.

Article IV. Limits of judicial assistance

1. This Treaty does not empower the authorities of either of the Parties to exercise, in the territory of the other, functions the competence of which is exclusively reserved for the authorities of that other Party in accordance with its national legislation.

2. The provisions of this Treaty do not empower natural or legal persons to obtain, remove or exclude evidence requested directly or indirectly by any authority or to prevent the execution of a request for judicial assistance.

3. Similarly, this Treaty does not apply to:

   (a) The detention of persons for extradition purposes or for the execution of requests for extradition;

   (b) The execution of criminal judgements, including the transfer of sentenced persons; or

   (c) The granting of direct judicial assistance to third States.

Article V. Precautionary or interim measures

1. At the written request of the Requesting Party, and if the procedure requested in the request for judicial assistance is admissible, in accordance with the national legislation of the

Requested Party, the latter may implement the corresponding precautionary or interim measures in order to maintain the existing de facto and de jure situation, thus protecting the threatened legal interests or preserving related evidence.

2. In urgent cases, precautionary or interim measures may be processed following the announcement of a request for judicial assistance, as long as sufficient information has been provided to determine that the conditions for the request for precautionary or interim measures have been satisfied and shall be cancelled if the Requesting Party fails to formalize the request for judicial assistance within a reasonable period of time.

Article VI. Processing and content of the request for judicial assistance

1. Requests for judicial assistance shall be made in writing.

2. The Requested Party shall immediately start to process the request for judicial assistance upon receiving it by fax, electronic mail or other similar means of communication, the Requesting Party being under the obligation to transmit the request formally within a reasonable period of time after transmission by the aforementioned means.

3. The Requested Party shall inform the Requesting Party of the results of the execution of the request for judicial assistance after formal receipt thereof. However, if the Requesting Party states that the judicial assistance is urgent, the absence of a formal submission of the request for judicial assistance shall not prejudice notification by the Requested Party of the results thereof.

4. Requests for judicial assistance shall include:

(a) The name of the institution and the competent authority conducting the investigation or criminal proceedings to which the request relates;

(b) The purpose of the request and a description thereof;

(c) A description of the facts under investigation or subject to criminal proceedings, transcripts of the legal provisions in effect that criminalize the conduct as a punishable offence and of those that establish the jurisdiction and, where necessary, the document that indicates the amount of the damage caused;

(d) The basis and description of any particular proceeding that the Requesting Party wishes to be conducted in executing the request for judicial assistance, provided that it is not contrary to the national legislation of the Requested Party;

(e) The period of time within which the Requesting Party wishes its request for judicial assistance to be executed, which shall be determined by the Central Authorities, in accordance with the national legislation of the Requested Party;

(f) Where necessary, the request for representatives of the competent authorities of the Requesting Party to attend the execution of the request for judicial assistance;

(g) The identity of persons subject to criminal investigation or proceedings;

(h) The full name or any other information, such as date of birth, address or telephone number, that would help to identify and locate the persons to be served and their relationship to the investigation or judicial proceedings under way;

(i) The location or description of the place to be searched or inspected;

(j) The location and description of the property or assets to be seized, confiscated or deposited;

(k) The questions to be asked when taking testimony or an expert opinion; and

(l) Such other information as may be useful to the Requested State in the execution of the request for judicial assistance.

5. If the Requested Party considers that the information contained in the request for judicial assistance is not sufficient, it may request additional information.

Article VII. Refusal or deferral of the request for judicial assistance

1. The request for judicial assistance may be refused when:

(a) Its execution could affect the security or public order of the Requested Party;

(b) Its execution is contrary to the national legislation of the Requested Party or is not in accordance with the provisions of this Treaty or is in breach of the international obligations of the Requested Party;

(c) The request for judicial assistance relates to actions or omissions in respect of which the person subject to investigation or criminal proceedings in the Requesting Party has already been convicted or acquitted of the same acts in the Requested Party or the criminal proceedings are time-barred;

(d) The request for judicial assistance relates to military offences that are not covered by ordinary criminal law;

(e) The offence in respect of which judicial assistance is requested is regarded by the Requested Party as an offence of a political character/nature. For the purposes of this Treaty, the following shall not be considered offences of a political character/nature and, therefore, requests for judicial assistance shall be processed:

1. Any crime against the life, physical integrity or freedom of a foreign Head of State or Government, or against his or her family members;
2. Genocide, war crimes committed against the peace and security of mankind;
3. Acts of terrorism, such as:
    i. Attacks on the life, physical integrity or freedom of individuals who are entitled to international protection, including diplomatic agents;
    ii. Hostage-taking or kidnapping;
    iii. Attacks on persons or property committed with the use of bombs, grenades, rockets, mines, firearms, explosives or similar devices;
    iv. Acts of unlawful seizure of ships or aircraft;
    v. Any act of violence not included among the aforementioned acts directed against the life, physical integrity or freedom of individuals, or that could affect institutions.
4. Offences committed by public officials in the exercise of his or her duties or by active subjects linked or related to public servants; and
5. Attempts to commit the offences referred to in this article or participation as a principal or an accomplice of a person who commits or attempts to commit such offences.

(f) There are substantial grounds for believing that the request for assistance has been made for the purpose of prosecuting a person on account of that person's race, sex, religion, nationality, ethnic origin, membership of a particular social group or political opinions or that the person's position may be prejudiced for any of those reasons;

(g) There is the possibility that, as a result of the criminal proceedings in respect of which judicial assistance is requested, a sentence could be imposed or executed that is prohibited by the national legislation of the Requested Party, unless the Requesting Party undertakes not to apply it; and

(h) The request for judicial assistance does not meet the requirements of this Treaty.

2. Bank or tax secrecy may not be used as an argument to refuse judicial assistance.

3. The Requested Party may refuse or defer execution of the request for judicial assistance when it considers that its execution may harm or impede an investigation or legal proceeding under way in its territory.

4. Before refusing or deferring the execution of a request for judicial assistance, the Requested Party shall consider whether it may grant the judicial assistance subject to such conditions as it may deem necessary. If the Requesting Party accepts the judicial assistance subject to such conditions, it shall be executed in accordance thereto.

5. If the Requested Party decides to refuse or defer judicial assistance, it shall so inform the Requesting Party through its Central Authority, stating the reasons for that decision as soon as possible.

Article VIII. Validity of documents

1. The documents submitted under this Treaty and certified by the competent or Central Authorities of the Party of origin shall be considered to be authentic without the need for any legalization or formalization.

Notwithstanding the above, if the request contains a requirement for documents to be in a specific form, the Requested Party shall send them in that form, if not precluded by its national legislation.

2. For the purposes of this Treaty, the documents recognized as official in the territory of one of the Parties are recognized as such in the territory of the other Party.

Article IX. Confidentiality and limitations on the use of information

1. The Requested Party shall keep confidential the receipt of a request for judicial assistance, its contents and any proceeding undertaken pursuant thereto, unless knowledge thereof is necessary for the execution of the request.

If execution of a request for judicial assistance makes it necessary to breach confidentiality, the Requested Party shall seek the authorization of the Requesting Party in writing. Without such authorization, the request for judicial assistance will not be executed.

2. The Requesting Party shall not use any information or evidence obtained under this Treaty for purposes other than those stated in the request for judicial assistance without prior authorization from the Requested Party.

3. In particular cases, if the Requesting Party needs to disclose and use, in whole or in part, the information or evidence for purposes other than those specified, it shall request authorization therefor from the Requested Party, which may accede to or deny that request in whole or in part.

4. The use of any information or evidence that has been obtained in accordance with this Treaty, and which has been made public in the Requesting Party during the course of the investigation or proceeding described in the request for judicial assistance, shall not be subject to the restrictions referred to in the paragraph above.

Article X. Execution of the request for judicial assistance

1. The fulfilment of the request for judicial assistance shall be conducted in accordance with the national legislation of the Requested Party and in accordance with the provisions of this Treaty. Requests for judicial assistance shall be executed promptly.

2. The Requested Party shall execute the request for judicial assistance in accordance with the special forms and procedures stated therein by the Requesting Party, unless they are incompatible with the national legislation of the Requested Party.

3. The Central Authority of the Requested Party shall promptly transmit to the Central Authority of the Requesting Party the information and evidence resulting from the execution of the request for judicial assistance.

4. When it is not possible to comply with the request for judicial assistance, in whole or in part, the Central Authority of the Requested Party shall immediately so inform the Central Authority of the Requesting Party, stating the reasons that prevent compliance.

Article XI. Presence of representatives of the Requesting Party in the execution of the request for judicial assistance

1. The Requesting Party may request the Requested Party to facilitate the presence of representatives of its competent authorities as observers during execution of the request for judicial assistance, which could require that, during the presentation or processing of testimonial or expert evidence, its representatives ask questions through the competent authority of the Requested Party and in accordance with the national legislation of both Parties.

2. The presence of representatives shall be previously authorized by the Requested Party, which shall advise the Requesting Party in advance of the date, time and place of the execution of the request for judicial assistance.

3. The Requesting Party shall transmit a list of the names, functional titles and reasons for the presence of its representatives as well as the questionnaires to be used in the examination of the witness or expert, reasonably far enough in advance of the date of execution of the request for judicial assistance.

Article XII. Notification and service of documents

1. Pursuant to the request for judicial assistance, the Central Authority of the Requested Party shall, within a reasonable period of time, serve or arrange to have served procedural documents.

2. The fulfilment of the request for judicial assistance shall be attested in a document of service, dated and signed by the recipient, or by means of a statement from the competent authority of the Requested Party containing the fact, date and form of notification and service.

Article XIII. Immunities and rights

1. If an individual who may be affected by the execution of the request for judicial assistance invokes immunity or a right in accordance with the national legislation of the Requested Party, this claim shall be resolved by the competent authority of the Requested Party prior to the execution of the request for judicial assistance and communicated to the Requesting Party through the Central Authority.

2. If the individual invokes immunity or a right in accordance with the national legislation of the Requesting Party, the respective Central Authorities shall communicate such claim, so that the competent authorities of the Requesting Party might reach a decision in that regard.

Article XIV. Obtaining of evidence in the Requested Party

1. The Requested Party shall take, in its territory, witness and victim statements, expert opinions, documents, objects and other evidence mentioned in the request for judicial assistance, in accordance with its national legislation, and shall transmit them to the Requesting Party.

2. At the request of the Requesting Party, the Central Authority of the Requested Party shall inform the Central Authority of the other Party of the date, time and place where the corresponding testimony or evidence will be taken.

3. In accordance with paragraph 1 of this article, the Requested Party shall deliver to the Requesting Party the records of proceedings, as well as the documents, records, files, evidence or objects in respect of which the request was made for judicial assistance.

4. For the purpose of executing the request for judicial assistance, the competent authority of the Requested Party may compel, by means of a summons, the person whose presence is required to appear and testify or present documents, records or objects under the same conditions as would apply in criminal investigations or proceedings in that Party.

5. The Requesting Party shall comply with any condition agreed upon with the Requested Party related to the documents or objects that it delivers, including the legal protection of third parties in the case of such documents and objects.

6. Unless original documents are expressly requested, copies certified by the Central or competent Authority of the Requested Party shall be provided. The Requested Party may refuse delivery of the original documents if they are needed in a criminal proceeding under way in its territory.

7. At the Requested Party's request, the Requesting Party shall return as soon as possible the originals of the documents and objects that have been delivered, in accordance with paragraph 1 of this article.

Article XV. Location and identification of persons and objects

At the Requesting Party's request, the competent authorities of the Requested Party shall take all measures under its national legislation to locate and identify persons and objects mentioned in the request for judicial assistance.

Article XVI. Appearance of persons in the Requesting Party

1. When the Requesting Party requests the appearance of a person as a witness, victim or expert who is in the territory of the Requested Party to give testimony or an expert opinion or otherwise act in trial proceedings in its territory, the Requested Party shall proceed to summoning and transferring that person in accordance with the request for judicial assistance made.

2. The person must provide his or her written consent for the transfer to take place. Moreover, that person shall enjoy the following guarantees in the Requesting Party:

(a) Coercive measures or sanctions shall not be applied in case of failure to appear in the Requesting Party;

(b) The said person shall not be prosecuted, detained or subjected to any other restriction on personal freedom in that Party for any criminal offence committed prior to departure from the Requested Party. However, the said person will be responsible for the content of the testimony or expert opinion given.

The guarantee provided for in this subparagraph shall not apply if the person, being free to voluntarily leave the territory of the Requesting Party, does not leave within a period of 30 days after having been officially notified that his or her presence is no longer required or, after having left, returns voluntarily to the territory of the Requesting Party; and

(c) The person shall not be compelled to testify in any proceedings other than those referred to in the request for judicial assistance.

3 The Requested Party shall inform the person to be transferred, by means of a summons, which must contain the guarantees referred to in the preceding subparagraph and indicate that the costs of transfer shall be borne by the Requesting Party, in accordance with article XXIII.

4. The Requested Party may not impose sanctions upon the person or apply coercive measures if he or she fails to appear before the court.

Article XVII. Temporary transfer of persons in custody

1. Any person in custody in the Requested Party, regardless of his or her nationality, may be temporarily transferred to the Requesting Party with the consent of the Central Authority of the Requested Party, to be heard as a witness or victim or for other court proceedings mentioned in the request for judicial assistance, on the condition that the detainee shall be returned to the Requested Party within the time frame established by the latter.

The initial time frame for the transfer, stay and return of the person shall not exceed 60 days. The length of the stay of the transferred person may be extended by the Central Authority of the Requested Party by means of a duly substantiated request from the Central Authority of the Requesting Party.

The formalities and conditions of the transfer and return of the person shall be agreed upon between the Central Authorities.

2. The transfer shall be denied:

(a) If the person in custody does not consent to it in writing;

(b) If the presence of the person is required for the continuation of criminal proceedings under way in the territory of the Requested Party;

(c) If the length of the stay of the person in the Requesting Party could exceed the term established for the completion of a custodial sentence in the Requested Party; or

(d) If the transfer of the person to the territory of the Requesting Party threatens the person's safety, health or life.

3. The Requesting Party shall hold the transferred person in custody while the person remains in its territory. If the authorities of the Requested Party lift the measure restricting the liberty of the transferred person, the Requesting Party must return the transferred person immediately to the Requested Party.

4. The length of the stay of the transferred person outside the territory of the Requested Party shall be considered to be time served as part of the criminal sentence delivered in the Requested Party.

5. A person in custody who does not consent to appear before the Requesting Party may not be subjected to any coercive measure or sanction as a result.

Article XVIII. Protection of persons summonsed or transferred to the Requesting Party

When necessary, the Requesting Party shall ensure the protection of the persons summonsed or transferred to its territory, in accordance with articles XVI and XVII of this Treaty.

Article XIX. Hearing by videoconference

1. The Requesting Party may request that the statement of a person in the territory of the Requested Party be given through a hearing by videoconference.

2. The Requested Party shall consent to the hearing by videoconference, provided that this is not contrary to its national legislation. If the Requested Party does not have the technical means for videoconferencing, the Requesting Party may make such means available.

3. The following rules shall apply to hearings by videoconference:

(a) The hearing shall be conducted in the presence of a competent authority of the Requested Party. This authority is also responsible for identifying the person giving the statement and for respecting the fundamental principles provided for in the national legislation of the Requested Party. If the authority of the Requested Party considers that the fundamental principles of its law are not being respected during the hearing, it shall take immediate steps to ensure that the hearing is conducted in accordance with its law;

(b) The competent authorities of the Parties shall agree, if necessary, on measures relating to the protection of the person giving the statement;

(c) The hearing shall be held directly by the Requesting Party or under its direction, in accordance with its national legislation; and

(d) At the conclusion of the hearing, the competent authority of the Requested Party shall produce a record, indicating the date, time and place thereof, the identity of the person who gave the statement, its content and the identities and capacities of any other persons who participated in the hearing. This document shall be transmitted to the Requesting Party.

Article XX. Special cases of assistance

In special cases, the Requested Party shall submit, insofar as its competent authorities can obtain them, extracts of criminal records and/or documents or objects that might be needed in an investigation and/or criminal proceedings, except those documents and objects that contain State secrets.

Article XXI. Spontaneous transmission of evidence and information

1. Through the Central Authorities and within the limits of their national legislation, the competent authorities of each Party may, without a request for judicial assistance in that regard having been submitted, exchange information and evidence in respect of criminally punishable acts where they consider that this transmission is of such a nature that it would allow the other Party:

(a) To submit a request for judicial assistance under this Treaty;

(b) To initiate criminal proceedings; or

(c) To facilitate the conduct of an ongoing criminal investigation.

2. The Party providing the information may, in accordance with its national legislation, make its use by the Receiving Party subject to certain conditions. The Receiving Party shall be under the obligation to comply with those conditions.

Article XXII. Restriction on the ownership of objects, proceeds or instruments of crime

1. The Requested Party, at the Requesting Party's request, shall conduct proceedings and investigations required to ascertain whether objects, proceeds or instruments of a crime or related to crime are in its territory and shall inform the Requesting Party of the results thereof. When making the request, the Requesting Party shall inform the Requested Party of the reasons which lead it to believe that objects, profits, proceeds or instruments of a crime or related to crime may be located in its territory.

2. Once the profits or proceeds of crime or objects related to crime have been located, in accordance with paragraph 1 of this article, the Requested Party, at the request of the Requesting Party, shall take the measures provided for in its national legislation to safeguard them and shall take the necessary measures to prevent their transaction, transfer or disposal or destruction.

3. To the extent permitted by its national legislation and subject to a request from the Requesting Party, the Requested Party must request, as a matter of priority, the return to the Requesting Party of the profits and/or proceeds of crime, with a view, in particular, to

compensating victims or returning them to the rightful owner, without prejudice to the rights of bona fide third parties.

4. The delivery of the profits and/or proceeds of crime will take place subject to a sharing agreement, in accordance with the national legislation of the Parties. Profits and/or proceeds will be shared pursuant to an agreement between the Central Authorities, which must be reached before the decision on the termination of ownership and transfer of the profits and/or proceeds of crime becomes enforceable.

5. Delivery shall be made in accordance with the national legislation of the Requested Party, after deduction of administration expenses and payment of any taxes and fees to which they might be subject.

6. This request for judicial assistance also includes instruments used to commit crime.

Article XXIII. Costs

1. The Requested Party shall bear the ordinary costs of executing requests for judicial assistance, except in the following cases in which they shall be borne by the Requesting Party:

(a) The costs associated with the transfer of persons from or to their territory, in accordance with articles XVI and XVII of this Treaty, and their stay in the territory of the Requesting Party, and other personal costs related to the execution of judicial assistance;

(b) Costs and fees for expert witnesses;

(c) Costs relating to the transport and stay of representatives of the competent authorities of the Requesting Party during execution of the request for judicial assistance, in accordance with article XI, paragraph 1, of this Treaty; and

(d) Costs associated with the shipping and return of objects transferred from the territory of the Requested Party to the territory of the Requesting Party.

2. If expenses of a substantial or extraordinary nature are or will be required to fulfil the request for judicial assistance, the Central Authorities shall consult one another to determine the conditions under which the request is to be executed, as well as the manner in which the costs are to be borne.

Article XXIV. Other legal agreements or instruments

2. The provisions of this Treaty shall not affect any request for more extensive judicial assistance that might have been or that might be agreed upon between the Parties in other legal agreements or instruments or deriving from their national legislation.

3. The Parties shall ensure the adoption of all measures necessary to give effect to the provisions of this Treaty.

Article XXV. Consultations and settlement of disputes

1. The Central Authorities of the Parties shall hold consultations, upon a proposal from either of them, concerning the interpretation or application of this Treaty in general or on a specific request for judicial assistance.

2. Any dispute arising out of the interpretation or application of this Treaty shall be resolved amicably through the diplomatic channel.

Article XXVI. Entry into force, amendments and termination

1. This Treaty shall enter into force 30 days after the date of receipt of the last notification by means of which the Parties inform each other, in writing and through the diplomatic channel, of the completion of the formalities required by their national legislations and shall remain in force for a period of indefinite duration.

2. Upon the entry into force of this Treaty, the Treaty on Cooperation between the Government of the United Mexican States and the Government of the Republic of Cuba on Mutual Judicial Assistance in Criminal Matters, done in Mexico City on 23 April 1996, will cease to be valid.

3. This Treaty may be amended by mutual consent of the Parties, formally communicated in writing through the diplomatic channel. Such amendments shall enter into force in accordance with the procedure laid down in paragraph 1 of this article.

4. Either Party may terminate this Treaty, at any time, by means of a written notification delivered to the other Party through the diplomatic channel. The Treaty will cease to be valid 180 days after the date of receipt of such notification.

5. The termination of this Treaty will not affect the completion of requests for judicial assistance received during its term.

SIGNED at Mexico City on 1 November 2013, in duplicate, in the Spanish language, both texts being equally authentic.

For the United Mexican States:
JESÚS MURILLO KARAM
Attorney-General of the Republic

For the Republic of Cuba:
BRUNO RODRÍGUEZ PARRILLA
Minister for Foreign Affairs

[TRANSLATION – TRADUCTION]

TRAITÉ D'ENTRAIDE JUDICIAIRE EN MATIÈRE PÉNALE ENTRE LES ÉTATS-UNIS DU MEXIQUE ET LA RÉPUBLIQUE DE CUBA

Les États-Unis du Mexique et la République de Cuba, ci-après dénommés « Parties »,

Souhaitant améliorer et renforcer la collaboration entre les deux pays dans le but de réprimer la criminalité et de lutter contre l'impunité de ses acteurs,

Désireux de coopérer plus étroitement sur la base des principes de respect mutuel, de souveraineté et d'égalité,

Animés par le désir de promouvoir des actions conjointes de prévention, de contrôle et de répression de la criminalité sous toutes ses formes, par la coordination des actions visant à rationaliser les mécanismes traditionnels d'aide judiciaire,

S'appuyant sur le respect mutuel de la souveraineté et de l'égalité entre les États,

Sont convenus de ce qui suit :

Article premier. Champ d'application

1. Les Parties s'accordent mutuellement, conformément aux dispositions du présent Traité, une aide judiciaire en matière pénale.

2. Les Parties se prêtent assistance même si les actes ou omissions qui donnent lieu aux demandes d'entraide judiciaire ne sont pas considérés comme des infractions par la législation nationale de la Partie requise, sauf dans les cas où ces demandes sont présentées pour l'application de mesures de précaution ou conservatoires (prise ferme, saisie, perquisition, occupation ou dépôt).

3. Le présent Traité s'étend aux enquêtes et procédures pénales relatives à toute infraction prévue par la législation nationale de l'une ou l'autre Partie.

4. L'entraide judiciaire est également accordée lorsque la demande a trait à des infractions relatives aux impôts, aux droits de douane, au contrôle des changes et à d'autres infractions fiscales.

5. Le présent Traité s'applique à toute demande d'entraide judiciaire présentée après son entrée en vigueur, y compris lorsque les actes ou omissions en cause ont eu lieu avant cette date.

Article II. Autorités centrales

1. Afin d'assurer une coopération adéquate entre les Parties dans la fourniture de l'entraide judiciaire qui fait l'objet du présent Traité, le Bureau du Procureur général de la République, pour ce qui est des États-Unis du Mexique, et le Ministère de la justice, pour ce qui est de la République de Cuba, sont désignés comme autorités centrales. Les Parties se notifient sans délai, par la voie diplomatique, tout changement concernant leurs autorités centrales et leurs domaines de compétence.

2. Les autorités centrales des Parties transmettent et reçoivent directement les demandes d'entraide judiciaire visées par le présent Traité et les réponses qui y sont apportées.

3. L'autorité centrale de la Partie requise exécute promptement les demandes d'entraide judiciaire ou les transmet pour exécution à l'autorité compétente, en encourageant cette dernière à donner rapidement et convenablement suite à la demande d'entraide judiciaire de la Partie requérante.

Article III. Portée de l'entraide judiciaire

L'entraide judiciaire comprend :

1. La notification et la remise des actes de procédure;
2. La remise de documents, d'objets et d'éléments de preuve;
3. L'échange de renseignements;
4. La localisation et l'identification de personnes et de biens;
5. Le recueil des déclarations et des témoignages;
6. La conduite des expertises ou d'autres actes de procédure prévus par la législation nationale, en rapport avec les enquêtes en question;
7. L'exécution des mesures de précaution ou conservatoires à l'égard d'avoirs ou de biens, conformément à la législation du pays requis, notamment les ordonnances de saisie ou de séquestre, de perquisition, de fouille, d'occupation ou de dépôt relatives aux biens ou objets ayant servi à la commission de l'infraction et à ceux qui proviennent directement ou indirectement de l'infraction, ainsi que leur restitution et leur répartition;
8. La convocation et le transfèrement de témoins, de victimes et d'experts en vue de leur comparution volontaire devant l'autorité compétente de la Partie requérante;
9. Le transfèrement temporaire de personnes détenues en vue de leur comparution sur le territoire de la Partie requérante dans le cadre d'une procédure pénale en tant que témoins ou victimes, ou pour d'autres actes de procédure, déterminés au préalable dans la demande d'entraide judiciaire;
10. L'autorisation de la présence de représentants des autorités compétentes de la Partie requérante en qualité d'observateurs pendant l'exécution d'une demande d'entraide judiciaire; et
11. Toute autre forme d'entraide judiciaire conforme aux objectifs du présent Traité et compatible avec la législation nationale de la Partie requise.

Article IV. Limitations de l'entraide judiciaire

1. Le présent Traité n'autorise pas les autorités d'une Partie à exercer sur le territoire de l'autre Partie des fonctions qui relèvent exclusivement de la compétence des autorités de cette autre Partie, aux termes de sa législation nationale.

2. Les dispositions du présent Traité n'accordent aucun droit aux personnes physiques ou morales de recueillir, d'éliminer ou d'exclure des éléments de preuve demandés directement ou indirectement par une autorité ou d'empêcher l'exécution d'une demande d'entraide judiciaire.

3. De la même manière, le présent Traité n'est pas applicable :

a) À l'arrestation de personnes aux fins d'extradition, ni à l'exécution de demandes d'extradition;

b) À l'exécution de décisions pénales, y compris le transfèrement des personnes condamnées; ou

c) À la fourniture d'une aide judiciaire directe à des États tiers.

Article V. Mesures de précaution ou conservatoires

1. Sur demande écrite de la Partie requérante et lorsque la procédure requise dans la demande d'entraide judiciaire est admissible en vertu de la législation nationale de la Partie requise, celle-ci peut prendre les mesures de précaution ou conservatoires appropriées dans le but de maintenir la situation de fait et de droit existante, de protéger les intérêts juridiques menacés ou de préserver les éléments de preuve à cet égard.

2. En cas d'urgence, les mesures de précaution ou conservatoires peuvent être prises dès l'annonce d'une demande d'entraide judiciaire, à condition que des renseignements suffisants aient été fournis pour établir que les conditions requises pour une demande de mesures de précaution ou conservatoires sont satisfaites, et sont annulées si la Partie requérante ne formule pas formellement la demande d'entraide judiciaire dans un délai raisonnable.

Article VI. Traitement et contenu de la demande d'entraide judiciaire

1. La demande d'entraide judiciaire est présentée par écrit.

2. La Partie requise entame immédiatement le traitement de la demande d'entraide judiciaire dès réception de la demande par télécopie, courrier électronique ou autre moyen de communication analogue, et la Partie requérante transmet la demande de manière formelle dans un délai raisonnable à compter de son envoi par les moyens susmentionnés.

3. La Partie requise informe la Partie requérante des résultats de l'exécution de la demande d'entraide judiciaire après l'avoir reçue de manière formelle. Toutefois, si la Partie requérante exprime l'urgence de l'entraide judiciaire, l'absence de présentation formelle de la demande d'entraide judiciaire n'empêche pas la Partie requise de notifier les résultats de la demande d'entraide judiciaire.

4. La demande d'entraide judiciaire contient :

a) Le nom de l'institution et de l'autorité compétente chargée de l'enquête ou de la procédure pénale dont découle la demande;

b) L'objet et la description de la demande;

c) L'exposé des faits qui font l'objet de l'enquête ou de la procédure pénale, la transcription des dispositions juridiques en vigueur qui qualifient le comportement d'acte punissable et de celles qui établissent la compétence et, s'il y a lieu, le document indiquant l'étendue des dommages causés;

d) Le fondement et la description de toute procédure spéciale que la Partie requérante souhaite voir mener dans le cadre de l'exécution de la demande d'entraide judiciaire, à condition qu'elle ne soit pas contraire à la législation nationale de la Partie requise;

e) Le délai dans lequel la Partie requérante souhaite que la demande d'entraide judiciaire soit exécutée, lequel est fixé par les autorités centrales, conformément à la législation nationale de la Partie requise;

f) Le cas échéant, la demande pour que des représentants des autorités compétentes de la Partie requérante assistent à l'exécution de la demande d'entraide judiciaire;

g) L'identification des personnes faisant l'objet d'une enquête ou d'une procédure pénale;

h) Le nom complet ou tout autre renseignement tel que la date de naissance, le lieu de résidence, le numéro de téléphone, permettant d'identifier et de localiser les personnes à notifier et leur lien avec l'enquête ou la procédure judiciaire en cours;

i) L'emplacement ou la description du lieu à perquisitionner ou à inspecter;

j) L'emplacement et la description des biens ou avoirs à sécuriser, à occuper ou à déposer;

k) Les questions à poser lors du témoignage ou de l'expertise; et

l) Tout autre renseignement susceptible d'être utile à la Partie requise lors de l'exécution de la demande d'entraide judiciaire.

5. Si la Partie requise estime que les renseignements contenus dans la demande d'entraide judiciaire sont insuffisants pour donner suite à la demande d'entraide judiciaire, elle peut demander un complément d'information.

Article VII. Refus ou report de la demande d'entraide judiciaire

1. La demande d'entraide judiciaire peut être refusée :

a) Si l'exécution de la demande peut porter atteinte à la sécurité ou à l'ordre public de la Partie requise;

b) Si l'exécution de la demande est contraire à la législation nationale de la Partie requise ou n'est pas conforme aux dispositions du présent Traité ou est contraire aux obligations internationales de la Partie requise;

c) Si la demande concerne des actes ou des omissions pour lesquels la personne faisant l'objet d'une enquête ou d'une procédure pénale sur le territoire de la Partie requérante a déjà été condamnée ou acquittée sur le territoire de la Partie requise pour les mêmes faits ou si l'action pénale est prescrite;

d) Si la demande vise des infractions au regard de la loi militaire, qui ne constituent pas des infractions au regard de la loi pénale ordinaire;

e) Si l'infraction pour laquelle l'entraide judiciaire est demandée est considérée par la Partie requise comme une infraction de caractère ou de nature politique. Aux fins du présent Traité, les infractions ci-après ne sont pas considérées comme des infractions de caractère ou de nature politique et il est donc donné suite à la demande d'entraide judiciaire :

   1. Toute atteinte à la vie, à l'intégrité physique ou à la liberté d'un chef d'État ou de gouvernement étranger, ou des membres de sa famille;

   2. Le génocide, les crimes de guerre commis contre la paix et la sécurité de l'humanité;

   3. Les actes de terrorisme tels que :

i. L'attentat contre la vie, l'intégrité physique ou la liberté des personnes qui ont droit à une protection internationale, y compris les agents diplomatiques;

ii. La prise d'otages ou l'enlèvement de personnes;

iii. L'attentat contre des personnes ou des biens commis au moyen de bombes, de grenades, de roquettes, de mines, d'armes à feu, d'explosifs ou de dispositifs analogues;

iv. Les actes de capture illicite de navires ou d'aéronefs;

v. Tout acte de violence non compris dans ce qui précède et qui est dirigé contre la vie, l'intégrité physique ou la liberté des personnes, ou qui affecterait les institutions.

4. Les infractions commises par des fonctionnaires dans l'exercice de leurs fonctions ou par des sujets actifs liés ou apparentés à des fonctionnaires; et

5. La tentative de commettre les infractions visées au présent article ou la participation en tant qu'acteur ou complice d'une personne qui commet ou tente de commettre ces infractions.

f) Si la Partie requise à de sérieux motifs de croire que la demande d'entraide judiciaire a été présentée en vue de poursuivre une personne en raison de sa race, de son sexe, de sa religion, de sa nationalité, de son origine ethnique, de son appartenance à un groupe social déterminé ou de ses opinions politiques, ou qu'il pourrait être porté atteinte à la situation de cette personne pour l'une de ces raisons;

g) S'il existe une possibilité que, à la suite de la procédure pénale pour laquelle l'entraide judiciaire est demandée, une peine interdite par la législation nationale de la Partie requise soit prononcée ou exécutée, à moins que la Partie requérante s'engage à ne pas l'appliquer; et

h) Si la demande d'entraide judiciaire ne répond pas aux exigences du présent Traité.

2. Le secret bancaire ou fiscal ne peut pas être invoqué pour refuser l'entraide judiciaire.

3. La Partie requise peut opposer un refus à une demande d'entraide judiciaire ou différer son exécution quand elle estime que l'exécution de cette demande pourrait nuire ou faire obstacle à une enquête ou à une procédure judiciaire en cours sur son territoire.

4. Avant d'opposer un refus à une demande d'entraide judiciaire ou de différer son exécution, la Partie requise examine si elle ne pourrait pas y consentir sous certaines conditions qu'elle estime nécessaires. Si la Partie requérante souscrit à ces conditions, elle est tenue de les observer.

5. Si la Partie requise décide d'opposer un refus à une demande d'entraide judiciaire ou d'en différer l'exécution, elle en informe la Partie requérante par l'intermédiaire de son autorité centrale en précisant les motifs de cette décision dans les plus brefs délais.

Article VIII. Validité des documents

1. Les documents transmis en application du présent Traité et certifiés par les autorités compétentes ou centrales de la Partie d'origine sont réputés authentiques sans qu'il soit nécessaire de les légaliser ou de les formaliser.

Nonobstant ce qui précède, si la demande exige que les documents soient présentés sous une forme spécifique, la Partie requise les transmet sous cette forme si sa législation interne ne l'interdit pas.

2. Aux fins du présent Traité, les documents reconnus comme officiels sur le territoire d'une Partie sont également reconnus comme tels sur le territoire de l'autre Partie.

Article IX. Confidentialité et limitations dans l'utilisation des renseignements

1. La Partie requise assure la confidentialité de la demande d'entraide judiciaire reçue, de son contenu et de toute mesure prise en vertu de la demande, à moins que sa connaissance ne soit nécessaire pour exécuter la demande.

S'il est nécessaire de violer la confidentialité pour exécuter la demande d'entraide judiciaire, la Partie requise demande par écrit l'autorisation de la Partie requérante. La demande d'entraide judiciaire n'est pas exécutée sans cette autorisation.

2. La Partie requérante n'utilise aucun renseignement ou élément de preuve obtenu en application du présent Traité à d'autres fins que celles déclarées dans la demande d'entraide judiciaire sans l'autorisation préalable de la Partie requise.

3. Dans des cas particuliers, si la Partie requérante doit divulguer et utiliser, en tout ou en partie, les renseignements ou les éléments de preuve à des fins autres que celles spécifiées, elle demande l'autorisation correspondante à la Partie requise, qui peut y accéder ou la refuser, en tout ou en partie.

4. L'utilisation de tout renseignement ou élément de preuve obtenus conformément aux dispositions du présent Traité et ayant un caractère public sur le territoire de la Partie requérante dans le cadre de l'enquête ou de la procédure décrite dans la demande d'entraide judiciaire n'est pas soumise à la restriction visée au paragraphe précédent.

Article X. Exécution de la demande d'entraide judiciaire

1. La demande d'entraide judiciaire est exécutée conformément à la législation nationale de la Partie requise et aux dispositions du présent Traité. La demande d'entraide judiciaire est exécutée dans les meilleurs délais.

2. La Partie requise donne suite à la demande d'entraide judiciaire conformément aux moyens et procédures spéciaux indiqués dans la demande par la Partie requérante, sauf si ceux-ci sont incompatibles avec la législation nationale de la Partie requise.

3. L'autorité centrale de la Partie requise transmet en temps voulu à l'autorité centrale de la Partie requérante les renseignements et les éléments de preuve obtenus à l'issue de l'exécution de la demande d'entraide judiciaire.

4. Lorsqu'il n'est pas possible de donner suite à la demande d'entraide judiciaire, en tout ou en partie, l'autorité centrale de la Partie requise en informe immédiatement l'autorité centrale de la Partie requérante et indique les raisons qui l'empêchent de donner suite à la demande.

Article XI. Présence de représentants de la Partie requérante pendant l'exécution de la demande d'entraide judiciaire

1. La Partie requérante peut demander à la Partie requise que des représentants de ses autorités compétentes soient présents, en qualité d'observateurs, lors de l'exécution de la demande d'entraide judiciaire, et peut exiger que, lors de la présentation ou du traitement des témoignages ou des preuves d'expertise, ses représentants formulent des questions par l'intermédiaire de l'autorité compétente de la Partie requise et conformément à la législation nationale des deux Parties.

2. La présence de représentants est autorisée au préalable par la Partie requise, qui informe à l'avance la Partie requérante de la date, de l'heure et du lieu d'exécution de la demande d'entraide judiciaire.

3. La Partie requérante transmet la liste indiquant les noms de ses représentants, leurs fonctions et le motif de leur présence ainsi que les questionnaires à utiliser lors de l'audition du témoin ou de l'expert dans un délai raisonnable avant la date d'exécution de la demande d'entraide judiciaire.

Article XII. Notification et remise de documents

1. Conformément à la demande d'entraide judiciaire, l'autorité centrale de la Partie requise procède, dans un délai raisonnable, à la signification ou à la remise des actes de procédure.

2. L'exécution de la demande d'entraide judiciaire est attestée par un document de remise daté et signé par le destinataire ou au moyen d'une déclaration de l'autorité compétente de la Partie requise indiquant le fait, la date et du mode de notification et de remise.

Article XIII. Immunités et droits

1. Si un individu qui pourrait être affecté par l'exécution de la demande d'entraide judiciaire invoque une immunité ou un droit aux termes de la législation nationale de la Partie requise, cette invocation fait l'objet d'une décision de l'autorité compétente de la Partie requise avant l'exécution de la demande d'entraide judiciaire et est communiquée à la Partie requérante par l'intermédiaire de l'autorité centrale.

2. Si l'individu invoque une immunité ou un droit aux termes de la législation nationale de la Partie requérante, cette invocation est signalée par l'intermédiaire des autorités centrales respectives afin que les autorités compétentes de la Partie requérante puissent se prononcer sur la question.

Article XIV. Obtention d'éléments de preuve sur le territoire de la Partie requise

1. La Partie requise recueille sur son territoire les déclarations de témoins et de victimes, les expertises, les documents, les objets et autres éléments de preuve mentionnés dans la demande d'entraide judiciaire, conformément à sa législation nationale, et les transmet à la Partie requérante.

2. À la demande de la Partie requérante, l'autorité centrale de la Partie requise notifie à l'autorité centrale de l'autre Partie la date, l'heure et le lieu où les témoignages ou les éléments de preuve en question seront recueillis.

3. Conformément au paragraphe 1 du présent article, la Partie requise remet à la Partie requérante les procès-verbaux concernant les procédures, ainsi que les documents, procès-verbaux, dossiers, éléments de preuve ou objets pour lesquels la demande d'entraide judiciaire a été formulée.

4. Aux fins de l'exécution de la demande d'entraide judiciaire, l'autorité compétente de la Partie requise peut, au moyen d'une citation à comparaître, citer la personne dont la présence est requise pour qu'elle comparaisse et témoigne ou produise des documents, dossiers ou objets, dans les mêmes conditions que dans le cadre d'enquêtes ou de procédures pénales dans cette Partie.

5. La Partie requérante satisfait à toute condition convenue avec la Partie requise en ce qui concerne les documents ou objets qu'elle lui remet, notamment pour ce qui est de la protection des droits de tiers sur ces documents et objets.

6. À moins que les documents originaux ne soient expressément demandés, l'autorité centrale ou compétente de la Partie requise fournit des copies certifiées. La Partie requise peut refuser de fournir les documents originaux si ceux-ci sont nécessaires pour une procédure pénale en cours sur son territoire.

7. À la demande de la Partie requise, la Partie requérante restitue dans les plus brefs délais les originaux des documents et objets qui lui ont été remis, conformément au paragraphe 1 du présent article.

Article XV. Localisation et identification des personnes et des objets

À la demande de la Partie requérante, les autorités compétentes de la Partie requise prennent toutes les mesures prévues dans leur législation nationale pour localiser et identifier les personnes et les objets visés dans la demande d'entraide judiciaire.

Article XVI. Comparution de personnes sur le territoire de la Partie requérante

1. Lorsque la Partie requérante demande la comparution d'une personne qui se trouve sur le territoire de la Partie requise en qualité de témoin, de victime ou d'expert, aux fins d'une déposition, d'un témoignage d'expert ou d'autres actes de procédure sur son territoire, la Partie requise convoque et transfère cette personne conformément à la demande d'entraide judiciaire formulée.

2. La personne ne peut être transférée que si elle y consent par écrit. La personne bénéficie également des garanties suivantes sur le territoire de la Partie requérante :

a) Aucune mesure de contrainte ou de sanction n'est appliquée en cas de non-comparution dans la Partie requérante;

b) Elle ne peut être poursuivie, arrêtée ou soumise à toute autre restriction de sa liberté individuelle sur le territoire de cette Partie pour toute infraction commise avant son départ du territoire de la Partie requise. Toutefois, elle est responsable de la teneur du témoignage ou de l'expertise qu'elle fournit.

La garantie prévue au présent alinéa ne s'applique pas si la personne, étant libre de quitter le territoire de la Partie requérante, n'est pas partie dans un délai de 30 jours après qu'il lui a été officiellement notifié que sa présence plus nécessaire ou si, de sa propre volonté, elle est retournée dans le territoire de la Partie requérante après l'avoir quitté; et

c) Elle n'est pas tenue de témoigner dans le cadre d'une procédure autre que celle à laquelle se rapporte la demande d'entraide judiciaire.

3. La Partie requise notifie la personne à transférer au moyen d'une citation à comparaître qui contient les garanties visées au paragraphe précédent et indique que les frais de son transfèrement sont à la charge de la Partie requérante, conformément à l'article XXIII.

4. La Partie requise ne peut pas sanctionner la personne ou appliquer des mesures de contrainte à son égard en cas de non-comparution.

Article XVII. Transfèrement provisoire de personnes détenues

1. Toute personne détenue sur le territoire de la Partie requise, indépendamment de sa nationalité, peut être transférée temporairement sur le territoire de la Partie requérante, avec le consentement de l'autorité centrale de la Partie requise, pour déposer en qualité de témoin ou de victime ou pour d'autres actes de procédure mentionnés dans la demande d'entraide judiciaire, à condition qu'elle soit renvoyée dans la Partie requise dans le délai indiqué par cette dernière.

La durée initiale du transfèrement, du séjour et du retour de la personne n'excède pas 60 jours. La période de séjour de la personne transférée peut être prolongée par l'autorité centrale de la Partie requise sur demande motivée de l'autorité centrale de la Partie requérante.

Les modalités et conditions du transfèrement et du retour de la personne sont convenues entre les autorités centrales.

2. Le transfèrement est refusé :

a) Si la personne détenue n'y consent pas par écrit;

b) Si la présence de la personne est nécessaire à la poursuite d'une procédure pénale sur le territoire de la Partie requise;

c) Si la durée du séjour de la personne sur le territoire de la Partie requérante peut excéder la durée prévue pour l'exécution d'une peine de privation de liberté dans la Partie requise; ou

d) Si le transfèrement de la personne sur le territoire de la Partie requérante présente un risque pour sa sécurité, sa santé ou sa vie.

3. La Partie requérante assure la garde de la personne transférée pendant son séjour sur son territoire. Si les autorités de la Partie requise lèvent la mesure restrictive de liberté à l'égard de la personne transférée, la Partie requérante renvoie immédiatement cette personne sur le territoire de la Partie requise.

4. La durée du séjour de la personne transférée en dehors du territoire de la Partie requise est prise en compte aux fins de l'exécution de la peine prononcée dans cette dernière.

5. Une personne détenue qui ne consent pas à comparaître devant la Partie requérante ne peut faire l'objet d'aucune mesure de contrainte ou de sanction de ce fait.

Article XVIII. Protection de personnes citées à comparaître ou transférées sur le territoire de la Partie requérante

En cas de besoin, la Partie requérante assure la protection des personnes citées à comparaître ou transférées sur son territoire, conformément aux articles XVI et XVII du présent Traité.

Article XIX. Audition par visioconférence

1. La Partie requérante peut demander que le témoignage d'une personne qui se trouve sur le territoire de la Partie requise soit recueilli au moyen d'une audition par visioconférence.

2. La Partie requise consent à la tenue de l'audition par visioconférence dans la mesure où cette méthode n'est pas contraire à sa législation nationale. Si la Partie requise ne dispose pas des moyens techniques nécessaires pour organiser une visioconférence, la Partie requérante peut les mettre à sa disposition.

3. L'audition par visioconférence est menée selon les règles suivantes :

a) L'audition se déroule en présence d'une autorité compétente de la Partie requise. Cette autorité est également responsable de l'identification de la personne entendue et du respect des principes fondamentaux prévus par la législation nationale de la Partie requise. Si l'autorité de la Partie requise estime que les principes fondamentaux prévus par son droit ne sont pas respectés lors de l'audition, elle prend immédiatement les mesures nécessaires pour que l'audition se déroule conformément à son droit;

b) Les autorités compétentes des Parties conviennent, selon que de besoin, des mesures concernant la protection de la personne à entendre;

c) L'audition est menée directement par la Partie requérante ou sous sa direction, conformément à sa législation nationale; et

d) Au terme de l'audition, l'autorité compétente de la Partie requise dresse un procès-verbal indiquant la date, l'heure et le lieu de l'audition, l'identité de la personne dont la déclaration a été recueillie, la teneur de sa déclaration, ainsi que l'identité et la qualité des autres personnes ayant participé à l'audition. Ce document est transmis à la Partie requérante.

Article XX. Cas particuliers d'entraide

La Partie requise soumet dans des cas particuliers, dans la mesure où ses autorités compétentes peuvent les obtenir, des extraits de casiers judiciaires et/ou des documents ou objets qui sont nécessaires dans le cadre d'une enquête et/ou d'une procédure pénale, à l'exception des documents et objets contenant des renseignements qui relèvent du secret d'État.

Article XXI. Transmission spontanée d'éléments de preuve et de renseignements

1. Les autorités compétentes de chaque Partie peuvent, par l'intermédiaire des autorités centrales et dans les limites de leur législation nationale, sans qu'une demande d'entraide judiciaire ait été présentée à cet effet, échanger des renseignements et des éléments de preuve

relatifs à des infractions pénales quand elles estiment que cet échange est de nature à permettre à l'autre Partie :

a) De présenter une demande d'entraide judiciaire conformément au présent Traité;

b) D'engager des poursuites pénales; ou

c) De faciliter le déroulement d'une enquête pénale en cours.

2. La Partie qui fournit les renseignements peut, conformément à sa législation nationale, subordonner leur utilisation à certaines conditions. La Partie destinataire est tenue de respecter ces conditions.

Article XXII. Restriction de la propriété des objets, produits ou instruments du crime

1. La Partie requise, à la demande de la Partie requérante, effectue les démarches et les enquêtes nécessaires pour déterminer si des objets, des produits ou des instruments d'une infraction ou liés à une infraction se trouvent sur son territoire et informe la Partie requérante des résultats de ces démarches et enquêtes. Lors de la présentation de la demande, la Partie requérante informe la Partie requise des motifs qui l'incitent à croire que des objets, des revenus, des produits ou des instruments d'une infraction ou liés à une infraction peuvent se trouver sur le territoire de la Partie requise.

2. Une fois que les revenus ou les produits du crime ou les objets qui y sont liés ont été localisés conformément au paragraphe 1 du présent article, la Partie requise prend, à la demande de la Partie requérante, les mesures prévues dans sa législation nationale pour les sécuriser et fait le nécessaire pour éviter leur échange, leur transfert ou leur aliénation ou destruction.

3. Dans la mesure où sa législation nationale le permet et à la demande de la Partie requérante, la Partie requise demande en priorité à la Partie requérante la restitution des revenus et/ou des produits des infractions, en particulier en vue d'indemniser les victimes ou de les restituer à leur propriétaire légitime, sans préjudice des droits de tiers de bonne foi.

4. La remise des gains et/ou des produits du crime est effectuée après accord sur le partage de ces revenus et/ou de ces produits du crime, conformément à la législation nationale des Parties. Le partage des revenus et/ou des produits est effectué par le biais d'un accord entre les autorités centrales, qui est conclu avant que la décision relative à la confiscation et à la remise des revenus et/ou des produits du crime ne devienne exécutoire.

5. La remise est effectuée conformément à la législation nationale de la Partie requise et après déduction des frais de gestion et du paiement de tous les impôts et droits auxquels ils sont soumis.

6. Cette demande d'entraide judiciaire s'étend également aux instruments utilisés pour commettre l'infraction.

Article XXIII. Frais

1. Les frais ordinaires liés à l'exécution des demandes d'entraide judiciaire sont supportés par la Partie requise, sauf dans les cas suivants, où ils sont pris en charge par la Partie requérante :

a) Les frais relatifs au transfèrement des personnes à destination et en provenance de son territoire conformément aux articles XVI et XVII du présent Traité, et à leur séjour sur le territoire de la Partie requérante, ainsi que les autres frais personnels relatifs à l'exécution de l'entraide judiciaire;

b) Les frais et les honoraires d'experts;

c) Les frais relatifs au transport et au séjour des représentants d'autorités compétentes de la Partie requérante pendant l'exécution de la demande d'entraide judiciaire, conformément au paragraphe 1 de l'article XI du présent Traité; et

d) Les frais relatifs à l'envoi et à la restitution d'objets transférés du territoire de la Partie requise au territoire de la Partie requérante.

2. Si la demande d'entraide judiciaire nécessite des dépenses exceptionnelles ou extraordinaires, les autorités centrales se consultent pour déterminer les conditions de l'exécution de la demande d'entraide judiciaire ainsi que les modalités de la prise en charge des frais.

Article XXIV. Autres accords ou instruments juridiques

1. Les dispositions du présent Traité n'affectent pas les demandes d'entraide judiciaire de portée plus étendue qui ont été ou seraient convenues entre les Parties dans d'autres accords ou instruments juridiques ou qui découlent de leur législation nationale.

2. Les Parties veillent à ce que toutes les mesures nécessaires soient prises pour donner effet aux dispositions du présent Traité.

Article XXV. Consultations et règlement des différends

1. Les autorités centrales des Parties, sur proposition de l'une ou l'autre d'entre elles, se consultent sur les questions liées à l'interprétation ou à l'application du présent Traité en général ou sur une demande d'entraide judiciaire particulière.

2. Tout différend découlant de l'interprétation ou de l'application du présent Traité est réglé à l'amiable par la voie diplomatique.

Article XXVI. Entrée en vigueur, modifications et dénonciation

1. Le présent Traité entre en vigueur 30 jours après la date de réception de la dernière des notifications par lesquelles les Parties s'informent, par écrit et par la voie diplomatique, de l'accomplissement des formalités requises par leur législation nationale, et reste en vigueur pour une durée indéterminée.

2. Dès l'entrée en vigueur du présent Traité, le Traité de coopération entre le Gouvernement des États-Unis du Mexique et le Gouvernement de la République de Cuba relatif à l'entraide judiciaire en matière pénale, conclu à Mexico le 23 avril 1996, cesse de produire ses effets.

3. Le présent Traité peut être modifié par consentement mutuel des Parties, formalisé par des communications écrites et par la voie diplomatique. Ces modifications entrent en vigueur conformément à la procédure prévue au paragraphe 1 du présent article.

4. Chacune des Parties peut dénoncer le présent Traité à tout moment par notification écrite adressée à l'autre Partie par la voie diplomatique. Le Traité prend fin 180 jours après la date de réception de cette notification.

5. La dénonciation du présent Traité n'affecte pas l'exécution des demandes d'entraide judiciaire reçues pendant qu'il était en vigueur.

SIGNÉ à Mexico, le 1er novembre 2013, en double exemplaire en langue espagnole, les deux textes faisant également foi.

Pour les États-Unis du Mexique :

JESÚS MURILLO KARAM
Procureur général

Pour la République de Cuba :

BRUNO RODRÍGUEZ PARRILLA
Ministre des affaires étrangères

No. 52843

Mexico
and
Cuba

Agreement between the Government of the United Mexican States and the Government of the Republic of Cuba on the mutual recognition and revalidation of certificates, diplomas and higher education studies. Mexico City, 1 November 2013

Entry into force: *9 July 2015, in accordance with article 15*

Authentic text: *Spanish*

Registration with the Secretariat of the United Nations: *Mexico, 5 August 2015*

Mexique
et
Cuba

Accord entre le Gouvernement des États-Unis du Mexique et le Gouvernement de la République de Cuba relatif à la reconnaissance et à la revalidation mutuelles des titres, des diplômes et des études de l'enseignement supérieur. Mexico, 1er novembre 2013

Entrée en vigueur : *9 juillet 2015, conformément à l'article 15*

Texte authentique : *espagnol*

Enregistrement auprès du Secrétariat de l'Organisation des Nations Unies : *Mexique, 5 août 2015*

[SPANISH TEXT – TEXTE ESPAGNOL]

ACUERDO ENTRE EL GOBIERNO DE LOS ESTADOS UNIDOS MEXICANOS Y EL GOBIERNO DE LA REPÚBLICA DE CUBA SOBRE RECONOCIMIENTO Y REVALIDACIÓN MUTUOS DE TÍTULOS, DIPLOMAS Y ESTUDIOS DE EDUCACIÓN SUPERIOR

El Gobierno de los Estados Unidos Mexicanos y el Gobierno de la República de Cuba, en lo sucesivo denominados las "Partes";

ANIMADAS por el deseo de mejorar y ampliar sus relaciones de cooperación en materia educativa;

TENIENDO PRESENTE las disposiciones del Convenio de Cooperación en los campos de la Educación, la Cultura, la Juventud, la Cultura Física y el Deporte entre los Estados Unidos Mexicanos y la República de Cuba, firmado en la ciudad de La Habana, Cuba, el 10 de abril de 2012;

Han acordado lo siguiente:

ARTÍCULO 1

El presente Acuerdo tiene como objetivo establecer el reconocimiento y la revalidación mutuos de los certificados de estudios, títulos, diplomas de nivel superior o grados académicos expedidos por las Instituciones o Centros de Educación Superior, pertenecientes a los sistemas educativos oficiales de los Estados Unidos Mexicanos y de la República de Cuba.

Las Partes reconocen como organismos estatales competentes los siguientes:

a) Por el Gobierno de los Estados Unidos Mexicanos: La Secretaría de Educación Pública.

b) Por el Gobierno de la República de Cuba: El Ministerio de Educación Superior.

ARTÍCULO 2

Para los efectos del presente Acuerdo, se entenderá por reconocimiento, la validez oficial que cada una de las Partes otorgue a los estudios realizados en las Instituciones o Centros de Educación Superior reconocidas por la otra Parte, acreditados por certificados de estudios, títulos, diplomas o grados académicos y científicos.

ARTÍCULO 3

Las Partes por conducto de sus respectivas autoridades educativas, intercambiarán en el plazo de dos (2) meses, a partir de la fecha de entrada en vigor del presente Acuerdo, la lista de sus Instituciones o Centros de Educación Superior reconocidos y los planes de estudio que se imparten dentro sus respectivos sistemas educativos oficiales.

ARTÍCULO 4

El reconocimiento de los certificados de estudios, títulos, diplomas o grados académicos, previsto por el presente Acuerdo, no exime a sus titulares de la obligación de cumplir con los requisitos de la legislación del país receptor, para el ingreso a las Instituciones o Centros de Educación Superior o para el ejercicio profesional.

ARTÍCULO 5

Las Partes reconocerán y concederán igual validez a los Certificados o Diplomas de estudios de bachillerato o bachiller y Técnico Medio Superior expedidos en los Centros de Educación Media Superior de los Estados Unidos Mexicanos y de la República de Cuba, los cuales dan derecho a sus titulares a ingresar a las Instituciones o Centros de Educación Superior de las Partes.

ARTÍCULO 6

Las Partes reconocerán y concederán igual validez al título de Técnico Superior Universitario expedido en los Estados Unidos Mexicanos, y el equivalente expedido en Centros de Educación Media Superior y Superior en la República de Cuba, para el ejercicio técnico profesional, de acuerdo con la calificación (o nivel profesional) obtenido y/o para ingresar en las Instituciones o Centros de Educación Superior de las Partes del presente Acuerdo, así como en los programas conducentes a la expedición de los Títulos de Licenciatura o profesionales cuyos planes de estudios son al menos de cuatro (4) años de estudio, en los Estados Unidos Mexicanos y en la República de Cuba.

ARTÍCULO 7

Las Partes reconocerán y concederán igual validez a los certificados parciales expedidos por los Centros de Enseñanza Superior en los Estados Unidos Mexicanos y los equivalentes expedidos por los Centros de Educación Superior de la República de Cuba. Asimismo, otorgarán el derecho de continuar con los estudios en sus Instituciones o Centros de Educación Superior, según los programas conducentes a la expedición del grado de Licenciado o Título Profesional en los Estados Unidos Mexicanos y a los Títulos de Licenciado, Ingeniero, Doctor en Medicina y otros títulos profesionales que confieren los Centros de Educación Superior en la República de Cuba, y cuya duración son de cuatro (4) años o más de estudios superiores.

ARTÍCULO 8

Las Partes reconocerán y concederán igual validez al Título de Licenciado y otros títulos profesionales expedidos en los Centros de Educación Superior de los Estados Unidos Mexicanos y a los expedidos en los Centros de Educación Superior de la República de Cuba para la continuación de los estudios de posgrado de Educación Superior y para el ejercicio de actividades profesionales.

ARTÍCULO 9

Las Partes reconocerán y concederán igual validez a los Títulos de Licenciado y otros títulos profesionales, Especialidad y Maestría expedidos en los Centros de Educación Superior de los Estados Unidos Mexicanos y a los expedidos en los Centros de Educación Superior de la República de Cuba, y cuya duración son de cuatro (4) años o más de estudios superiores. Dichos títulos darán derecho a sus titulares a ingresar en Programas de Posgrado, Maestría y Doctorado en las instituciones de nivel superior de los Estados Unidos Mexicanos y en las instituciones de nivel superior de la República de Cuba.

ARTÍCULO 10

Las Partes reconocerán y concederán igual validez al Título de Doctorado expedido en las instituciones de nivel superior de los Estados Unidos Mexicanos, considerando a éste como el que se otorga después de la Licenciatura y la Maestría, y al expedido por las instituciones de nivel superior de la República de Cuba.

ARTÍCULO 11

Las Partes, por conducto de sus autoridades educativas competentes, se consultarán respecto de la legislación interna aplicable para el reconocimiento de los títulos y estudios de nivel superior, así como de sus sistemas educativos y se informarán sobre cualquier cambio que pudiera tener impacto en la aplicación del presente Acuerdo.

ARTÍCULO 12

Las Partes, de estimarlo conveniente, alentarán la participación de otras instituciones públicas y privadas, cuyas actividades incidan directamente en las áreas de cooperación, con el propósito de fortalecer y ampliar los mecanismos que apoyen el objetivo del presente Acuerdo.

ARTÍCULO 13

Para lograr las mejores condiciones de aplicación, seguimiento y evaluación de las actividades de cooperación del presente Acuerdo, las Partes establecerán, en un plazo no mayor de sesenta (60) días, a partir de la fecha de entrada en vigor del presente Acuerdo, una Comisión Bilateral Técnica, para lo cual designarán a un Coordinador por cada una de Ellas.

La Comisión Bilateral se reunirá periódicamente, al menos una vez al año, a fin de evaluar los aspectos derivados de la aplicación del presente Acuerdo, teniendo a su cargo las funciones siguientes:

a) establecer los mecanismos de intercambio de información, consulta y asistencia que se requieran para la mejor ejecución del presente Acuerdo;

b) definir los términos de referencia en que podrá otorgarse el reconocimiento de los certificados de estudios, títulos y grados académicos y especificar los procedimientos que deberán cubrirse en cada país; y

c) realizar el seguimiento y evaluación en el cumplimiento y propósito del presente Acuerdo.

La Comisión Bilateral Técnica formulará informes sobre los avances obtenidos en el presente Acuerdo y los someterá a la consideración de las Partes. Una vez aprobados, se harán del conocimiento de sus respectivas Cancillerías y de las instancias gubernamentales que estimen pertinentes.

ARTÍCULO 14

Cualquier controversia derivada de la aplicación o cumplimiento de las disposiciones contenidas en el presente Acuerdo, se resolverá entre las Partes de común acuerdo, mediante consultas y negociaciones amistosas a través de la vía diplomática.

ARTÍCULO 15

El presente Acuerdo entrará en vigor treinta (30) días después de la fecha de recepción de la última notificación, mediante la cual las Partes se comuniquen por escrito, a través de la vía diplomática, el cumplimiento de los requisitos exigidos por su legislación nacional para tal efecto.

El presente Acuerdo podrá ser modificado por mutuo consentimiento, a solicitud de cualquiera de las Partes. Las modificaciones entrarán en vigor de conformidad con el procedimiento establecido en el primer párrafo del presente Artículo.

El presente Acuerdo tendrá vigencia indefinida y cualquiera de las Partes podrá darlo por terminado, mediante comunicación escrita dirigida a la otra Parte, a través de la vía diplomática, con ciento ochenta (180) días de antelación.

La terminación del presente Acuerdo no afectará el reconocimiento y la revalidación mutuos de los certificados de estudios, títulos, diplomas y grados académicos, que se hubieran expedido durante su vigencia, ni afectará a los estudiantes que hayan llegado a los Estados Unidos Mexicanos o a la República de Cuba antes de la expiración de dicho Acuerdo. Los títulos de estudios y grados académicos otorgados a sus titulares, durante la vigencia del presente Acuerdo, se reconocerán de conformidad con los términos del mismo.

Firmado en la Ciudad de México, el primero de noviembre de dos mil trece, en dos ejemplares originales en idioma español, siendo ambos textos igualmente auténticos.

POR EL GOBIERNO DE LOS ESTADOS UNIDOS MEXICANOS

Enrique del Val y Blanco
Subsecretario de Planeación y Evaluación de Políticas Educativas de la Secretaría de Educación Pública

POR EL GOBIERNO DE LA REPÚBLICA DE CUBA

Dagoberto Rodríguez Barrera
Embajador de la República de Cuba en los Estados Unidos Mexicanos

[TRANSLATION – TRADUCTION]

AGREEMENT BETWEEN THE GOVERNMENT OF THE UNITED MEXICAN STATES AND THE GOVERNMENT OF THE REPUBLIC OF CUBA ON THE MUTUAL RECOGNITION AND REVALIDATION OF CERTIFICATES, DIPLOMAS AND HIGHER EDUCATION STUDIES

The Government of the United Mexican States and the Government of the Republic of Cuba, hereinafter referred to as "the Parties",

Motivated by the desire to improve and expand their cooperative relations in educational matters,

Bearing in mind the provisions of the Agreement for cooperation in the fields of education, culture, youth, physical education and sports between the United Mexican States and the Republic of Cuba, signed in Havana, Cuba, on 10 April 2012,

Have agreed as follows:

Article 1

This Agreement is intended to establish mutual recognition and revalidation of certificates of studies, qualifications, higher level diplomas or academic degrees issued by higher education institutions or establishments belonging to the official education systems of the United Mexican States and the Republic of Cuba.

The Parties recognize the following as competent State agencies:

(a) For the Government of the United Mexican States: The Ministry of Public Education;

(b) For the Government of the Republic of Cuba: The Ministry of Higher Education.

Article 2

For the purposes of this Agreement, recognition shall be understood to be the official validity that each Party grants to studies pursued in higher education institutions or establishments recognized by the other Party, accredited by academic and scientific certificates of studies, qualifications, diplomas or degrees.

Article 3

The Parties, through their respective educational authorities, shall exchange within two months, from the date of entry into force of this Agreement, the list of their recognized higher education institutions or establishments and the curricula taught in their respective official educational systems.

Article 4

The recognition of certificates of academic studies, qualifications, diplomas or degrees provided for by this Agreement does not exempt holders of the obligation to comply with the requirements of the legislation of the host country as regards admission to institutions or establishments of higher education or for the practice of g a profession.

Article 5

The Parties shall recognize and grant equal validity to high school and higher technical school certificates or diplomas issued by the establishments of higher secondary education of the United Mexican States and the Republic of Cuba, which entitle holders to enter the higher education institutions or establishments of the Parties.

Article 6

The Parties shall recognize and grant equal validity to the higher technical university qualification issued in the United Mexican States and the equivalent qualification issued by higher secondary and higher education establishments in the Republic of Cuba for the exercise of technical professions, in accordance with the qualification (or professional level) obtained and/or to enter the higher education institutions or establishments of the Parties to this Agreement, as well as programmes leading to the issuance of a bachelor's or professional degree that comprise at least four years of study in the United Mexican States or in the Republic of Cuba.

Article 7

The Parties shall recognize and grant equal validity to partial certificates issued by the higher education establishments in the United Mexican States and the equivalent certificates issued by the higher education establishments of the Republic of Cuba. In addition, they shall grant the right to pursue studies in their higher education institutions or establishments, following programmes leading to the issuance of a bachelor's degree or professional certificate in the United Mexican States and the bachelor's, engineering and medical doctor's degree and other professional qualifications conferred by higher education establishments in the Republic of Cuba, and whose duration are four or more years of higher education.

Article 8

The Parties shall recognize and grant equal validity to the bachelor's degree and other professional qualifications issued by the establishments of higher education of the United Mexican States and those issued by the establishments of higher education of the Republic of Cuba for the continuation of postgraduate higher education studies and the exercise of professional activities.

Article 9

The Parties shall recognize and grant equal validity to bachelor's degrees and other professional and specialization certificates and master's degrees issued by the higher education establishments of the United Mexican States and to those issued by the higher education establishments of the Republic of Cuba, with a course duration of four or more years of higher education. The holders of those qualifications will be entitled to enter postgraduate, master's and doctoral degree programmes in the higher-level institutions of the United Mexican States and in the higher-level institutions of the Republic of Cuba.

Article 10

The Parties shall recognize and grant equal validity to the doctoral degree issued in the higher-level institutions of the United Mexican States, which is the degree granted subsequently to a bachelor's or master's degree and issued by the higher-level institutions of the Republic of Cuba.

Article 11

The Parties, through their competent educational authorities, shall consult each other with respect to the domestic legislation applicable to the recognition of higher education certificates and studies and their education systems and shall inform each other of any changes that might have an impact on the implementation of this Agreement.

Article 12

The Parties, should they deem it appropriate, shall encourage the participation of other public and private institutions whose activities have a direct impact on the areas of cooperation, in order to strengthen and expand the mechanisms that support the objective of this Agreement.

Article 13

In order to achieve the best conditions for the implementation, follow-up and evaluation of the cooperative activities under this Agreement, the Parties shall establish, within a period not exceeding 60 days from the date of entry into force of this Agreement, a bilateral Technical Commission, for which they shall each appoint a coordinator.

The Bilateral Commission shall meet regularly, at least once a year, to evaluate issues arising from the application of this Agreement, with responsibility for the following functions:

(a) Establishing the mechanisms for information-sharing, consultation and assistance required for the best implementation of this Agreement;

(b) Defining the terms of reference in which the recognition of certificates of studies, qualifications and academic degrees may be granted and specifying the procedures to be followed in each country; and

(c) Monitoring and evaluating the implementation and purpose of this Agreement.

The Bilateral Technical Commission will produce reports on the progress achieved under this Agreement and will submit them for consideration by the Parties. Once adopted, they shall be sent to their respective Ministries of Foreign Affairs and to the Government agencies that they deem appropriate.

Article 14

Any dispute arising out of the application or implementation of the provisions contained in this Agreement shall be settled by mutual agreement of the Parties, by means of friendly consultations and negotiations through the diplomatic channel.

Article 15

This Agreement shall enter into force 30 days after the date of receipt of the last notification by which the Parties notify each other in writing, through the diplomatic channel, of the completion of the formalities required by their national legislation for that purpose.

This Agreement may be amended by mutual consent at the request of either of the Parties. Such amendments shall enter into force in accordance with the procedure laid down in the first paragraph of this article.

This Agreement shall remain in effect for a period of indefinite duration and may be terminated by either Party by means of a written notification addressed to the other Party, through the diplomatic channel, with a notice period of 180 days.

Termination of this Agreement shall not affect the mutual recognition and revalidation of certificates of studies, qualifications, diplomas, degrees and academic degrees issued while it was in force, nor shall it affect students who have arrived in the United Mexican States or the Republic of Cuba before the expiration of the Agreement. The certificates of studies and academic degrees granted to their holders during the term of this Agreement shall be recognized in accordance with the terms thereof.

SIGNED at Mexico City on 1 November 2013, in duplicate, in the Spanish language, both texts being equally authentic.

For the Government of the United Mexican States:

ENRIQUE DEL VAL Y BLANCO
Deputy Minister for Educational Policy Planning and Evaluation
Ministry of Public Education

For the Government of the Republic of Cuba:

DAGOBERTO RODRÍGUEZ BARRERA
Ambassador of the Republic of Cuba in the United Mexican States

[TRANSLATION – TRADUCTION]

ACCORD ENTRE LE GOUVERNEMENT DES ÉTATS-UNIS DU MEXIQUE ET LE GOUVERNEMENT DE LA RÉPUBLIQUE DE CUBA RELATIF À LA RECONNAISSANCE ET À LA REVALIDATION MUTUELLES DES TITRES, DES DIPLÔMES ET DES ÉTUDES DE L'ENSEIGNEMENT SUPÉRIEUR

Le Gouvernement des États-Unis du Mexique et le Gouvernement de la République de Cuba, ci-après dénommés « Parties »,

Animés par le désir d'améliorer et d'étendre leurs relations de coopération dans le domaine de l'éducation,

Gardant à l'esprit les dispositions de la Convention de coopération dans les domaines de l'enseignement, de la culture, de la jeunesse, de l'éducation physique et des sports entre les États-Unis du Mexique et la République de Cuba, signé dans la ville de La Havane, à Cuba, le 10 avril 2012,

Sont convenus de ce qui suit :

Article premier

Le présent Accord a pour objet d'établir la reconnaissance et la revalidation mutuelles des certificats d'études, des titres, des diplômes d'études supérieures ou des grades académiques délivrés par des établissements ou centres d'enseignement supérieur appartenant aux systèmes éducatifs officiels des États-Unis du Mexique et de la République de Cuba.

Les Parties reconnaissent comme organismes publics compétents :

a) Pour le Gouvernement des États-Unis du Mexique : le Ministère de l'enseignement public;

b) Pour le Gouvernement de la République de Cuba : le Ministère de l'enseignement supérieur.

Article 2

Aux fins du présent Accord, le terme « reconnaissance » désigne la validité officielle que chaque Partie accorde aux études effectuées dans des établissements ou centres d'enseignement supérieur reconnus par l'autre Partie, sanctionnées par des certificats d'études, des titres, des diplômes ou des grades académiques et scientifiques.

Article 3

Les Parties, par l'intermédiaire de leurs autorités éducatives respectives, échangent, dans un délai de deux mois à compter de la date d'entrée en vigueur du présent Accord, la liste de leurs établissements ou centres d'enseignement supérieur reconnus ainsi que les programmes d'études proposés dans leurs systèmes éducatifs officiels respectifs.

Article 4

La reconnaissance des certificats d'études, des titres, des diplômes ou des grades académiques prévue par le présent Accord ne dispense pas leurs titulaires de l'obligation de se conformer aux exigences de la législation du pays d'accueil en ce qui concerne l'admission dans les établissements ou centres d'enseignement supérieur ou pour l'exercice d'une profession.

Article 5

Les Parties reconnaissent et accordent la même validité aux certificats ou diplômes d'études secondaires ou d'études secondaires et techniques de second cycle délivrés dans les centres d'enseignement secondaire de second cycle des États-Unis du Mexique et de la République de Cuba, qui permettent à leurs titulaires d'entrer dans les établissements ou centres d'enseignement supérieur des Parties.

Article 6

Les Parties reconnaissent et accordent la même validité au diplôme universitaire technique supérieur délivré aux États-Unis du Mexique et à son équivalent délivré par les centres d'enseignement secondaire de second cycle et d'enseignement supérieur de la République de Cuba, pour la pratique professionnelle technique, en fonction de la qualification (ou du niveau professionnel) obtenue, et/ou pour entrer dans les établissements ou centres d'enseignement supérieur des Parties au présent Accord, ainsi que dans les programmes conduisant à la délivrance de licences ou de diplômes professionnels dont le cursus est d'au moins quatre années d'études, aux États-Unis du Mexique et dans la République de Cuba.

Article 7

Les Parties reconnaissent et accordent la même validité aux certificats partiels délivrés par les centres d'enseignement supérieur des États-Unis du Mexique et aux équivalents délivrés par les centres d'enseignement supérieur de la République de Cuba. De même, elles accordent le droit de poursuivre des études dans leurs établissements ou centres d'enseignement supérieur, en suivant les programmes menant à l'obtention de la licence ou diplôme professionnel aux États-Unis du Mexique et aux diplômes de licence, d'ingénieur, de docteur en médecine et autres diplômes professionnels délivrés par les centres d'enseignement supérieur de la République de Cuba, et dont le cursus est de quatre ans d'études supérieures ou plus.

Article 8

Les Parties reconnaissent et accordent la même validité à la licence et aux autres diplômes professionnels délivrés dans les centres d'enseignement supérieur des États-Unis du Mexique et à ceux délivrés dans les centres d'enseignement supérieur de la République de Cuba pour la poursuite des études de troisième cycle dans l'enseignement supérieur et pour l'exercice d'activités professionnelles.

Article 9

Les Parties reconnaissent et accordent la même validité aux licences et aux autres titres professionnels, de spécialisation et de maîtrise délivrés dans les centres d'enseignement supérieur des États-Unis du Mexique et à ceux délivrés dans les centres d'enseignement supérieur de la République de Cuba, et dont le cursus est de quatre ans d'études supérieures ou plus. Ces diplômes permettent à leurs titulaires d'accéder à des programmes de troisième cycle, de maîtrise et de doctorat dans les établissements d'enseignement supérieur des États-Unis du Mexique et dans les établissements d'enseignement supérieur de la République de Cuba.

Article 10

Les Parties reconnaissent et accordent la même validité au diplôme de doctorat délivré par les établissements d'enseignement supérieur des États-Unis du Mexique, qu'elles considèrent comme le diplôme délivré après la licence et la maîtrise, et au diplôme délivré par les établissements d'enseignement supérieur de la République de Cuba.

Article 11

Les Parties, par l'intermédiaire de leurs autorités éducatives compétentes, se consultent sur la législation nationale applicable à la reconnaissance des diplômes et des études d'enseignement supérieur, ainsi que sur leurs systèmes d'éducation, et s'informent de tout changement susceptible d'avoir une incidence sur l'application du présent Accord.

Article 12

Les Parties, si elles le jugent approprié, encouragent la participation d'autres établissements publics et privés dont les activités ont une incidence directe sur les domaines de coopération, en vue de renforcer et d'élargir les mécanismes qui soutiennent l'objectif du présent Accord.

Article 13

Afin de créer les meilleures conditions pour la mise en œuvre, le suivi et l'évaluation des activités de coopération visées par le présent Accord, les Parties établissent, dans un délai n'excédant pas 60 jours à compter de la date d'entrée en vigueur du présent Accord, une Commission bilatérale technique, pour laquelle elles désignent un coordonnateur pour chacune d'entre elles.

La Commission bilatérale se réunit périodiquement, au moins une fois par an, afin d'évaluer les aspects découlant de l'application du présent Accord, et est chargée des fonctions suivantes :

a) Établir les mécanismes d'échange de renseignements, de consultation et d'assistance nécessaires à une meilleure mise en œuvre du présent Accord;

b) Définir les termes de référence en vertu desquels la reconnaissance des certificats d'études, des titres et des grades académiques peut être accordée et spécifier les procédures à suivre dans chaque pays; et

c) Suivre et évaluer la mise en œuvre et l'objectif du présent Accord.

La Commission bilatérale technique élabore des rapports sur les progrès réalisés dans le cadre du présent Accord et les soumet aux Parties pour examen. Une fois approuvés, ils sont portés à la connaissance de leurs Ministères des affaires étrangères respectifs et des organismes gouvernementaux qu'ils jugent pertinents.

Article 14

Tout différend découlant de l'application ou de la mise en œuvre des dispositions contenues dans le présent Accord est réglé d'un commun accord entre les Parties, par des consultations et des négociations à l'amiable par la voie diplomatique.

Article 15

Le présent Accord entre en vigueur 30 jours après la date de réception de la dernière des notifications écrites par lesquelles les Parties s'informent mutuellement, par la voie diplomatique, de l'accomplissement des formalités requises à cet effet par leur législation nationale.

Le présent Accord peut être modifié par consentement mutuel, à la demande de l'une ou l'autre Partie. Les modifications entrent en vigueur conformément à la procédure visée au paragraphe 1 du présent article.

Le présent Accord reste en vigueur pour une durée indéterminée et peut être dénoncé par une Partie moyennant un préavis écrit de 180 jours adressé à l'autre Partie par la voie diplomatique.

La dénonciation du présent Accord n'affecte pas la reconnaissance et la revalidation mutuelles des certificats d'études, titres, diplômes et grades académiques délivrés pendant qu'il était en vigueur ni les étudiants arrivés aux États-Unis du Mexique ou en République de Cuba avant l'expiration dudit Accord. Les titres d'études et grades académiques décernés à leurs titulaires pendant la durée du présent Accord sont reconnus conformément aux dispositions du présent Accord.

SIGNÉ à Mexico, le 1er novembre 2013, en double exemplaire en langue espagnole, les deux textes faisant également foi.

Pour le Gouvernement des États-Unis du Mexique :

ENRIQUE DEL VAL Y BLANCO
Ministre adjoint chargé de la planification et de l'évaluation de la politique éducative
Ministère de l'enseignement public

Pour le Gouvernement de la République de Cuba :

DAGOBERTO RODRIGUEZ BARRERA
Ambassadeur de la République de Cuba auprès des États-Unis du Mexique

No. 52844

Mexico
and
Turkey

Agreement between the Government of the United Mexican States and the Government of the Republic of Turkey on mutual administrative assistance and exchange of information on customs matters. Ankara, 17 December 2013

Entry into force: *16 July 2015, in accordance with article 23*

Authentic texts: *English, Spanish and Turkish*

Registration with the Secretariat of the United Nations: *Mexico, 5 August 2015*

Mexique
et
Turquie

Accord entre le Gouvernement des États-Unis du Mexique et le Gouvernement de la République turque relatif à l'assistance mutuelle administrative et à l'échange de renseignements en matière douanière. Ankara, 17 décembre 2013

Entrée en vigueur : *16 juillet 2015, conformément à l'article 23*

Textes authentiques : *anglais, espagnol et turc*

Enregistrement auprès du Secrétariat de l'Organisation des Nations Unies : *Mexique, 5 août 2015*

[English text – Texte anglais]

AGREEMENT BETWEEN THE GOVERNMENT OF THE UNITED MEXICAN STATES AND THE GOVERNMENT OF THE REPUBLIC OF TURKEY ON MUTUAL ADMINISTRATIVE ASSISTANCE AND EXCHANGE OF INFORMATION ON CUSTOMS MATTERS

The Government of the United Mexican States and the Government of the Republic of Turkey, hereinafter referred to as the "Parties"

AWARE OF the offences against Customs Legislation are prejudicial to the economic, tax, financial, social, cultural and commercial interests of their respective countries;

CONSIDERING the importance of assuring the accurate assessment of Customs duties, taxes, other charges and fees, collected on the importation or exportation of goods, with the correct determination of their tariff classification, value and origin, as well as the proper enforcement of the provisions of prohibition, restriction and control;

RECOGNIZING the importance of international cooperation in matters related to the application and enforcement of their Customs Legislation;

CONVINCED that efforts to prevent offences against Customs Legislation and efforts to ensure accurate collection of import and export duties, taxes, fees and other charges may be rendered more effectively through cooperation between the Customs Authorities;

CONCERNED about the scales and growth tendencies of the illicit traffic of narcotic drugs and psychotropic substances, which constitute a danger to public health and to society;

TAKING INTO CONSIDERATION to the Single Convention on Narcotic Drugs of 1961 amended by its Protocol of 1972 and the Convention on Psychotropic Substances of 1971, created under the auspices of the United Nations, as well as the United Nations Convention against the Illicit Traffic in Narcotic Drugs and Psychotropic Substances of 1988;

HAVING REGARD to the obligations imposed under international conventions already accepted or applied by the Parties;

Have agreed as follows:

CHAPTER I
GENERAL PROVISIONS

ARTICLE 1
Definitions

For the purposes of this Agreement:

1) "Customs Authority" shall mean in the United Mexican States, the Ministry of Finance and Public Credit and, in the Republic of Turkey, the Ministry of Customs and Trade;

2) "Customs duties" shall mean all duties, taxes, fees or any other charges which are levied in the territories of the Parties in the application of the Customs Legislation excluding fees and charges for services rendered;

3) "Customs Legislation" shall mean the statutory and regulatory provisions relating to the importation, exportation, movement or storage of goods, the administration and enforcement of which are specifically entrusted to the Customs Authorities, and any regulations made by Customs Authorities under their statutory powers;

4) "Customs offence" shall mean any violation or attempted violation of Customs Legislation;

5) "Information" shall mean any data, whether or not processed or analyzed, documents, reports, certified or authenticated copies thereof or other communications, including electronic data;

6) "International trade supply chain " shall mean any process in which the cross-border movement of goods from the place of origin to its final destination is involved;

7) "Official" shall mean any Customs officer or other Government agent designated by a Customs Authority;

8) "Person" shall mean any natural or legal person;

9) "Personal data" shall mean any information concerning an identified or identifiable natural person;

10) "Requesting Customs Authority" shall mean the Customs Authority which requests assistance in Customs matters;

11) "Requested Customs Authority" shall mean the Customs Authority which receives a request for assistance in Customs matters, and

12) "Territory" shall mean:

a) regarding the United Mexican States, the territory of the United Mexican States as it is defined in its Political Constitution, including any area beyond its territorial sea on which the United Mexican States can exercise sovereign rights of exploration and exploitation of the natural resources of the depth of the sea, subsoil and the overlapping waters, and the air space above those areas, according to the International Law, and

b) regarding the Republic of Turkey, the land territory, the territorial sea and the air space above them, as well as the sea and submarine areas over which Turkey is entitled to exercise, in conformity with international law, sovereignity and jurisdiction.

ARTICLE 2

Scope of the Agreement

1) The Parties shall, through their Customs Authorities, provide each other with mutual assistance in accordance with the terms set out in this Agreement, for the proper application of the Customs Legislation and for the prevention, investigation, and repression of Customs offences and to protect the security of the international trade supply chain.

2) Assistance, as provided for in this Agreement, shall also be extended on a Party's own initiative or upon request for the purposes of assessing Customs duties and other taxes or charges with respect to the Customs Legislation, and enforcing controls within the Customs Authority.

3) Any action carried out under this Agreement by either Party will be performed in accordance with its national legal and administrative provisions and within the limits of its Customs Authority's competence and economic available resources.

4) No provision in this Agreement shall be interpreted in a manner that would restrict an agreement relating to mutual assistance and cooperation that is already in force between the Parties.

5) The provisions of this Agreement shall not give rise to a right to any private person to obtain, suppress or exclude any evidence or to impede the execution of a request for assistance.

6) The assistance as provided in the present Agreement does not include requesting the arrest of people or the collection of Customs duties, charges, fines or any other amounts determined by the Customs Authority of one of the Parties.

CHAPTER II
GENERAL ASSISTANCE PROCEDURES

ARTICLE 3
Form and Substance of Requests for Assistance

1) Requests for assistance under this Agreement shall be communicated directly between the Customs Authorities concerned. Each Customs Authority shall designate an official contact point for this purpose and shall communicate this information and any updates thereof to the other Customs Authority.

2) Requests for assistance under this Agreement shall be made in writing or electronically, and shall be accompanied by any information or documents deemed useful for the execution of such requests. The Requested Custom Authority will be able to request the confirmation in writing of electronic requests. When required because of the exigency of the situation, requests may be made verbally but shall be confirmed in writing as expeditiously as possible, but no later than ten (10) days from the date of the oral requests.

3) The request shall be made in English. Any documents accompanying such requests shall be translated, to the extent necessary, into English.

4) Requests made pursuant to paragraph 2 of this Article shall include the following information:

a) the name of the Requesting Customs Authority;

b) type of assistance requested;

c) the object and the reasons for the request;

d) a brief description of the case under consideration and the legal and administrative provisions that apply, and

e) the names and addresses of the persons to whom the request relates, if known.

5) If a request does not meet the format requirements, its correction or completion may be demanded. The ordering of precautionary measures shall not be affected thereby.

6) Where the Requesting Customs Authority requests that a certain procedure be followed, the Requested Customs Authority shall comply with such a request, in accordance with its legislation in force.

ARTICLE 4

Spontaneous Assistance

In cases that could involve substantial damage to the economy, public health, public security, including the security of the international trade supply chain, or other vital interests of the Parties, the Customs Authority of any Party shall, wherever possible, provide assistance on its own initiative without delay.

CHAPTER III

INFORMATION

ARTICLE 5

Communication of Information

1) The Customs Authorities shall, upon request or by own initiative, furnish each other with all information, which may help to ensure accuracy in:

a) the collection of Customs duties levied by the Customs Authorities and, in particular, information which may help to assess the value of goods for customs purposes and to establish their tariff classification;

b) the enforcement of the measures of prohibition, restriction and other controls, preferences or exemptions relating to the importation, exportation, transit of goods and other Customs regimes, and

c) the verification of the country of origin of the goods.

2) If the Requested Customs Authority does not have the information asked for, it shall be notified to the Requesting Party promptly.

3) The Requested Customs Authority shall seek the information as if it were acting on its own account.

ARTICLE 6
Particular Types of Information

1) On request, the Customs Authorities shall inform each other:

a) whether goods imported into the territory of the requesting Party have been lawfully exported from the territory of the other Party, and

b) whether goods exported from the territory of the requesting Party have been lawfully imported into the territory of the other Party.

2) Such information shall also specify the customs procedure used for the clearance of the goods.

ARTICLE 7
Information for the Application and Enforcement of Customs Legislation

The Customs Authorities shall provide each other, either on request or on their own initiative, with information which helps to ensure proper application of Customs Legislation and the prevention, investigation and combating of Customs offences and to ensure the security of the international trade supply chain. Such information may include:

a) new Customs enforcement techniques having proved their effectiveness;

b) new trends, means or methods of committing Customs offences, as well as those that attempt to hide the origin or the correct value of goods;

c) goods known to be subject of Customs offences, as well as transport and storage methods used in respect of those goods;

d) information of persons known to have committed a Customs offence or suspected of being about to commit a Customs offence, as long as the legislation of the Parties related to the protection of personal information, allows the exchange of that information even by means of exception;

e) any other information that can assist Customs Authorities with the proper application of its Customs Legislation, and

f) any other information that can assist Customs Authorities with risk analysis for control and facilitation purposes.

ARTICLE 8

Exchange of Customs Information

1) The information already processed through the risk analysis and that may result in some kind of alert shall be sent and shared between the Parties, in an expeditiously manner in order to take measures.

2) The Parties shall exchange the information regarding the seizure of goods and money, including detection methods and hiding procedures.

ARTICLE 9

Information Relating to Customs Offences

The Customs Authorities of the Parties shall, upon request or on their own initiative, furnish each other information on activities planned, ongoing, or completed which provide reasonable grounds to believe that a Customs offence has been committed or will be committed in the territory of the Party concerned. In serious cases which could involve substantial damage to the economy, public health, public security or any other vital interest of the other Party, such information shall be supplied without being requested.

ARTICLE 10

Information for the Assessment of Customs Duties

1) On request, the Requested Customs Authority shall, without prejudice to Article 17 in order to support the proper application of Customs Legislation or in the prevention of Customs offences, provide information to assist the Requesting Customs Authority that has reasons to doubt the truth or accuracy of a declaration of goods.

2) The request shall specify the verification procedures that the Requesting Customs Authority has undertaken or attempted and the specific information requested.

ARTICLE 11
Intellectual Property Information Exchange

The Customs Authorities of the Parties may exchange information related to intellectual property and copyright offences. This information exchange shall have the objective to share data that will ease the detection of behaviors that attempt against the industrial property rights, intellectual property rights or copyrights, and transmit that information to the competent authorities in the territory of each of the Parties.

ARTICLE 12
Conduct of Assistance

1) Assistance shall be carried out in direct communication between officials designated by the Heads of the respective Customs Authorities.

2) If the Requested Customs Authority is not the competent authority to obtain the requested information, it shall identify and transmit the request to the competent authority and notify promptly this fact to the Requesting Customs Authority.

ARTICLE 13
Files, Documents and Other Materials

The Requested Customs Authority may provide copies of documentation necessary for the execution of requests; in particular the Requesting Customs Authority shall provide indications of background facts and the reasons for the requests. The Requested Customs Authority, when considered necessary, may provide export prices declared by enterprises of the requested party or copies of export declaration documents upon request.

CHAPTER IV
SPECIAL ASSISTANCE

ARTICLE 14
Surveillance of Goods and Means of Transport

1) On request, the Requested Customs Authority shall, to the extent of its ability and in consistency with its national laws and regulations maintain surveillance and provide the Requesting Customs Authority with information on:

a) Goods either in transport or in storage known to have been used or suspected of being used to commit a Customs offence in the territory of the Requesting Customs Authority;

b) Means of transport known to have been used or suspected of being used to commit a Customs offence in the territory of the Requesting Customs Authority, and

c) Premises in the territory of the Requested Customs Authority known to have been used or suspected of being used in connection with the commission of a Customs offence in the territory of the Requesting Customs Authority.

2) The Customs Authority of any Party may maintain such surveillance on its own initiative if it has reason to believe that planned, ongoing or completed activities appear to constitute a Customs offence in the territory of the other Party.

ARTICLE 15
Presence of Officials in the Territory of the Other Party

1) On request, officials specially designated by the Requesting Customs Authority may, with the authorization of the Requested Customs Authority and subject to conditions the latter may impose, according to its national legislation, and for the purpose of investigating a Customs offence, be present during an inquiry conducted by the Requested Customs Authority in its territory when is relevant to the Requesting Customs Authority. These officials shall only have an advisory role.

2) Regarding to the arrangements for visiting officials;

a) When officials of a Party should be present in the territory of the other Party, under the terms of this Agreement, they must furnish, in an acceptable language to both Parties, proof of their official identity and status in their Customs Authority and of their official status as granted in the territory of the Requested Customs Authority.

b) Officials shall, while in the territory of the other Party and under the terms of this Agreement, be responsible for any offence they may commit and shall enjoy, to the extent provided by that Party's national legislation, the same protection as accorded to its own officials.

CHAPTER V

USE, COFIDENTIALITY AND PROTECTION OF INFORMATION

ARTICLE 16

Use of Information

1) Information, documents and other materials obtained under this Agreement shall be used only by the Customs Authorities of the Parties and solely for the purpose of administrative assistance under the terms set out in this Agreement.

2) On request, the Party that supplied the information may, notwithstanding paragraph 1 of this Article, authorize its use for other purpose or by other authorities, subject to any terms and conditions, which may be specified. Such use shall be in accordance with the legal administrative provisions of the Party which seeks to use the information.

ARTICLE 17

Confidentiality and Protection of Information

1) Any information communicated under this Agreement shall be treated as confidential and shall, at least, be subject to the same protection and confidentiality granted to the same kind of information subject to the national, legal and administrative provisions of the Party where it is received.

2) The Customs Authorities shall inform each other of any change in their data protection laws occurring after the entry into force of this Agreement.

3) Any information received under this Agreement shall be used only by the Customs Authorities of the Parties under the terms set out in this Agreement.

4) Information obtained shall be used solely for the purposes of this Agreement. Where one of the Parties wishes to use such information for other purposes, it shall obtain the prior written consent of the Customs Authority which provided the information. Such use shall till then be subject to any restriction laid down by that Authority.

CHAPTER VI
EXEMPTIONS AND COSTS

ARTICLE 18
Exemptions from Assistance

1) In cases where the Requested Customs Authority is of the opinion that compliance with a request would infringe upon its sovereignty, security, public policy or other substantive national interest, or prejudice any legitimate commercial or professional interest or is contrary to its national legislation, assistance can be refused or compliance may be made subject to the satisfaction of certain conditions or requirements.

2) In cases where a request is made with which the Requesting Customs Authority itself would be unable to comply if requested by the other Customs Authority, the Requesting Customs Authority shall draw attention to this fact in its request. The compliance of such request shall be within the discretion of the Requested Customs Authority.

3) The Requested Customs Authority may postpone assistance on the ground that it will interfere with an ongoing investigation, prosecution or proceeding. In such instance the Requested Customs Authority shall consult with the Requesting Customs Authority to determine if assistance can be given subject to such terms and conditions as the Requested Customs Authority may require.

4) .Where assistance is declined or postponed, the Requesting Customs Authority shall be notified, without delay and as early as possible, the reasons for declining or postponing shall be given.

ARTICLE 19
Costs

1) The Customs Authorities shall waive all claims for reimbursement of costs incurred in the execution of this Agreement, with the exception of expenses for the experts as well as costs of translators and interpreters, other than Government employees.

2) If expenses of an exceptional and extraordinary nature are or will be required, in order to execute a request, the Customs Authorities shall consult each other to determine the terms and conditions under which the request will be executed as well as the manner in which the costs shall be borne.

CHAPTER VII
FINAL PROVISIONS

ARTICLE 20
Territorial Applicability

This Agreement shall be applicable in the territory of the United Mexican States and in the territory of the Republic of Turkey.

ARTICLE 21
Dispute Settlement

Any matter arising from the application or interpretation of this Agreement shall be resolved by common agreement between the Customs Authorities of the Parties. In case Customs Authorities fail to resolve disputes arising from the interpretation or implementation of this Agreement, such disputes shall be settled through diplomatic channels.

ARTICLE 22
Review

The Parties shall meet in order to review this Agreement, on request or at the end of five (5) years from the date of its entry into force; unless they notify each other in writing that such review is not necessary.

ARTICLE 23
Entry into Force, Amendment and Termination

1) This Agreement shall enter into force thirty (30) days after the date of receipt of the last written notification by which the Parties notify each other, through diplomatic channels, of the completion of their internal legal procedures required for the entry into force of this Agreement.

2) This Agreement may be amended as necessary by mutual consent between the Parties. Such amendments shall enter into force in accordance with the procedure provided for in paragraph 1.

3) This Agreement shall remain in force for successive periods of five (5) years and it shall be extended automatically for further periods of five (5) years unless one of the Parties gives written notification through diplomatic channels about its intention to terminate this Agreement. Termination shall take effect three (3) months from the date of the notification of termination to the other Party. The termination of this Agreement shall not affect any ongoing cooperative activities undertaken prior to the date of termination.

Signed in Ankara on the seventeenth day of December of two thousand and thirteen, in two originals, in the Spanish, Turkish and English languages, all text being equally authentic. In case of divergence of interpretation, the English text shall prevail.

FOR THE GOVERNMENT OF THE UNITED MEXICAN STATES	FOR THE GOVERNMENT OF THE REPUBLIC OF TURKEY
José Antonio Meade Kuribreña Minister of Foreign Affairs	Hayati Yazıcı Minister of Customs and Trade

[SPANISH TEXT – TEXTE ESPAGNOL]

ACUERDO ENTRE EL GOBIERNO DE LOS ESTADOS UNIDOS MEXICANOS Y EL GOBIERNO DE LA REPÚBLICA DE TURQUÍA SOBRE ASISTENCIA ADMINISTRATIVA MUTUA E INTERCAMBIO DE INFORMACIÓN SOBRE ASUNTOS ADUANEROS

El Gobierno de los Estados Unidos Mexicanos y el Gobierno de la República de Turquía, en lo sucesivo denominados como las "Partes";

CONSCIENTES que las infracciones en contra de la Legislación Aduanera son perjudiciales para los intereses económicos, fiscales, financieros, sociales, culturales y comerciales de sus respectivos países;

CONSIDERANDO la importancia de asegurar la determinación exacta de los aranceles, impuestos aduaneros, otros gravámenes y derechos, recaudados por la importación o exportación de mercancías, a través de la correcta determinación de su clasificación arancelaria, valor y origen, así como el adecuado cumplimiento de las disposiciones sobre prohibición, restricción y control;

RECONOCIENDO la importancia de la cooperación internacional en asuntos relativos a la aplicación y cumplimiento de su Legislación Aduanera;

CONVENCIDOS de que los esfuerzos para prevenir las infracciones en contra de la Legislación Aduanera y para asegurar la recaudación correcta de aranceles, impuestos, derechos y otros gravámenes por la importación y la exportación, puedan llevarse a cabo de manera más efectiva a través de la cooperación entre las Autoridades Aduaneras;

PREOCUPADOS por la escalada y las tendencias de crecimiento del tráfico ilícito de estupefacientes y sustancias psicotrópicas, que constituyen un peligro para la salud pública y para la sociedad;

TENIENDO EN CONSIDERACIÓN la Convención Única de 1961 sobre Estupefacientes, enmendada por su Protocolo de 1972 y el Convenio sobre Sustancias Sicotrópicas de 1971, elaborado bajo los auspicios de las Naciones Unidas, así como la Convención de las Naciones Unidas contra el Tráfico Ilícito de Estupefacientes y Sustancias Sicotrópicas de 1988;

TOMANDO EN CUENTA las obligaciones establecidas a través de las convenciones internacionales aceptadas o aplicadas por las Partes;

Han acordado lo siguiente:

CAPÍTULO I
DISPOSICIONES GENERALES

ARTÍCULO 1
Definiciones

Para los efectos de este Acuerdo:

1) "Autoridad Aduanera" significa para los Estados Unidos Mexicanos, la Secretaría de Hacienda y Crédito Público y para la República de Turquía, el Ministerio de Aduanas y Comercio;

2) "Impuestos aduaneros" significa los aranceles, impuestos, derechos y otros gravámenes que se recaudan en el territorio de las Partes en aplicación de la Legislación Aduanera, excluyendo los derechos y gravámenes por servicios prestados;

3) "Legislación Aduanera" significa las disposiciones legales y administrativas relacionadas con la importación, exportación, movimiento y almacenaje de mercancías, cuya administración y aplicación esté a cargo de las Autoridades Aduaneras, así como cualquier disposición emitida por dichas Autoridades de conformidad con sus atribuciones;

4) "Infracción Aduanera" significa cualquier violación o intento de violación a la Legislación Aduanera;

5) "Información" significa aquellos datos, estén o no procesados o analizados, documentos, informes, copias certificadas o autenticadas de los mismos u otras comunicaciones, incluyendo datos electrónicos;

6) "Cadena logística de comercio internacional" significa cualquier proceso en el que se encuentre involucrado el movimiento transfronterizo de mercancías del lugar de origen a su destino final;

7) "Funcionario" significa cualquier servidor público de la Autoridad Aduanera u otro empleado gubernamental designado por dicha Autoridad;

8) "Persona" significa cualquier persona física o moral;

9) "Datos personales" significa cualquier información concerniente a una persona física identificada o identificable;

10) "Autoridad Aduanera Requirente" significa la Autoridad Aduanera que realiza una solicitud de asistencia en asuntos aduaneros;

11) "Autoridad Aduanera Requerida" significa la Autoridad Aduanera que recibe la solicitud de asistencia en asuntos aduaneros, y

12) "Territorio" significa:

a) respecto de los Estados Unidos Mexicanos, el territorio de los Estados Unidos Mexicanos tal como se define en su Constitución Política, incluyendo cualquier área más allá de su mar territorial sobre la cual los Estados Unidos Mexicanos puede ejercer derechos soberanos de exploración y explotación de los recursos naturales del fondo marino, subsuelo y las aguas suprayacentes, y el espacio aéreo situado sobre dichas áreas, de conformidad con el derecho internacional, y

b) respecto de la República de Turquía, el territorio continental. el mar territorial y el espacio aéreo situado sobre éstos, así como las áreas marinas y submarinas sobre las que Turquía tiene derecho a ejercer su jurisdicción y soberanía, de conformidad con el derecho internacional.

ARTÍCULO 2

Alcance del Acuerdo

1) Las Partes se proporcionarán, a través de sus Autoridades Aduaneras, asistencia mutua de conformidad con las disposiciones de este Acuerdo, para la correcta aplicación de su Legislación Aduanera y para prevenir, investigar y combatir las Infracciones aduaneras, así como para proteger la seguridad de la cadena logística de comercio internacional.

2) La asistencia en el marco de este Acuerdo, deberá brindarse por las Partes, por iniciativa propia o previa solicitud, con la finalidad de determinar los Impuestos aduaneros y otros impuestos o gravámenes relacionados con la Legislación Aduanera, y con el propósito de aplicar controles que sean competencia de la Autoridad Aduanera.

3) Cualquier acción ejecutada en el marco de este Acuerdo por alguna de las Partes, deberá realizarse de conformidad con su legislación y disposiciones administrativas nacionales y dentro de los límites de competencia de la Autoridad Aduanera y los recursos económicos disponibles.

4) Ninguna disposición de este Acuerdo será interpretada de manera que pueda restringir un acuerdo sobre asistencia mutua y cooperación que se encuentre en vigor entre las Partes.

5) Las disposiciones de este Acuerdo no crearán un derecho a favor de persona alguna para obtener, suprimir o excluir cualquier prueba o impedir la ejecución de una solicitud de asistencia.

6) La asistencia brindada en el marco de este Acuerdo no incluye la solicitud para arrestar a una persona o el cobro de Impuestos aduaneros, gravámenes, multas o cualquier otra cantidad determinada por la Autoridad Aduanera de una de las Partes.

CAPÍTULO II
PROCEDIMIENTOS GENERALES DE ASISTENCIA

ARTÍCULO 3
Forma y Contenido de las Solicitudes de Asistencia

1) Las solicitudes de asistencia formuladas en el marco de este Acuerdo, deberán ser comunicadas directamente entre las Autoridades Aduaneras involucradas. Cada Autoridad Aduanera designará un punto de contacto oficial para este propósito y comunicará esta información y cualquier actualización a la otra Autoridad Aduanera.

2) Las solicitudes de asistencia conforme a este Acuerdo deberán formularse por escrito o electrónicamente y deberán acompañarse de cualquier información o documentos considerados útiles para su ejecución. La Autoridad Aduanera Requerida podrá solicitar confirmación por escrito de las solicitudes electrónicas. Cuando las circunstancias así lo requieran, las solicitudes se podrán formular verbalmente, pero deberán ser confirmadas por escrito de la manera más expedita posible, sin exceder un plazo de diez (10) días a partir de la fecha en que se haya realizado la solicitud verbal.

3) La solicitud deberá formularse en idioma inglés. Cualesquier documentos que la acompañen se traducirán, de ser necesario, al idioma inglés.

4) La solicitud a que se refiere el párrafo 2 de este Artículo deberá incluir la información siguiente:

a) el nombre de la Autoridad Aduanera Requirente;

b) la medida solicitada;

c) el objeto y motivo de la solicitud;

d) una breve descripción del caso sometido a consideración y las disposiciones legales y administrativas aplicables, y

e) los nombres y direcciones de las personas relacionadas con la solicitud, si se conocen.

5) Si la solicitud no cumple con los requerimientos de forma, podrá solicitarse su corrección o complementación. La imposición de medidas preventivas no se verá afectada.

6) Cuando la Autoridad Aduanera Requirente solicite seguir un procedimiento en particular, la Autoridad Aduanera Requerida deberá cumplir con dicha solicitud, de conformidad con su legislación vigente.

ARTÍCULO 4
Asistencia Espontánea

La Autoridad Aduanera de cualquiera de las Partes deberá, en la medida de lo posible, proporcionar asistencia por iniciativa propia y sin demora, en aquellos casos que pudieran representar daños considerables a la economía, la salud pública, la seguridad pública, incluyendo la seguridad de la cadena logística de comercio internacional u otros intereses esenciales de cualquiera de las Partes.

CAPÍTULO III
INFORMACIÓN

ARTÍCULO 5
Comunicación de la Información

1) Las Autoridades Aduaneras deberán proporcionarse, por iniciativa propia o previa solicitud, toda la información que ayude a asegurar la correcta aplicación en:.

a) la recaudación de impuestos aduaneros por parte de las Autoridades Aduaneras y, en particular, la información que pueda ayudar a determinar el valor de las mercancías para propósitos aduaneros y establecer su clasificación arancelaria;

b) la implementación de medidas de prohibición, restricción y otros controles, preferencias o exenciones relacionados con la importación, exportación, tránsito de mercancías y otros regímenes aduaneros, y

c) la verificación del país de origen de las mercancías

2) Si la Autoridad Aduanera Requerida no cuenta con la información solicitada deberá notificarlo a la Autoridad Aduanera Requirente, lo antes posible.

3) La Autoridad Aduanera Requerida deberá obtener la información como si estuviera actuando por cuenta propia.

ARTÍCULO 6
Información Especial

1) Las Autoridades Aduaneras, previa solicitud, deberán informarse:

a) si los bienes importados al territorio de la Parte requirente han sido legalmente exportados desde el territorio de la otra Parte, y

b) si los bienes exportados desde el territorio de la Parte requirente han sido legalmente importados al territorio de la otra Parte.

2) La información deberá incluir el procedimiento aduanero utilizado para el despacho de las mercancías.

ARTÍCULO 7
Información para la Aplicación y Cumplimiento de la Legislación Aduanera

Las Autoridades Aduaneras deberán proporcionarse, por iniciativa propia o previa solicitud, información que ayude a asegurar la correcta aplicación de la Legislación Aduanera y la prevención, investigación y combate de las Infracciones aduaneras, así como para garantizar la seguridad de la cadena logística de comercio internacional. Dicha información podrá incluir:

a) nuevas técnicas de aplicación de controles aduaneros que hayan probado su efectividad;

b) nuevas tendencias, medios o métodos utilizados para cometer Infracciones aduaneras, así como aquellas que intenten ocultar el origen o el valor correcto de las mercancías;

c) mercancías susceptibles de ser objeto de Infracciones aduaneras, así como métodos de transporte y almacenamiento utilizados en relación con dichas mercancías;

d) información de las personas que hayan cometido una Infracción aduanera o sean sospechosas de cometerla, siempre que la legislación de las Partes relacionada con la protección de la información personal, permita el intercambio de esa información, incluso en vía de excepción;

e) cualquier otra información que pueda ser útil a las Autoridades Aduaneras para la correcta aplicación de la Legislación Aduanera, y

f) cualquier otra información que pueda ayudar a las Autoridades Aduaneras en el análisis de riesgo para propósitos de control y facilitación.

ARTÍCULO 8

Intercambio de Información Aduanera

1) La información que haya sido procesada a través del análisis de riesgo y que pudiera resultar en algún tipo de alerta deberá ser enviada y compartida entre las Partes, de una manera expedita, a fin de que se adopten las medidas necesarias.

2) Las Partes intercambiarán la información relativa al embargo de bienes y dinero, incluidos los métodos de detección y procedimientos de ocultamiento.

ARTÍCULO 9

Información Relacionada con Infracciones Aduaneras

Las Autoridades Aduaneras de las Partes se proporcionarán, por iniciativa propia o previa solicitud, información sobre actividades planeadas, en curso o consumadas que otorguen bases suficientes para creer que una Infracción aduanera ha sido o será cometida en el territorio de la otra Parte. En casos graves, que puedan suponer un perjuicio sustancial a la economía, la salud pública, la seguridad pública o cualquier otro interés esencial de la otra Parte, dicha información se proporcionará sin mediar solicitud.

ARTÍCULO 10

Información para la Determinación de Impuestos Aduaneros

1) La Autoridad Aduanera Requerida proporcionará, previa solicitud y sin perjuicio de lo establecido en el Artículo 17, información para asistir a la Autoridad Aduanera Requirente que tenga razones para dudar de la veracidad o la certeza de una declaración de mercancías, con la finalidad de apoyar la correcta aplicación de la Legislación Aduanera o la prevención de Infracciones aduaneras.

2) La solicitud deberá especificar los procedimientos de verificación que la Autoridad Aduanera Requirente aplicó o intentó aplicar, así como la información específica solicitada.

ARTÍCULO 11
Intercambio de Información de Propiedad Intelectual

Las Autoridades Aduaneras de las Partes podrán intercambiar información relacionada con la propiedad intelectual y los delitos de derecho de autor. Este intercambio de información tendrá el objetivo de compartir los datos que faciliten la detección de conductas que atentan contra los derechos de propiedad industrial, derechos de propiedad intelectual o derechos de autor, y transmitir esa información a las autoridades competentes en el territorio de cada una de las Partes.

ARTÍCULO 12
Conducto de la Asistencia

1) La asistencia deberá llevarse a cabo mediante la comunicación directa entre los funcionarios designados por los titulares de las respectivas Autoridades Aduaneras.

2) En caso que la Autoridad Aduanera Requerida no sea la autoridad competente para obtener la información solicitada, deberá identificar y transmitir la solicitud a la autoridad competente y notificar este hecho a la Autoridad Aduanera Requirente, lo antes posible.

ARTÍCULO 13
Expedientes, Documentos y Otros Materiales

La Autoridad Aduanera Requerida podrá proporcionar copias de la documentación necesaria para la ejecución de las solicitudes; en particular, la Autoridad Aduanera Requirente proporcionará los antecedentes y las razones de la solicitud. La Autoridad Aduanera Requerida podrá proporcionar, cuando estime necesario y previa solicitud, los precios de exportación declarados por las empresas de la parte requerida o copias de los documentos de declaración de exportación.

CAPÍTULO IV
ASISTENCIA ESPECIAL

ARTÍCULO 14
Vigilancia de Mercancías y Medios de Transporte

1) La Autoridad Aduanera Requerida deberá, previa solicitud, en la medida de sus posibilidades y de conformidad con sus leyes y reglamentos nacionales, mantener la vigilancia y proporcionar a la Autoridad Aduanera Requirente información sobre:

a) mercancías en transporte o en almacenamiento que han sido utilizadas o se sospeche que han sido utilizadas, para cometer Infracciones aduaneras en el territorio de la Autoridad Aduanera Requirente;

b) medios de transporte que han sido utilizados o se sospeche que han sido utilizados para cometer una Infracción aduanera en el territorio de la Autoridad Aduanera Requirente, y

c) instalaciones en el territorio de la Autoridad Aduanera Requerida identificadas por haber sido utilizadas o se sospeche que fueron utilizadas para cometer una Infracción aduanera en el territorio de la Autoridad Aduanera Requirente.

2) La Autoridad Aduanera de cualquiera de las Partes podrá mantener dicha vigilancia por cuenta propia, si tiene razones para creer que las actividades planeadas, en curso o consumadas pueden constituir una Infracción aduanera en el territorio de la otra Parte.

ARTÍCULO 15
Presencia de Funcionarios en el Territorio de la Otra Parte

1) Con el propósito de investigar una Infracción aduanera, funcionarios especialmente designados por la Autoridad Aduanera Requirente podrán, previa solicitud, con autorización de la Autoridad Aduanera Requerida y sujeto a las condiciones que esta última pueda imponer de conformidad con su legislación nacional, estar presentes durante la investigación llevada a cabo por la Autoridad Aduanera Requerida en su territorio, cuando sea relevante para la Autoridad Aduanera Requirente. Estos funcionarios tendrán únicamente una función consultiva.

2) En relación con los arreglos para la visita de funcionarios:

a) Cuando los funcionarios de una Parte debieran estar presentes en el territorio de la otra Parte, de conformidad con los términos de este Acuerdo, deberán estar en aptitud de acreditar en un idioma aceptable para ambas Partes, su identificación oficial y función en sus Autoridades Aduaneras, así como su rango oficial otorgado en el territorio de la Autoridad Aduanera Requerida.

b) Los funcionarios, mientras se encuentren en el territorio de la otra Parte y de conformidad con los términos de este Acuerdo, serán responsables de cualquier infracción que puedan cometer y gozarán, de conformidad con la legislación nacional de esa Parte, de la misma protección otorgada a sus funcionarios.

CAPÍTULO V
USO, CONFIDENCIALIDAD Y PROTECCIÓN DE LA INFORMACIÓN

ARTÍCULO 16
Uso de la Información

1) La información, documentos y otros materiales obtenidos en el marco de este Acuerdo, deberán ser utilizados exclusivamente por las Autoridades Aduaneras de las Partes, únicamente para el propósito de asistencia administrativa, según los términos establecidos en este Acuerdo.

2) En la solicitud, la Parte que proporcionó la información puede, no obstante lo dispuesto en el párrafo 1 del presente Artículo, autorizar su uso para otros fines o por otras autoridades, con sujeción a los términos y condiciones que puedan ser especificados. Dicha utilización se realizará de conformidad con las disposiciones legales y administrativas de la Parte que pretende utilizar la información.

ARTÍCULO 17
Confidencialidad y Protección de la Información

1) Cualquier información comunicada en el marco de este Acuerdo deberá ser tratada con carácter confidencial y gozará, por lo menos, de la misma protección y confidencialidad que se otorgue a dicha información, de conformidad con las disposiciones legales y administrativas nacionales de la Parte que la recibe.

2) Las Autoridades Aduaneras deberán informarse sobre cualquier modificación a sus leyes en materia de protección de datos que se realice con posterioridad a la entrada en vigor de este Acuerdo.

3) Cualquier información recibida de conformidad con este Acuerdo, deberá ser utilizada únicamente por las Autoridades Aduaneras de las Partes, de conformidad con los términos establecidos en este Acuerdo.

4) La información obtenida se utilizará únicamente para los efectos de este Acuerdo. Cuando una de las Partes desee utilizar dicha información para otros fines, deberá obtener el consentimiento previo por escrito de la Autoridad Aduanera que la haya provisto. Dicha utilización hasta ese momento estará sujeta a las restricciones de esa Autoridad.

CAPÍTULO VI
EXCEPCIONES Y COSTOS

ARTÍCULO 18
Excepciones al Suministro de Asistencia

1) En los casos en que la Autoridad Aduanera Requerida considere que el cumplimiento de alguna solicitud pudiera afectar su soberanía, seguridad, políticas públicas u otro interés nacional substantivo, o perjudicar cualquier interés comercial o profesional legítimo, o entre en conflicto con su legislación nacional, la asistencia podrá negarse o sujetarse al cumplimiento de ciertas condiciones o requisitos.

2) En los casos en que la Autoridad Aduanera Requirente formule una solicitud que ella misma no podría cumplir, de haberla formulado la otra Autoridad Aduanera, deberá indicar tal circunstancia en su solicitud. El cumplimiento de dicha solicitud estará sujeto a la discrecionalidad de la Autoridad Aduanera Requerida.

3) La Autoridad Aduanera Requerida podrá diferir la asistencia en caso de que ésta pudiera interferir con alguna investigación, juicio o procedimiento en curso. En tal caso, la Autoridad Aduanera Requerida consultará con la Autoridad Aduanera Requirente para determinar si la asistencia puede ser proporcionada, de conformidad con los términos y condiciones que la Autoridad Aduanera Requerida pueda establecer.

4) Cuando la asistencia sea negada o diferida, la Autoridad Aduanera Requirente deberá ser notificada sin demora y tan pronto como sea posible, dando a conocer las razones por las cuales se negó o difirió dicha asistencia.

ARTÍCULO 19
Costos

1) Las Autoridades Aduaneras renunciarán a cualquier reclamo de reembolso de los costos incurridos en la ejecución de este Acuerdo, excepto por los gastos pagados a expertos, así como los honorarios de los traductores e intérpretes, que no sean empleados gubernamentales.

2) Si se requiere o pudiera requerirse el pago de gastos de naturaleza excepcional y extraordinarios para la ejecución de una solicitud, las Autoridades Aduaneras deberán consultarse para determinar los términos y condiciones conforme a los cuales dicha solicitud será ejecutada, así como la forma en que los costos deberán ser solventados.

CAPÍTULO VII
DISPOSICIONES FINALES

ARTÍCULO 20
Aplicabilidad Territorial

Este Acuerdo será aplicable en el territorio de los Estados Unidos Mexicanos y en el territorio de la República de Turquía.

ARTICULO 21
Solución de Controversias

Cualquier asunto derivado de la aplicación o interpretación de este Acuerdo deberá ser resuelto por convenio mutuo entre las Autoridades Aduaneras de las Partes. En caso que las Autoridades Aduaneras no pueden resolver las controversias derivadas de la interpretación o aplicación de este Acuerdo, tales controversias se resolverán por la vía diplomática.

ARTÍCULO 22
Revisión

Las Partes se reunirán con el propósito de revisar este Acuerdo, a petición o al término de cinco (5) años a partir de la fecha de su entrada en vigor, a menos que se comuniquen por escrito, que dicha revisión no es necesaria.

ARTÍCULO 23
Entrada en Vigor, Modificación y Terminación

1) Este Acuerdo entrará en vigor treinta (30) días después de la fecha de recepción de la última notificación escrita entre las Partes, en la que se comuniquen por la vía diplomática, el cumplimiento de sus procedimientos legislativos internos necesarios para la entrada en vigor de este Acuerdo.

2) Este Acuerdo podrá ser modificado conforme sea necesario, por consentimiento mutuo entre las Partes. Las enmiendas entrarán en vigor de conformidad con el procedimiento previsto en el párrafo 1.

3) Este Acuerdo permanecerá vigente por periodos sucesivos de cinco (5) años y se prorrogará automáticamente por períodos de cinco (5) años, salvo que una de las Partes notifique por escrito, a través de la vía diplomática, su intención de dar por terminado este Acuerdo. La terminación de este Acuerdo surtirá efectos tres (3) meses después de la fecha de la notificación de terminación de la otra Parte. La terminación de este Acuerdo no afectará las actividades de cooperación acordadas antes de la fecha de su terminación.

Firmado en Ankara el diecisiete de diciembre de dos mil trece, en dos ejemplares originales, en los idiomas español, turco e inglés, siendo todos los textos igualmente auténticos. En caso de diferencias derivadas de la interpretación, el texto en inglés prevalecerá.

POR EL GOBIERNO DE LOS ESTADOS UNIDOS MEXICANOS	POR EL GOBIERNO DE LA REPÚBLICA DE TURQUÍA
José Antonio Meade Kuribreña Secretario de Relaciones Exteriores	Hayati Yazici Ministro de Aduanas y Comercio

[TURKISH TEXT – TEXTE TURC]

BİRLEŞİK MEKSİKA DEVLETLERİ HÜKÜMETİYLE TÜRKİYE CUMHURİYETİ HÜKÜMETİ ARASINDA GÜMRÜK KONULARINDA KARŞILIKLI İDARİ YARDIM VE BİLGİ PAYLAŞIMI ANLAŞMASI

Bundan sonra "Taraflar" olarak anılacak olan Birleşik Meksika Devletleri Hükümetiyle, Türkiye Cumhuriyeti Hükümeti

Gümrük mevzuatına karşı işlenen suçların, Tarafların ülkelerinin ekonomik, vergiyle ilgili, mali, sosyal, kültürel ve ticari çıkarlarına zarar verdiğini **DİKKATE ALARAK;**

Eşyanın tarife sınıflandırmasının, kıymet ve menşeinin doğru olarak tespit edilmesiyle birlikte, eşyanın ithalatında ya da ihracatında toplanan Gümrük vergilerinin doğru bir şekilde tahakkuk etmesinin ve yasaklama, kısıtlama ve kontrol hükümlerinin muntazaman uygulanmasının taşıdığı önemin **BİLİNCİNDE OLARAK;**

Tarafların Gümrük Mevzuatlarının uygulanmasıyla ilgili konularda uluslararası işbirliğinin önemini **KABUL EDEREK;**

Gümrük Mevzuatına karşı işlenen suçların önlenmesine ve ithalat ve ihracat vergi, resim, ücret ve diğer harçların doğru bir şekilde tahsilinin sağlanmasına yönelik çabaların, Gümrük İdarelerinin işbirliği ile daha etkin hale getirileceğine **İKNA OLARAK;**

Kamu sağlığı ve toplum için tehlike teşkil eden uyuşturucu ve psikotrop maddelerin yasadışı trafiğinin mevcut çapından ve artma eğiliminden **ENDİŞE DUYARAK;**

1972 yılına ait Protokol'le üzerinde değişiklik yapılan 1961 Uyuşturucu Maddeler Tek Sözleşmesi'ne ve Birleşmiş Milletler'in himayesinde oluşturulan 1971 Psikotrop Maddeler Sözleşmesiyle 1988 Birleşmiş Milletler Uyuşturucu ve Psikotrop Maddelerin Yasadışı Trafiğiyle Mücadele Sözleşmesi'ni **GÖZ ÖNÜNDE BULUNDURARAK;**

Tarafların hali hazırda kabul ettiği ya da uyguladığı uluslararası sözleşmeler çerçevesinde getirilen yükümlülüklere **ATIFTA BULUNARAK**;

Aşağıdaki hususlarda mutabakata varmışlardır:

BÖLÜM I
GENEL HÜKÜMLER

MADDE 1
TANIMLAR

Bu Anlaşmada geçen:

1) "Gümrük İdaresi" deyimi, Birleşik Meksika Devletleri'nde, Maliye ve Kamu Kredileri Bakanlığı; Türkiye Cumhuriyeti'nde ise Gümrük ve Ticaret Bakanlığı;

2) "Gümrük vergileri" deyimi, Tarafların topraklarında, Gümrük Mevzuatı'nın uygulanması dâhilinde tarh edilen; ancak verilen hizmetler karşılığında alınan ücret ve harçların dâhil olmadığı, tüm vergi, resim, ücret ya da harçlar;

3) "Gümrük Mevzuatı" deyimi, idaresi ve uygulanması, özellikle Gümrük İdarelerine verilen, eşyanın ithalatı, ihracatı, dolaşımı ya da depolanmasıyla ilgili kanuni ve düzenleyici hükümler; ve Gümrük İdarelerinin, kendi kanuni yetkileri çerçevesinde yaptıkları düzenlemeler;

4) "Gümrük suçu" deyimi, Gümrük Mevzuatı'nın ihlali ya da ihlaline yönelik teşebbüs;

5) "Bilgi" deyimi, işlemden geçirilmiş ya da tahlil edilmiş olsun ya da olmasın her tür veri, belge, rapor, bunların onaylı ya da tasdikli örnekleri ya da elektronik veri de dâhil olmak üzere diğer iletiler;

6) "Uluslararası ticaret arz zinciri" deyimi, eşyanın, menşe yerinden nihai varış yerine sınır aşan hareketinin söz konusu olduğu her tür süreç;

7) "Görevli" deyimi, bir Gümrük İdaresi'nin tayin ettiği Gümrük memuru ya da diğer Hükümet görevlisi;

8) "Kişi" deyimi, gerçek ya da tüzel kişi;

9) "Kişisel veri" deyimi, teşhis edilen ya da teşhis edilebilir özel kişiyle ilgili bilgiler;

10) "Talepte Bulunan Gümrük İdaresi" deyimi, Gümrük konularında yardım talep eden Gümrük İdaresi;

11) "Talepte Bulunulan Gümrük İdaresi" deyimi, Gümrük konularında yapılan yardım talebini alan Gümrük İdaresi;

12) "Toprak" deyimi:

a) Birleşik Meksika Devletleri'nde, Uluslararası Hukuka göre Birleşik Meksika Devletlerinin denizin derinliklerindeki, toprak altındaki ve birbiriyle çakışan sulardaki ve bu alanlar üzerindeki hava sahasındaki doğal kaynakları araştırma ve kullanma üzerindeki egemenlik hakkından yararlandığı kara suları ötesindeki alanlar da dâhil olmak üzere, Birleşik Meksika Devletleri'nin Siyasi Anayasası'nda tanımlanan Birleşik Meksika Devletleri toprağı; ve

b) Türkiye Cumhuriyeti'nde, kara, kara suları ve bunların yukarısında bulunan hava sahası ile Türkiye'nin, uluslararası hukuk, egemenlik, yargı yetkisine uygun şekilde kullanım hakkı olan deniz ve deniz altı alanlar anlamına gelir.

MADDE 2

ANLAŞMANIN KAPSAMI

1) Taraflar, Gümrük Mevzuatının muntazaman uygulanması ve Gümrük suçlarının önlenmesi, soruşturulması ve bastırılması için ve uluslararası ticaret arz güvenliğini korumak amacıyla, Gümrük İdareleri vasıtasıyla, bu Anlaşma'da belirtilen koşullar gereği, birbirlerine karşılıklı yardım sağlarlar.

2) Bu Anlaşma'da öngörülen yardımın kapsamı, Taraflardan birinin kendi inisiyatifiyle ya da talep üzerine, Gümrük Mevzuatıyla ilgili olarak Gümrük vergi ve diğer resim veya harçlarının tahakkukuna ve Gümrük İdaresi dâhilinde kontrollerin yürütülmesine ilişkin tüm bilgileri içerecek şekilde genişletilir.

3) Taraftardan birinin, işbu Anlaşma kapsamında yürüttüğü faaliyetler, söz konusu Tarafın ulusal yasal ve idari hükümlerine uygun olarak ve bu Tarafın Gümrük İdaresi'nin yetkileri ve mevcut ekonomik kaynakları dâhilinde gerçekleştirilecektir.

4) Bu Anlaşma'da geçen hiçbir hüküm, Taraflar arasında hali hazırda yürürlükte olan karşılıklı yardım ve işbirliğiyle ilgili bir mutabakatı kısıtlayacak şekilde yorumlanmaz.

5) Bu Anlaşma'nın hükümleri, özel kişilere, delil elde etme, delili gizleme ya da dikkate almayarak kapsam dışı tutma hakkını; ya da bir yardım talebinin uygulanmasını engelleme hakkını vermez.

6) Bu Anlaşma'da öngörülen yardım, kişilerin tutuklanmasının ya da Gümrük vergilerinin, harçlarının, cezalarının ya da Taraflardan birinin Gümrük İdaresi'nin belirlediği diğer meblağların tahsilinin talep edilmesini içermez.

BÖLÜM II
GENEL YARDIM PROSEDÜRLERİ

MADDE 3
YARDIM TALEPLERİNİN ŞEKLİ VE ÖZÜ

1) Bu Anlaşma kapsamında yapılan yardım talepleri, doğrudan ilgili Gümrük İdareleri arasında iletilir. Her Gümrük İdaresi, bu amaçla resmi bir irtibat kişisi tayin eder ve bu bilgiyi ve bu bilgiye ilişkin güncellemeleri, diğer Gümrük İdaresi'ne iletir.

2) Bu Anlaşma kapsamında yapılan yardım talepleri, yazılı olarak ya da elektronik ortamda yapılır ve yardım taleplerinin gereğinin yapılması için yararlı olduğu düşünülen bilgi ya da belgeler, yardım taleplerine eklenir. Talepte Bulunulan Gümrük İdaresi, elektronik yoldan gönderilen taleplerin yazılı teyidini isteyebilecektir. Durumun acil olması sebebiyle gerekli görülmesi halinde, talepler sözlü olarak da yapılabilir; ancak sözlü taleplerin, yapıldıkları tarihten itibaren en geç on (10) gün içerisinde ivedilikle yazıyla teyit edilmesi gerekir.

3) Talep, İngilizce yapılır. Taleplerle birlikte verilen belgeler, gerekli olduğu ölçüde, İngilizce'ye tercüme edilir.

4) Bu Madde'nin 2. fıkrası çerçevesinde yapılan taleplerde aşağıdaki bilgiler yer alır:

a) Talepte Bulunan Gümrük İdaresi'nin adı;

b) Talep edilen yardım türü;

c) Talebin konusu ve gerekçeleri;

d) İncelenmekte olan konunun kısa bir tanımı ve ilgili hukuki ve idari hükümler; ve

e) Bilinmesi halinde, talebin ilgili olduğu kişilerin isim ve adresleri.

5) Bir talebin, talep formatı koşullarını karşılamaması halinde; talebin düzeltilmesi ya da talepteki eksikliklerin tamamlanması istenebilir. İhtiyati tedbirlerin düzenlenişi, bu durumdan etkilenmez.

6) Talepte Bulunan Gümrük İdaresi'nin belli bir prosedürün takip edilmesini talep ettiği durumlarda, Talepte Bulunulan Gümrük İdaresi, yürürlükte olan mevzuatı çerçevesinde bu talebin gereğini yapar.

MADDE 4
KENDİLİĞİNDEN YARDIM

Uluslararası ticaret arz zincirinin güvenliği de dâhil olmak üzere Tarafların ekonomisinin, kamu sağlığının, kamu güvenliğinin ya da diğer hayati çıkarlarının ciddi zarar görebileceği hallerde, Taraflardan birinin Gümrük İdaresi, mümkün olması halinde, herhangi bir gecikme olmaksızın, kendi inisiyatifiyle yardım sağlar.

BÖLÜM III
BİLGİLER

MADDE 5
BİLGİLERİN İLETİLMESİ

1) Gümrük İdareleri, talep üzerine ya da kendi inisiyatifleriyle,

a) Gümrük İdarelerinin tarh ettiği Gümrük vergilerinin toplanması ve özellikle de Gümrük amaçlı eşyanın kıymetini takdir etmeye ve eşyanın tarife sınıflandırmasını belirlemeye yardımcı olacak bilgiler;

b) Eşyanın ithalatı, ihracatı, transit edilmesi ve diğer gümrük rejimleriyle ilgili yasaklama, kısıtlama ve diğer kontrol, tercih ya da muafiyet tedbirlerinin uygulanması; ve

c) Eşyanın menşe ülkesinin teyidi

hususlarının doğruluğunun sağlanmasına yardımcı olacak tüm bilgileri birbirlerine sağlarlar.

2) Talepte Bulunulan Gümrük İdaresi'nin, talep edilen bilgiye sahip olmaması halinde, bu durum, Talepte Bulunan Taraf'a derhal iletilir.

3) Talepte Bulunulan Gümrük İdaresi, söz konusu bilgileri, kendi hesabına hareket ediyormuş gibi araştırır.

MADDE 6

ÖZEL BİLGİ TÜRLERİ

1) Gümrük İdareleri, talep üzerine;

a) Talepte Bulunan Tarafın topraklarına ithal edilen eşyanın, diğer Tarafın topraklarından yasalara uygun bir şekilde ihraç edilip edilmediği; ve

b) Talepte Bulunan Tarafın topraklarından ihraç edilen eşyanın, diğer Tarafın topraklarına yasalara uygun şekilde ithal edilip edilmediği hususlarında birbirlerini bilgilendirirler.

2) Bu bilgilerde, eşyanın Gümrük işlemlerine tabi tutulmasında kullanılan Gümrük prosedürü de yer alır.

MADDE 7

GÜMRÜK MEVZUATININ UYGULANMASI VE YÜRÜTÜLMESİNE İLİŞKİN BİLGİLER

Gümrük İdareleri, Gümrük Mevzuatı'nın muntazaman uygulanmasını ve Gümrük suçlarının önlenmesini, soruşturulmasını ve bu suçlarla mücadele edilmesini ve uluslararası ticaret arz zincirinin güvenliğini sağlamada yardımcı olan bilgileri, talep üzerine ya da kendiliğinden birbirlerine temin ederler. Bu bilgiler, aşağıdaki hususları kapsar:

a) etkinlikleri kanıtlanmış olan yeni Gümrük muhafaza teknikleri;

b) gümrük suçu işlemede ve eşyanın menşeini ya da doğru kıymetini gizlemeye yönelik teşebbüslerde başvurulan yeni eğilimler, yol ya da yöntemler;

c) gümrük suçlarına konu olduğu bilinen eşya ile bu eşyayla ilgili olarak kullanılan nakliye ve depolama yöntemleri;

d) tarafların kişisel bilgilerinin korunmasına ilişkin mevzuatları tarafından istisnai yöntemlerle bile bilgi paylaşımına izin verildiği sürece, Gümrük suçu işlediği bilinen ya da Gümrük suçu işlemek üzere olduğundan şüphelenilen kişiler;

e) gümrük İdarelerine, Gümrük Mevzuatlarının muntazaman uygulanmasında yardımcı olabilecek diğer bilgiler; ve

f) kontrol ve kolaylaştırma amacıyla, risk analizi hususunda Gümrük İdarelerine yardımcı olabilecek diğer bilgiler.

MADDE 8
GÜMRÜK BİLGİLERİNİN PAYLAŞIMI

1) Risk analizi yoluyla hali hazırda işleme tabi tutulmuş olan ve dikkatli olmayı gerektirecek nitelikteki bilgiler, önleyici tedbirlerin alınmasını sağlamak amacıyla ivedilikle Taraflar arasında gönderilir ve paylaşılır.

2) Taraflar, tespit yöntemleri ve saklama usulleri de dâhil olmak üzere, eşya ve paraya el konulmasıyla ilgili bilgileri birbiriyle paylaşırlar.

MADDE 9
GÜMRÜK SUÇLARINA İLİŞKİN BİLGİLER

Tarafların Gümrük İdareleri, talep üzerine ya da kendi inisiyatifleriyle, ilgili Tarafın topraklarında bir Gümrük suçunun işlendiğine ya da işleneceğine inanmak için makul gerekçeler sunan, planlanan, devam eden ya da tamamlanmış faaliyetlerle ilgili olarak, birbirlerine bilgi sağlarlar. Diğer Tarafın ekonomisine, kamu sağlığına, kamu güvenliğine ya da diğer hayati çıkarlarına önemli ölçüde zarar verebilecek ciddi durumlarda, bu bilgiler, talep edilmeden sağlanır.

MADDE 10

GÜMRÜK VERGİLERİNİN TAHAKKUKUNA İLİŞKİN BİLGİLER

1) Talep üzerine, Talepte Bulunulan Gümrük İdaresi, 17nci Madde hükümleri saklı kalmak üzere, Gümrük mevzuatının muntazaman uygulanmasını desteklemek ya da Gümrük suçlarının önlenmesi amacıyla eşya beyannamesinin gerçekliğinden ya da doğruluğundan şüphelenmek iain gerekçeleri olan Talepte Bulunan İdareye bilgi temin eder.

2) Talepte Bulunan İdarenin üstlendiği ya da üstlenme girişiminde bulunduğu doğrulama işlemleri ile talep edilen özel bilgiler, Talepte belirtilmelidir.

MADDE 11

FİKRİ MÜLKİYETLE İLGİLİ BİLGİLERİN PAYLAŞIMI

Tarafların Gümrük İdareleri, fikri mülkiyet ve telif hakkı suçlarıyla ilgili bilgileri birbiriyle paylaşabilir. Bu bilgi paylaşımının amacı, sınai mülkiyet haklarına, fikri mülkiyet haklarına ya da telif haklarına aykırı davranışların tespit edilmesini kolaylaştıracak verilerin paylaşılması ve bu bilgilerin, Tarafların her birinin topraklarındaki yetkili makamlarına iletilmesidir.

MADDE 12

YARDIMIN YÜRÜTÜLMESİ

1) Yardım, Tarafların Gümrük İdarelerinin Başkanlarının tayin ettiği görevliler arasında doğrudan iletişim yoluyla yürütülür.

2) Talepte Bulunulan İdarenin, talep edilen bilgileri elde etmek için yetkili merci olmaması halinde, Talepte Bulunulan İdare, bu talebi, yetkili merciye iletir ve bu hususu Talepte Bulunan Gümrük İdaresi'ne derhal bildirir.

MADDE 13
DOSYALAR, BELGELER VE DİĞER MATERYALLER

Talepte Bulunulan Gümrük İdaresi, taleplerin yerine getirilmesi için gerekli olan belgelerin örneklerini sağlayabilir; Talepte Bulunan Gümrük idaresi, özellikle, konunun arka planına ilişkin bulguları ve taleplerin gerekçelerini temin eder. Talepte Bulunulan Gümrük idaresi, gerekli gördüğü hallerde, talepte bulunulan tarafın işletmelerinin beyan ettiği ihracat fiyatlarını ya da ihracat beyannamesinin örneklerini, talep üzerine, sağlayabilir.

BÖLÜM IV
ÖZEL YARDIM

MADDE 14
EŞYANIN VE TAŞIMA ARAÇLARININ GÖZETİMİ

1) Talep durumunda, Talepte Bulunulan Gümrük İdaresi, imkânları ölçüsünde ve ulusal kanun ve yönetmelikleriyle uyumlu olacak şekilde, aşağıdaki hususlar üzerinde gözetim sağlar ve bu hususlarla ilgili bilgileri Talepte Bulunan Gümrük İdaresine temin eder:

a) Talepte Bulunan Gümrük İdaresi'nin topraklarında bir Gümrük suçunun işlenmesinde kullanıldığı bilinen veya kullanıldığından şüphe edilen nakliye halindeki ya da depodaki eşya;

b) Talepte Bulunan Gümrük İdaresi'nin topraklarında bir Gümrük suçunun işlenmesinde kullanıldığı bilinen veya kullanıldığından şüphe edilen taşıma araçları; ve

c) Talepte Bulunan Gümrük İdaresi'nin topraklarında bir Gümrük suçunun işlenmesiyle bağlantılı olarak kullanıldığı bilinen veya kullanıldığından şüphe edilen, Talepte Bulunulan Tarafın topraklarında yer alan binalar.

2) Tarafların herhangi birinin Gümrük İdaresi, planlanmış, devam etmekte olan veya tamamlanmış faaliyetlerin diğer Tarafın topraklarında Gümrük suçu teşkil ediyor gözüktüğüne inanmak için makul gerekçelere sahipse, kendi inisiyatifiyle, anılan türde bir gözetimde bulunabilir.

MADDE 15

GÖREVLİLERİN DİĞER TARAFIN TOPRAKLARINDA BULUNMASI

1) Talepte Bulunan Gümrük İdaresi tarafından özel olarak tayin edilen görevliler, talep olması halinde, Talepte Bulunulan Gümrük İdaresinin izniyle ve bu idarenin ulusal mevzuatına göre getirebileceği koşullara tabi olarak, bir Gümrük suçunu soruşturmak amacıyla, Talepte Bulunulan Gümrük İdaresi'nin kendi topraklarında yürüttüğü ve Talepte Bulunan Gümrük İdaresi'ni ilgilendiren bir incelemede hazır bulunabilirler. Bu görevliler, sadece danışmanlık sıfatına sahiptirler.

2) Ziyarette bulunan görevlilere ilişkin düzenlemelerle ilgili olarak

a) Bir Tarafın görevlileri, bu Anlaşma'nın şartları uyarınca diğer Tarafın topraklarında hazır bulundukları zaman, Gümrük idarelerindeki resmi kimlik ve statülerini ve kendilerine Talepte Bulunulan Gümrük İdaresi'nin topraklarında verilen resmi statüyü gösterir delilleri, her iki Tarafın kabul edeceği bir dilde, her zaman gösterebilmelidirler.

b) Görevliler, bu Anlaşma'nın şartları uyarınca, diğer Tarafın topraklarında hazır bulundukları sırada işleyebilecekleri herhangi bir suçtan sorumlu tutulurlar ve söz konusu Tarafın, ulusal mevzuatı kapsamında kendi görevlilerine tanıdığı korumadan yararlanırlar.

BÖLÜM V

BİLGİLERİN KULLANIMI, GİZLİLİĞİ VE KORUNMASI

MADDE 16

BİLGİLERİN KULLANIMI

1) Bu Anlaşma kapsamında alınan bilgi, belge ve diğer materyaller, sadece Tarafların Gümrük İdareleri tarafından ve yalnızca bu Anlaşma'da belirtilen koşullar çerçevesinde, idari yardım amacıyla kullanılır.

2) Bu Madde'nin 1inci fıkrası hükümlerine rağmen, talep üzerine, bilgiyi sağlayan Taraf, getirebileceği koşullara tabi olmak üzere, bilginin, başka amaçlar doğrultusunda veya başka makamlarca kullanımına izin verebilir. Bilginin bu şekilde kullanımı, bilgiyi kullanmak isteyen Tarafın hukuki idari hükümlerine uygun olmalıdır.

MADDE 17

BİLGİLERİN GİZLİLİĞİ VE KORUNMASI

1) Bu Anlaşma kapsamında iletilen bilgilere gizlilik muamelesi yapılır ve bu bilgiler, bilgileri alan Tarafın ulusal hukuki ve idari hükümleri uyarınca, asgari olarak, aynı tür bilgilere sağladığı koruma ve gizliliğe tabi tutulur.

2) Gümrük İdareleri, veri koruma yasalarında, bu Anlaşma'nın yürürlüğe girmesinden sonra oluşan değişikliklerden birbirlerini haberdar ederler.

3) Bu Anlaşma kapsamında alınan bilgiler, bu Anlaşma'nın koşulları uyarınca, sadece Tarafların Gümrük İdareleri tarafından kullanılır.

4) Elde edilen bilgiler, sadece bu Anlaşma amaçları doğrultusunda kullanılır. Taraflardan biri, bu bilgiyi başka amaçlar için kullanmayı istemesi halinde, bilgiyi sağlayan Gümrük İdaresinin önceden yazılı rızasını alır. Bu durumda, bilginin kullanımı, söz konusu Gümrük İdaresi'nin getirebileceği kısıtlamalara tabi tutulur.

BÖLÜM VI

İSTİSNALAR VE MALİYETLER

MADDE 18

YARDIMA İLİŞKİN İSTİSNALAR

1) Talepte Bulunulan Gümrük İdaresi, bir talebin karşılanmasının kendi egemenliğine, güvenliğine, kamu politikasına ya da diğer asli ulusal çıkarlarına aykırı olacağı ya da meşru ticari ya da mesleki çıkarlara halel getireceği ya da ulusal mevzuatına aykırı olacağı kanısında olması halinde, yardım talebi reddedilebilir ya da yardımın gereğinin yapılması, belli şart ya da koşulların karşılanmasına tabi olabilir.

2) Talepte Bulunan Gümrük İdaresi'nin diğer Gümrük İdaresi'nin kendisinden talep etmesi halinde karşılayamayacağı bir talepte bulunulması halinde, Talepte Bulunan Gümrük İdaresi, talebinde buna dikkat çeker. Bu tür bir talebin karşılanması, Talepte Bulunulan Gümrük İdaresi'nin takdirindedir.

3) Talepte Bulunulan Gümrük İdaresi, devam etmekte olan bir soruşturma, kovuşturma ya da adli işlemi engelleyeceği gerekçesiyle, yardım sağlamayı erteleyebilir. Bu durumda, Talepte Bulunulan Gümrük İdaresi, yardımın Talepte Bulunulan Gümrük İdaresi'nin gerekli görebileceği şart ve koşullara tabi olacak şekilde sağlanıp sağlanmamasını belirlemek amacıyla, Talepte Bulunan Gümrük İdaresiyle istişarede bulunur.

4) Yardımın reddedilmesi ya da ertelenmesi halinde, Talepte Bulunan Gümrük İdaresi, gecikmeye mahal vermeden ve mümkün olan en erken sürede durumdan haberdar edilir; yardımın reddinin ya da ertelenmesinin gerekçeleri de belirtilir.

MADDE 19

MALİYETLER

1) Uzmanların masraflarıile Hükümet görevlileri dışındaki mütercim ve tercümanların maliyetleri hariç olmak üzere, Gümrük İdareleri, bu Anlaşma'nın yürütülmesinden kaynaklanan maliyetlerin geri ödenmesi konusundaki tüm taleplerinden vazgeçerler.

2) İstisnai ve olağandışı mahiyetteki masrafların gerekmesi ya da gerekecek olması halinde, bir talebin gereğinin yapılması amacıyla, Gümrük İdareleri, talebin gereğinin yapılacağı koşullarla, maliyetleri karşılama biçimini belirlemek için birbirleriyle istişarede bulunurlar.

BÖLÜM VII
NİHAİ HÜKÜMLER

MADDE 20
ÜLKESEL UYGULAMA

Bu Anlaşma, Birleşik Meksika Devletleri'nin topraklarında ve Türkiye Cumhuriyeti'nin topraklarında uygulanır.

MADDE 21
ANLAŞMAZLIKLARIN ÇÖZÜMLENMESİ

Bu Anlaşma'nın uygulanmasından ya da yorumlanmasından kaynaklanan meseleler, Tarafların Gümrük İdareleri arasındaki müşterek mutabakatla çözüme kavuşturulur. Gümrük İdarelerinin, bu Anlaşma'nın yorumlanmasından ya da uygulanmasından kaynaklanan anlaşmazlıklarını çözüme kavuşturamaması halinde, bu anlaşmazlıklar, diplomatik yollarla çözülür.

MADDE 22
GÖZDEN GEÇİRME

Taraflar, Anlaşmanın gözden geçirilmesinin gerekli olmadığını yazılı olarak birbirlerine bildirmedikleri sürece, bu Anlaşmayı gözden geçirmek için, talep üzerine ya da Anlaşmanın yürürlüğe girdiği tarihten itibaren beş (5) yıllık sürenin sonunda bir araya gelirler.

MADDE 23
ANLAŞMANIN YÜRÜRLÜĞE GİRMESİ, ANLAŞMADA DEĞİŞİKLİK YAPILMASI VE ANLAŞMANIN FESHİ

1) İşbu Anlaşma, Tarafların anılan belgenin yürürlüğe girmesi için gerekli iç yasal usullerin tamamlandığını birbirlerine diplomatik yollarla bildirdikleri son yazılı bildirimin alındığı tarihten otuz (30) gün sonra yürürlüğe girer.

2) Bu Anlaşmada, Tarafların karşılıklı rızasıyla değişiklik yapılabilir. Yapılan bu değişiklikler, 1. fıkrada öngörülen prosedüre göre yürürlüğe girer.

3) Bu Anlaşma, müteakip beş (5) yıllık sürelerle yürürlükte kalacak ve Akit Taraflardan herhangi biri, bu Anlaşmayı feshetme niyetini diplomatik kanallar aracılığıyla diğer Tarafa yazıyla tebliğ etmediği sürece, Anlaşma kendiliğinden ilave beş (5) yıllık sürelerle uzatılacaktır. Anlaşmanın feshi, feshe dair ihbarın diğer Akit Tarafa bildirildiği tarihten üç (3) ay sonra yürürlüğe girer. Bu Anlaşmanın feshedilmesi, fesih öncesinde başlatılan ve devam etmekte olan işbirliği faaliyetlerini etkilemez.

Bu Anlaşma, bütün metinler eşit derecede geçerli olmak üzere, Ankara'da, 17 Aralık 2013'de İspanyolca, Türkçe ve İngilizce dillerinde iki nüsha olarak imzalanmıştır. Metinler arasında yorum ihtilafı olması halinde, İngilizce metin geçerli sayılır.

BİRLEŞİK MEKSİKA DEVLETLERİ HÜKÜMETİ ADINA	TÜRKİYE CUMHURİYETİ HÜKÜMETİ ADINA
José Antonio Meade Kuribreña Dışişleri Bakanı	Hayati Yazıcı Gümrük ve Ticaret Bakanı

[TRANSLATION – TRADUCTION]

ACCORD ENTRE LE GOUVERNEMENT DES ÉTATS-UNIS DU MEXIQUE ET LE GOUVERNEMENT DE LA RÉPUBLIQUE TURQUE RELATIF À L'ASSISTANCE MUTUELLE ADMINISTRATIVE ET À L'ÉCHANGE DE RENSEIGNEMENTS EN MATIÈRE DOUANIÈRE

Le Gouvernement des États-Unis du Mexique et le Gouvernement de la République turque, ci-après dénommés « Parties »,

Conscients du fait que les infractions à la législation douanière portent préjudice aux intérêts économiques, fiscaux, financiers, sociaux, culturels et commerciaux de leurs pays respectifs,

Considérant qu'il importe d'assurer l'évaluation exacte des droits de douane, taxes, autres redevances et impositions, prélevés à l'importation ou à l'exportation de marchandises, avec la détermination correcte de leur classement tarifaire, de leur valeur et de leur origine, ainsi que l'application appropriée des dispositions de prohibition, de restriction et de contrôle,

Reconnaissant l'importance de la coopération à l'échelon international au sujet des questions liées à l'application de leur législation douanière,

Convaincus que les initiatives visant à prévenir les infractions à la législation douanière et à assurer la perception exacte des droits, taxes, redevances et autres impositions à l'importation et à l'exportation peuvent être rendues plus efficaces grâce à la coopération entre les autorités douanières,

Préoccupés par l'ampleur et les tendances à la croissance du trafic illicite de stupéfiants et de substances psychotropes, qui constituent un danger pour la santé publique et la société,

Prenant en considération la Convention unique sur les stupéfiants de 1961 modifiée par son Protocole de 1972 et la Convention sur les substances psychotropes de 1971, créées sous les auspices de l'Organisation des Nations Unies, ainsi que la Convention des Nations Unies contre le trafic illicite de stupéfiants et de substances psychotropes de 1988,

Tenant compte des obligations imposées par les conventions internationales déjà acceptées ou appliquées par les Parties,

Sont convenus de ce qui suit :

CHAPITRE PREMIER. DISPOSITIONS GÉNÉRALES

Article premier. Définitions

Aux fins du présent Accord :

1) L'expression « autorité douanière » désigne, aux États-Unis du Mexique, le Ministère des finances et du crédit public et, en République turque, le Ministère des douanes et du commerce;

2) L'expression « droits de douane » désigne tous les droits, taxes, redevances ou impositions diverses perçus sur les territoires des Parties en application de la législation douanière, à l'exception des redevances et impositions pour services rendus;

3) L'expression « législation douanière » désigne les dispositions d'ordre juridique ou administratif concernant l'importation, l'exportation, le mouvement ou le stockage des marchandises dont l'administration et l'application sont spécifiquement confiées aux autorités douanières, ainsi que les règlements établis par les autorités douanières en vertu de leurs pouvoirs statutaires;

4) L'expression « infraction douanière » désigne toute infraction ou tentative d'infraction à la législation douanière;

5) Le terme « renseignement » désigne les données, qu'elles soient traitées ou analysées ou non, les documents, les rapports, leurs copies certifiées conformes ou autres communications, y compris électroniques;

6) L'expression « chaîne logistique internationale » désigne l'ensemble des processus concernant les mouvements transfrontaliers des marchandises du lieu d'origine à celui de destination finale;

7) Le terme « fonctionnaire » désigne tout fonctionnaire des douanes ou d'un autre service public désigné par une autorité douanière;

8) Le terme « personne » désigne toute personne physique ou morale;

9) L'expression « données à caractère personnel » désigne toute donnée concernant une personne physique dûment identifiée ou identifiable;

10) L'expression « autorité douanière requérante » désigne l'autorité douanière qui formule une demande d'assistance en matière douanière;

11) L'expression « autorité douanière requise » désigne l'autorité douanière qui reçoit une demande d'assistance en matière douanière;

12) Le terme « territoire » désigne :

a) Pour les États-Unis du Mexique, le territoire des États-Unis du Mexique tel qu'il est défini dans sa Constitution, y compris toute zone au-delà de sa mer territoriale sur laquelle les États-Unis du Mexique peuvent exercer leurs droits souverains aux fins d'exploration et d'exploitation des ressources naturelles du fond marin, du sous-sol et des eaux surjacentes, ainsi que l'espace aérien qui surplombe ces zones, conformément au droit international; et

b) Pour la République turque, le territoire terrestre, la mer territoriale et l'espace aérien qui les surplombe, ainsi que les zones maritimes et sous-marines sur lesquelles la Turquie peut exercer ses droits souverains et juridictionnels, conformément au droit international.

Article 2. Champ d'application de l'Accord

1) Les Parties se prêtent mutuellement assistance par l'intermédiaire de leurs autorités douanières conformément aux conditions fixées dans le présent Accord, en vue d'appliquer comme il convient la législation douanière et de prévenir, de rechercher et de sanctionner les infractions douanières, ainsi que d'assurer la sécurité de la chaîne logistique internationale.

2) L'assistance prévue par le présent Accord est également accordée, de la propre initiative d'une Partie ou sur demande, aux fins de l'évaluation des droits de douane et autres taxes ou impositions en vertu de la législation douanière, et de l'exécution des contrôles au sein de l'autorité douanière.

3) Toute action menée dans le cadre du présent Accord par l'une ou l'autre Partie est exécutée conformément aux dispositions juridiques et administratives nationales qu'elle applique et dans la limite de la compétence et des ressources économiques dont dispose son autorité douanière.

4) Aucune disposition du présent Accord n'est interprétée de manière à restreindre un accord relatif à l'assistance mutuelle et à la coopération déjà en vigueur entre les Parties.

5) Les dispositions du présent Accord ne donnent à aucun particulier le droit d'obtenir, de supprimer ou d'exclure des éléments de preuve ou de faire obstacle à l'exécution d'une demande d'assistance.

6) L'assistance visée par le présent Accord ne comprend pas la demande d'arrestation de personnes ou la perception de droits de douane, d'impositions, d'amendes ou de tout autre montant déterminé par l'autorité douanière de l'une des Parties.

CHAPITRE II. PROCÉDURES GÉNÉRALES D'ASSISTANCE

Article 3. Forme et contenu des demandes d'assistance

1) Les demandes d'assistance visées au présent Accord sont communiquées directement entre les autorités douanières concernées. Chaque autorité douanière désigne un point de contact officiel à cet effet et communique les renseignements et toute mise à jour de ceux-ci à l'autre autorité douanière.

2) Les demandes d'assistance formulées conformément au présent Accord sont adressées par écrit ou par voie électronique, accompagnées de tous les renseignements ou documents jugés utiles aux fins de l'exécution de ces demandes. L'autorité douanière requise pourra exiger la confirmation par écrit des demandes formulées par voie électronique. Lorsque les circonstances le justifient, les demandes peuvent être formulées verbalement, mais doivent être confirmées par écrit dans les meilleurs délais, et au plus tard 10 jours à compter de la date à laquelle les demandes sont formulées verbalement.

3) Les demandes sont formulées en anglais. Tous les documents accompagnant ces demandes sont, dans la mesure du possible, traduits en anglais.

4) Les demandes formulées conformément aux dispositions du paragraphe 2 du présent article comportent les renseignements ci-après :

a) Le nom de l'autorité douanière requérante;

b) Le type d'assistance demandée;

c) L'objet et les motifs de la demande;

d) Un exposé sommaire de la question en cause et ses éléments d'ordre administratif et juridique; et

e) Les noms et adresses des personnes visées par la demande, s'ils sont connus.

5) Si une demande ne respecte pas les exigences de présentation, il est possible de demander qu'elle soit corrigée ou complétée. L'adoption de mesures conservatoires n'en est pas affectée.

6) Lorsque l'autorité douanière requérante demande qu'une certaine procédure soit suivie, l'autorité douanière requise fait droit à cette demande, conformément à sa législation en vigueur.

Article 4. Assistance spontanée

Dans les cas risquant de porter gravement atteinte à l'économie, à la santé publique, à la sécurité publique, y compris à la sécurité de la chaîne logistique internationale, ou à tout autre intérêt vital des Parties, l'autorité douanière de l'une ou l'autre Partie fournit, chaque fois que possible, une assistance de sa propre initiative et sans délai.

CHAPITRE III. RENSEIGNEMENTS

Article 5. Communication de renseignements

1) Les autorités douanières se communiquent, sur demande ou de leur propre initiative, tous les renseignements qui peuvent permettre de garantir l'exactitude :

a) Du recouvrement des droits de douane perçus par les autorités douanières et, en particulier, les renseignements qui peuvent aider à évaluer la valeur des marchandises à des fins douanières et à établir leur classement tarifaire;

b) De l'application des mesures de prohibition, de restriction et autres contrôles, préférences ou exemptions relatifs à l'importation, à l'exportation, au transit des marchandises et autres régimes douaniers; et

c) De la vérification du pays d'origine des marchandises.

2) Si l'autorité douanière requise ne dispose pas des renseignements demandés, la Partie requérante en est informée dans les plus brefs délais.

3) L'autorité douanière requise recherche les renseignements comme si elle agissait pour son propre compte.

Article 6. Types de renseignements particuliers

1) Sur demande, les autorités douanières s'informent mutuellement sur :

a) La régularité de l'exportation, à partir du territoire de la Partie requérante, des marchandises importées dans le territoire douanier de l'autre Partie; et

b) La régularité de l'importation, dans le territoire de la Partie requérante, des marchandises exportées du territoire douanier de l'autre Partie.

2) Ces renseignements précisent également le régime douanier utilisé pour le dédouanement des marchandises.

Article 7. Renseignements concernant l'application de la législation douanière

Les autorités douanières se communiquent, sur demande ou de leur propre initiative, les renseignements qui peuvent contribuer à appliquer comme il convient la législation douanière et à prévenir, rechercher et réprimer les infractions douanières, ainsi qu'à assurer la sécurité de la chaîne logistique internationale. Ces renseignements peuvent porter sur :

a) De nouvelles techniques de lutte contre la fraude douanière dont l'efficacité a été prouvée;

b) De nouvelles tendances, techniques ou méthodes en matière d'infractions douanières, ainsi que celles qui visent à dissimuler l'origine ou la valeur exacte des marchandises;

c) Des marchandises connues pour faire l'objet d'infractions douanières, ainsi que les méthodes utilisées pour transporter et stocker ces marchandises;

d) Des renseignements concernant des personnes dont on sait qu'elles ont commis une infraction douanière ou soupçonnées d'être sur le point de commettre une telle infraction, pour autant que la législation des Parties relative à la protection des données à caractère personnel permette l'échange de ces renseignements, même par voie d'exception;

e) Tout autre renseignement susceptible d'aider les autorités douanières à appliquer comme il convient leur législation douanière; et

f) Tout autre renseignement susceptible d'aider les autorités douanières à évaluer les risques aux fins du contrôle et de la facilitation.

Article 8. Échange de renseignements douaniers

1) Les informations déjà traitées dans le cadre de l'analyse des risques et susceptibles de déclencher une alerte sont envoyées et échangées entre les Parties, dans les meilleurs délais, afin de prendre des mesures.

2) Les Parties échangent des renseignements relatifs à la saisie de marchandises et de capitaux, y compris les méthodes de détection et les procédures de dissimulation.

Article 9. Renseignements relatifs aux infractions douanières

Les autorités douanières des Parties se communiquent, sur demande ou de leur propre initiative, des renseignements sur les activités planifiées, en cours ou réalisées qui constituent une présomption raisonnable portant à croire qu'une infraction douanière a été ou sera commise sur le territoire de la Partie concernée. Dans les cas graves risquant de porter gravement atteinte à l'économie, à la santé publique, à la sécurité publique ou à tout autre intérêt vital de l'autre Partie, ces renseignements sont fournis sans qu'il soit nécessaire d'en faire la demande.

Article 10. Renseignements aux fins de l'établissement des droits de douane

1) Sur demande, l'autorité douanière requise communique, sans préjudice des dispositions de l'article 17, aux fins de l'application appropriée de la législation douanière ou de la prévention des infractions douanières, des renseignements susceptibles d'aider l'autorité douanière requérante qui a des raisons de douter de la véracité ou de l'exactitude d'une déclaration de marchandises.

2) La demande spécifie les procédures de vérification que l'autorité douanière requérante a appliquées ou tenté d'appliquer, ainsi que les renseignements spécifiques demandés.

Article 11. Échange de renseignements relatifs à la propriété intellectuelle

Les autorités douanières des Parties peuvent échanger des renseignements relatifs aux infractions en matière de propriété intellectuelle et de droits d'auteur. Cet échange de renseignements a pour objectif de partager les données qui faciliteront la détection des comportements qui portent atteinte aux droits de propriété industrielle, aux droits de propriété intellectuelle ou aux droits d'auteur, et de transmettre ces renseignements aux autorités compétentes sur le territoire de chacune des Parties.

Article 12. Fourniture de l'assistance

1) L'assistance est fournie par communication directe entre les fonctionnaires désignés par les chefs des autorités douanières respectives.

2) Si l'autorité douanière requise n'est pas l'autorité compétente pour obtenir les renseignements demandés, elle identifie l'autorité compétente et lui transmet la demande, et en informe sans délai l'autorité douanière requérante.

Article 13. Dossiers, documents et autres matériels

L'autorité douanière requérante peut fournir des copies des documents nécessaires à l'exécution des demandes; en particulier, l'autorité douanière requérante fournit des indications sur les circonstances générales et les motifs des demandes. L'autorité douanière requise peut, lorsque cela est jugé nécessaire, fournir les prix à l'exportation déclarés par les entreprises de la Partie requise ou des copies des documents de déclaration d'exportation, sur demande.

CHAPITRE IV. ASSISTANCE SPÉCIALE

Article 14. Surveillance des marchandises et des moyens de transport

1) Sur demande, l'autorité douanière requise, dans la mesure de ses moyens et conformément à ses lois et règlements nationaux, exerce une surveillance et fournit à l'autorité douanière requérante des renseignements concernant :

a) Les marchandises transportées ou entreposées que l'on sait avoir été utilisées ou que l'on soupçonne d'être utilisées dans le cadre d'infractions douanières sur le territoire de l'autorité douanière requérante;

b) Les moyens de transport que l'on sait avoir été utilisés ou que l'on soupçonne d'être utilisés pour commettre des infractions douanières sur le territoire de l'autorité douanière requérante; et

c) Les locaux situés sur le territoire de l'autorité douanière requise que l'on sait avoir été utilisés ou que l'on soupçonne d'être utilisés dans le cadre d'une infraction douanière commise sur le territoire de l'autorité douanière requérante.

2) L'autorité douanière de l'une ou l'autre Partie peut exercer cette surveillance de sa propre initiative si elle a des raisons de croire que les activités planifiées, en cours ou réalisées semblent constituer une infraction douanière sur le territoire de l'autre Partie.

Article 15. Présence de fonctionnaires sur le territoire de l'autre Partie

1) Sur demande, des fonctionnaires désignés spécialement par l'autorité douanière requérante peuvent, avec l'autorisation de l'autorité douanière requise et sous réserve des

conditions que cette dernière peut leur imposer, conformément à sa législation nationale et aux fins de l'enquête concernant une infraction douanière, assister à une enquête effectuée par l'autorité douanière requise sur son territoire lorsque cela est pertinent pour l'autorité douanière requérante. Ces fonctionnaires jouent un rôle purement consultatif.

2) En ce qui concerne les dispositions relatives aux fonctionnaires en visite :

a) Lorsque des fonctionnaires d'une Partie doivent être présents sur le territoire de l'autre Partie aux termes du présent Accord, ils doivent fournir, dans une langue acceptable par les deux Parties, la preuve de leur identité et de leur qualité officielles au sein de leur autorité douanière ainsi que de leur qualité officielle accordée sur le territoire de l'autorité douanière requise;

b) Durant leur présence sur le territoire de l'autre Partie et conformément aux dispositions du présent Accord, les fonctionnaires sont responsables de toute infraction qu'ils peuvent commettre et bénéficient, dans la limite prévue par la législation nationale de cette Partie, de la même protection que celle accordée à ses propres fonctionnaires.

CHAPITRE V. UTILISATION, CONFIDENTIALITÉ ET PROTECTION DES RENSEIGNEMENTS

Article 16. Utilisation des renseignements

1) Les renseignements, documents et autres matériels obtenus au titre du présent Accord sont utilisés uniquement par les autorités douanières des Parties et aux seules fins de l'assistance administrative dans les conditions fixées par le présent Accord.

2) Sur demande, la Partie qui a fourni les renseignements peut, nonobstant le paragraphe 1 du présent article, autoriser leur utilisation à d'autres fins ou par d'autres autorités, sous réserve de modalités et de conditions qui peuvent être précisées. L'utilisation des renseignements à d'autres fins se fait conformément aux dispositions administratives et juridiques de la Partie qui cherche à utiliser les renseignements.

Article 17. Confidentialité et protection des renseignements

1) Les renseignements communiqués conformément au présent Accord sont traités comme étant confidentiels et bénéficient d'une protection et d'un degré de confidentialité au moins équivalents à ceux prévus pour les renseignements de même nature dans les dispositions juridiques et administratives nationales de la Partie qui les reçoit.

2) Les autorités douanières s'informent de toute modification de leurs lois en matière de protection des données intervenant après l'entrée en vigueur du présent Accord.

3) Les renseignements reçus en vertu du présent Accord sont utilisés uniquement par les autorités douanières des Parties conformément aux conditions fixées dans le présent Accord.

4) Les renseignements obtenus sont utilisés uniquement aux fins du présent Accord. Lorsqu'une Partie souhaite utiliser les renseignements à d'autres fins, elle obtient l'accord préalable écrit de l'autorité douanière qui a fourni les renseignements. Cette utilisation est jusqu'alors soumise à toute restriction imposée par cette autorité.

CHAPITRE VI. DÉROGATIONS ET FRAIS

Article 18. Dérogations à l'obligation de prêter assistance

1) Lorsque l'autorité douanière requise estime que l'exécution d'une demande pourrait porter atteinte à sa souveraineté, à sa sécurité, à l'ordre public ou à d'autres intérêts nationaux essentiels, ou porter préjudice aux intérêts commerciaux ou professionnels légitimes ou qu'elle est contraire à sa législation nationale, l'assistance peut être refusée ou l'exécution peut être subordonnée à la satisfaction de certaines conditions ou exigences.

2) Lorsque l'autorité douanière requérante formule une demande à laquelle elle ne serait pas elle-même en mesure d'accéder si elle avait été formulée par l'autre autorité douanière, l'autorité douanière requérante signale le fait dans l'exposé de sa demande. L'autorité douanière requise a alors toute latitude pour déterminer la suite à donner à cette demande.

3) L'autorité douanière requise peut différer l'assistance au motif qu'elle perturbera une enquête, des poursuites judiciaires ou une procédure en cours. Dans ce cas, l'autorité douanière requise consulte l'autorité douanière requérante pour déterminer si l'assistance peut être apportée sous réserve du respect des conditions éventuellement exigées par l'autorité douanière requise.

4) Lorsque l'assistance est refusée ou différée, l'autorité douanière requérante en est informée, sans délai et dès que possible, et les raisons de ce refus ou de ce report lui sont communiquées.

Article 19. Frais

1) Les autorités douanières renoncent à toute demande de remboursement des frais encourus pour l'exécution du présent Accord, à l'exception des frais d'experts et des frais des traducteurs et interprètes, autres que les fonctionnaires.

2) Si des dépenses de nature exceptionnelle et extraordinaire sont ou seront nécessaires pour exécuter une demande, les autorités douanières se consultent pour déterminer les modalités et conditions dans lesquelles la demande sera exécutée ainsi que la manière dont les frais seront supportés.

CHAPITRE VII. DISPOSITIONS FINALES

Article 20. Applicabilité territoriale

Le présent Accord est applicable sur le territoire des États-Unis du Mexique et sur le territoire de la République turque.

Article 21. Règlement des différends

Tout différend découlant de l'application ou de l'interprétation du présent Accord est réglé d'un commun accord entre les autorités douanières des Parties. Si les autorités douanières ne parviennent pas à résoudre les différends découlant de l'interprétation ou de la mise en œuvre du présent Accord, ces différends sont réglés par la voie diplomatique.

Article 22. Examen

Les Parties se réunissent afin d'examiner le présent Accord, sur demande ou au terme d'un délai de cinq ans à compter de la date de son entrée en vigueur, sauf si elles se notifient mutuellement par écrit que cet examen est inutile.

Article 23. Entrée en vigueur, modification et dénonciation

1) Le présent Accord entre en vigueur 30 jours après la date de réception de la dernière des notifications écrites par lesquelles les Parties s'informent mutuellement, par la voie diplomatique, de l'accomplissement de leurs procédures juridiques internes nécessaires à cet effet.

2) Le présent Accord peut être modifié en tant que de besoin par consentement mutuel des Parties. Ces modifications entrent en vigueur conformément à la procédure prévue au paragraphe 1.

3) Le présent Accord reste en vigueur pour des périodes successives de cinq ans et il est tacitement reconduit pour de nouvelles périodes de cinq ans, à moins que l'une des Parties ne notifie par écrit, par la voie diplomatique, son intention de dénoncer le présent Accord. La dénonciation prend effet trois mois après la date de la notification de dénonciation adressée à l'autre Partie. La dénonciation du présent Accord n'affecte pas les activités de coopération en cours entreprises avant la date de dénonciation.

SIGNÉ à Ankara, le 17 décembre 2013, en double exemplaire, en langues espagnole, turque et anglaise, tous les textes faisant également foi. En cas de divergence d'interprétation, le texte anglais prévaut.

Pour le Gouvernement des États-Unis du Mexique :
JOSÉ ANTONIO MEADE KURIBREÑA
Ministre des affaires étrangères

Pour le Gouvernement de la République turque :
HAYATI YACIZI
Ministre des douanes et du commerce

No. 52845

Germany and Central African Forests Commission

Agreement between the Government of the Federal Republic of Germany and the Central African Forests Commission concerning Financial Cooperation in 2011. Yaoundé, 12 June 2015

Entry into force: *12 June 2015 by signature, in accordance with article 5*

Authentic texts: *French and German*

Registration with the Secretariat of the United Nations: *Germany, 12 August 2015*

Not published in print, in accordance with article 12(2) of the General Assembly regulations to give effect to Article 102 of the Charter of the United Nations, as amended, and the publication practice of the Secretariat.

Allemagne et Commission des forêts d'Afrique centrale

Accord de coopération financière entre le Gouvernement de la République fédérale d'Allemagne et la Commission des Forêts d'Afrique Centrale 2011. Yaoundé, 12 juin 2015

Entrée en vigueur : *12 juin 2015 par signature, conformément à l'article 5*

Textes authentiques : *français et allemand*

Enregistrement auprès du Secrétariat de l'Organisation des Nations Unies : *Allemagne, 12 août 2015*

Non disponible en version imprimée, conformément au paragraphe 2 de l'article 12 du règlement de l'Assemblée générale destiné à mettre en application l'Article 102 de la Charte des Nations Unies, tel qu'amendé, et à la pratique du Secrétariat en matière de publication.

No. 52846

Germany
and
United States of America

Arrangement between the Government of the Federal Republic of Germany and the Government of the United States of America regarding the granting of exemptions and benefits to enterprises charged with providing Troop Care Services to the United States Forces stationed in the Federal Republic of Germany – "Choctaw Professional Resources Enterprise (DOCPER-TC-35-02) (VN 134)". Berlin, 25 June 2015

Entry into force: *25 June 2015, in accordance with its provisions*

Authentic texts: *English and German*

Registration with the Secretariat of the United Nations: *Germany, 12 August 2015*

Not published in print, in accordance with article 12(2) of the General Assembly regulations to give effect to Article 102 of the Charter of the United Nations, as amended, and the publication practice of the Secretariat.

Allemagne
et
États-Unis d'Amérique

Arrangement entre le Gouvernement de la République fédérale d'Allemagne et le Gouvernement des États-Unis d'Amérique relatif à l'octroi d'exemptions et d'allocations aux entreprises chargées de fournir des services de soin aux forces américaines stationnées dans la République fédérale d'Allemagne – « Choctaw Professional Resources Enterprise (DOCPER-TC-35-02) (VN 134) ». Berlin, 25 juin 2015

Entrée en vigueur : *25 juin 2015, conformément à ses dispositions*

Textes authentiques : *anglais et allemand*

Enregistrement auprès du Secrétariat de l'Organisation des Nations Unies : *Allemagne, 12 août 2015*

Non disponible en version imprimée, conformément au paragraphe 2 de l'article 12 du règlement de l'Assemblée générale destiné à mettre en application l'Article 102 de la Charte des Nations Unies, tel qu'amendé, et à la pratique du Secrétariat en matière de publication.

No. 52847

International Bank for Reconstruction and Development and Georgia

Loan Agreement (First Inclusive Growth Development Policy Operation) between Georgia and the International Bank for Reconstruction and Development (with schedules, appendix and International Bank for Reconstruction and Development General Conditions for Loans, dated 12 March 2012). Tbilisi, 22 May 2015

Entry into force: *12 June 2015 by notification*

Authentic text: *English*

Registration with the Secretariat of the United Nations: *International Bank for Reconstruction and Development, 13 August 2015*

Not published in print, in accordance with article 12(2) of the General Assembly regulations to give effect to Article 102 of the Charter of the United Nations, as amended, and the publication practice of the Secretariat.

Banque internationale pour la reconstruction et le développement et Géorgie

Accord de prêt (Première opération relative à la politique de développement pour une croissance inclusive) entre la Géorgie et la Banque internationale pour la reconstruction et le développement (avec annexes, appendice et Conditions générales applicables aux prêts de la Banque internationale pour la reconstruction et le développement, en date du 12 mars 2012). Tbilissi, 22 mai 2015

Entrée en vigueur : *12 juin 2015 par notification*

Texte authentique : *anglais*

Enregistrement auprès du Secrétariat de l'Organisation des Nations Unies : *Banque internationale pour la reconstruction et le développement, 13 août 2015*

Non disponible en version imprimée, conformément au paragraphe 2 de l'article 12 du règlement de l'Assemblée générale destiné à mettre en application l'Article 102 de la Charte des Nations Unies, tel qu'amendé, et à la pratique du Secrétariat en matière de publication.

No. 52848

International Bank for Reconstruction and Development and Georgia

Loan Agreement (First Programmatic Private Sector Competitiveness Development Policy Operation) between Georgia and the International Bank for Reconstruction and Development (with schedules, appendix and International Bank for Reconstruction and Development General Conditions for Loans, dated 12 March 2012). Tbilisi, 22 May 2015

Entry into force: *12 June 2015 by notification*

Authentic text: *English*

Registration with the Secretariat of the United Nations: *International Bank for Reconstruction and Development, 13 August 2015*

Not published in print, in accordance with article 12(2) of the General Assembly regulations to give effect to Article 102 of the Charter of the United Nations, as amended, and the publication practice of the Secretariat.

Banque internationale pour la reconstruction et le développement et Géorgie

Accord de prêt (Première opération relative à la politique de développement de la compétitivité programmatique du secteur privé) entre la Géorgie et la Banque internationale pour la reconstruction et le développement (avec annexes, appendice et Conditions générales applicables aux prêts de la Banque internationale pour la reconstruction et le développement, en date du 12 mars 2012). Tbilissi, 22 mai 2015

Entrée en vigueur : *12 juin 2015 par notification*

Texte authentique : *anglais*

Enregistrement auprès du Secrétariat de l'Organisation des Nations Unies : *Banque internationale pour la reconstruction et le développement, 13 août 2015*

Non disponible en version imprimée, conformément au paragraphe 2 de l'article 12 du règlement de l'Assemblée générale destiné à mettre en application l'Article 102 de la Charte des Nations Unies, tel qu'amendé, et à la pratique du Secrétariat en matière de publication.

No. 52849

Germany
and
Central African Forests Commission

Agreement between the Government of the Federal Republic of Germany and the Central African Forests Commission concerning Financial Cooperation in 2014. Yaoundé, 12 June 2015

Entry into force: *12 June 2015 by signature, in accordance with article 5*

Authentic texts: *French and German*

Registration with the Secretariat of the United Nations: *Germany, 12 August 2015*

Not published in print, in accordance with article 12(2) of the General Assembly regulations to give effect to Article 102 of the Charter of the United Nations, as amended, and the publication practice of the Secretariat.

Allemagne
et
Commission des forêts d'Afrique centrale

Accord de coopération financière entre le Gouvernement de la République fédérale d'Allemagne et la Commission des Forêts d'Afrique Centrale 2014. Yaoundé, 12 juin 2015

Entrée en vigueur : *12 juin 2015 par signature, conformément à l'article 5*

Textes authentiques : *français et allemand*

Enregistrement auprès du Secrétariat de l'Organisation des Nations Unies : *Allemagne, 12 août 2015*

Non disponible en version imprimée, conformément au paragraphe 2 de l'article 12 du règlement de l'Assemblée générale destiné à mettre en application l'Article 102 de la Charte des Nations Unies, tel qu'amendé, et à la pratique du Secrétariat en matière de publication.

No. 52850

Germany
and
United States of America

Arrangement between the Government of the Federal Republic of Germany and the Government of the United States of America regarding the granting of exemptions and benefits to enterprises charged with providing Troop Care Services to the United States Forces stationed in the Federal Republic of Germany – "Leidos, INC. (DOCPER-TC-06-07) (VN 551)". Berlin, 25 June 2015

Entry into force: *25 June 2015, in accordance with its provisions*

Authentic texts: *English and German*

Registration with the Secretariat of the United Nations: *Germany, 12 August 2015*

Not published in print, in accordance with article 12(2) of the General Assembly regulations to give effect to Article 102 of the Charter of the United Nations, as amended, and the publication practice of the Secretariat.

Allemagne
et
États-Unis d'Amérique

Arrangement entre le Gouvernement de la République fédérale d'Allemagne et le Gouvernement des États-Unis d'Amérique relatif à l'octroi d'exemptions et d'allocations aux entreprises chargées de fournir des services de soin aux forces américaines stationnées dans la République fédérale d'Allemagne – « Leidos, INC. (DOCPER-TC-06-07) (VN 551) ». Berlin, 25 juin 2015

Entrée en vigueur : *25 juin 2015, conformément à ses dispositions*

Textes authentiques : *anglais et allemand*

Enregistrement auprès du Secrétariat de l'Organisation des Nations Unies : *Allemagne, 12 août 2015*

Non disponible en version imprimée, conformément au paragraphe 2 de l'article 12 du règlement de l'Assemblée générale destiné à mettre en application l'Article 102 de la Charte des Nations Unies, tel qu'amendé, et à la pratique du Secrétariat en matière de publication.

No. 52851

Germany
and
Democratic Republic of the Congo

Agreement between the Government of the Federal Republic of Germany and the Government of the Democratic Republic of the Congo concerning Financial Cooperation in 2013. Kinshasa, 3 December 2014

Entry into force: *3 December 2014 by signature, in accordance with article 5*

Authentic texts: *French and German*

Registration with the Secretariat of the United Nations: *Germany, 12 August 2015*

Not published in print, in accordance with article 12(2) of the General Assembly regulations to give effect to Article 102 of the Charter of the United Nations, as amended, and the publication practice of the Secretariat.

Allemagne
et
République démocratique du Congo

Accord de coopération financière entre le Gouvernement de la République fédérale d'Allemagne et le Gouvernement de la République démocratique du Congo 2013. Kinshasa, 3 décembre 2014

Entrée en vigueur : *3 décembre 2014 par signature, conformément à l'article 5*

Textes authentiques : *français et allemand*

Enregistrement auprès du Secrétariat de l'Organisation des Nations Unies : *Allemagne, 12 août 2015*

Non disponible en version imprimée, conformément au paragraphe 2 de l'article 12 du règlement de l'Assemblée générale destiné à mettre en application l'Article 102 de la Charte des Nations Unies, tel qu'amendé, et à la pratique du Secrétariat en matière de publication.

No. 52852

Mexico
and
Turkey

Air Services Agreement between the Government of the United Mexican States and the Government of the Republic of Turkey (with annexes). Ankara, 17 December 2013

Entry into force: *16 July 2015, in accordance with article 23*

Authentic texts: *English, Spanish and Turkish*

Registration with the Secretariat of the United Nations: *Mexico, 5 August 2015*

Mexique
et
Turquie

Accord relatif aux services aériens entre le Gouvernement des États-Unis du Mexique et le Gouvernement de la République turque (avec annexes). Ankara, 17 décembre 2013

Entrée en vigueur : *16 juillet 2015, conformément à l'article 23*

Textes authentiques : *anglais, espagnol et turc*

Enregistrement auprès du Secrétariat de l'Organisation des Nations Unies : *Mexique, 5 août 2015*

[ENGLISH TEXT – TEXTE ANGLAIS]

AIR SERVICES AGREEMENT BETWEEN THE GOVERNMENT OF THE UNITED MEXICAN STATES AND THE GOVERNMENT OF THE REPUBLIC OF TURKEY

The Government of the United Mexican States and the Government of the Republic of Turkey, hereinafter referred to as "the Contracting Parties";

BEING parties to the Convention on International Civil Aviation and International Air Services Transit Agreement both opened for signature at Chicago on the seventh day of December 1944;

DESIRING to facilitate the expansion of international air services opportunities;

RECOGNISING that efficient and competitive international air service enhance economic growth, trade, tourism, investment and the welfare of consumers;

DESIRING to ensure the highest degree of safety and security in international air services and reaffirming their grave concern about acts or threats against the security of aircraft, which jeopardise the safety of persons or property, adversely affect the operation of air services, and undermine public confidence in the safety of civil aviation, and

DESIRING to conclude an Agreement for the purpose of establishing and operating air services between their respective territories,

Have agreed as follows:

ARTICLE 1
Definitions

For the purpose of this Agreement, unless the context otherwise requires:

a. "Aeronautical Authorities" means, in the case of the United Mexican States, the Secretariat of Communications and Transport through the Directorate General of Civil Aviation and in the case of the Republic of Turkey, the Ministry of Transport, Maritime Affairs and Communications through the Directorate General of Civil Aviation, or in both cases, any person or body authorised to exercise the functions presently assigned to the said authorities;

b. "Agreement" means this Agreement, its Annex and any amendments thereto;

c. "Agreed services" means the international air services which can be operated, according to provisions of present Agreement on the specified routes;

d. "Annex" means the Annex to this Agreement or as amended in accordance with the provisions of Article 18 (Consultations and Amendment) of this Agreement. The Annex forms an integral part of this Agreement and all references to the Agreement shall include the Annex except where explicitly agreed otherwise;

e. "Air service", "international air service", "airline" and "stop for non-traffic purposes" have the meanings specified in Article 96 of the Convention;

f. "Capacity" means:

- in relation to an aircraft, the payload of that aircraft available on the route or section of a route;

- in relation to a specified air service, the capacity of the aircraft used on such service multiplied by the frequency operated by such aircraft over a given period on a route or section of a route;

g. "Convention" means the Convention on International Civil Aviation opened for signature at Chicago on the seventh day of December, 1944 and includes any Annex adopted under Article 90 of that Convention and any amendment of the Annexes of the Convention under Articles 90 and 94 thereof, so far as those Annexes and amendments have become effective for or been ratified by both Contracting Parties;

h. "Designated airline(s)" means any airline(s) which has/have been designated and authorized in accordance with Article 3 (Designation and Authorization) of this Agreement;

i. "Ground-handling" includes but is not limited to passenger, cargo and baggage handling, and the provision of catering facilities and/or services;

j. "ICAO" means the International Civil Aviation Organization;

k. "International air transportation" means air transportation which passes through the air space over the territory of more than one State;

l. "Marketing airline" means an airline that offers air transportation on an aircraft operated by another airline, through code-sharing;

m. "Schedule" means the schedule of the routes to operate air transportation services annexed to the present Agreement and any modifications thereto as agreed in accordance with the provisions of Article 18 of the present Agreement;

n. "Specified routes" means the routes established or to be established in the Annex to this Agreement;

o. "Spare parts" means articles of a repair or replacement nature for incorporation in an aircraft, including engines;

p. "Tariff" means the price charged for the transportation of passengers, baggage and cargo, as well as the conditions and rules that regulate the application of transportation cost depending on the characteristics of the service rendered, under which that amount shall be applied, excluding the remuneration and other conditions relative to the carriage of mail;

q. "Territory" has the meaning specified in Article 2 of the Convention;

r. "Traffic" means, passengers, baggage, cargo and mail;

s. "Regular equipment" means articles, other than stores and spare parts of a removable nature, for use on board an aircraft during flight, including first aid and survival equipment;

t. "User charges" means fees or rates levied for the use of airports, navigational facilities and other related services offered by one Contracting Party to the Other.

ARTICLE 2

Grant of Rights

1. Each Contracting Party grants to the other Contracting Party the following rights for the conduct of scheduled international air services on the routes specified in Annex I to this Agreement by the designated airlines of the other Contracting Party:

a. the right to fly without landing across the territory of the other Contracting Party,

b. the right to make stops in the said territory for non-traffic purposes,

c. the right to make stops in the said territory at the points specified for that route in Annex I to this Agreement for the purpose of putting down and taking up international traffic in combination or separately,

d. the rights otherwise specified in this Agreement.

2. Nothing in paragraph (1) of this Article shall be deemed to confer on the airlines of one Contracting Party the privilege of taking up, in the territory of the other Contracting Party, traffic carried for remuneration or hire and destined for another point in the territory of that other Contracting Party.

ARTICLE 3

Designation and Authorization

1. Each Contracting Party shall have the right to designate one or more airlines for the purpose of operating the agreed services on the specified routes. Such designation shall be effected by virtue of a written notification through diplomatic channels.

2. On receipt of such designation, the aeronautical authorities of the other Contracting Party shall, subject to paragraphs (3) and (4) of this Article, grant without delay to the designated airline(s) the appropriate operating authorization.

3. The aeronautical authorities of one Contracting Party may require an airline(s) designated by the other Contracting Party to satisfy that it is (they are) qualified to fulfill the conditions prescribed under the laws and regulations normally and reasonably applied to the operations of international services by such authorities in conformity with the provisions of the Convention.

4. Each Contracting Party shall have the right to refuse to grant the operating authorizations referred in paragraph (2) of this Article, or to impose such conditions as it may deem necessary on the exercise by a designated airline of the rights specified in Article 2 (Grant of Rights) of this Agreement, in any case where the Contracting Party is not satisfied that:

a. substantial ownership and effective control of that airline are vested in the Contracting Party designating the airline or in its nationals; and/or

b. the Government designating the airline is maintaining and administering the standards set forth in Article 13 (Aviation Safety) and Article 14 (Aviation Security) of this Agreement.

5. When an airline has been so designated and authorized, it may begin at any time to operate the agreed services, provided that a capacity agreed upon and a tariff established in accordance with the provisions of Article 5 (Capacity) and Article 6 (Tariffs) of this Agreement is in force in respect of that service.

ARTICLE 4

Revocation or Suspension of Operating Authorization

1. Each Contracting Party shall have the right to revoke an operating authorization or to suspend the exercise of the rights specified in Article 2 (Grant of Rights) of this Agreement by an airlines/s designated by the other Contracting Party, or to impose such conditions as it may deem necessary on the exercise of these rights:

a. in any case where it is not satisfied that substantial ownership and effective control of that airline is vested in the Contracting Party designating the airline or in its nationals, or

b. in case of failure by that airline to comply with the laws or regulations of the Contracting Party granting the rights, or

c. in case that airline otherwise fails to operate in accordance with the conditions prescribed under this Agreement.

2. Unless immediate revocation, suspension or imposition of the conditions mentioned in paragraph (1) of this Article is essential to prevent further infringements of laws or regulations, such right shall be exercised only after consultations aeronautical authorities of the State of other Contracting Party. In such a case consultations shall begin within a period of sixty (60) days from the date of request made by either Contracting Party for consultations.

ARTICLE 5

Capacity

1. The designated airline(s) of each Contracting Party shall enjoy fair and equal opportunity for the operation of air services for the carriage of traffic between the territories of the two Contracting Parties.

2. In the operation by the designated airline(s) of either Contracting Party of the specified air services, the interests of the airline of the other Contracting Party shall be taken into consideration so as not to affect unduly the services which the latter provides on all or part of the same route.

3. The agreed services provided by the designated airlines of the Contracting Parties shall bear close relationship to the requirements of the public for transportation on the specified routes and shall have as their primary objective the provision, at a reasonable load factor, of capacity adequate to carry the current and reasonably anticipated requirements of passengers and cargo including mail between the territories of the Contracting Parties.

4. In the operation of the agreed services, the total capacity to be provided and the frequency of the services to be operated by the designated airlines of each Contracting Party shall be, at the outset, be mutually determined by the aeronautical authorities of the Contracting Parties before the services are inaugurated. Such capacity and frequency of services initially determined may be reviewed and revised from time to time by the said authorities.

ARTICLE 6
Tariffs

1. Each Contracting Party shall allow the tariffs for international air services operated to/from its territory to be established by the designated airlines at reasonable levels, due regard being paid to all relevant factors, including cost of operation, reasonable profit and the tariffs of other airlines. The Contracting Parties may intervene for the:

a. prevention of unreasonably discriminatory prices or practices;

b. protection of consumers from prices that are unreasonably high or restrictive due to the abuse of a dominant position; and

c. protection of airlines from prices that are artificially low due to direct or indirect governmental subsidy or support.

2. The designated airlines of one Contracting Party shall fulfill the requirements established under paragraph (1) and file the tariffs to the other Contracting Party.

3. Neither Contracting Party shall allow its designated airline or airlines, in the establishment of tariffs, either in conjunction with any other airline or airlines or separately, to abuse market power in a way which has or is likely or intended to have the effect of severely weakening a competitor, being a designated airline of the other Contracting Party, or excluding such competitor from a route.

4. The Contracting Parties agree that the following airline practices, in relation to the establishment of tariffs, may be regarded as possible unfair competitive practices which may merit closer examination:

a. charging fares and rates on routes at levels which are, in the aggregate, insufficient to cover the costs of providing the services to which they relate;

b. the practices in question are sustained rather than temporary;

c. the practices in question have a serious economic effect on, or cause significant damage to, designated airline(s) of the other Contracting Party; and

d. behavior indicating an abuse of dominant position on the route.

5. In the event that either aeronautical authority is dissatisfied with a tariff in effect for an airline of the other Contracting Party, the aeronautical authorities will endeavour to settle the matter through consultations, if so requested by either authority. In any event, the aeronautical authority of a Contracting Party shall not take unilateral action to prevent the coming into effect or.continuation of a tariff of an airline of the other Contracting Party.

6. Notwithstanding the foregoing, the designated airlines of one Contracting Party shall provide, on request, to the aeronautical authorities of the other Contracting Party the information relating to the establishment of the tariffs, in a manner and format as specified by such authorities.

7. No Contracting Party shall impose on the other Contracting Party's designated airlines a first-refusal requirement, uplift ratio, no-objection fee, or any other requirement with respect to capacity, frequency or traffic that would be inconsistent with the purposes of this Agreement.

ARTICLE 7

Customs Duties and Other Charges

1. Aircraft operating on international air services by the designated airline of either Contracting Party, as well as their regular equipment, spare parts (including engines), supplies of fuels, lubricants and aircraft stores (including but not limited to such items as food, beverages, tobacco and products intended for sale or use of passenger during the flight) which are on board such aircraft, shall be exempt by the other Contracting Party on the basis of reciprocity and in accordance with applicable law, from all customs duties, inspection fees and other similar charges on arriving in the territory of the other Contracting Party, provided such equipment, spare parts, stores and supplies remain on board the aircraft until such time as they are re-exported or are used on board aircraft on the part of the journey to be performed over that territory.

2. The following equipment and items shall be exempted by the other Contracting Party on the basis of reciprocity and in accordance with applicable law from all customs duties, inspection fees and other similar charges not based on the cost of services provided on arrival, including:

a. regular equipment, fuel, lubricants, consumable technical supplies, aircraft stores (including but not limited to such items as food, beverages and tobacco) introduced into the territory of the other Contracting Party by or on behalf of a designated airline or taken on board the aircraft operated by that designated airline intended for use on aircraft operated in international air services, even when such regular equipment and such other items are to be used on any part of a journey performed over the territory of the other Contracting Party;

b. spare parts (including engines) introduced into the territory of the other Contracting Party by or on behalf of a designated airline or taken on board an aircraft operated by that designated airline for the maintenance or repair of aircraft operated in international air services by that designated airline; and

c. printed ticket stock, air waybills, any printed material which bears insignia of a designated airline of one Contracting Party and usual publicity material distributed without charge by that designated airline.

Material referred to in sub-paragraphs (a), (b) and (c) above shall be required to be kept under customs supervision or control.

3. The regular airborne equipment, spare parts (including engines), aircraft stores and supplies of fuels and lubricants (including hydraulic fluids) as well as the materials and supplies retained on board the aircraft of either Contracting Party may be unloaded in the territory of the other Contracting Party only with the approval of the customs authorities of such territory. In such case, they shall be placed under the supervision of the said authorities up to such time as they are re-exported or otherwise disposed of in accordance with customs regulations of that Contracting Party.

4. Charges corresponding to the services performed storage and customs clearance will be charged in accordance with the national laws and regulations of either Contracting Party.

ARTICLE 8
Direct Transit

Subject to the laws and regulations of each Contracting Party, passengers, baggage and cargo in direct transit across the territory of one Contracting Party and not leaving the area of the airport reserved for such purposes shall, unless security measures against violence, air piracy and smuggling of narcotic drugs require differently, only be subject to no more than a very simplified control. Baggage and cargo in direct transit shall be exempt from customs duties and other similar charges.

ARTICLE 9
User Charges

1. Airports, aviation security and other related facilities and services that are provided in the territory of one Contracting Party shall be available for use by the airlines of the other Contracting Party on terms no less favourable than the most favourable terms available to any airline engaged in similar international air services at the time arrangements for use are made.

2. The designated airline or airlines of one Contracting Party shall be permitted, in accordance with the domestic laws and regulations of both Contracting Parties, on the basis of reciprocity, to perform its own specified ground handling services in the territory of the other Contracting Party and, at its option, to have ground handling services provided in whole or in part by any agent authorized, if required by domestic laws and regulations, by the competent authorities of the other Contracting Party to provide such services.

3. The setting and collection of fees and charges imposed in the territory of one Contracting Party on an airline of the other Contracting Party for the use of airports, aviation security and other related facilities and services shall be just and fair. Any such fees and charges shall be assessed on an airline of the other Contracting Party on terms no less favourable than the most favourable terms available to any airline engaged in similar international air services at the time the fees or charges are imposed.

4. Each Contracting Party shall encourage discussions between its competent charging authorities and the airlines using the services and facilities, or where practicable, through airlines' representative organizations. Users shall be informed, with as much notice as possible, of any proposals for changes in user charges, to enable them to express their views before the changes are made.

ARTICLE 10

Non-National Personnel and Access to Local Services

1. In accordance with the laws and regulations of the other Contracting Party relating to entry, residence and employment the designated airline or airlines of one Contracting Party shall be entitled to bring in and to maintain in the territory of the other Contracting Party their own administrative, commercial, sales, operational, technical and other specialist staff who are required for the operation of the agreed services.

2. These staff requirements may, at the option of the designated airline or airlines of one Contracting Party, be satisfied by its own personnel or by using the services and personnel of any other organization, company or airline operating in the territory of the other Contracting Party and which has been authorized to perform such services for other airlines.

3. The representatives and staff shall be subject to the laws and regulations in force of the other Contracting Party. Consistent with such laws and regulations each Contracting Party shall, on the basis of reciprocity and with the minimum of delay, grant the necessary employment authorizations, visitor visas or other similar documents to the representatives and staff referred to in paragraph (1) of this Article.

ARTICLE 11

Currency Conversion and Remittance of Earnings

1. Each designating airline(s) shall have the right to sell and issue its own transportation documents in the territory of the other Contracting Party through its sales offices and, at its discretion, through its agents. Such airlines shall have the right to sell such transportation, and any person shall be free to purchase such transportation in any freely usable currency and/or in local currency, in accordance with the applicable national laws and regulations.

2. Each designated airline(s) shall have the right to convert and remit to its country, the revenues over expenditures achieved in connection with the carriage of traffic. In the absence of appropriate provisions of a payments agreement between the Contracting Parties, the above mentioned transfer shall be made in freely usable currencies and in accordance with the applicable national laws and foreign exchange regulations.

3. The conversion and remittance of such revenues shall be permitted without restriction at the rate of exchange applicable to current transactions which is in effect at the time such revenues are presented for conversion and remittance, and shall not be subject to any charges except those normally made by banks for carrying out such conversation and remittance.

4. The designated airline(s) of each Contracting Party shall have the right at their discretion to pay for local expenses, including purchases of fuel, in the territory of the other Contracting Party in local currency or, provided these accords with local currency regulations, in freely usable currencies.

ARTICLE 12
Mutual Recognition of Certificates and Licenses

1. Certificates of airworthiness, certificates of competency and licenses, issued or rendered valid by one Contracting Party and still in force shall be recognized as valid by the other Contracting Party for the purpose of operating the agreed services on the specified routes provided that the requirements under which such certificates or licenses were issued or rendered valid are equal to or above the minimum standards which are or may be established pursuant to the Convention. However, each Contracting Party reserves the right to refuse to recognize, for the purpose of flights above its own territory, certificates of competency and licenses granted to its own nationals or rendered valid for them by the other Contracting Party or any other State.

2. If the privileges or conditions of the licenses or certificates referred to in paragraph (1) above, issued by the aeronautical authorities of one Contracting Party to any person or designated airline or in respect of an aircraft used in the operation of the agreed services, should permit a difference from the minimum standards established under the Convention, and which difference has been filed with the ICAO, the other Contracting Party may request consultations between the aeronautical authorities with a view to clarifying the practice in question. Failure to reach satisfactory agreement shall constitute grounds for the application of Article 4 (Revocation or Suspension of Operating Authorization) of this Agreement.

ARTICLE 13
Aviation Safety

1. Each Contracting Party may request consultations at any time concerning safety standards in any area relating to aeronautical facilities and services, to aircrew, aircraft or their operation adopted by the other Contracting Party. Such consultations shall take place within thirty (30) days of that request.

2. If, following such consultations, one Contracting Party finds that the other Contracting Party does not effectively maintain and administer, in the aspects mentioned in paragraph (1) of this Article, safety standards in any such area that are at least equal to the minimum standards established at that time pursuant to the Convention, the first Contracting Party shall notify the other Contracting Party of those findings and the steps considered necessary to conform with those minimum ICAO standards, and that other Contracting Party shall take appropriate corrective action within an agreed period. Failure to take appropriate action within the agreed period shall be grounds for the application of Article 4 (Revocation or Suspension of Operating Authorization) of this Agreement.

3. Notwithstanding the obligations mentioned in Article 16 of the Convention, it is agreed that any aircraft operated by or on behalf of the airline of one Contracting Party on services to or from the territory of the State of the other Contracting Party may, while within the territory of the State of the other Contracting Party, may be made subject of an examination (in this Article called "ramp inspection"), without unreasonable delay. This would be an inspection by the authorized representatives of the other Contracting Party, on board and around the aircraft. However the obligations mentioned in Article 33 of the Convention, the objective of this inspection will be to check both the validity of the aircraft documents and those of its crew and the apparent condition of the aircraft and its equipment, in accordance with the established effective norms on the base of the Convention.

4. If any such ramp inspection or series of ramp inspections gives rise to:

a. serious concerns that an aircraft or the operation of an aircraft does not comply with the minimum standards established at that time pursuant to the Convention, or

b. serious concerns that there is a lack of effective maintenance and administration of safety standards established at that time pursuant to the Convention,

the Contracting Party carrying out the inspection shall, for the purposes of Article 33 of the Convention, be free to conclude that the requirements under which the certificate or licenses in respect of that aircraft or in respect of the crew of that aircraft had been issued or rendered valid, or that the requirements under which that aircraft is operated, are not equal to or above the minimum standards established pursuant to the Convention.

5. In the event that access for the purpose of undertaking a ramp inspection of an aircraft operated by the designated airline of a Contracting Party in accordance with paragraph (3) above is denied by the representative of that airline, the other Contracting Party shall be free to infer that serious concerns of the type referred to in paragraph (4) above arise and draw the conclusions referred in that paragraph.

6. Each Contracting Party reserves the right to suspend or vary the operating authorization of the airline of the other Contracting Party immediately in the case the first Contracting Party concludes, whether as a result of a ramp inspection, the denial of an access to a ramp inspection or a series of ramp inspection, consultation or otherwise, that immediate action is essential to the safety of an airline operation.

7. Any action by one Contracting Party in accordance with paragraphs (2) or (6) above shall be discontinued once the basis of the taking of that action ceases to exist.

ARTICLE 14

Aviation Security

1. Consistent with their rights and obligations under international law, the Contracting Parties reaffirm that their obligation to each other to protect the security of civil aviation against acts of unlawful interference forms an integral part of this Agreement. Without limiting the generality of their rights and obligations under international law, the Contracting Parties shall in particular act in conformity with the provisions of the Convention on Offenses and Certain Other Acts Committed on Board Aircraft, signed at Tokyo on 14 September 1963; the Convention for the Suppression of Unlawful Seizure of Aircraft, signed at the Hague on 16 December 1970; the Convention for the Suppression of Unlawful Acts Against the Safety of Civil Aviation, signed at Montreal on 23 September 1971; the Protocol for the Suppression of Unlawful Acts of Violence at Airports Serving International Civil Aviation, signed at Montreal on 24 February 1988 and the Convention on the Marking of Plastic Explosives for the Purpose of Detection, done at Montreal on 1 March 1991, or any other Convention on aviation security to which the Contracting Parties are parties.

2. Upon request, the Contracting Parties shall provide all necessary assistance to each other to prevent acts of unlawful seizure of civil aircraft and other unlawful acts against the safety of such aircraft, their passengers and crew, of airports and air navigation facilities, and to address any other threat to the security of civil aviation.

3. The Contracting Parties, in their mutual relations, shall act in conformity with all aviation security standards and appropriate recommended practices established by ICAO and designated as Annexes to the Convention on International Civil Aviation to the extent that such security provisions are applicable to the Contracting Parties. They shall require that operators of aircraft of their registry or operators of aircraft who have their principal place of business or permanent residence in their territory and the operators of airports in their territory act in conformity with such aviation security provisions as are applicable to the Contracting Parties. Accordingly each Contracting Party shall advise the other Contracting Party of any difference between its national regulations and practices and the aviation security standards of the Annexes referred to above. Either Contracting Party may request immediate consultations with the other Contracting Party at any time to discuss any such differences which shall be held in accordance with paragraph (2) of Article 18 of the present Agreement.

4. Each Contracting Party agrees that such operators of aircraft may be required to observe the aviation security provisions referred to in paragraph (3) above required by the other Contracting Party for entry into, departure from, or while within, the territory of that other Contracting Party. Each Contracting Party shall secure that adequate measures are effectively applied within its territory to protect the aircraft and to inspect passengers, crew, carry-on items, baggage, cargo and aircraft stores prior to and during boarding or loading. Each Contracting Party shall also give sympathetic consideration to any request from the other Contracting Party for reasonable special security measures to meet a particular threat.

5. When an incident or threat of an incident of unlawful seizure of civil aircraft or other unlawful acts against the safety to such aircraft, their passengers and crew, airports or air navigation facilities occurs, the Contracting Parties shall assist each other by facilitating communications and other appropriate measures intended to terminate rapidly and safely such incident or threat thereof, with minimum risk to life.

6. Each Contracting Party shall take such measures, as it may find practicable, to ensure that an aircraft subject to an act of unlawful seizure or other acts of unlawful interference, which has landed in the territory of the respective State is detained on the ground unless its departure is necessitated by the overriding duty to protect human life. Wherever practicable, such measures shall be taken on the basis of mutual consultations.

ARTICLE 15
Flight Schedule Submission

1. The designated airline(s) of each Contracting Party shall submit its envisaged flight schedules for approval to the aeronautical authorities of the other Contracting Party at least thirty (30) days prior to the operation of the agreed services.

2. For supplementary flights which the designated airline of one Contracting Party wishes to operate on the agreed services outside the approved flight schedule, that airline has to request prior permission from the aeronautical authorities of the other Contracting Party. Such requests shall be submitted in accordance with the national laws and regulations of the Contracting Parties. The same procedure shall be applied to any modification thereof.

ARTICLE 16
Statistics

The aeronautical authorities of either Contracting Party shall supply to the aeronautical authorities of the other Contracting Party at their request, such periodic or other statements of statistics as may be reasonably required for the purpose of reviewing the capacity provided on the agreed services by the designated airlines of the first Contracting Party. Such statements shall include all information required to determine the amount of traffic carried by that airline on the agreed services and the origins and destinations of such traffic.

ARTICLE 17
Application of National Laws and Regulations

1. The laws and regulations of a Contracting Party relating to the entry into, sojourn in or departure from its territory of aircraft engaged in international air services, or to the operation and navigation of such aircraft or flights of such aircraft over that territory shall be applied to aircraft of the airline designated by the other Contracting Party.

2. The laws and regulations of one Contracting Party governing entry into, sojourn in or departure from its territory of passengers, crew, baggage or cargo, including mail, such as formalities relating to entry, exit, clearance, emigration and immigration, aviation security, passports, customs, currency, health and quarantine, and postal shall be complied with by or on behalf of such passengers, crew, baggage, cargo or mail carried by the aircraft of the designated airlines of the other Contracting Party while they are within the said territory.

3. Each Contracting Party shall, upon request of the other Contracting Party, supply copies of the relevant laws, regulations and procedures referred to in this Agreement.

ARTICLE 18

Consultations and Amendment

1. In a spirit of close co-operation, the aeronautical authorities of the Contracting Parties shall consult each other from time to time with a view to the implementation, interpretation, application or amendment of this Agreement and the Annex thereto.

2. Should one Contracting Party request consultations with a view to modify the present Agreement or its Annexes, such consultations shall begin at the earliest possible date but not later than sixty (60) days from the date the other Contracting Party receives the written request, unless otherwise agreed by the Contracting Parties. Such consultations may be conducted through discussion or by correspondence. Each Contracting Party shall prepare and present during such consultations relevant evidence in support of its position in order to facilitate rational and economic decisions to be taken.

3. If either of the Contracting Parties considers it desirable to amend any provision of this Agreement, such modification shall enter into force thirty (30) days after the date on which the Contracting Parties notify each other the fulfillment of the necessary requirements established by their respective national legislation for such purpose.

4. Amendments to the Annex I may be by direct agreement between the aeronautical authorities of the Contracting Parties. They shall be applied from the date they have been agreea upon and enter into force when confirmed by an exchange of diplomatic notes.

ARTICLE 19

Settlement of Disputes

1. If any dispute arises between the Contracting Parties relating to the interpretation or application of this Agreement, the Contracting Parties shall in first place endeavor to settle their dispute by negotiations between their aeronautical authorities.

2. If the said aeronautical authorities fail to reach a settlement by negotiation, the dispute shall be settled through diplomatic channels.

3. If the Contracting Parties fail to reach a settlement pursuant to paragraphs (1) and (2) above, either Contracting Party may in accordance with its relevant laws and regulations refer the dispute to an arbitral tribunal of three arbitrators, one to be named by each Contracting Party and the third arbitrator, who shall be the umpire, to be agreed upon by the two arbitrators so chosen, provided that such arbitrator shall not be a national of either Contracting Party and shall be a national of a State having diplomatic relations with each of the Contracting Parties at the time of appointment.

Each Contracting Parties shall nominate its arbitrator within a period of sixty (60) days from the date of receipt, through registered mail, of a notice of arbitration. The umpire shall be appointed within a further period of sixty (60) days following the appointment of the arbitrator by each of the Contracting Parties.

If a Contracting Party fails to nominate its arbitrator within the specified period or in case the chosen arbitrators fail to agree on the umpire within the mentioned period, each Contracting Party may request the President of the Council of ICAO to appoint the umpire or the arbitrator representing the failing Contracting Party, as the case may require.

4. The Vice-President or a senior member of the Council of ICAO, not being a national of either of the Contracting Parties, as the case may be, shall replace the President of ICAO in its arbitral duties, as mentioned in paragraphs (3) of this Article, in case of absence or incompetence of the latter.

5. The arbitral tribunal shall determine its procedures and the place of arbitration subject to provisions agreed upon between the Contracting Parties.

6. The decisions of the arbitral tribunal shall be final and binding upon the Contracting Parties to the dispute.

7. If either Contracting Party or the designated airline of either Contracting Party fails to comply with the decision given under paragraph (2) of this Article, the other Contracting Party may limit, suspend or revoke any rights or privileges which have been granted by virtue of this Agreement to the Contracting Party in default.

8. Each Contracting Party shall bear the expenses of its own arbitrator. The expenses of the umpire, including his fees and any expenses incurred by ICAO in connection with the appointment of the umpire and/or the arbitrator of the failing Contracting Party as referred to in paragraph (3) of this Article shall be shared equally by the Contracting Parties.

9. Pending the submission to arbitration and thereafter until the arbitral tribunal publishes its award, the Contracting Parties shall, except in the event of termination, continue to perform all their obligations under this Agreement without prejudice to a final adjustment in accordance with the said award.

ARTICLE 20

Registration

This Agreement, its Annexes and all amendments thereto shall be registered with ICAO.

ARTICLE 21

Multilateral Agreements

In the event of conclusion of multilateral convention or agreement concerning air transport to which both Contracting Parties adhere, this Agreement shall be modified to conform with the provisions of such convention or agreement.

ARTICLE 22

Termination

This Agreement is concluded for an indefinite period of time.

Either Contracting Party may at any time give notice to the other Contracting Party to its decision to terminate this Agreement. Such notice shall simultaneously be communicated to ICAO.

In such case, the Agreement shall terminate twelve (12) months after the date of receipt of the notice by the other Contracting Party unless the notice to terminate is withdrawn by mutual agreement before the expiry of this period. In the absence of acknowledgement of receipt by the other Contracting Party, the notice shall be deemed to have been received fourteen (14) working days after the date on which ICAO shall have received communication thereof.

ARTICLE 23

Entry into Force

This Agreement shall enter into force thirty (30) days after the Contracting Parties have notified to each other through the diplomatic channels the fulfillment of their constitutional formalities for such purpose.

In witness thereof the undersigned plenipotentiaries, being duly authorized thereto by their respective Governments, have signed this Agreement comprising twenty three (23) Articles and two (2) Annexes.

Done in Ankara on this seventeenth day of December of two thousand and thirteen, in duplicate, in the Spanish, Turkish and English languages. All texts are being equally authentic. In case of any divergence of implementation or interpretation, the English text shall prevail.

FOR THE GOVERNMENT OF THE UNITED MEXICAN STATES	FOR THE GOVERNMENT OF THE REPUBLIC OF TURKEY
José Antonio MEADE KURIBREÑA Secretary of Foreign Affairs	Hayati YAZICI Minister of Customs and Trade

ANNEX I
ROUTE SCHEDULE

1. The airlines designated by the United Mexican States shall be entitled to operate air services in both directions as follows:

From	Intermediate Points	To	Beyond Points
Points in the United Mexican States	Any Point(s)	Points in Turkey	Any Point(s)

2. The airlines designated by the Republic of Turkey shall be entitled to operate air services in both directions as follows:

From	Intermediate Points	To	Beyond Points
Points in Turkey	Any Point(s)	Points in the United Mexican States	Any Point(s)

Notes:

1. Intermediate and beyond points may be omitted by the designated airline(s) on any or all flights at their discretion provided that such services on this route shall start and terminate in the territory of the Contracting Party designating the airline.

2. The designated airlines shall be allowed to exercise full 3rd and 4th freedom traffic rights.

3. The designated airlines may only exercise 5th freedom traffic rights when agreed upon and previously authorized by the aeronautical authorities of both Contracting Parties.

4. The designated airline(s) of both Contracting Parties shall submit for approval to the aeronautical authority of the other Contracting Party at least thirty (30) days prior to the inauguration of its services, the timetable of intended services, specifying the frequency, the type of aircraft, and period of validity. Minor schedule changes of temporary nature may be requested forty eight (48) hours in advance.

ANNEX II

CODE SHARING

1. The designated airline(s) of either Contracting Party may enter into marketing arrangements such as blocked space, code sharing or other commercial arrangements with:

a) an airline or airlines of the same Contracting Party,

b) an airline or airlines of the other Contracting Party,

c) an airline or airlines of a third country.

provided that all airlines in the above arrangements hold the appropriate route and traffic rights, and, in respect of each ticket sold, the purchaser is informed at the point of sale which airline will operate each section of the service.

2. It is the common understanding of both Contracting Parties that code-share services are not counted against the frequency entitlement of the marketing carrier.

3. No service shall be held out by an airline of one Contracting Party for the carriage of local passengers between a point in the territory of the other Contracting Party and a point in a third State unless that airline has the necessary traffic rights to operate and carry traffic between those two points.

[SPANISH TEXT – TEXTE ESPAGNOL]

CONVENIO SOBRE SERVICIOS AÉREOS ENTRE EL GOBIERNO DE LOS ESTADOS UNIDOS MEXICANOS Y EL GOBIERNO DE LA REPÚBLICA DE TURQUÍA

El Gobierno de los Estados Unidos Mexicanos y el Gobierno de la República de Turquía, en adelante "las Partes Contratantes";

SIENDO partes de la Convención sobre Aviación Civil Internacional y del Convenio Relativo al Tránsito de los Servicios Aéreos Internacionales, abiertos a firma en Chicago el 7 de diciembre de 1944;

DESEANDO facilitar la expansión de oportunidades en los servicios aéreos internacionales;

RECONOCIENDO que los servicios aéreos internacionales eficientes y competitivos mejoran el crecimiento económico, el comercio, el turismo, la inversión y el bienestar de los consumidores;

DESEANDO asegurar el más alto grado de seguridad operacional y seguridad de la aviación en los servicios aéreos internacionales y reafirmando su grave preocupación sobre los actos o amenazas contra la seguridad de las aeronaves, que ponen en peligro la seguridad de las personas o los bienes, afectando negativamente la operación de los servicios aéreos y socavando la confianza del público en la seguridad de la aviación civil, y

DESEANDO concluir un Convenio con el propósito de establecer y operar servicios aéreos entre sus respectivos territorios,

Han acordado lo siguiente:

ARTÍCULO 1
Definiciones

Para el propósito de este Convenio, salvo que el contexto lo requiera de otra manera:

a. "Autoridades Aeronáuticas" significa, para el caso de los Estados Unidos Mexicanos, la Secretaría de Comunicaciones y Transportes, a través de la Dirección General de Aeronáutica Civil y para el caso de la República de Turquía, el Ministerio de Transportes, Asuntos Marítimos y Comunicaciones, a través de la Dirección General de Aviación Civil, o en ambos casos, cualquier persona o entidad autorizada para ejercer las funciones actualmente asignadas a dichas autoridades;

b. "Convenio" significa este Convenio, sus Anexos y las enmiendas a éstos;

c. "Servicios convenidos" significa los servicios aéreos internacionales que pueden ser operados de conformidad con las disposiciones del presente Convenio en las rutas especificadas;

d. "Anexos" significan los Anexos a este Convenio o sus enmiendas de conformidad con las disposiciones del Artículo 18 (Consultas y Enmiendas) de este Convenio. Los Anexos forman parte integrante del presente Convenio y toda referencia al Convenio incluirá los Anexos, salvo acuerdo expreso en contrario;

e. "Servicio aéreo", "servicio aéreo internacional", "línea aérea" y "escala para fines no comerciales" tienen los significados especificados en el Artículo 96 de la Convención;

f. "Capacidad" significa:

- en relación con una aeronave, la capacidad de carga disponible en una aeronave para una ruta o sección de una ruta;

- en relación con un servicio aéreo especificado, la capacidad utilizada de una aeronave en dicho servicio, multiplicado por la frecuencia operada por la aeronave sobre un periodo determinado, en una ruta o sección de una ruta;

g. "Convención" significa la Convención sobre Aviación Civil Internacional abierta a firma en Chicago el 7 de diciembre de 1944, incluyendo cualquier Anexo adoptado bajo el Artículo 90 de esa Convención y cualquier enmienda a los Anexos de la Convención, de conformidad con los Artículos 90 y 94 de la misma, en la medida en que dichos Anexos y enmiendas hayan entrado en vigor o hayan sido ratificados por ambas Partes Contratantes;

h. "Línea(s) aérea(s) designada(s)" significa cualquier línea(s) aérea(s) que haya(n) sido designada(s) y autorizada(s) de conformidad con el Artículo 3 (Designación y Autorización) de este Convenio;

i. "Asistencia en tierra" incluye, pero no se limita, a los pasajeros, carga y equipaje, y el suministro de instalaciones y/o servicios de avituallamiento;

j. "OACI" significa la Organización de Aviación Civil Internacional;

k. "Transporte aéreo internacional" significa el transporte aéreo que pasa a través del espacio aéreo sobre el territorio de más de un Estado;

l. "Línea aérea de comercialización" significa una línea aérea que ofrece transportación aérea en una aeronave operada por otra línea aérea, por virtud de código compartido;

m. "Itinerario" significa el cuadro de las rutas para operar servicios de transporte aéreo, anexo al presente Convenio y cualquier modificación realizada de conformidad con las disposiciones del Artículo 18 del presente Convenio;

n. "Rutas especificadas" significa las rutas establecidas o a ser establecidas en el Anexo a este Convenio;

o. "Refacciones" significa los artículos para reparar o de remplazo para su incorporación en una aeronave, incluyendo motores;

p. "Tarifa" significa el precio cobrado para la transportación de pasajeros, equipaje y carga, así como las condiciones y reglas que regulan la aplicación del costo de la transportación sobre las características del servicio prestado, bajo las cuales esa cantidad será aplicada, excluyendo la remuneración y otras condiciones relativas al transporte de correo;

q. "Territorio" tiene el significado especificado en el Artículo 2 de la Convención;

r. "Tráfico" significa, pasajeros, equipaje, carga y correo;

s. "Equipo regular" significa los artículos distintos a provisiones, refacciones de naturaleza removible, para uso a bordo de una aeronave durante el vuelo, incluyendo primeros auxilios y equipo de supervivencia;

t. "Cargos al usuario" significa las tarifas y cargos cobrados por el uso de aeropuertos, servicios de navegación y otros servicios conexos, ofrecidos por una Parte Contratante a la Otra.

ARTÍCULO 2

Otorgamiento de Derechos

1. Cada Parte Contratante otorga a la otra Parte Contratante los siguientes derechos para la operación de servicios aéreos regulares internacionales, por las líneas aéreas designadas de la otra Parte Contratante, en las rutas especificadas en el Anexo I del presente Convenio:

a. el derecho a sobrevolar el territorio de la otra Parte Contratante, sin aterrizar en el mismo,

b. el derecho a realizar escalas en dicho territorio para fines no comerciales,

c. el derecho a realizar escalas en dicho territorio, en los puntos especificados para esa ruta en el Anexo I del presente Convenio con el propósito de desembarcar y embarcar tráfico internacional en combinación o por separado,

d. los demás derechos especificados en este Convenio.

2. Nada de lo dispuesto en el numeral (1) de este Artículo será interpretado en el sentido de conferir a las líneas aéreas de una Parte Contratante, el privilegio de llevar a bordo, en el territorio de la otra Parte Contratante, tráfico transportado mediante remuneración o renta y llevado a otro punto en el territorio de esa otra Parte Contratante.

ARTÍCULO 3
Designación y Autorización

1. Cada Parte Contratante tendrá el derecho de designar a una o más líneas aéreas con el propósito de operar los servicios convenidos en las rutas especificadas. Tal designación será efectuada mediante notificación escrita a través de la vía diplomática.

2. Al recibir dicha designación, las autoridades aeronáuticas de la otra Parte Contratante otorgarán a la(s) línea(s) aérea(s) designada(s), sin demora, la autorización de operación correspondiente, de conformidad con los numerales (3) y (4) de este Artículo.

3. Las autoridades aeronáuticas de una Parte Contratante podrán requerir a la(s) línea(s) aérea(s) designada(s) de la otra Parte Contratante, comprobar que está(n) calificadas para cumplir con las condiciones prescritas por las leyes y reglamentos, que son normal y razonablemente aplicados por dichas autoridades a las operaciones de servicios aéreos internacionales, de conformidad con las disposiciones de la Convención.

4. Cada Parte Contratante tendrá el derecho de negar el otorgamiento de las autorizaciones de operación referidas en el numeral (2) de este Artículo, o de imponer las condiciones que considere necesarias sobre el ejercicio de los derechos especificados en el Artículo 2 (Otorgamiento de Derechos) del presente Convenio, por parte de una línea aérea designada, en cualquier caso en que la Parte Contratante no le satisfaga que:

a. la propiedad sustancial y control efectivo de la línea aérea pertenezcan a la Parte Contratante que designó a la línea aérea o a sus nacionales; y/o

b. el Gobierno que ha designado la línea aérea, sigue manteniendo y administrando las normas establecidas en el Artículo 13 (Seguridad Operacional) y Artículo 14 (Seguridad de la Aviación) de este Convenio.

5. Cuando una línea aérea haya sido designada y autorizada, podrá iniciar en cualquier momento la operación de los servicios aéreos convenidos, siempre y cuando la capacidad acordada y las tarifas establecidas de conformidad con las disposiciones del Artículo 5 (Capacidad) y del Artículo 6 (Tarifas) de este Convenio, se encuentren en vigor con respecto de ese servicio.

ARTÍCULO 4

Revocación o Suspensión de la Autorización de Operación

1. Cada Parte Contratante tendrá el derecho de revocar una autorización de operación o suspender el ejercicio de los derechos especificados en el Artículo 2 (Otorgamiento de Derechos) de este Convenio, a la(s) línea(s) aérea(s) designada(s) por la otra Parte Contratante, o imponer las condiciones que considere necesarias sobre el ejercicio de esos derechos:

a. en cualquier caso en que no se compruebe que la propiedad substancial y el control efectivo de esa línea aérea son mantenidos por la Parte Contratante que designa a la línea aérea o por sus nacionales, o

b. en caso de incumplimiento de esa línea aérea, de las leyes o reglamentos de la Parte Contratante que otorga los derechos, o

c. en caso que la línea aérea no opere conforme a las condiciones prescritas en el presente Convenio.

2. A menos que la inmediata revocación, suspensión o imposición de las condiciones mencionadas en el numeral (1) de este Artículo sea necesaria para prevenir nuevas violaciones a las leyes o reglamentos, dicho derecho será ejercido sólo después de haber celebrado consultas con las autoridades aeronáuticas del Estado de la otra Parte Contratante. En tal caso, las consultas comenzarán en un periodo de sesenta (60) días a partir de la fecha de solicitud de las mismas, realizada por cualquiera de las Partes Contratantes

ARTÍCULO 5
Capacidad

1. La(s) línea(s) aérea(s) designada(s) de cada Parte Contratante gozarán de oportunidades justas y equitativas para la operación de servicios aéreos, para el transporte de tráfico entre los territorios de las dos Partes Contratantes.

2. En la operación de los servicios aéreos especificados, por parte de las línea(s) aérea(s) designada(s) de cualquiera de las Partes Contratantes, se considerarán los intereses de la línea aérea de la otra Parte Contratante, a fin de no afectar indebidamente los servicios que esta última línea aérea preste en la misma ruta o en una sección de ésta.

3. Los servicios prestados por las líneas aéreas designadas de las Partes Contratantes, se apegarán a las necesidades del público transportado en las rutas especificadas y tendrán como objetivo principal proporcionar, a un factor de carga razonable, la capacidad adecuada para responder a las necesidades actuales y razonablemente previsibles para el transporte de pasajeros, carga y correo entre los territorios de las Partes Contratantes.

4. En la operación de los servicios convenidos, la capacidad total que será prestada y la frecuencia de los servicios operados por las líneas aéreas designadas de cada Parte Contratante, serán mutuamente determinados por las autoridades aeronáuticas de las Partes Contratantes, antes del inicio de operaciones. La capacidad y la frecuencia de los servicios inicialmente determinados podrán ser revisados y modificados periódicamente, por dichas autoridades.

ARTÍCULO 6
Tarifas

1. Cada Parte Contratante permitirá que las tarifas para los servicios aéreos internacionales, operados hacia o desde su territorio, sean establecidas por las líneas aéreas designadas a niveles razonables, tomando debidamente en cuenta todos los factores relevantes, incluyendo el costo de operación, ganancias razonables y las tarifas de otras líneas aéreas. Las Partes Contratantes podrán intervenir en:

a. la prevención de prácticas o precios discriminatorios irracionales;

b. la protección a los consumidores, de precios que sean irracionalmente altos o restrictivos, debido al abuso de una posición dominante; y

c. la protección a las líneas aéreas de precios que sean artificialmente bajos, debido al subsidio o apoyo gubernamental.

2. Las líneas aéreas designadas de una Parte Contratante cumplirán con los requisitos establecidos en el numeral (1) y presentarán las tarifas a la otra Parte Contratante.

3. Ninguna Parte Contratante permitirá que su(s) línea(s) aérea(s) designada(s) abusen de su poder de mercado en el establecimiento de tarifas, ya sea en conjunto con cualquier otra línea(s) aérea(s) o por separado, de modo que haya(n) debilitado o intentado debilitar gravemente a un competidor, al ser línea aérea designada de la otra Parte Contratante o excluyendo a dicho competidor de una ruta.

4. Las Partes Contratantes acuerdan que las siguientes prácticas realizadas por las líneas aéreas, en relación con el establecimiento de tarifas, podrán ser consideradas como posibles prácticas de competencia desleal, que podrían ser objeto de un examen más detallado:

a. las tarifas y tasas sobre rutas, cuyo precio total sea insuficiente para cubrir los costos para la prestación de los servicios de que se trate;

b. que las prácticas en cuestión sean reiteradas y no temporales;

c. que las prácticas en cuestión tengan un grave efecto económico o que causen daños significativos a la(s) las línea(s) aérea(s) designada(s) de la otra Parte Contratante; y

d. las conductas que indiquen el abuso de una posición dominante en una ruta.

5. En el supuesto de que cualquier autoridad aeronáutica no esté de acuerdo con una tarifa en vigor de una línea aérea de la otra Parte Contratante, las autoridades aeronáuticas resolverán el asunto a través de consultas, si es solicitado por cualquiera de las autoridades. En cualquier caso, la autoridad aeronáutica de una Parte Contratante no implementará acciones unilaterales para prevenir la aplicación o la continuación de una tarifa de una línea aérea de la otra Parte Contratante.

6. No obstante lo anterior, las líneas aéreas designadas de una Parte Contratante proporcionarán, a solicitud de las autoridades aeronáuticas de la otra Parte Contratante, la información relacionada con el establecimiento de las tarifas, conforme a las condiciones y formatos especificados por tales autoridades.

7. Ninguna Parte Contratante impondrá a las líneas aéreas designadas de la otra Parte Contratante el requisito de un primer rechazo, la relación de elevación, con cargo de no objeción, o cualquier otro requisito en relación con la capacidad, frecuencia o tráfico que pudieran resultar inconsistentes con los propósitos del presente Convenio.

ARTÍCULO 7
Derechos Aduaneros y Otros Gravámenes

1. Las aeronaves utilizadas por la línea aérea designada de cualquier Parte Contratante en la operación de servicios aéreos internacionales, así como su equipo regular, piezas de repuesto (incluyendo motores), suministros de combustibles, lubricantes, así como provisiones de la aeronave (incluyendo pero no limitado a artículos tales como alimentos, bebidas, tabaco y productos destinados para su venta o consumo de los pasajeros durante el vuelo) que estén a bordo de dicha aeronave, estarán exentos por la otra Parte Contratante, sobre la base de reciprocidad y de conformidad con la legislación aplicable, de todos los derechos aduaneros, cuotas de inspección y otros gravámenes similares, al arribar al territorio de la otra Parte Contratante, a condición de que dicho equipo, piezas de repuesto, provisiones y suministros de la aeronave permanezcan a bordo de la aeronave hasta el momento en que sean re-exportados o sean utilizados a bordo de la aeronave en una parte del viaje realizado sobre ese territorio.

2. Los siguientes artículos y equipo estarán exentos por la otra Parte Contratante, sobre la base de reciprocidad y de conformidad con la legislación aplicable, de todos los derechos aduaneros, cuotas de inspección y otros cargos similares que no se basen en los costos de los servicios suministrados a la llegada, incluyendo:

a. el equipo regular, combustible, lubricantes, suministros técnicos consumibles, provisiones de la aeronave (incluyendo pero no limitado a artículos tales como alimentos, bebidas y tabaco), introducidos al territorio de la otra Parte Contratante o en nombre de una línea aérea designada o llevados a bordo de la aeronave operada por esa línea aérea designada, destinados al uso de la aeronave en servicios aéreos internacionales, incluso cuando dicho equipo regular y los otros artículos sean usados en cualquier parte del viaje realizado sobre el territorio de la otra Parte Contratante.

b. los repuestos (incluyendo los motores) introducidos al territorio de la otra Parte Contratante por o en nombre de una línea aérea designada o llevados a bordo de una aeronave operada por la línea aérea designada para el mantenimiento o reparación de la aeronave operada en servicios aéreos internacionales por esa línea aérea designada; y

c. boletos impresos, guías aéreas, cualquier material impreso que porte la insignia de la línea aérea designada de una Parte Contratante y material publicitario distribuido gratuitamente por esa línea aérea designada.

El material referido en los incisos (a), (b) y (c) antes mencionados, deberá permanecer bajo control o supervisión aduanero.

3. El equipo regular de la aeronave, piezas de repuesto (incluyendo motores), provisiones y suministros de combustibles y lubricantes de la aeronave (incluyendo fluidos hidráulicos), así como materiales y suministros mantenidos a bordo de la aeronave de cualquiera de las Partes Contratantes, podrán ser descargados en el territorio de la otra Parte Contratante, sólo con la autorización de las autoridades aduaneras de dicho territorio. En tal caso, serán puestos bajo supervisión de dichas autoridades, hasta el momento en que sean re-exportados o, de otra manera, como lo disponga la legislación aduanera de esa Parte Contratante.

4. Los cargos correspondientes a los servicios prestados por almacenamiento y despacho de aduana serán cobrados de conformidad con las leyes y reglamentos nacionales de cualquiera de las Partes Contratantes.

ARTÍCULO 8
Tránsito Directo

Sujeto a las leyes y reglamentos de cada Parte Contratante, los pasajeros, equipaje y carga en tránsito directo a través del territorio de una Parte Contratante y que no abandonen el espacio del aeropuerto reservado para dichos propósitos, sólo estarán sujetos a un control simplificado, a menos que las medidas de seguridad contra agresiones, piratería aérea y tráfico de narcóticos requieran un tratamiento distinto. El equipaje y la carga en tránsito directo estarán exentos de derechos aduaneros y otros gravámenes similares.

ARTÍCULO 9

Cargos al Usuario

1. Los aeropuertos, seguridad de la aviación y otras instalaciones y servicios conexos que sean prestados en el territorio de una Parte Contratante estarán disponibles para uso de las líneas aéreas de una Parte Contratante en condiciones no menos favorables que las más favorables disponibles para cualquier línea aérea que preste servicios aéreos internacionales similares en el momento en que sean realizados los arreglos para su uso.

2. La(s) línea(s) aérea(s) designada(s) de una Parte Contratante estará(n) autorizada(s), de conformidad con las leyes y reglamentos nacionales de ambas Partes Contratantes y sobre la base de reciprocidad, a prestar su propio servicio en tierra en el territorio de la otra Parte Contratante y, opcionalmente, a obtener tales servicios, total o parcialmente, de cualquier agente autorizado por las autoridades aeronáuticas de la otra Parte Contratante para la prestación de tales servicios, de así ser requerido por sus leyes y reglamentos nacionales.

3. Las condiciones y la recaudación de tarifas y cargos impuestos en el territorio de una Parte Contratante sobre una línea aérea de la otra Parte Contratante, por la utilización de aeropuertos, seguridad de la aviación y otros servicios e instalaciones conexos, serán justas y equitativas. Cualquier tarifa o cargo impuesto a una línea aérea de la otra Parte Contratante será gravado sobre un trato no menos favorable que el trato más favorable que se conceda a una línea aérea que preste servicios aéreos internacionales similares en el momento en que las tarifas o cargos sean impuestos.

4. Cada Parte Contratante promoverá la realización de consultas entre sus autoridades tributarias y las líneas aéreas que utilizan las instalaciones y servicios o, cuando sea propicio, a través de las organizaciones de representación de las líneas aéreas. Los usuarios serán informados de cualquier propuesta de modificación a los cargos al usuario, con la mayor antelación posible, a efecto de permitirles expresar sus puntos de vista antes de que los cambios sean efectuados.

ARTÍCULO 10
Personal Extranjero y Acceso a Servicios Locales

1. De conformidad con las leyes y reglamentos de la otra Parte Contratante relacionados con la entrada, residencia y empleo, la(s) línea(s) aérea(s) designada(s) de una Parte Contratante estará(n) autorizada(s) para traer y mantener en el territorio de la otra Parte Contratante su propio personal administrativo, comercial, de ventas, operacional, técnico y otro tipo de personal especializado, necesario para la operación de los servicios convenidos.

2. Los requisitos para este personal podrán ser cumplidos, a elección de la(s) línea(s) aérea(s) designada(s) de una Parte Contratante, por su propio personal o por medio del personal y servicios de cualquier otra organización, empresa o línea aérea que opere en el territorio de la otra Parte Contratante y que haya sido autorizada para proporcionar dichos servicios a otras líneas aéreas.

3. Los representantes y personal estarán sujetos a las leyes y reglamentos en vigor de la otra Parte Contratante. De conformidad con dichas leyes y reglamentos, cada Parte Contratante otorgará, sobre la base de reciprocidad y con un mínimo de retraso, las autorizaciones de empleo necesarias, las visas de visitante u otros documentos similares, a los representantes y personal referidos en el numeral (1) del presente Artículo.

ARTÍCULO 11
Conversión de Moneda y Transferencia de Utilidades

1. Cada una de las líneas aéreas designadas tendrá el derecho de vender y expedir su propia documentación de transportación en el territorio de la otra Parte Contratante a través de sus oficinas de ventas y, a su discreción, a través de sus agentes. Tales líneas aéreas tendrán el derecho de comercializar el transporte y cualquier persona estará en libertad para adquirirlo en cualquier moneda de libre uso y/o en la moneda de dicho país, de conformidad con las leyes y reglamentos nacionales aplicables.

2. Cada una de las líneas aéreas designadas tendrá el derecho de convertir y transferir a su país, los ingresos respecto de los gastos obtenidos en relación con el transporte de tráfico. A falta de disposiciones adecuadas de un acuerdo de pagos entre las Partes Contratantes, las transferencias antes mencionadas se realizarán en divisas de libre uso y de conformidad con la legislación nacional y la regulación cambiaria extranjera aplicable.

3. La conversión y transferencia de dichos ingresos se permitirá sin restricción al tipo de cambio aplicable a esas transacciones en la fecha en que estos ingresos sean presentados para su conversión y transferencia, y no estará sujeta a gravamen alguno, excepto a aquéllos normalmente aplicados por los bancos para la realización de dichas conversiones y transferencias.

4. La(s) línea(s) aérea(s) designada(s) de cada Parte Contratante tendrá(n) el derecho de pagar, a su discreción, gastos locales incluyendo compras de combustible en el territorio de la otra Parte Contratante, en moneda local o, siempre y cuando concuerde con la legislación monetaria nacional, en divisas de libre uso.

ARTÍCULO 12

Convalidación de Certificados y Licencias

1. Los certificados de aeronavegabilidad, certificados de competencia y licencias, expedidos o convalidados por una Parte Contratante y que se encuentren en vigor, serán convalidados por la otra Parte Contratante para el propósito de operar los servicios convenidos en las rutas especificadas, siempre que los requisitos bajo los cuales fueron expedidos o convalidados dichos certificados o licencias, sean iguales o superiores a las normas mínimas que sean o puedan ser establecidas de conformidad con la Convención. No obstante, cada Parte Contratante se reserva el derecho de no reconocer, para los vuelos sobre su territorio, los certificados de competencia y licencias expedidos o convalidados a sus propios nacionales, por la otra Parte Contratantes o cualquier otro Estado.

2. Si los privilegios o condiciones de las licencias o certificados referidos en el numeral (1) del presente Artículo, expedidos por las autoridades aeronáuticas de una Parte Contratante a cualquier persona o línea aérea designada o respecto de una aeronave utilizada en la operación de los servicios convenidos, debe permitir una diferencia entre las normas mínimas establecidas conforme a la Convención y aquéllas que hayan sido presentadas ante la OACI, la otra Parte Contratante podrá solicitar consultas entre las autoridades aeronáuticas con la intención de esclarecer la práctica en cuestión. La falta de un acuerdo satisfactorio será motivo para la aplicación del Artículo 4 (Revocación o Suspensión de la Autorización de Operación) del presente Convenio.

ARTÍCULO 13
Seguridad Operacional

1. Cada Parte Contratante podrá solicitar consultas en cualquier momento respecto de las normas de seguridad adoptadas por la otra Parte Contratante en cualquier área relacionada con los servicios e instalaciones aeronáuticas, tripulaciones, aeronaves o su operación. Tales consultas tendrán lugar dentro de los (30) días siguientes a dicha solicitud.

2. Si tras haberse celebrado las consultas, una Parte Contratante encuentra que la otra Parte Contratante no mantiene ni administra efectivamente, en los aspectos mencionados en el numeral 1 del presente Artículo, las normas de seguridad en cualquier área y que sean por lo menos, iguales a las normas mínimas establecidas en ese momento de conformidad con la Convención, la primera Parte Contratante notificará a la otra Parte Contratante los hallazgos y los pasos que considere necesarios para cumplir con las normas mínimas de la OACI. La otra Parte Contratante adoptará las acciones correctivas pertinentes en el periodo que sea acordado. La falta de adopción de medidas pertinentes dentro del periodo acordado, será motivo para la aplicación del Artículo 4 (Revocación o Suspensión de la Autorización de Operación) del presente Convenio.

3. No obstante las obligaciones mencionadas en el Artículo 16 de la Convención, se acuerda que cualquier aeronave operada por o en nombre de la línea aérea de una Parte Contratante en servicios hacia o desde el territorio del Estado de la otra Parte Contratante, podrá ser objeto de una inspección (en este Artículo denominada "inspección en rampa") mientras se encuentre en el territorio del Estado de la otra Parte Contratante, siempre que ello no cause demoras innecesarias. Se trataría de una inspección por parte de los representantes autorizados de la otra Parte Contratante, a bordo y alrededor de la aeronave. No obstante las obligaciones mencionadas en el Artículo 33 de la Convención, el objetivo de esta inspección será comprobar tanto la validez de los documentos de la aeronave y los de su tripulación, como el estado visible de la aeronave y su equipo, de conformidad con las normas efectivamente establecidas sobre la base de la Convención.

4. Si alguna inspección o series de inspecciones en rampa arrojaran:

a. graves indicios de que una aeronave o la operación de una aeronave no cumple con las normas mínimas establecidas en ese momento conforme a la Convención, o

b. graves indicios de la falta de mantenimiento efectivo y la administración de las normas de seguridad operacional establecidas en ese momento de conformidad con la Convención,

la Parte Contratante que realice la inspección, para los fines del Artículo 33 de la Convención, estará en libertad para concluir que los requisitos bajo los cuales los certificados o licencias respecto de esa aeronave o de la tripulación de esa aeronave han sido expedidos o convalidados, o que los requisitos bajo los cuales dicha aeronave es operada, no son similares o superiores a las normas mínimas establecidas de conformidad con la Convención.

5. En caso que los representantes de la línea aérea nieguen el acceso a una aeronave operada por la línea aérea designada de una Parte Contratante, para la realización de una inspección en rampa de conformidad con el numeral (3) del presente Artículo, la otra Parte Contratante estará en libertad para inferir que existen indicios graves, como los referidos en el numeral (4) del presente Artículo y determinar las conclusiones referidas en dicho numeral.

6. Cada Parte Contratante se reserva el derecho de suspender o modificar inmediatamente la autorización de operación de la línea aérea de la otra Parte Contratante en caso de que la primera Parte Contratante concluya que, como resultado de una inspección en rampa, la denegación de acceso para la realización de una o varias inspecciones en rampa, consultas o de otra forma, la acción inmediata referida es necesaria para la seguridad operacional de una línea aérea.

7. Cualquier acción realizada por una Parte Contratante, de conformidad con los numerales (2) o (6) antes referidos, será suspendida una vez que cesen las razones que la motivaron.

ARTÍCULO 14
Seguridad de la Aviación

1. De conformidad con los derechos y obligaciones que les impone el derecho internacional, las Partes Contratantes reafirman que su obligación mutua de proteger la seguridad de la aviación civil contra actos de interferencia ilícita, constituye parte integrante de este Convenio. Sin limitar la validez general de sus derechos y obligaciones en virtud del derecho internacional, las Partes Contratantes actuarán, en particular, de conformidad con las disposiciones del Convenio sobre las Infracciones y Ciertos Otros Actos Cometidos a Bordo de las Aeronaves, firmado en Tokio el 14 de septiembre de 1963; del Convenio para la Represión del Apoderamiento Ilícito de Aeronaves, firmado en La Haya el 16 de diciembre de 1970; del Convenio para la Represión de Actos Ilícitos contra la Seguridad de la Aviación Civil, firmado en Montreal el 23 de septiembre de 1971; del Protocolo para la Represión de Actos Ilícitos de Violencia en los Aeropuertos que Presten Servicio a la Aviación Civil Internacional, firmado en Montreal el 24 de febrero de 1988, y del Convenio sobre la Marcación de Explosivos Plásticos para los Fines de Detección, hecho en Montreal el 1° de marzo de 1991 o cualquier otra convención sobre seguridad de la aviación de la que las Partes Contratantes sean partes.

2. Previa solicitud, las Partes Contratantes se prestarán toda la ayuda necesaria para prevenir actos de apoderamiento ilícito de aeronaves y otros actos ilícitos contra la seguridad operacional de dichas aeronaves, sus pasajeros y tripulación, aeropuertos e instalaciones de navegación aérea y para atender cualquier otra amenaza contra la seguridad de la aviación civil.

3. Las Partes Contratantes actuarán en sus relaciones mutuas de conformidad con todas las normas de seguridad de la aviación y las prácticas pertinentes recomendables de la OACI, referidas como Anexos a la Convención sobre Aviación Civil Internacional, en la medida en que esas disposiciones sobre seguridad sean aplicables a las Partes Contratantes. Éstas solicitarán que los operadores de aeronaves de su matrícula o que los operadores de aeronaves que tengan su principal centro de negocios o residencia permanente en su territorio, y a los operadores de aeropuertos en su territorio, actuar de conformidad con las disposiciones de seguridad de la aviación aplicables a las Partes Contratantes. En consecuencia, cada Parte Contratante dará aviso a la otra Parte Contratante sobre cualquier diferencia entre su reglamentación y prácticas nacionales y las normas de seguridad de la aviación establecidas en los Anexos antes referidos. Cualquiera de las Partes Contratantes podrá solicitar, en cualquier momento, consultas de manera inmediata con la otra Parte Contratante, para discutir cualquier diferencia, las cuales deberán realizarse de conformidad con el numeral (2) del Artículo 18 del presente Convenio.

4. Cada Parte Contratante podrá exigir a los operadores de aeronaves que observen las disposiciones sobre seguridad de la aviación que se mencionan en el numeral (3) anterior, exigidas por la otra Parte Contratante para la entrada, salida o durante la estancia en el territorio de la otra Parte Contratante. Cada Parte Contratante se asegurará de que en su territorio se apliquen efectivamente las medidas adecuadas para proteger la aeronave e inspeccionar a sus pasajeros, tripulación, los efectos personales, el equipaje, la carga y los suministros de la aeronave antes y durante el embarque o la estiba. Además, cada Parte Contratante considerará favorablemente cualquier solicitud de la otra Parte Contratante relacionadas con medidas razonables especiales de seguridad para afrontar una amenaza determinada.

5. Cuando se produzca un incidente o amenaza de incidente de apoderamiento ilícito de aeronaves civiles o de otros actos ilícitos contra la seguridad operacional de dichas aeronaves, sus pasajeros y tripulación, los aeropuertos o las instalaciones de navegación aérea, las Partes Contratantes se asistirán facilitando las comunicaciones y otras medidas apropiadas destinadas a detener en forma rápida y segura dicho incidente o amenaza, con el menor riesgo para la vida.

6. Cada Parte Contratante adoptará las medidas referidas como lo considere necesario, para asegurar que una aeronave sujeta a un acto de apoderamiento ilícito u otros actos de interferencia ilícita, que haya aterrizado en el territorio de su respectivo Estado, sea retenida a menos que su partida sea necesaria por el imperioso deber de proteger la vida humana. Cuando sea necesario, dichas medidas serán adoptadas sobre la base de consultas mutuas.

ARTÍCULO 15
Itinerarios

1. La(s) línea(s) aérea(s) designada(s) de cada Parte Contratante presentarán su proyecto de itinerario para aprobación de las autoridades aeronáuticas de la otra Parte Contratante, por lo menos treinta (30) días antes del inicio de operaciones de los servicios convenidos.

2. La línea aérea de una Parte Contratante que pretenda operar servicios complementarios en los servicios convenidos, adicionales a los contenidos en el itinerario aprobado, tendrá que solicitar previamente el permiso de las autoridades aeronáuticas de la otra Parte Contratante. Dichas solicitudes serán presentadas de conformidad con las leyes y reglamentos de las Partes Contratantes. El mismo procedimiento será aplicable a cualquier modificación que se realice al itinerario.

ARTÍCULO 16
Estadísticas

Las autoridades aeronáuticas de cualquiera de las Partes Contratantes proporcionarán a las autoridades aeronáuticas de la otra Parte Contratante, previa solicitud, estadísticas periódicas o de otro tipo, que puedan ser razonablemente requeridas con el propósito de revisar la capacidad prestada por las líneas aéreas designadas de la primera Parte Contratante, en los servicios convenidos. Tales estadísticas incluirán toda la información requerida para determinar la cantidad de tráfico transportado por esa línea aérea en los servicios convenidos y el origen y destino de dicho tráfico.

ARTÍCULO 17
Aplicación de Leyes y Reglamentos Nacionales

1. Las leyes y reglamentos de una Parte Contratante relativas a la entrada, permanencia o salida de aeronaves destinadas a la prestación de servicios aéreos internacionales desde su territorio, o a la operación y navegación de tales aeronaves o vuelos de dichas aeronaves sobre ese territorio, serán aplicables a las aeronaves de la línea aérea designada por la otra Parte Contratante.

2. Las leyes y reglamentos de una Parte Contratante que rigen la entrada, permanencia o salida de su territorio, de pasajeros, tripulación, equipaje o carga, incluyendo correo, así como las formalidades relativas a la entrada, salida, internación, emigración e inmigración, seguridad aérea, pasaportes, aduanas, moneda, salubridad y cuarentena, y correo, serán cumplidos por o en nombre de dichos pasajeros, tripulación, equipaje, carga o correo transportado por las aeronaves de las líneas aéreas designadas de la otra Parte Contratante, mientras se encuentren dentro de dicho territorio.

3. Cada Parte Contratante, a petición de la otra Parte Contratante, proporcionará copias de las leyes, reglamentos y procedimientos pertinentes, a que se refiere el presente Convenio.

ARTÍCULO 18
Consultas y Enmiendas

1. Las autoridades aeronáuticas de las Partes Contratantes, en un espíritu de estrecha cooperación, se consultarán mutuamente de manera periódica en relación con la implementación, la interpretación, la aplicación o la enmienda de este Convenio y sus Anexos.

2. En caso que una Parte Contratante solicite consultas con la intención de modificar el presente Convenio o sus Anexos, tales consultas iniciarán a la brevedad posible, sin exceder de sesenta (60) días a partir de la fecha en que la otra Parte Contratante reciba la solicitud por escrito, salvo acuerdo en contrario entre las Partes Contratantes. Tales consultas podrán realizarse de manera presencial o por correspondencia. Cada Parte Contratante preparará y presentará en dichas consultas, evidencia relevante que apoye su posición a fin de facilitar la toma de decisiones racionales y económicas.

3. Si cualquiera de las Partes Contratantes considera conveniente enmendar cualquier disposición de este Convenio, dicha modificación entrará en vigor treinta (30) días después de la fecha en que las Partes Contratantes se notifiquen el cumplimiento de los requisitos necesarios establecidos por su respectiva legislación nacional para tal efecto.

4. Las enmiendas al Anexo I podrán ser efectuadas por acuerdo directo entre las autoridades aeronáuticas de las Partes Contratantes. Tales enmiendas serán aplicables a partir de la fecha en que hayan sido acordadas y entrarán en vigor cuando sean confirmadas a través de un intercambio de notas diplomáticas.

ARTÍCULO 19
Solución de Controversias

1. Cualquier controversia que pudiera surgir entre las Partes Contratantes respecto de la interpretación o aplicación de este Convenio, las Partes Contratantes procurarán resolverla, en primera instancia, a través de negociaciones entre sus autoridades aeronáuticas.

2. Si tales autoridades aeronáuticas no lograran una solución a través de la negociación, la controversia se resolverá a través de los canales diplomáticos.

3. Si las Partes Contratantes no alcanzaran una solución de conformidad con los numerales (1) y (2) anteriores, cualquiera de las Partes Contratantes podrá, de conformidad con sus leyes y reglamentos aplicables, someter la controversia a un tribunal arbitral conformado por tres árbitros, uno nombrado por cada Parte Contratante y el tercer árbitro acordado por los dos árbitros nombrados por las Partes Contratantes, siempre que el tercer árbitro no sea nacional de cualquiera de las Partes Contratantes y sea nacional de un Estado que tenga relaciones diplomáticas con cada una de las Partes Contratantes en el momento del nombramiento.

Cada Parte Contratante nominará su árbitro dentro de un periodo de sesenta (60) días a partir de la fecha de recepción de la notificación de arbitraje, por medio de correo certificado. El tercer árbitro será nombrado en un periodo no mayor de sesenta (60) días, después del nombramiento del árbitro de cada una de las Partes Contratantes.

Si una Parte Contratante no lograre nombrar su árbitro dentro del periodo especificado o, en el supuesto de que los dos árbitros elegidos no lograren ponerse de acuerdo con respecto del tercer árbitro en el periodo referido, cada Parte Contratante podrá solicitar al Presidente del Consejo de la OACI que nombre al tercer árbitro o al árbitro de la Parte Contratante que no lo ha nombrado, según sea el caso.

4. En caso de ausencia o incompetencia del Presidente de la OACI, el Vice-presidente o un miembro de alto rango en el Consejo de la OACI, que no sea nacional de ninguna de las Partes Contratantes, según sea el caso, sustituirá al Presidente de la OACI en sus deberes arbitrales mencionados en el numeral (3) de este Artículo.

5. El tribunal arbitral determinará sus procedimientos y la sede del arbitraje, sujeto a las disposiciones acordadas entre las Partes Contratantes

6. Las decisiones del tribunal arbitral serán definitivas y vinculantes para las Partes Contratantes en la controversia.

7. Si cualquier Parte Contratante o línea aérea designada de cualquier Parte Contratante no cumple con la determinación establecida conforme al numeral (2) de este Artículo, la otra Parte Contratante podrá limitar, suspender o revocar los derechos o privilegios que hayan sido otorgados con base en este Convenio, a la Parte Contratante que incumple.

8. Cada Parte Contratante sufragará los gastos de su propio árbitro. Los gastos del tercer árbitro, incluyendo sus honorarios y cualquier gasto en que incurra la OACI en relación con el nombramiento del tercer árbitro y/o el árbitro de una de las Partes Contratantes, mencionado en el numeral (3) de este Artículo, serán compartidos en partes iguales entre las Partes Contratantes.

9. Durante el sometimiento del arbitraje y hasta que el tribunal arbitral publique su laudo, las Partes Contratantes continuarán cumpliendo sus obligaciones conforme a este Convenio, salvo en caso de terminación del mismo y sin perjuicio de un ajuste final, de conformidad con el referido laudo.

ARTÍCULO 20
Registro

El presente Convenio, sus Anexos y todas las enmiendas a los mismos, serán registrados ante la OACI.

ARTÍCULO 21
Convenios Multilaterales

En el supuesto de la celebración de una convención o convenio multilateral respecto al transporte aéreo en el cual ambas Partes Contratantes se adhieran, el presente Convenio será modificado conforme a las disposiciones de dicha convención o convenio.

ARTÍCULO 22
Terminación

El presente Convenio ha sido celebrado por un periodo de tiempo indefinido.

Cualquier Parte Contratante podrá, en cualquier momento, notificar a la otra Parte Contratante su decisión de dar por terminado el presente Convenio. Dicha notificación será comunicada simultáneamente a la OACI.

En tal caso, el Convenio terminará doce (12) meses después de la fecha de recepción de la notificación de la otra Parte Contratante, a menos que la notificación de terminación sea mutuamente acordada antes de que termine el periodo señalado. A falta de acuse de recibo de la otra Parte Contratante, la notificación se considerará recibida catorce (14) días hábiles después de la fecha en que la OACI haya recibido dicha notificación.

ARTÍCULO 23
Entrada en Vigor

El presente Convenio entrará en vigor treinta (30) días después de que las Parte Contratantes se hayan notificado, a través de la vía diplomática, el cumplimiento de sus formalidades constitucionales para tal efecto.

En fe de lo cual, los plenipotenciarios abajo señalados, debidamente autorizados por sus respectivos Gobiernos, han firmado el presente Convenio que ›mprende veintitrés (23) Artículos y dos (2) Anexos.

Hecho en Ankara el diecisiete de diciembre de dos mil trece, en duplicado, en los idiomas español, turco e inglés. Siendo todos los textos igualmente auténticos. En caso de divergencia en la aplicación o interpretación, el texto en inglés prevalecerá.

POR EL GOBIERNO DE LOS ESTADOS UNIDOS MEXICANOS	POR EL GOBIERNO DE LA REPÚBLICA DE TURQUÍA
José Antonio MEADE KURIBREÑA Secretario de Relaciones Exteriores	Hayati YAZICI Ministro de Aduanas y Comercio

ANEXO I

CUADRO DE RUTAS

1. Las líneas aéreas designadas por los Estados Unidos Mexicanos tendrán derecho para operar servicios aéreos en ambas direcciones de la siguiente forma:

De	Puntos Intermedios	Hacia	Puntos más allá
Puntos en los Estados Unidos Mexicanos	Cualesquier puntos	Puntos en Turquía	Cualesquier puntos

2. Las líneas aéreas designadas de la República de Turquía tendrán derecho para operar servicios aéreos en ambas direcciones de la siguiente forma:

De	Puntos Intermedios	Hacia	Puntos más allá
Puntos en Turquía	Cualesquier puntos	Puntos en los Estados Unidos Mexicanos	Cualesquier puntos

Notas:

1. Los puntos intermedios y más allá podrán ser omitidos de manera discrecional por la(s) línea(s) aérea(s) designadas en cualquiera o todos los vuelos, siempre y cuando dichos servicios en esa ruta inicien o terminen en el territorio de la Parte Contratante que designa a la(s) línea(s) aérea(s).

2. A las líneas aéreas designadas se les permitirá el pleno ejercicio de los derechos de 3ª y 4ª libertades de tráfico.

3. Las líneas aéreas designadas sólo podrán ejercer los derechos de 5ª libertad de tráfico, cuando esto haya sido acordado y autorizado previamente por las autoridades aeronáuticas de ambas Partes Contratantes.

4. La(s) línea(s) aérea(s) designada(s) de ambas Partes Contratantes podrán presentar para aprobación de las autoridades aeronáuticas de la otra Parte Contratante, al menos treinta (30) días antes del inicio de sus servicios, el itinerario de los servicios que se pretenden prestar, especificando la frecuencia, el tipo de aeronave y la vigencia. Los cambios menores en los horarios, de carácter temporal, podrán ser solicitados con cuarenta y ocho (48) horas de antelación.

ANEXO II

CÓDIGO COMPARTIDO

1. La(s) línea(s) aérea(s) designada(s) de cualquiera de las Partes Contratantes podrá(n) celebrar acuerdos comerciales tales como bloqueo de espacios, código compartido u otro tipo de acuerdo con:

a) una línea aérea o líneas aéreas de la misma Parte Contratante,

b) una línea aérea o líneas aéreas de la otra Parte Contratante,

c) una línea aérea o líneas aéreas de un tercer país.

siempre que todas las líneas aéreas participantes en dichos acuerdos posean rutas y derechos de tráfico apropiados y, respecto de cada boleto vendido, el comprador sea informado en el punto de venta qué línea aérea operará cada sección del servicio.

2. Las Partes Contratantes entienden, mutuamente, que los servicios de código compartido no son contabilizados contra el número de frecuencias otorgadas al transportista comercializador.

3. Ningún servicio se extenderá a la línea aérea de una Parte Contratante para el transporte de pasajeros locales entre un punto en el territorio de la otra Parte Contratante y un punto en un tercer Estado, a menos que la línea aérea haya obtenido los derechos de tráfico requeridos para operar y transportar tráfico entre esos dos puntos.

[TURKISH TEXT – TEXTE TURC]

BİRLEŞİK MEKSİKA DEVLETLERİ HÜKÜMETİ VE TÜRKİYE CUMHURİYETİ HÜKÜMETİ ARASINDA HAVA ULAŞTIRMA ANLAŞMASI

Bundan sonra "Akit Taraflar" olarak nitelendirilecek olan Birleşik Meksika Devletleri Hükümeti ve Türkiye Cumhuriyeti Hükümeti;

7 Aralık 1944 tarihinde Şikago'da imzaya açılan Uluslararası Sivil Havacılık Sözleşmesine ve Uluslararası Hava Hizmetleri Transit Anlaşmasına taraf olarak;

Uluslararası hava hizmetlerine ilişkin fırsatların genişletilmesini kolaylaştırmak isteyerek;

Etkin ve rekabetçi uluslararası hava hizmetlerinin ekonomik büyümeyi, ticareti, turizmi, yatırımı ve tüketicilerin refahını arttırdığının bilicinde olarak;

Hava araçlarının güvenliğine karşı yapılan, kişilerin ve mülklerin emniyetini tehdit eden, hava hizmetlerini olumsuz etkileyen ve sivil havacılığın emniyeti konusunda halkın güvenini sarsan eylemler ve tehlikeler konusundaki ciddi endişelerini teyit ederek ve uluslararası hava hizmetlerinde en üst seviyede emniyet ve güvenliği sağlamayı isteyerek;

Kendi ülkeleri arasında hava hizmetleri tesis etmek ve yürütmek amacıyla bir anlaşmaya varmayı arzu ederek,

AŞAĞIDAKİ MADDELERDE ANLAŞMIŞLARDIR:

MADDE 1

TANIMLAR

İşbu Anlaşmanın amacı doğrultusunda, metin içeriği aksini gerektirmediği takdirde:

a. "Havacılık otoriteleri" terimi, Birleşik Meksika Devletleri Sivil Havacılık Genel Müdürlüğü vasıtasıyla Haberleşme ve Ulaştırma Bakanlığını ve Türkiye Cumhuriyeti için, Sivil Havacılık Genel Müdürlüğü vasıtasıyla Ulaştırma, Denizcilik ve Haberleşme Bakanlığını veya bahse konu her iki ülke için hâlihazırda bu otoritelere tevdi edilmiş olan görevleri yerine getirmeye yetkili herhangi bir kurum veya kişiyi ifade etmektedir;

b. "Anlaşma" terimi işbu Anlaşmayı, Ek'ini ve bunlarda yapılacak herhangi bir değişikliği ifade etmektedir;

c. "Mutabık kalınan hizmetler" terimi işbu Anlaşma hükümlerine göre, belirlenmiş hatlarda sunulabilecek uluslararası hava hizmetlerini ifade etmektedir;

d. "Ek" terimi, işbu Anlaşmanın Ekini veya işbu Anlaşmanın 18. Maddesinin (İstişareler ve Değişiklikler) hükümleri doğrultusunda bu Ek üzerinde yapılan değişiklikleri ifade etmektedir. Ek işbu Anlaşmanın ayrılmaz bir parçasını oluşturmaktadır ve aksi kararlaştırılmadıkça Anlaşmaya yapılan tüm atıflar Ek'i de kapsayacaktır;

e. "hava hizmetleri", "uluslararası hava hizmetleri", "havayolu şirketleri" ve "trafik amacı dışındaki duraklama" terimleri, Sözleşmenin 96. Maddesinde tanımlanan anlamlarında kullanılmaktadır;

f. "Kapasite" terimi:

- hava aracı için, bu hava aracı tarafından hatta veya hattın belirli bir kısmında taşınabilen yükü;

- belirlenmiş bir hava hizmeti için, bu hizmette kullanılan hava aracının kapasitesinin, bu hava aracı için bir hatta veya hattın bir kısmında belli bir dönemde işletilen frekans sayısının çarpımını ifade etmektedir;

g. "Sözleşme" terimi 7 Aralık 1944 tarihinde Şikago'da imzaya açılan Uluslararası Sivil Havacılık Sözleşmesini ifade etmekte ve her iki Akit Tarafça yürürlüğe konması veya kabul edilmesi koşuluyla, Sözleşmenin 90. Maddesi altında kabul edilen tüm Ekleri ve 90. ve 94. Maddeler uyarınca Sözleşmenin Eklerinde yapılan tüm değişiklikleri içermektedir;

h. "Tayin edilen havayolu (havayolları)" terimi, işbu Anlaşmanın 3. Maddesi (Tayin ve Yetkilendirme) uyarınca tayin edilmiş ve yetkilendirilmiş havayolunu (havayollarını) ifade etmektedir;

i. "Yer hizmetleri" terimi, yolcu, kargo ve bagaj hizmetleri ve ikram servisleri ve/veya hizmetleri de dahil olmak ancak bunlarla sınırlı kalmamak kaydıyla çeşitli hizmetlerin teminini ifade etmektedir;

j. "ICAO" terimi, Uluslararası Sivil Havacılık Örgütünü ifade etmektedir;

k. "Uluslararası hava taşımacılığı" terimi, birden fazla Devletin ülkesi üzerindeki hava sahasının kullanıldığı hava taşımacılığını ifade etmektedir;

l. "Pazarlamacı havayolu " terimi, kod paylaşımı vasıtasıyla başka bir havayolu tarafından işletilen bir hava aracı ile hava taşımacılığı ulaşım hizmeti sunan havayolunu ifade etmektedir;

m. "Hat Çizelgesi" terimi, işbu Anlaşmanın 18. Maddesindeki hükümlere uygun olarak işbu Anlaşmaya eklenen, hava taşımacılığı hizmetinin yapılacağı hatların çizelgesini ve bu çizelge üzerinde yapılacak her türlü değişikliği ifade etmektedir;

n. "Belirlenen hatlar" terimi, işbu Anlaşmanın Ekinde onaylanmış veya onaylanacak hatları ifade etmektedir;

o. "Yedek parçalar" terimi, motorlar da dâhil olmak üzere, yenileme veya onarım amacı ile hava aracına monte edilecek aksamı ifade etmektedir;

p. "Ücret tarifesi" terimi, postanın taşınmasına ilişkin ücretler ve koşullar hariç tutulmak kaydıyla, yolcuların, bagajların ve kargonun taşınmasında uygulanacak bilet ücretini ve taşımacılık giderlerinin tatbik edileceği hizmetin özelliklerine bağlı olarak taşımacılık giderlerinin tatbikinin tabi olduğu şartları ve kuralları ifade etmektedir;

q. "Ülke" terimi, Sözleşmenin 2. Maddesinde tanımlanan anlamlarında kullanılmaktadır;

r. "Trafik" terimi; yolcular, bagaj, kargo ve postayı ifade etmektedir;

s. "Olağan teçhizat" terimi çıkartılabilir nitelikteki yedek parçalar ve malzemeler dışında, ilk yardım ve yaşamsal teçhizat da dâhil olmak üzere, uçuş sırasında kullanılan tüm malzemeleri ifade etmektedir;

t. 'Kullanıcı ücretleri" terimi, bir Akit Tarafça diğerine sağlanan havalimanlarının, seyrüsefer tesislerinin ve ilgili diğer hizmetlerin kullanımı için tahsil edilen harçları ve ücretleri ifade etmektedir.

MADDE 2
HAKLARIN TANINMASI

1. Her bir Akit Taraf, diğer Akit Tarafça tayin edilmiş havayolu şirketlerinin işbu Anlaşma'nın Ek I' inde belirlenen hatlar üzerinde tarifeli uluslararası hava hizmetlerini yürütebilmesi için diğer Akit Tarafa aşağıda belirtilen hakları tanımaktadır:

a. diğer Akit Tarafın ülkesi üzerinden iniş yapmaksızın uçma hakkı,

b. söz konusu devletin ülkesinde trafik dışındaki amaçlar için duraklama hakkı,

c. uluslararası trafiği birlikte veya birbirinden ayrı olarak indirmek ve almak amacıyla işbu Anlaşmanın Ek I' inde belirtilen hat için ilgili ülkede belirlenen noktalarda duraklama hakkı,

d. İşbu Anlaşmada belirtilen sair haklar.

2. İşbu Maddenin (1.) fıkrasında yer verilen hiçbir husus, bir Akit Tarafın havayolu şirketlerine, diğer Akit Tarafın ülkesinde, bu diğer tarafın ülkesindeki başka bir noktaya ücret veya kira karşılığı taşınmak üzere trafik alma ayrıcalığını verdiği şeklinde anlaşılamaz.

MADDE 3
TAYİN VE YETKİLENDİRME

1. Her bir Akit Taraf, belirlenen hatlarda, mutabık kalınan hizmetleri yürütmesi amacıyla bir veya daha fazla havayolu şirketi tayin etme hakkına sahip olacaktır. Bu tayin, diplomatik kanallar aracılığıyla yazılı bildirim yoluyla gerçekleştirilecektir.

2. Söz konusu tayin bildiriminin tebellüğ edilmesi üzerine, diğer Akit Tarafın havacılık otoriteleri işbu Maddenin (3.) ve (4.) fıkralarına tabi olarak, gereken işletme yetkisini gecikmeksizin tayin edilen havayolu şirketine (şirketlerine) tanıyacaktır.

3. Bir Akit Tarafın Havacılık Otoriteleri, diğer Akit Tarafça tayin edilen havayolu şirketinin (şirketlerinin), sözü geçen havacılık otoritelerince, Sözleşmenin hükümleri doğrultusunda, uluslararası hava hizmetlerinin yürütülmesinde normal ve makul bir şekilde uygulanan yasa ve yönetmeliklerin şartlarını yerine getirebilecek yeterlilikte olduğunu (olduklarını) kanıtlamasını talep edebilecektir.

4. Her bir Akit Taraf, aşağıda belirtilen koşulların sağlandığından emin olamaması halinde, işbu Maddenin (2.) fıkrasında atıfta bulunulan işletme yetkilerini tanımayı reddedebilecek veya tayin edilen havayolu şirketinin işbu Anlaşmanın 2. Maddesinde (Hakların Tanınması) belirlenen hakları kullanabilmesi için birtakım şartlar uygulanmasını gerekli görebilecektir:

a. söz konusu havayolu şirketinin mülkiyetinin büyük bir kısmının ve etkin kontrolünün söz konusu havayolu şirketini tayin eden Akit Tarafın kendisinde veya uyruğundakilerin yetkisinde olması, ve/veya

b. söz konusu havayolu şirketini tayin eden Hükümetin, işbu Anlaşmanın 13. Maddesinde (Havacılık Emniyeti) ve 14. Maddesinde (Havacılık Güvenliği) belirtilen standartlara sahip olması ve bu standartları uyguluyor olması.

5. Bu şekilde tayin edilip yetkilendirilmiş bir havayolu şirketi, işbu Anlaşmanın 5. Maddesindeki (Kapasite) ve 6. Maddesindeki (Ücret Tarifeleri) hükümler uyarınca, söz konusu hizmetle ilgili olarak üzerinde mutabakata varılan bir kapasitenin ve saptanmış bir ücret tarifesinin yürürlükte olması koşuluyla, mutabık kalınan hizmetleri sunmaya istediği herhangi bir zamanda başlayabilecektir.

MADDE 4
İŞLETME YETKİSİNİN İPTALİ VEYA ASKIYA ALINMASI

1. Her bir Akit Taraf, aşağıdaki hallerde, diğer Akit Tarafça tayin edilen havayolu şirketine (şirketlerine) verilmiş bulunan işletme yetkisini iptal etme veya bu havayolu şirketi (şirketleri) tarafından işbu Anlaşmanın 2. Maddesinde (Hakların Tanınması) belirtilen hakların kullanılmasını askıya alma veya bu hakların kullanılmasına yönelik olarak gerekli gördüğü şartları tatbik etme hakkına sahip olacaktır:

a. söz konusu havayolu şirketinin mülkiyetinin büyük bir kısmının ve etkin kontrolünün söz konusu havayolu şirketini tayin eden Akit Tarafın kendisinde veya uyruğundakilerin yetkisinde olduğuna kanaat getirememesi veya,

b. tayin edilen havayolu şirketinin kendisine bu hakları tanıyan Akit Tarafın kanun ve yönetmeliklerine uymaması veya,

c. tayin edilen havayolu şirketinin işbu Anlaşma'da belirtilen koşullara göre işletilmemesi halinde.

2. İptalin, askıya alma işleminin veya bu Maddenin (1.) fıkrasında belirtilen hükümlerin derhal uygulanması kanun ve yönetmeliklerin ihlalinin devam etmesini önlemek açısından zaruri değilse, sözü geçen hak, ancak diğer Akit Taraf Devletin havacılık otoriteleri ile istişare edildikten sonra kullanılabilecektir. Bu durumda istişarelerin, herhangi bir Akit Tarafın talep tarihinden itibaren altmış (60) günlük bir süre içerisinde başlaması gerekmektedir.

MADDE 5
KAPASİTE

1. Akit Taraflarca tayin edilen havayollarına , iki Akit Devletin ülkeleri arasında trafiğin taşınmasına yönelik hava hizmetlerini yürütmeleri için adil ve eşit düzeyde imkân sağlanacaktır.

2. Belirlenen hava hizmetlerinin herhangi bir Akit Tarafça tayin edilen havayolu tarafından işletilmesinde, aynı hatların tümünde veya bir kısmında sunduğu hizmetlerin haksız yere etkilenmesini önlemek amacı ile, diğer Akit Tarafça tayin edilen havayolu şirketinin çıkarları dikkate alınacaktır.

3. Akit Taraflarca tayin edilmiş havayolları tarafından sunulan, mutabık kalınan hizmetler, Akit Tarafların vatandaşlarının belirlenen hatlardaki ulaşım ihtiyaçları ile yakından ilintili olacak ve bu hava hizmetlerinin asli amacı Akit Tarafların ülkeleri arasında yolcular ve posta da dâhil olmak üzere kargo için mevcut ve makul olarak beklenen ulaşım ihtiyaçlarını makul bir yük faktörü ile karşılayacak bir kapasiteyi sağlamak olacaktır.

4. Mutabık kalınan hizmetlerin işletilmesinde her bir Akit Tarafça tayin edilen havayolları tarafından sağlanacak toplam kapasite ve hizmet frekansları, söz konusu hizmetlerin sunulmasına başlanmadan önce Akit Tarafların havacılık otoriteleri tarafından karşılıklı olarak belirlenecektir. Başlangıçta belirlenen kapasite ve hizmetlerin frekansı söz konusu otoriteler tarafından zaman içerisinde gözden geçirilebilecek ve yeniden düzenlenebilecektir.

MADDE 6
ÜCRET TARİFELERİ

1. Her bir Akit Taraf kendi ülkesine veya kendi ülkesinden sunulacak uluslararası hava hizmetleri için uygulanacak ücret tarifelerinin, tayin edilen havayolları tarafından, işletme maliyeti, makul bir kar oranı ve diğer havayollarının tarifeleri de dâhil olmak üzere ilgili tüm etkenlerin dikkate alınması suretiyle makul seviyelerde belirlenmesine izin verecektir. Akit Taraflar aşağıda belirtilen amaçlarla müdahalede bulunabileceklerdir:

a. makul olmayan ölçülerdeki ayrımcı ücret ve uygulamaları önlemek,

b. pazardaki hakim konumun kötüye kullanılmasından kaynaklanan çok yüksek veya kısıtlayıcı ücretlerden tüketicileri korumak ve

c. havayolu şirketlerini doğrudan veya dolaylı devlet sübvansiyonundan veya desteğinden kaynaklanan düşük ücretlerden korumak.

2. Akit Taraflarca tayin edilen havayolu şirketleri (1) fıkrada öngörülen şartlara uyacak ve belirledikleri ücret tarifelerini diğer Akit Tarafa bildireceklerdir.

3. Akit Taraflar, tayin ettikleri havayollarının ücret tarifelerini tek başlarına veya diğer havayolu şirketleri ile birlikte belirlerken, diğer Akit Tarafça tayin edilmiş havayolu şirketi olan rakibini ciddi bir biçimde zayıflatacak veya onu hat dışı bırakabilecek bir biçimde pazar gücünü suiistimal etmesine izin vermeyecektir.

4. Akit Taraflar, ücret tarifelerinin havayolları tarafından belirlenmesine ilişkin olarak aşağıda belirtilen uygulamaların daha yakından incelenmesi gerekebilecek, haksız rekabet uygulamaları olarak değerlendirilebileceği hususunda mutabıktır:

a. belirlenen hatlardaki hizmetlerin sağlanabilmesi için gereken maliyetleri tümüyle karşılamayacak ücretlerin ve fiyatların tatbik edilmesi;

b. söz konusu uygulamaların geçici olmak yerine süreklilik arz etmesi,

c. söz konusu uygulamaların diğer Akit Tarafça tayin edilmiş havayolu şirketi (şirketleri) üzerinde önemli ekonomik etkileri olması veya bu şirketi (şirketleri) önemli ölçüde zarara uğratması, ve

d. hattaki hakim konumun suiistimaline işaret eden davranışlar.

5. Havacılık otoritelerinden herhangi birinin, diğer Akit Tarafça tayin edilen havayolu tarafından önerilen veya uygulamada olan ücret tarifesinden memnun olmaması halinde, içlerinden herhangi birinin talebi üzerine, havacılık otoriteleri sorunu istişare yoluyla çözmeye çalışacaklardır. Akit Taraflardan herhangi birinin

havacılık otoritesi hiçbir surette diğer Akit Tarafın havayolunun ücret tarifesinin yürürlüğe girmesini veya hâlihazırda yürürlükte bulunan ücret tarifesinin uygulanmasının sürdürülmesini önlemek amacıyla tek taraflı müdahalede bulunmayacaktır.

6. Yukarıdaki hükümlere bakılmaksızın, bir Akit Tarafça tayin edilen havayolu , talep edilmesi halinde, diğer Akit Tarafın havacılık otoritelerine bu otoritelerin belirlediği şekil ve düzen çerçevesinde, ücret tarifelerinin oluşturulmasına dair bilgi verecektir.

7. Akit Taraflardan hiçbiri, diğer Akit Tarafça tayin edilen havayollarına, kapasite, frekans veya trafiğe ilişkin olarak, işbu Anlaşmanın amaçlarına ters düşecek nitelikte rüçhan hakkı zorunluluğu, uçuş kotası, itiraz hakkından feragat tazminatı veya sair şartlar uygulayamaz.

MADDE 7
GÜMRÜK HARÇLARI
VE DİĞER ÜCRETLERDEN MUAFİYET

1. Herhangi bir Akit Tarafça tayin edilen havayolunun uluslararası hava hizmetlerinde işletilen bir hava aracı, beraberindeki olağan teçhizatı, yedek parçaları (motorlar da dahil olmak üzere), yakıt, yağ stokları ve ikmal malzemeleri (hava aracında bulunan yiyecek, içecek, alkol ve sigara da dahil olmak üzere) ile birlikte diğer Akit Tarafın ülkesine varışta, bu teçhizat, yedek parçalar ve stoklar yeniden ihraç edilene veya bu ülke üzerinden yapılacak yolculuğun bir kısmında hava aracının içerisinde kullanılana kadar hava aracında kalmak ve mütekabiliyet esasına ve ilgili kanunlara tabi olmak kaydıyla her türlü gümrük harcından, muayene ücretinden ve diğer harç veya vergilerden muaf olacaktır.

2. Aşağıda belirtilen teçhizat ve maddeler, diğer Akit Tarafça, mütekabiliyet esasına ve ilgili kanunlara tabi olmak tabi olmak kaydıyla, her türlü gümrük harcından, muayene ücretinden ve varışta sunulan hizmetlerin maliyetlerinden kaynaklananlar dışında diğer harç veya vergilerden muaf tutulacaktır:

a. diğer Akit Tarafın ülkesi üzerindeki uçuşların bir kısmında kullanılacak olsalar dahi, tayin edilmiş bir hava yolu şirketi tarafından veya bu hava yolu şirketi adına diğer Akit Tarafın ülkesine getirilen ya da bu hava şirketi tarafından işletilen bir hava aracına alınan ve uluslararası hizmetlerde işletilen hava aracında kullanılması amaçlanan olağan teçhizat, yakıt, yağlar, teknik sarf malzemeleri, ikmal malzemeleri (yiyecek, içecek ve tütün gibi maddeler de dahil olmak üzere),

b. motorlar da dahil olmak üzere, tayin edilen bir havayolu tarafından uluslararası hava hizmetlerinde işletilen bir hava aracının bakım ve onarımı için bu havayolu tarafından veya bu havayolu adına diğer Akit Tarafın ülkesine getirilen veya bu havayolu tarafından işletilen bir hava aracına alınan yedek parçalar ve olağan havacılık teçhizatı,

c. herhangi bir Akit Tarafça tayin edilen havayolunun amblemini taşıyan basılı bilet stokları, havayolu konşimentoları ve sair basılı materyaller ile tayin edilen havayolu tarafından ücretsiz dağıtılan mutat tanıtım materyalleri.

Yukarıda (a), (b) ve (c) bentlerinde atıfta bulunulan maddelerin gümrük nezaretinde veya kontrolünde tutulması gerekecektir.

3. Herhangi bir Akit Tarafın hava aracında bulundurulan olağan havacılık teçhizatı, yedek parçalar (motorlar da dâhil olmak üzere), ikmal malzemeleri, yakıt ve yağ stokları (hidrolik sıvılar da dâhil olmak üzere) ile sair teçhizat ve malzemeler diğer Akit Tarafın ülkesine sadece o ülkenin gümrük otoritelerinin onayı ile indirilebilir. Bu durumda, bu teçhizat ve malzemeler söz konusu Akit Tarafın gümrük mevzuatın göre yeniden ihraç edilene veya sair şekillerde elden çıkartılana kadar söz konusu otoritelerin gözetiminde tutulacaktır.

4. Depolama ve gümrüklemeye ilişkin hizmetler için tarh edilen harçlar Akit Tarafların ulusal yasa ve yönetmeliklerine uygun olarak tahsil edilecektir.

MADDE 8

TRANSİT GEÇİŞ

Akit Tarafların yasa ve yönetmeliklerine tabi olmak kaydıyla, bir Akit Tarafın ülkesinden transit geçişlerde, havalimanının bu amaçla ayrılan kısmını terk etmemek kaydıyla yolcular, bagajlar ve kargo şiddete, hava korsanlığına ve narkotik madde kaçakçılığına karşı alınan güvenlik önlemleri aksini gerektirmedikçe sadece basitleştirilmiş bir kontrole tabi tutulacaklardır. Transit geçiş yapan bagajlar ve kargo gümrük harçlarından ve sair benzeri harçlardan muaf tutulacaklardır.

MADDE 9

KULLANICI ÜCRETLERİ

1. Bir Akit Tarafın kendi ülkesinde bulunan havalimanları, havacılık güvenliği tesisleri ve diğer ilgili tesisler ve hizmetler, diğer Akit Tarafın havayollarının kullanımına, kullanım anlaşmalarının yapıldığı tarih itibariyle benzer uluslararası hava hizmetleri ile iştigal eden herhangi bir havayoluna sağlanan en iyi koşullardan daha az avantajlı koşullarla sunulmayacaktır.

2. Bir Akit Tarafça tayin edilen havayolunun veya havayollarının, mütekabiliyet esasına tabi olmak kaydıyla, her iki Akit Tarafın ulusal yasa ve yönetmeliklerine uygun bir şekilde, diğer Akit Tarafın ülkesinde kendisi tarafından belirlenmiş yer hizmetlerini yürütmesine ve kendi tercihi doğrultusunda, yerel kanun ve yönetmelikler uyarınca gerekli görülmesi halinde, tamamen ya da kısmen, diğer Akit Tarafın yetkili makamları tarafından yetkilendirilmiş herhangi bir acenteden sağlanan yer hizmetlerini almasına izin verilecektir.

3. Bir Akit Tarafın ülkesinde, diğer Akit Tarafın havayoluna, havalimanlarının, havacılık güvenliği tesislerinin ve diğer ilgili tesislerin ve hizmetlerin kullanımı için belirlenen edilen ücretler ve harçlar hakkaniyetli ve adil bir şekilde belirlenecek ve tahsil edilecektir. Bu ücretler ve harçlar diğer Akit Tarafın havayolu şirketine, bu ücretlerin ve harçların tarh edildiği tarih itibariyle, benzer uluslararası hava hizmetleri ile iştigal eden herhangi bir havayolu şirketine sağlanan en iyi koşullardan daha az avantajlı koşullarda tarh edilmeyecektir.

4. Akit Taraflar, söz konusu ücretleri ve harçları tarh eden yetkili mercileri ile söz konusu hizmetlerden ve tesislerden faydalanan havayolları arasında veya pratikte mümkün olması halinde, söz konusu havayolunu temsil eden kuruluşlar arasında görüşmeler ve müzakereler yapılmasını destekleyecekler ve teşvik edeceklerdir. Kullanıcılar, değişiklikler yapılmadan önce görüşlerini belirtebilmelerini sağlamak üzere, kullanıcı ücretlerindeki her değişiklik teklifi hakkında mümkün olduğu kadar önceden bilgilendirilecektir.

MADDE 10
YABANCI PERSONEL VE YEREL HİZMETLERE ERİŞİM

1. Bir Akit Tarafça tayin edilen havayolu veya havayolları, mutabık kalınan hizmetlerin yürütülmesi için gerekli olan idari, ticari, satış, operasyonel, teknik ve diğer uzman personelini, diğer Akit Tarafın ülkesine giriş, ikamet ve istihdamla ilgili yasa ve yönetmeliklerine uygun bir şekilde, diğer Akit Tarafın ülkesine getirme ve burada bulundurma hakkına sahip olacaktır.

2. Bu personel ihtiyaçları, Akit Taraflarca tayin edilmiş havayollarının tercihleri doğrultusunda bu şirketlerin kendi personeli vasıtasıyla veya diğer Akit Tarafın ülkesinde diğer havayollarına bu tür hizmetler sunulması konusunda yetkilendirilmiş herhangi bir kuruluş, şirket veya havayolu tarafından sunulan hizmetlerden ve personelden faydalanmak suretiyle karşılanabilecektir.

3. Bu temsilciler ve personel diğer Akit Tarafın yürürlükteki yasalarına ve yönetmeliklerine tabi olacaklardır. Her bir Akit Taraf bu yasalar ve yönetmelikler doğrultusunda ve mütekabiliyet esasına tabi olmak kaydıyla, gerekli çalışma izinlerini, ziyaretçi vizelerini veya benzeri dokümanları gereksiz gecikmelere mahal vermeksizin, işbu Madde'nin (1.) fıkrasında belirtilen temsilcilere ve personele temin edecektir.

MADDE 11

DÖVİZ DÖNÜŞÜMÜ VE KAZANÇLARIN TRANSFERİ

1. Tayin edilen tüm havayolları, kendi taşımacılık belgelerini, diğer Akit Tarafın ülkesinde satış ofisleri veya tamamen kendi takdirlerinde olmak kaydıyla, acenteleri aracılığıyla satma ve tanzim etme hakkına sahip olacaktır. Yürürlükte olan ulusal yasalara ve yönetmeliklere tabi olmak kaydıyla, havayolları, sundukları taşımacılık hizmetlerini serbestçe kullanılabilen para birimleri ve/veya yerel para birimi üzerinden satma hakkına sahip olacaklar ve bu taşımacılık hizmetleri herkes tarafından yukarıda belirtilen para birimleri üzerinden serbestçe satın alınabilecektir.

2. Tayin edilen havayolları trafiğin taşınması ile ilgili olarak üstlendikleri giderlerden artan gelirleri çevirerek ülkelerine havale etme hakkına sahip olacaktır. Akit Taraflar arasında ödemelerle ilgili olarak uygun hükümlere sahip bir anlaşma akdedilmemiş ise, yukarıda belirtilen havale, serbestçe kullanılabilen para birimleri üzerinden ve yürürlükteki ulusal yasalara ve kambiyo düzenlemelerine uygun şekilde gerçekleştirilecektir.

3. Bu gelirlerin çevrilmesine ve havalesine o anda geçerli olan döviz kuru üzerinden, herhangi bir sınırlama getirilmeden izin verilecektir ve bu işlemler bankalar tarafından bu tür çevrilme ve havale işlemlerine uygulanan ücretler dışında başka bir ücrete veya harca tabi olmayacaktır.

4. Akit Taraflarca tayin edilen havayolları, tamamen kendi takdirlerinde olmak kaydıyla, yakıt alımı dâhil olmak üzere diğer Akit Tarafın ülkesinde üstlendikleri yerel giderleri, yerel para birimi üzerinden veya ulusal döviz mevzuatına uygun olmak kaydıyla serbestçe kullanılabilen bir para birimi üzerinden ödeme hakkına sahip olacaklardır.

MADDE 12
SERTİFİKA VE LİSANSLARIN KARŞILIKLI TANINMASI

1. Bir Akit Tarafça tanzim edilen veya geçerli kılınan ve hâlihazırda yürürlükte olan uçuşa elverişlilik sertifikaları, yeterlilik sertifikaları ve lisanslar, söz konusu sertifikaların veya lisansların tanzim edildiği veya geçerli sayıldığı koşulların, Sözleşme uyarınca belirlenen asgari standartlara eşit seviyede veya daha yüksek seviyede olması halinde, mutabık kalınan hizmetlerin belirlenen hatlarda yürütülmesi amacıyla diğer Akit Tarafça da tanınacaktır. Ancak Akit Taraflar, kendi ülkelerinin üzerinde yapılan uçuşlar ile ilgili olarak kendi vatandaşlarına diğer Akit Tarafça veya başka bir Devlet tarafından tanzim edilen veya geçerli kılınan yeterlilik sertifikalarını ve lisansları tanımayı reddetme hakkını saklı tutmaktadır.

2. Akit Taraflardan herhangi birinin havacılık otoriteleri tarafından herhangi bir kişiye veya tayin edilen bir havayolu şirketine ya da mutabık kalınan hizmetlerin yürütülmesinde kullanılan bir hava aracına verilen ve yukarıda (1.) fıkrada atıfta bulunulan lisans ve sertifikalarla ilgili imtiyazlar ve koşullar, Sözleşmeye uygun olarak belirlenen asgari standartlardan farklı bir standardın uygulanmasına izin veriyorsa ve bu fark konusunda Uluslararası Sivil Havacılık Örgütü'ne (ICAO) başvuruda bulunulmuş ise, diğer Akit Taraf, bu muallak uygulamanın açıklığa kavuşturulması amacıyla havacılık otoritelerinin istişarede bulunmasını talep edebilecektir. Uygun bir anlaşmaya varılamaması durumu, bu Anlaşmanın 4. Maddesinin (Yetkilendirmenin İptali veya Askıya Alınması) uygulanmasına gerekçe oluşturacaktır.

MADDE 13
HAVACILIK EMNİYETİ

1. Akit Taraflardan herhangi biri, diğer Akit Tarafça havacılık tesislerine ve hizmetlerine, mürettebata, hava aracına veya bunların işletilmesine ilişkin herhangi bir alanda benimsenmiş bulunan emniyet standartları ile ilgili olarak herhangi bir zamanda istişarelerde bulunmayı talep etme hakkına sahip olacaktır. Bu istişareler, talep tarihinden itibaren otuz (30) gün içerisinde gerçekleştirilecektir.

2. Bu istişareleri müteakiben, Akit Taraflardan herhangi birinin diğer Akit Tarafın işbu Maddenin (1.) fıkrasında belirtilen hususlara ilişkin emniyet standartlarını en azından ilgili tarihte Sözleşme uyarınca belirlenen asgari standartlara eşit şekilde sağlamadığını ve uygulamadığını tespit etmesi halinde, sözü geçen Akit Taraf bu tespitlerini ve asgari ICAO standartlarına uygunluğun sağlanması için atılması gereken adımları diğer akit Tarafa bildirecek ve diğer Akit Taraf da müştereken belirlenen süre içerisinde gereken düzeltici önlemleri alacaktır. Diğer Akit Tarafın belirlenenden daha uzun bir süre içerisinde gerekli düzeltici önlemleri almaması, bu Anlaşmanın 4. Maddesinin (Yetkilendirmenin İptali veya Askıya Alınması) uygulanmasına temel teşkil edecektir.

3. Sözleşmenin 16. Maddesinde öngörülen yükümlülüklere bakılmaksızın, bir Akit Tarafın havayolu şirketi tarafından veya bu havayolu şirketi adına diğer Akit Taraf Devletin ülkesine inecek veya ülkesinden kalkacak şekilde gerçekleştirilen uçuşlarda işletilen bir hava aracının diğer Akit Taraf Devletin ülkesinde bulunduğu sırada, olağandışı bir gecikmeye yol açmamak şartıyla denetime (işbu Maddede "rampa denetimi" olarak adlandırılacaktır) tabi tutulabileceği konusunda mutabık kalınmıştır. Bu denetim hava aracının içinde veya çevresinde, diğer Akit Tarafın yetkili temsilcileri tarafından yapılacaktır. Ancak, Sözleşmenin 33. Maddesinde sözü edilen yükümlülükler uyarınca, söz konusu denetimin amacı, Sözleşme temelinde oluşturulan ve hâlihazırda yürürlükte bulunan normlara uygun olarak hava aracının ve mürettebatın belgelerinin geçerliliği ile hava aracının ve teçhizatının görünürdeki durumunu kontrol etmek olacaktır.

4. Bu şekilde icra edilen herhangi bir rampa denetimi ya da bir dizi rampa denetimi sırasında:

a) bir hava aracının veya bir hava aracının işletilmesinin, Sözleşme uyarınca belirlenmiş olan ve denetimin gerçekleştirildiği tarih itibariyle yürürlükte bulunan asgari standartlara uygun olmadığı yönünde ciddi kaygıların oluşması, veya

b) Sözleşme uyarınca belirlenmiş olan ve denetimin gerçekleştirildiği tarih itibariyle yürürlükte bulunan emniyet standartlarının etkin bir şekilde sağlanamadığı ve uygulanamadığı hususunda ciddi kaygıların oluşması halinde,

denetimi icra eden Akit Taraf Sözleşmenin 33. Maddesine göre, ilgili hava aracının veya mürettebatın sertifika ve lisanslarının tanzimine veya geçerli kılınmasına veya hava aracının işletilmesine esas koşulların, Sözleşmeye göre belirlenen asgari standartlara eşit seviyede veya daha üst seviyede olmadığı sonucunu çıkarmakta serbest olacaktır.

5. Yukarıda yer alan (3.) fıkra uyarınca bir Akit Tarafça tayin edilen havayolu şirketi tarafından işletilen hava aracına rampa denetimi uygulanmasına söz konusu havayolu şirketinin temsilcisi tarafından müsaade edilmemesi durumunda, diğer Akit Taraf yukarıda yer alan (4.) fıkrada belirtilen ciddi kaygıların oluştuğu sonucuna varabilecek ve söz konusu fıkrada belirtilen sonuçları çıkarabilecektir.

6. Herhangi bir Akit Tarafın, bir rampa denetimi sonucunda, bir veya bir dizi rampa denetiminin engellenmesi sonucunda, istişareler sonrasında ya da sair nedenlerle, hava aracının işletilmesinin emniyeti açısından derhal bir tedbir alınması gerektiği sonucuna varması durumunda, söz konusu Akit Taraf diğer Akit Tarafın havayolu şirketinin işletme yetkilerini derhal askıya alma veya tadil etme hakkına sahip olacaktır.

7. Akit Taraflardan herhangi birinin işbu Madde'nin (2.) veya (6.) fıkraları uyarınca aldığı tedbirler, bu tedbirin alınmasını gerektiren durumun ortadan kalkmasıyla sona erdirilecektir.

MADDE 14
HAVACILIK GÜVENLİĞİ

1. Akit Taraflar, uluslararası hukuktan doğan hak ve yükümlülükleri doğrultusunda, sivil havacılık güvenliğinin yasa dışı müdahalelere karşı korunması amacıyla birbirlerine karşı üstlendikleri yükümlülüğün, işbu Anlaşmanın ayrılmaz bir parçasını teşkil ettiğini teyit ederler. Akit Taraflar, uluslararası hukuka göre mevcut haklarının ve yükümlülüklerinin genel niteliklerini kısıtlamaksızın, özellikle 14 Eylül 1963 tarihinde Tokyo'da imzalanan Hava araçlarında İşlenen Suçlar ve Diğer Bazı Eylemlere ilişkin Sözleşme, 16 Aralık 1970 tarihinde Lahey'de imzalanan Hava araçlarının Yasadışı Yollarla Ele Geçirilmesinin Önlenmesine İlişkin Sözleşme, 23 Eylül 1971 tarihinde Montreal'de imzalanan Sivil Havacılık Güvenliğine Karşı İşlenen Suçların Önlenmesine ilişkin Sözleşme ve 24 Şubat 1988 tarihinde Montreal'de imzalanan Uluslararası Sivil Havacılığa Hizmet Veren Hava Limanlarında Yasadışı Şiddet Eylemlerinin Önlenmesine ilişkin Protokol, 1 Mart 1991'de Montreal'de düzenlenen Plastik Patlayıcıların Teşhisi Amacıyla İşaretlenmesi Sözleşmesi veya Akit Tarafların taraf oldukları sivil havacılık güvenliğine ilişkin diğer herhangi bir sözleşme hükümlerine uygun hareket edeceklerdir.

2. Akit Taraflar; sivil hava aracının yasadışı yollarla ele geçirilmesini önlemek, bu hava aracının, yolcularının ve mürettebatının, havalimanlarının ve hava seyrüsefer tesislerinin emniyetine karşı girişilebilecek diğer yasa dışı eylemleri ve sivil havacılığın güvenliğine ilişkin diğer tehditleri bertaraf etmek üzere, talep halinde birbirlerine gerekli her türlü yardımda bulunacaklardır.

3. Akit Taraflar karşılıklı ilişkilerinde, Akit Taraflara uygulanabilir olduğu ölçüde, ICAO tarafından tesis edilen ve Uluslararası Sivil Havacılık Sözleşmesine Ek olarak kabul edilen tüm havacılık güvenliği standartlarına ve tavsiye edilen uygulamalara uygun olarak hareket edeceklerdir. Akit Taraflar, kendi tescillerindeki hava aracı işletmecilerinin veya işyeri merkezi ya da daimi ikametgâhı kendi ülkelerinde bulunan hava aracı işletmecilerinin ve ülkelerindeki havalimanı

işletmecilerinin Akit Tarafları bağlayan bu tür havacılık güvenliği hükümlerine uygun hareket etmelerini sağlayacaklardır. Bu bağlamda her bir Akit Taraf, diğer Akit Tarafa kendi ulusal düzenlemeleri ve uygulamaları ile yukarıda belirtilen Ek'lerdeki havacılık güvenlik standartları arasındaki farklılıkları bildirmelidir. Her bir Akit Taraf herhangi bir zamanda diğer Akit Taraftan bu tip farklılıkları diğer Akit Tarafla görüşmek için işbu Anlaşmanın 18. Maddesinin 2. fıkrası hükümleri uyarınca gerçekleştirilmek üzere acil istişare talebinde bulunabilecektir.

4. Akit Taraflar söz konusu hava aracı işletmecilerinin, diğer Akit Tarafın ülkesine giriş için, bu devletin ülkesinden çıkış için veya bu devletin ülkesinde kalınan süre zarfında diğer Akit Tarafça, yukarıda yer alan (3.) fıkrada atıf yapılan havacılık güvenliği hükümlerine uymalarının istenebileceği hususunda mutabıktır. Akit Taraflardan her biri, kendi ülkelerinde hava aracının güvenliğinin sağlanması, yolcuların, mürettebatın, el bagajlarının, bagajların, kargonun ve ikmal malzemelerinin yükleme ve boşaltma sırasında ve öncesinde kontrol edilmesi amacıyla yeterli tedbirlerin alınmasını ve etkin şekilde uygulanmasını sağlayacaktır. Akit Taraflardan her biri, belirli bir tehdidin bertaraf edilmesi amacıyla diğer Akit Tarafın makul ölçülerde özel güvenlik tedbirleri alınması yolunda yapacağı herhangi bir talebi olumlu şekilde dikkate alacaktır.

5. Sivil hava aracının yasadışı yollarla ele geçirilmesi olayının veya bu doğrultuda bir tehdidin vuku bulması veya bu hava aracının, hava aracının yolcularının ve mürettebatının, havaalanlarının veya hava seyrüsefer tesislerinin emniyetine yönelik diğer yasadışı müdahalelerin meydana gelmesi halinde Akit Taraflar, haberleşmede ve bu tür bir olayın veya tehdidinin insan hayatı konusunda riski asgariye indirmek suretiyle hızlı ve emniyetli biçimde sona erdirilmesini amaçlayan diğer uygun tedbirlerin alınmasında kolaylık sağlayarak birbirlerine yardımcı olacaklardır.

6. Her bir Akit Taraf, kalkışı insan hayatını korumak için zaruri olmadıkça, yasadışı yollarla ele geçirilmiş veya diğer yasadışı müdahale eylemlerine maruz kalmış ve kendi ülkesine iniş yapmış olan bir hava aracının, yerde kalmasını sağlamak üzere pratikte mümkün olan gerekli önlemleri alacaktır. Mümkün olduğu durumlarda bu tip önlemler karşılıklı istişarelere dayanılarak alınacaktır.

MADDE 15
UÇUŞ PROGRAMLARININ SUNULMASI

1. Her bir Akit Tarafça tayin edilen havayolu şirketleri, planladıkları uçuş programlarını, mutabık kalınan hizmetlerin başlamasından en az otuz (30) gün önce diğer Akit Tarafın havacılık otoritelerine onay için sunacaktır.

2. Bir Akit Tarafça tayin edilen havayolu şirketi, onaylanmış uçuş programı dışında mutabık kalınan hizmetler doğrultusunda düzenlemek istediği ek uçuşlar için diğer Akit Tarafın havacılık otoritelerinden önceden izin talep etmelidir. Bu tür talepler, Akit Tarafların ulusal yasa ve yönetmeliklerine uygun şekilde sunulacaktır. Uçuş programları üzerinde yapılacak herhangi bir değişiklikte de aynı usul uygulanacaktır.

MADDE 16
İSTATİSTİKLER

Akit Tarafların havacılık otoriteleri, talep edilmesi halinde, diğer Akit Tarafın havacılık otoritelerine, birinci Akit Tarafça tayin edilmiş havayolları tarafından mutabık kalınan hizmetlerde sunulan kapasitenin değerlendirilmesi amacıyla makul ölçülerde gerekli olabilecek periyodik istatistiki raporlar veya sair istatistiki raporlar sunacaklardır. Bu raporlar söz konusu havayolunun mutabık kalınan hizmetler ile ilgili olarak taşımış olduğu trafik miktarını ve bu trafiğin başlangıç ve varış noktalarını belirlemek için gerekli tüm bilgileri içerecektir.

MADDE 17

ULUSAL YASALARIN VE YÖNETMELİKLERİN UYGULANMASI

1. Bir Akit Tarafın, uluslararası hava hizmetinde bulunan bir hava aracının, ülkesine girişi, kalışı ve çıkışı veya bu hava aracının işletilmesi ve seyrüseferi veya bu hava aracının bu ülke üzerindeki uçuşlarıyla ile ilgili yasa ve yönetmelikleri, diğer Akit Tarafça tayin edilen havayolunun hava araçlarının ilk Akit Tarafın ülkesine girişi, kalışı ve çıkışında da uygulanacaktır.

2. Bir Akit Tarafın yolcu, mürettebat, bagaj veya posta da dâhil olmak üzere kargonun ülkesine girişi, kalışı veya ayrılışıyla ilgili giriş, çıkış, gümrükleme, göç, havacılık güvenliği, pasaport, döviz, sağlık ve karantina ve posta gibi formaliteleri düzenleyen yasalarına ve düzenlemelerine, söz konusu ülke sınırları dahilinde bulundukları süre zarfında, diğer Akit Tarafça tayin edilen havayolu şirketinin hava araçları tarafından taşınan yolcu, mürettebat, bagaj, kargo veya posta tarafından veya onlar adına uyulacaktır.

3. Her bir Akit Taraf, diğer Akit Tarafın talebi üzerine işbu Anlaşmada belirtilen ilgili yasa, düzenleme ve prosedürlerin suretlerini karşı tarafa sunacaktır.

MADDE 18

İSTİŞARELER VE DEĞİŞİKLİKLER

1. Akit Tarafların Havacılık Otoriteleri, yakın işbirliği anlayışı içinde, zaman zaman işbu Anlaşmanın ve Eklerinin uygulanması, yorumlanması, tatbiki veya gerekli değişikliklerin yapılması konusunda birbirleriyle istişareler yürüteceklerdir.

2. Bir Akit Tarafın işbu Anlaşma veya Ekleri üzerinde değişiklik yapmak amacıyla istişarede bulunmayı talep etmesi durumunda, Akit Taraflarca aksi yönde bir karar alınmadığı müddetçe bu istişareler Akit Taraflardan birinin, diğer Akit Tarafça yazılı olarak yapılan talebi tebellüğ ettiği tarihten itibaren en kısa sürede ve her hâl ve kârda en geç altmış (60) gün içerisinde başlayacaktır. Bu istişareler müzakere veya yazışma yoluyla gerçekleştirilecektir. Her bir Akit Taraf bu istişareler sırasında makul ve ekonomik kararların alınabilmesini kolaylaştırmak amacıyla, tutumunu destekleyen ilgili gerekçeleri hazırlayacak ve sunacaktır.

3. Akit Taraflardan herhangi birinin, işbu Anlaşmanın herhangi bir hükmü üzerinde değişiklik yapılması gerektiğine kanaat getirmesi halinde, bu değişiklik her bir Akit Tarafın, kendi ulusal mevzuatında bu amaçla öngörülen koşulları yerine getirdiğini diğer tarafa bildirmesinin ardından otuz (30) gün sonra yürürlüğe girecektir.

4. Ek I üzerindeki değişiklikler Akit Tarafların havacılık otoritelerinin kendi aralarında doğrudan anlaşmasıyla da yapılabilecektir. Değişiklikler karşılıklı mutabakata varıldığı tarihten itibaren uygulanmaya başlanacak ve diplomatik nota teatisi ile teyit edildikten sonra yürürlüğe girecektir.

MADDE 19
İHTİLAFLARIN ÇÖZÜMÜ

1. İşbu Anlaşmanın yorumlanmasında veya uygulanmasında Akit taraflar arasında herhangi bir uyuşmazlık çıkması durumunda, Akit Taraflar öncelikle uyuşmazlıklarını her iki Akit Taraf Devletinin havacılık otoriteleri arasında müzakere yoluyla çözmeye çaba göstereceklerdir.

2. Söz konusu Havacılık Otoritelerinin müzakereler yoluyla çözüme ulaşamamaları halinde, uyuşmazlık diplomatik kanallar yoluyla çözüme kavuşturulacaktır.

3. Akit Tarafların, yukarıda yer alan (1.) ve (2.) fıkraların hükümleri doğrultusunda bir çözüme ulaşamamaları halinde, Akit Taraflardan herhangi biri söz konusu uyuşmazlığı, ilgili yasa ve yönetmeliklere uygun bir şekilde, birer üyesi her bir Akit Tarafça belirlenecek, üçüncü üyesi ise Akit Taraflardan birinin vatandaşı olmamak ve hakemlerin belirlendiği tarih itibariyle her iki akit Tarafın da diplomatik ilişkide olduğu bir Devletin vatandaşı olmak kaydıyla, bu iki hakem tarafından seçilecek, üç hakemden oluşan bir hakem heyetine sunabilecektir.

Akit Taraflar, uyuşmazlığın tahkime götürüleceğine dair bildirimi taahhütlü posta ile tebellüğ ettikleri tarihi izleyen altmış (60) gün içinde aday gösterecekleri hakemi belirleyeceklerdir. Hakem heyeti başkanı olarak görev yapacak olan üçüncü hakem Akit Tarafların hakemlerini belirledikleri tarihten itibaren altmış (60) gün içinde tayin edilecektir.

Akit Taraflardan herhangi birinin belirlenen süre içinde aday göstereceği hakemi belirleyememesi veya seçilen hakemlerin hakem heyeti başkanı olarak görev yapacak üçüncü hakemin belirlenmesine öngörülen sürede karar verememeleri halinde, duruma bağlı olarak, her bir Akit Taraf ICAO Konsey Başkanından üçüncü hakemi veya bir hakem tayin etmemiş olan Tarafın hakemini belirlemesini talep edebilecektir.

4. Akit Tarafların vatandaşı olmamak kaydıyla ICAO Konseyi Başkan Yardımcısı veya kıdemli bir üyesi, duruma bağlı olarak, ICAO Başkanının yokluğunda veya yetersizliği durumunda Başkanın tahkim süreci ile ilgili olarak işbu Maddenin (3.) fıkrasında belirtilen sorumluluklarını üstlenecektir.

5. Hakem Heyeti, usullerini ve tahkim işleminin yerini Akit Taraflar arasında mutabık kalınan hükümlere tabi olmak kaydıyla belirleyecektir.

6. Hakem Heyetinin kararları aralarında uyuşmazlık bulunan Akit Taraflar açısından nihai ve bağlayıcı nitelik taşıyacaktır.

7. Akit Taraflardan herhangi birinin veya Akit Taraflardan herhangi biri tarafından tayin edilen havayolu şirketinin işbu Maddenin (2.) fıkrası uyarınca verilen karara uymaması durumunda, diğer Akit Taraf, temerrüde düşen Akit Tarafa işbu Anlaşma uyarınca sağlanan hakları veya ayrıcalıkları sınırlandırabilecek, askıya alabilecek veya iptal edebilecektir.

8. Her bir Akit Taraf kendi hakeminin masraflarını karşılayacaktır. İşbu Maddenin (3.) fıkrası uyarınca, üçüncü hakemin ve/veya hakem tayin etmemiş Tarafça bildirilmeyen hakemin atanmasında ICAO'nun yapacağı her türlü masraflar da dâhil olmak üzere, hakem heyeti başkanı olarak görev yapacak üçüncü hakemin ücretleri ve masrafları Akit Taraflarca eşit olarak paylaşılacaktır.

9. Tahkime başvurulmasından itibaren hakem heyeti kararını açıklayana dek, Akit Taraflar fesih hali dışında, verilen nihai karar doğrultusunda yapılabilecek düzeltmelere halel getirmeksizin, işbu Anlaşmadan doğan tüm yükümlülüklerini yerine getirmeye devam edeceklerdir.

MADDE 20

TESCİL

İşbu Anlaşma, Ekleri ve bunlarda yapılacak tüm değişiklikler ICAO nezdinde tescil edilecektir.

MADDE 21

ÇOK TARAFLI ANLAŞMALAR

Her iki Akit Tarafın da hava ulaştırmasına dair çok taraflı bir sözleşme veya anlaşmaya taraf olmaları halinde, işbu Anlaşma söz konusu sözleşme veya anlaşmanın hükümlerine uyum sağlayacak şekilde değiştirilecektir.

MADDE 22

SONA ERME

İşbu Anlaşma süresiz olarak imzalanmıştır.

Akit Taraflar her an diğer Akit Tarafa işbu Anlaşmayı feshetmek istediklerini bildirebileceklerdir ve bu bildirim eş zamanlı olarak ICAO' ya da ulaştırılacaktır.

Bu durumda, fesih bildirimi karşılıklı mutabakatla süre bitiminden önce geri çekilmediği takdirde, işbu Anlaşma, sona erme bildiriminin diğer Akit Tarafça tebellüğ edildiği tarihten on iki (12) ay sonra sona erecektir. Diğer Akit Tarafın bildirimi tebellüğ ettiğini teyit etmemesi durumunda, bu bildirimin, ICAO'nun bildirimi tebellüğ ettiği tarihten on dört (14) iş günü sonra tebellüğ edilmiş olduğu kabul edilecektir.

MADDE 23

YÜRÜRLÜĞE GİRİŞ

İşbu Anlaşma, Akit Tarafların anayasal gerekliliklerini yerine getirdiklerini diplomatik kanallar yoluyla karşılıklı olarak birbirlerine bildirdikleri tarihten otuz (30) gün sonra yürürlüğe girecektir.

Yukarıdaki hususlar muvacehesinde, aşağıda imzaları bulunan ve kendi Hükümetleri tarafından usulüne uygun olarak yetkili kılınmış taraflar yirmi üç (23) Madde ve iki (2) Ekten oluşan işbu Anlaşmayı imzalamışlardır.

Ankara'da iki bin on üç yılının Aralık ayının on yedinci gününde İspanyolca, Türkçe ve İngilizce dillerinde çift nüsha halinde düzenlenmiştir. Tüm metinler birbirine eşdeğer niteliktedir. Herhangi bir uygulama veya yorumlama farklılığının oluşması durumunda İngilizce metin geçerli olacaktır.

BİRLEŞİK MEKSİKA DEVLETLERİ HÜKÜMETİ ADINA	TÜRKİYE CUMHURİYETİ HÜKÜMETİ ADINA
José Antonio Meade Kuribreña Dışişleri Bakanı	Hayati YAZICI Gümrük ve Ticaret Bakanı

EK I

HAT ÇİZELGESİ

1. Birleşik Meksika Devletleri tarafından tayin edilen havayolları her iki yönde aşağıda belirtilen hava hizmetlerini işletme hakkına sahip olacaktır:

Hareket Noktası	Ara Noktalar	Varış Noktası	İleri Noktalar
Birleşik Meksika Devletlerindeki noktalar	Herhangi bir nokta	Türkiye'deki noktalar	Herhangi bir nokta

2. Türkiye Cumhuriyeti tarafından tayin edilen havayolları her iki yönde aşağıda belirtilen hava hizmetlerini işletme hakkına sahip olacaktır:

Hareket Noktası	Ara Noktalar	Varış Noktası	İleri Noktalar
Türkiye'deki noktalar	Herhangi bir nokta	Birleşik Meksika Devletlerindeki noktalar	Herhangi bir nokta

Notlar:

1. İlgili güzergâhtaki hizmetlerin başlangıç ve bitiş noktasının, havayolunu tayin eden Akit Tarafın ülkesi içinde bulunması koşuluyla, tayin edilmiş havayolu ,tamamen kendi takdirinde olmak kaydıyla, herhangi bir uçuşta ya da hiç bir uçuşta ara noktaları ve ileri noktaları kullanmayabilecektir.

2. Tayin edilen havayolu şirketlerinin tam 3üncü ve 4üncü trafik haklarını kullanmalarına imkân sağlanacaktır.

3. Tayin edilen havayolu şirketleri 5inci trafik haklarını ancak her iki Tarafın havacılık otoritelerinin bu konuda mutabakata varmaları ve önceden gerekli izinleri vermeleri halinde kullanabileceklerdir.

4. Taraflarca tayin edilen havayolu şirketleri sunmayı planladıkları hizmetlere ilişkin uçuş tarifelerini, sunulacak hizmetin türüne, kullanılacak hava aracının tipine ve uçuş tarifesinin geçerlilik süresine ilişkin bilgileri de içerecek şekilde, bu hizmetleri sunmaya başlamadan en az otuz (30) gün önce onay için diğer tarafın havacılık otoritesine sunacaklardır. Uçuş programları üzerinde yapılacak geçici nitelik taşıyan küçük değişikliklerin kırk sekiz (48) saat önceden bildirilmesi gerekebilecektir.

EK II

KOD PAYLAŞIMI

1. Her bir Akit Tarafça tayin edilen havayolu ,

a) aynı Akit Tarafın havayolları;

b) diğer Akit Tarafın havayolları;

c) üçüncü bir ülkenin havayolları

ile, söz konusu tüm havayollarının uygun hat ve trafik haklarına sahip olmaları ve satılan her bilet için, alıcıyı satış noktasında hizmetin hangi kısmında hangi havayolunun görev yapacağı konusunda bilgilendirmeleri koşuluyla, bloke yer angajmanı, kod paylaşımı veya diğer ticari uygulamalar gibi pazarlama uygulamalarına katılabilecektir.

2. Kod Paylaşımı hizmetlerinin pazarlamacı havayolunun frekans hakkından sayılmayacağı hususu her iki Akit Tarafın ortak anlayışıdır.

3. Bu iki nokta arasında faaliyet göstermek ve trafik taşımak için gereken trafik haklarına sahip olmadığı taktirde, Akit Taraflardan herhangi birinin havayolu, diğer Akit Tarafın ülkesinde bulunan bir nokta ile üçüncü bir Devlette bulunan bir nokta arasında yerel yolcuların taşınmasına yönelik bir hizmet sunamayacaktır.

[TRANSLATION – TRADUCTION]

ACCORD RELATIF AUX SERVICES AÉRIENS ENTRE LE GOUVERNEMENT DES ÉTATS-UNIS DU MEXIQUE ET LE GOUVERNEMENT DE LA RÉPUBLIQUE TURQUE

Le Gouvernement des États-Unis du Mexique et le Gouvernement de la République turque, ci-après dénommés « Parties contractantes »,

Étant parties à la Convention relative à l'aviation civile internationale et à l'Accord relatif au transit des services aériens internationaux, ouverts à la signature à Chicago le 7 décembre 1944,

Désireux d'élargir l'offre en matière de transport aérien international,

Reconnaissant que des services aériens internationaux efficaces et concurrentiels favorisent la croissance économique, le commerce, le tourisme, les investissements et le bien-être des consommateurs,

Désireux de garantir une sécurité et une sûreté maximales aux services aériens internationaux, et réaffirmant leur profonde préoccupation face aux actes ou aux menaces dirigés contre la sûreté des aéronefs, qui compromettent la sécurité des personnes ou des biens, nuisent à l'exploitation des services aériens et affaiblissent la confiance du public en la sûreté de l'aviation civile, et

Désireux de conclure un Accord en vue d'établir et d'exploiter des services aériens entre leurs territoires respectifs,

Sont convenus de ce qui suit :

Article premier. Définitions

Aux fins du présent Accord, à moins que le contexte n'exige une autre interprétation :

a) L'expression « autorités aéronautiques » désigne, en ce qui concerne les États-Unis du Mexique, le Ministère des communications et des transports par l'intermédiaire de la Direction générale de l'aviation civile, et en ce qui concerne la République turque, le Ministère des transports, des affaires maritimes et des communications par l'intermédiaire de la Direction générale de l'aviation civile ou, dans les deux cas, toute personne ou entité habilitée à exercer les fonctions actuellement attribuées auxdites autorités;

b) Le terme « Accord » désigne le présent Accord, ses annexes et toute modification qui leur est apportée;

c) L'expression « services convenus » désigne les services aériens internationaux qui peuvent être exploités sur les routes spécifiées conformément aux dispositions du présent Accord;

d) Le terme « annexe » désigne une annexe au présent Accord, ou telle que modifiée conformément aux dispositions de l'article 18 (Consultations et amendement). Les annexes font partie intégrante du présent Accord et toute référence à l'Accord englobe ses annexes, sauf convention contraire explicite;

e) Les expressions « service aérien », « service aérien international », « compagnie aérienne » et « escale non commerciale » ont le sens qui leur est attribué à l'article 96 de la Convention;

f) Le terme « capacité » désigne :

- En ce qui concerne un aéronef, sa charge utile disponible sur une route ou un segment de route;
- En ce qui concerne un service aérien spécifié, la capacité de l'aéronef utilisé pour ce service, multipliée par la fréquence à laquelle cet aéronef est exploité pendant une période donnée sur une route ou un segment de route;

g) Le terme « Convention » désigne la Convention relative à l'aviation civile internationale ouverte à la signature à Chicago le 7 décembre 1944, y compris les annexes adoptées conformément aux dispositions de son article 90 et tout amendement desdites annexes à la Convention adopté en vertu des articles 90 et 94, dans la mesure où ces annexes et amendements ont pris effet pour les deux Parties contractantes ou ont été ratifiés par elles;

h) L'expression « compagnie aérienne désignée » désigne toute compagnie aérienne désignée et autorisée conformément à l'article 3 (Désignation et autorisation) du présent Accord;

i) L'expression « services d'escale » comprend, sans s'y limiter, la prise en charge des passagers, des marchandises et des bagages, et la fourniture d'installations et/ou de services de restauration;

j) Le terme « OACI » désigne l'Organisation de l'aviation civile internationale;

k) L'expression « transport aérien international » désigne un transport qui s'effectue en traversant l'espace aérien situé au-dessus du territoire de plus d'un État;

l) L'expression « compagnie de commercialisation » désigne une compagnie aérienne qui propose un transport aérien sur un aéronef exploité par une autre compagnie aérienne, grâce au partage de codes;

m) Le terme « tableau » désigne le tableau des routes pour exploiter les services de transport aérien joint en annexe au présent Accord et toute modification de celui-ci telle que convenue conformément aux dispositions de l'article 18 du présent Accord;

n) L'expression « routes spécifiées » désigne les routes qui sont ou seront établies dans l'annexe au présent Accord;

o) L'expression « pièces de rechange » désigne les éléments utilisés pour des réparations ou des remplacements et qui sont incorporés aux aéronefs, y compris les moteurs;

p) Le terme « tarif » désigne le prix appliqué pour le transport de passagers, de bagages et de marchandises, ainsi que les conditions et les normes régissant l'application du coût de transport en fonction des caractéristiques du service fourni, qui déterminent le montant appliqué, mais ne comprend pas la rémunération et les autres conditions relatives au transport du courrier;

q) Le terme « territoire » a le sens qui lui est attribué à l'article 2 de la Convention;

r) Le terme « trafic » désigne le transport de passagers, de bagages, de marchandises et de courrier;

s) L'expression « équipement ordinaire » désigne les articles, autres que les provisions et les pièces de rechange de nature amovible, destinés à être utilisés à bord d'un aéronef pendant le vol, y compris l'équipement de premiers secours et les dispositifs de survie;

t) L'expression « redevances d'usage » désigne les droits ou frais perçus pour l'utilisation d'installations aéroportuaires ou de navigation ainsi que d'autres services connexes qu'une Partie contractante propose à l'autre.

Article 2. Droits accordés

1) Chaque Partie contractante accorde à l'autre Partie contractante les droits suivants aux fins de l'exploitation par des compagnies aériennes désignées de l'autre Partie contractante des services aériens internationaux réguliers sur les routes spécifiées dans l'annexe I au présent Accord :

a) Le droit de survoler, sans y atterrir, le territoire de l'autre Partie contractante;

b) Le droit d'effectuer des escales non commerciales sur ledit territoire;

c) Le droit de faire escale sur ledit territoire aux points spécifiés pour cette route à l'annexe I du présent Accord afin de débarquer et d'embarquer du trafic international, conjointement ou séparément;

d) Les autres droits visés au présent Accord.

2) Aucune disposition du paragraphe 1 du présent article ne peut être interprétée comme conférant à une compagnie aérienne d'une Partie contractante le droit de d'embarquer, sur le territoire de l'autre Partie contractante, du trafic contre rémunération ou en vertu d'un contrat de location à destination d'un autre point situé sur le territoire de cette autre Partie contractante.

Article 3. Désignation et autorisation

1) Chaque Partie contractante a le droit de désigner une ou plusieurs compagnies aériennes chargées d'exploiter les services convenus sur les routes spécifiées. Cette désignation s'effectue par l'envoi d'une notification écrite par la voie diplomatique.

2) À la réception de cette désignation, les autorités aéronautiques de l'autre Partie contractante accordent sans délai l'autorisation d'exploitation appropriée aux compagnies aériennes désignées, sous réserve des dispositions des paragraphes 3 et 4 du présent article.

3) Les autorités aéronautiques d'une Partie contractante peuvent demander à une compagnie aérienne désignée par l'autre Partie contractante de prouver qu'elle est à même de respecter les conditions prescrites par les lois et règlements normalement et raisonnablement appliqués à l'exploitation de services aériens internationaux par ces autorités conformément aux dispositions de la Convention.

4) Chaque Partie contractante a le droit de refuser d'accorder l'autorisation d'exploitation visée au paragraphe 2 du présent article ou d'imposer les conditions qu'elle juge nécessaires à l'exercice par la compagnie aérienne désignée des droits visés à l'article 2 (Droits accordés) du présent Accord, lorsque la Parties contractante n'a pas la preuve que :

a) La propriété substantielle et le contrôle effectif de cette compagnie aérienne sont détenus par la Partie contractante qui a désigné la compagnie aérienne ou ses ressortissants; et/ou

b) Le Gouvernement qui a désigné la compagnie aérienne adopte ou assure les suivi des normes énoncées à l'article 13 (Sécurité aérienne) et à l'article 14 (Sûreté de l'aviation) du présent Accord.

5) La compagnie aérienne ainsi désignée et autorisée peut à tout moment commencer à assurer les services convenus, à condition qu'une capacité convenue et un tarif établi conformément aux dispositions des articles 5 (Capacité) et 6 (Tarifs) du présent Accord soient en vigueur pour ces services.

Article 4. Révocation ou suspension des autorisations d'exploitation

1) Chaque Partie contractante a le droit de révoquer une autorisation d'exploitation, de suspendre l'exercice des droits visés à l'article 2 (Droits accordés) du présent Accord par une compagnie aérienne désignée par l'autre Partie contractante ou d'imposer les conditions qu'elle estime nécessaires à l'exercice de ces droits :

a) Dans tous les cas où elle n'a pas la preuve que la propriété substantielle et le contrôle effectif de cette compagnie aérienne sont détenus par la Partie contractante qui l'a désignée ou ses ressortissants; ou

b) Si cette compagnie aérienne ne se conforme pas aux lois et règlements de la Partie contractante qui accorde ces droits; ou

c) Si cette compagnie aérienne n'est pas à même, de toute autre façon, de respecter les conditions prescrites dans le présent Accord.

2) À moins que des mesures immédiates de révocation, de suspension ou d'imposition de conditions visées au paragraphe 1 du présent article ne soient indispensables pour empêcher de nouvelles infractions aux lois ou règlements, ces droits ne sont exercés qu'après des consultations avec les autorités aéronautiques de l'État de l'autre Partie contractante. Dans ces cas, les consultations se tiennent dans les 60 jours suivant la date de la demande émise par une Partie contractante à cet effet.

Article 5. Capacité

1) La ou les compagnies aériennes désignées d'une Partie contractante bénéficient de possibilités équitables et égales d'exploiter des services aériens pour le transport de trafic entre les territoires des deux Parties contractantes.

2) Lors de l'exploitation des services aériens spécifiés par une compagnie aérienne désignée d'une Partie contractante, les intérêts de la compagnie aérienne de l'autre Partie contractante sont pris en considération afin de ne pas nuire indûment aux services assurés par cette dernière sur tout ou partie des mêmes routes.

3) Les services convenus exploités par les compagnies aériennes désignées des Parties contractantes doivent correspondre étroitement aux besoins du public en matière de transport sur les routes spécifiées et ont pour but essentiel de fournir, à un coefficient de remplissage raisonnable, une capacité suffisante pour répondre aux besoins actuels et raisonnablement prévisibles de transport de passagers et de marchandises (y compris le courrier) entre les territoires des Parties contractantes.

4) Pour l'exploitation des services convenus, la capacité totale à fournir et la fréquence des services à exploiter par la compagnie aérienne de chaque Partie contractante sont, dès le début, déterminés conjointement par les autorités aéronautiques des Parties contractantes avant l'inauguration des services. Lesdites autorités peuvent, de temps à autre, revoir et modifier la capacité et la fréquence initialement déterminées.

Article 6. Tarifs

1) Chaque Partie contractante permet aux compagnies aériennes désignées d'établir, à des taux raisonnables, les tarifs pour les services aériens internationaux assurés à destination ou en

provenance de son territoire, compte dûment de tous les éléments d'appréciation, notamment du coût d'exploitation, d'un bénéfice raisonnable et des tarifs des autres compagnies aériennes. Les Parties contractantes peuvent intervenir pour :

a) Prévenir les tarifs ou pratiques excessivement discriminatoires;

b) Protéger les consommateurs contre des tarifs excessivement élevés ou restrictifs en raison d'un abus de position dominante; et

c) Protéger les compagnies aériennes contre des tarifs artificiellement bas en raison de subventions ou d'aides publiques, directes ou indirectes.

2) Les compagnies aériennes désignées d'une Partie contractante doivent répondre aux exigences visées au paragraphe 1 du présent article et soumettre leurs tarifs à l'autre Partie contractante.

3) Les Parties contractantes n'autorisent pas leurs compagnies aériennes désignées, lors de l'établissement de tarifs, séparément ou conjointement avec une ou plusieurs autres compagnies aériennes, à abuser de leur position dominante sur le marché d'une manière qui affaiblirait, serait susceptible d'affaiblir ou viserait à affaiblir sérieusement un concurrent qui est une compagnie aérienne désignée de l'autre Partie contractante, ou à exclure ce concurrent d'une route.

4) Les Parties contractantes conviennent que, conformément aux pratiques des compagnies aériennes, lors de l'établissement des tarifs, les pratiques suivantes peuvent être considérées comme des pratiques concurrentielles éventuellement déloyales qui peuvent mériter un examen plus approfondi :

a) L'imposition de tarifs sur des routes à des niveaux qui sont globalement insuffisants pour couvrir les coûts associés à la prestation des services auxquels ils se rapportent;

b) Les pratiques en question sont appliquées durablement et pas seulement de manière temporaire;

c) Les pratiques en question ont une incidence économique importante sur une ou plusieurs compagnies aériennes désignées de l'autre Partie contractante, ou leur causent de graves préjudices; et

d) Tout comportement dénotant un abus de position dominante sur la route considérée.

5) Si une autorité aéronautique désapprouve un tarif appliqué par une compagnie aérienne de l'autre Partie contractante, les autorités aéronautiques s'efforcent de régler la question par voie de consultations, à la demande de l'une d'entre elles. En tout état de cause, l'autorité aéronautique d'une Partie contractante ne prend pas de mesures unilatérales pour empêcher l'entrée en vigueur d'un tarif d'une compagnie aérienne de l'autre Partie contractante ou son maintien.

6) Nonobstant ce qui précède, les compagnies aériennes désignées d'une Partie contractante communiquent, sur demande, aux autorités aéronautiques de l'autre Partie contractante, les renseignements relatifs à l'établissement des tarifs, de la façon et sous la forme demandées par ces autorités.

7) Aucune Partie contractante n'impose aux compagnies aériennes désignées de l'autre Partie contractante un droit de préférence, de rapport de partage du trafic, de redevance de non-opposition ou toute autre condition relative à la capacité, à la fréquence ou au trafic qui ne serait pas conforme aux objectifs du présent Accord.

Article 7. Droits de douane et autres taxes

1) Les aéronefs exploités pour des services aériens internationaux par la compagnie aérienne désignée d'une Partie contractante, ainsi que l'équipement ordinaire, les pièces de rechange (y compris les moteurs), le carburant, les lubrifiants et les provisions de bord (y compris, sans s'y limiter les denrées alimentaires, les boissons, le tabac et les produits destinés à la vente aux passagers ou à leur consommation pendant le vol) qui se trouvent à bord desdits aéronefs sont exonérés par l'autre Partie contractante, à l'arrivée sur son territoire, sur une base de réciprocité et conformément au droit applicable, de l'ensemble des droits de douane, frais de visite et autres taxes similaires, à condition que ces équipements, pièces de rechange et provisions restent à bord des aéronefs jusqu'à ce qu'ils soient réexportés ou utilisés à bord pendant la portion du voyage effectuée au-dessus de ce territoire.

2) Les équipements et articles suivants sont exonérés par l'autre Partie contractante, sur une base de réciprocité et conformément au droit applicable, de l'ensemble des droits de douane, frais de visite et autres taxes similaires qui ne sont pas dus au titre d'une prestation de services à l'arrivée, notamment :

a) L'équipement ordinaire, le carburant, les lubrifiants, les fournitures à usage technique consommables, les provisions de bord (y compris les denrées alimentaires, les boissons et le tabac) introduits sur le territoire de l'autre Partie contractante par une compagnie aérienne désignée ou pour son compte ou embarqués à bord de l'aéronef exploité par cette compagnie aérienne désignée afin d'être utilisés dans l'exploitation des services aériens internationaux, même lorsque cet équipement ordinaire et ces autres articles sont destinés à être utilisés pendant une portion du voyage effectuée au-dessus du territoire de l'autre Partie contractante;

b) Les pièces de rechange (y compris les moteurs) introduites sur le territoire de l'autre Partie contractante par une compagnie aérienne désignée, ou pour son compte, ou embarqués à bord d'un aéronef exploité par cette compagnie aérienne aux fins de l'entretien ou de la réparation d'aéronefs exploités pour des services aériens internationaux; et

c) Les stocks de billets imprimés, les lettres de transport aérien, les documents imprimés portant le logo de la compagnie aérienne désignée d'une Partie contractante ainsi que les supports publicitaires habituels qu'elle distribue gratuitement.

Les matériels visés aux alinéas a), b) et c) ci-dessus sont placés sous la surveillance ou le contrôle des services de douane.

3) L'équipement de bord ordinaire, ainsi que les pièces de rechange (y compris les moteurs), les provisions de bord, le carburant et les lubrifiants (y compris les liquides hydrauliques) ainsi que les matériels et fournitures qui sont conservés à bord des aéronefs d'une Partie contractante ne peuvent être déchargés sur le territoire de l'autre Partie contractante qu'avec l'approbation des autorités douanières de ce territoire. Dans ce cas, ils sont placés sous la surveillance de ces autorités jusqu'au moment où ils sont réexportés ou jusqu'à ce qu'il en soit autrement disposé conformément à la réglementation douanière de cette Partie contractante.

4) Les redevances pour les services fournis, le stockage et le dédouanement sont facturées conformément aux dispositions législatives et réglementaires nationales de chaque Partie contractante.

Article 8. Transit direct

Sous réserve des lois et règlements de chaque Partie contractante, les passagers, bagages et marchandises qui sont en transit direct par le territoire d'une Partie contractante et qui ne quittent pas la zone de l'aéroport réservée à cette fin ne subissent qu'un contrôle très simplifié, sauf si des mesures de sûreté contre les actes de violence, la piraterie aérienne et la contrebande de stupéfiants requièrent un contrôle plus strict. Les bagages et les marchandises en transit direct sont exonérés de droits de douane et autres taxes similaires.

Article 9. Redevances d'usage

1) Les installations et services aéroportuaires, de sûreté de l'aviation et autres installations et services connexes qui sont fournis sur le territoire d'une Partie contractante sont mis à la disposition des compagnies aériennes désignées de l'autre Partie contractante à des conditions non moins favorables que les conditions les plus favorables accordées à toute autre compagnie aérienne qui assure des services aériens internationaux semblables, au moment où les arrangements relatifs à leur utilisation sont pris.

2) La ou les compagnies aériennes désignées d'une Partie contractante peuvent, conformément aux lois et règlements nationaux des deux Parties et sur une base de réciprocité, assurer leurs propres services d'escale spécifiés sur le territoire de l'autre Partie contractante et, si elles le souhaitent, faire appel, pour exécuter tout ou partie desdits services, à un agent autorisé, si les lois et règlements nationaux l'exigent, par les autorités compétentes de l'autre Partie contractante à fournir de tels services.

3) L'établissement et la perception des droits et des taxes imposés sur le territoire d'une Partie contractante à une compagnie aérienne de l'autre Partie contractante pour l'utilisation des installations et services aéroportuaires, de sûreté de l'aviation ainsi que d'autres installations et services connexes sont justes et raisonnables. Ces droits et taxes sont établis à l'égard d'une compagnie aérienne de l'autre Partie contractante à des conditions qui ne sont pas moins favorables que les conditions les plus favorables accordées à toute compagnie aérienne qui assure des services aériens internationaux semblables au moment où ces droits et taxes sont imposés.

4) Chaque Partie contractante encourage les consultations entre ses autorités compétentes en matière d'imputation et les compagnies aériennes utilisant les services et les installations fournis ou, lorsque cela est possible, par l'intermédiaire d'organisations représentatives de ces compagnies aériennes. Les usagers sont informés, le plus tôt possible, des propositions de modification des redevances d'usage afin de leur permettre d'exprimer leurs vues avant que des changements ne soient apportés.

Article 10. Personnel étranger et accès aux services locaux

1) Conformément aux lois et règlements d'une Partie contractante en matière d'entrée et de séjour sur le territoire, et d'emploi, les compagnies aériennes désignées de l'autre Partie contractante ont le droit de faire entrer et de maintenir sur le territoire de l'autre Partie contractante leur propre personnel administratif, commercial, opérationnel, technique et tout autre personnel spécialisé nécessaire pour l'exploitation des services convenus.

2) La ou les compagnies aériennes désignées d'une Partie contractante peuvent à leur choix combler ces besoins en recourant à leur propre personnel ou aux services de toute autre

organisation, société ou compagnie aérienne exerçant des activités sur le territoire de l'autre Partie contractante et autorisée à fournir ces services à d'autres compagnies aériennes.

3) Les représentants et les membres du personnel sont soumis aux lois et règlements en vigueur dans l'autre Partie contractante. Conformément à ces lois et règlements, chacune des Parties contractantes, sur une base de réciprocité et avec un délai minimal, accorde au personnel visé au paragraphe 1 du présent article les autorisations d'emploi, visas de visiteur et autres documents similaires nécessaires.

Article 11. Conversion des devises et transfert des recettes

1) Les compagnies aériennes désignées ont le droit de vendre et de commercialiser leurs propres titres de transport sur le territoire de l'autre Partie contractante par l'intermédiaire de leurs bureaux de vente et, si elles le souhaitent, de leurs agents. Ces compagnies ont également le droit de vendre ces titres de transport, et toute personne est libre de les acheter, dans la monnaie du pays et/ou dans toute autre monnaie librement convertible, conformément aux lois et règlements nationaux applicables.

2) Les compagnies aériennes désignées ont le droit de convertir et de transférer dans leur pays l'excédent des recettes sur les dépenses qui a été réalisé dans le cadre du transport de trafic. En l'absence de dispositions appropriées dans un accord sur les paiements entre les Parties contractantes, le transfert susmentionné s'effectue dans des monnaies librement utilisables et conformément au droit interne et aux réglementations en matière de change applicables.

3) Les opérations de conversion et de transfert de ces recettes sont autorisées sans aucune restriction, au taux de change applicable aux transactions courantes en vigueur au moment où ces recettes sont présentées pour conversion et transfert, et ne donnent lieu à aucune commission autre que celle que les banques perçoivent normalement pour exécuter ce type d'opérations.

4) Les compagnies aériennes désignées des Parties contractantes ont le droit de régler, à leur discrétion, les dépenses locales, y compris l'achat de carburant, effectuées sur le territoire de l'autre Partie contractante, en monnaie locale ou, si cela est conforme aux réglementations monétaires locales applicables, en monnaies librement utilisables.

Article 12. Reconnaissance mutuelle des certificats et licences

1) Les certificats de navigabilité, les brevets d'aptitude et les licences délivrés ou validés par une Partie contractante et toujours en vigueur sont reconnus valables par l'autre Partie contractante aux fins de l'exploitation des services convenus sur les routes spécifiées, à condition que les normes selon lesquelles ces certificats, brevets ou licences ont été délivrés ou validés soient équivalentes ou supérieures aux normes minimales qui sont ou peuvent être établies conformément à la Convention. Chaque Partie contractante se réserve toutefois le droit de refuser de reconnaître, pour le survol de son territoire, les brevets d'aptitude et les licences délivrés à ses propres ressortissants ou validés pour eux par l'autre Partie contractante ou par tout autre État.

2) Si les privilèges ou conditions des licences, certificats ou brevets visés au paragraphe 1 ci-dessus, que les autorités aéronautiques d'une Partie contractante ont délivrés à une personne ou à une compagnie aérienne désignée ou pour un aéronef utilisé dans l'exploitation des services convenus, permettent une différence par rapport aux normes minimales établies en vertu de la Convention, différence qui a été notifiée à l'OACI, l'autre Partie contractante peut demander des

consultations entre les autorités aéronautiques afin de clarifier la pratique en question. L'absence d'accord satisfaisant constitue un motif pour appliquer les dispositions de l'article 4 (Révocation ou suspension des autorisations d'exploitation) du présent Accord.

Article 13. Sécurité aérienne

1) Chaque Partie contractante peut, en tout temps, demander des consultations au sujet des normes de sécurité adoptées par l'autre Partie contractante dans des domaines qui se rapportent aux services et installations aéronautiques, aux équipages, aux aéronefs ou à l'exploitation des aéronefs. Ces consultations ont lieu dans les 30 jours suivant la demande.

2) Si, à la suite de ces consultations, une Partie contractante découvre que l'autre Partie contractante n'adopte ni n'assure effectivement le suivi de normes de sécurité, dans les domaines mentionnés au paragraphe 1 du présent article, qui sont au moins aussi rigoureuses que les normes minimales établies à cette date conformément à la Convention, la première Partie contractante informe l'autre Partie contractante de ces conclusions et des démarches jugées nécessaires pour se conformer aux normes minimales de l'OACI et cette autre Partie contractante prend les mesures correctives appropriées qui s'imposent dans un délai convenu. Si ces mesures ne sont pas prises en temps utile, la première Partie contractante peut appliquer les dispositions de l'article 4 (Révocation ou suspension des autorisations d'exploitation) du présent Accord.

3) Nonobstant les obligations mentionnées à l'article 16 de la Convention, il est convenu que tout aéronef exploité par une compagnie aérienne d'une Partie contractante ou en son nom, à destination ou en provenance du territoire de l'État de l'autre Partie contractante peut, lorsqu'il se trouve sur le territoire de l'État de l'autre Partie contractante, faire l'objet d'une visite (dénommé, dans le présent article, « inspection sur piste »), sans retard excessif. Cette inspection est menée par les représentants autorisés de l'autre Partie contractante à bord et autour de l'aéronef. Nonobstant les obligations visées à l'article 33 de la Convention, l'objet de cette visite est de vérifier la validité des documents de l'aéronef et de son équipage et l'état apparent de l'aéronef et son équipement, conformément aux normes en vigueur établies en vertu de la Convention.

4) Si une inspection sur piste ou une série d'inspections sur piste donne des raisons sérieuses de penser que :

a) Un aéronef ou l'exploitation d'un aéronef n'est pas conforme aux normes minimales établies à cette date conformément à la Convention; ou

b) Les normes de sécurité définies à cette date conformément à la Convention ne sont pas adoptées effectivement et que leur suivi n'est pas effectivement assuré;

La Partie contractante qui procède à l'inspection est, aux fins de l'article 33 de la Convention, libre de conclure que les conditions qui ont régi la délivrance ou la validation des certificats, des brevets ou des licences pour cet aéronef ou son équipage, ou que les conditions en vertu desquelles cet aéronef est exploité, ne sont pas équivalentes ou supérieures aux normes minimales établies en vertu de la Convention.

5) Si le représentant de la compagnie aérienne désignée d'une Partie contractante refuse l'accès à un aéronef qu'elle exploite aux fins d'une inspection sur piste menée conformément aux dispositions du paragraphe 3 ci-dessus, l'autre Partie contractante est libre d'en déduire qu'il existe des raisons sérieuses du type visé au paragraphe 4 précédent et d'en tirer les conclusions qui y sont énoncées.

6) Chaque Partie contractante se réserve le droit de suspendre ou de modifier immédiatement l'autorisation d'exploitation de la compagnie aérienne de l'autre Partie contractante si la première Partie contractante conclut, à la suite d'une inspection sur piste, d'une série d'inspections sur piste ou d'un refus d'accès pour une inspection sur piste, de consultations ou pour toute autre raison, qu'une action immédiate est indispensable pour assurer la sécurité de l'exploitation d'une compagnie aérienne.

7) Toute mesure appliquée par une Partie contractante conformément au paragraphe 2 ou 6 ci-dessus est suspendue dès que les faits motivant cette mesure ont cessé d'exister.

Article 14. Sûreté de l'aviation

1) Conformément à leurs droits et obligations en vertu du droit international, les Parties contractantes réaffirment que leur obligation mutuelle de protéger l'aviation civile contre des actes d'intervention illicite, pour en assurer la sûreté, fait partie intégrante du présent Accord. Sans limiter la généralité de leurs droits et obligations en vertu du droit international, les Parties contractantes agissent en particulier conformément aux dispositions de la Convention relative aux infractions et à certains autres actes survenant à bord des aéronefs, signée à Tokyo le 14 septembre 1963, de la Convention pour la répression de la capture illicite d'aéronefs, signée à La Haye le 16 décembre 1970, de la Convention pour la répression d'actes illicites dirigés contre la sécurité de l'aviation civile, signée à Montréal le 23 septembre 1971, du Protocole pour la répression des actes illicites de violence dans les aéroports servant à l'aviation civile internationale, signé à Montréal le 24 février 1988 et de la Convention sur le marquage des explosifs plastiques et en feuilles aux fins de détection, signée à Montréal le 1er mars 1991, ou de toute autre convention relative à la sûreté de l'aviation à laquelle les Parties contractantes sont parties.

2) Les Parties contractantes se prêtent mutuellement, sur demande, toute l'assistance nécessaire pour prévenir les actes de capture illicite d'aéronefs civils et autres actes illicites dirigés contre la sécurité de ces aéronefs, de leurs passagers et équipages, des aéroports et des installations de navigation aérienne, et pour faire face à toute autre menace pour la sûreté de l'aviation civile.

3) Les Parties contractantes, dans leurs relations mutuelles, se conforment aux normes de sûreté de l'aviation et aux pratiques recommandées appropriées établies par l'OACI et qui sont désignées comme annexes à la Convention relative à l'aviation civile internationale, dans la mesure où ces dispositions relatives à la sûreté s'appliquent aux Parties contractantes. Elles exigent des exploitants d'aéronefs qui sont immatriculés par les Parties contractantes, ou des exploitants d'aéronefs qui ont leur établissement principal ou leur résidence permanente sur leur territoire et des exploitants d'aéroports situés sur leur territoire qu'ils se conforment aux dispositions en matière de sûreté de l'aviation qui s'appliquent aux Parties contractantes. En conséquence, chaque Partie contractante informe l'autre Partie contractante de toute divergence entre sa réglementation et ses pratiques nationales et les normes de sûreté de l'aviation des annexes susvisées. Une Partie contractante peut, à tout moment, demander à l'autre Partie contractante des consultations immédiates, tenues conformément au paragraphe 2 de l'article 18 du présent Accord, afin de discuter de ces divergences.

4) Chaque Partie contractante convient que ces exploitants d'aéronefs peuvent être tenus d'observer les dispositions relatives à la sûreté de l'aviation visées au paragraphe 3 ci-dessus que l'autre Partie contractante prescrit pour l'entrée et le séjour sur son territoire ainsi que pour la sortie de celui-ci. Chaque Partie contractante veille à ce que des mesures adéquates soient

appliquées effectivement sur son territoire pour protéger les aéronefs, et assurer l'inspection des passagers, des équipages, des bagages à main, des bagages, des marchandises et des provisions de bord avant et pendant l'embarquement ou le chargement. Chaque Partie contractante examine également avec bienveillance toute demande que lui adresse l'autre Partie contractante en vue d'obtenir que des mesures spéciales de sûreté soient prises pour faire face à une menace particulière.

5) En cas d'incident ou de menace d'incident de capture illicite d'aéronefs civils ou d'autres actes illicites dirigés contre la sûreté de ces aéronefs, de leurs passagers, de leurs membres d'équipage, des aéroports et des installations de navigation aérienne, les Parties contractantes s'entraident en facilitant les communications et autres mesures appropriées pour mettre fin avec rapidité et sécurité à cet incident ou à cette menace.

6) Chaque Partie contractante prend les mesures qu'elle estime réalisables pour s'assurer qu'un aéronef qui fait l'objet d'un acte de capture illicite ou d'un autre acte d'interférence illicite qui a atterri sur son territoire, est retenu au sol, à moins que son départ ne constitue une nécessité impérieuse pour protéger la vie humaine. Ces mesures sont prises, chaque fois que possible, en concertation.

Article 15. Soumission du programme de vols

1) La ou les compagnies aériennes désignées d'une Partie contractante soumettent les programmes de vols envisagés pour approbation aux autorités aéronautiques de l'autre Partie contractante, au moins 30 jours avant que les services convenus ne soient assurés.

2) Si la compagnie aérienne désignée d'une Partie contractante souhaite assurer des vols supplémentaires sur les services convenus en dehors du programme approuvé, cette compagnie aérienne demande l'autorisation préalable des autorités aéronautiques de l'autre Partie contractante. Ces demandes sont présentées conformément aux lois et règlements nationaux des Parties contractantes. La même procédure s'applique à toute modification y relative.

Article 16. Statistiques

Les autorités aéronautiques de chaque Partie contractante communiquent à celles de l'autre Partie contractante, à leur demande, les relevés statistiques périodiques ou autres qui peuvent être raisonnablement requis pour vérifier la capacité fournie par les compagnies aériennes désignées de la première Partie contractante sur les services convenus. Ces relevés contiennent tous les renseignements nécessaires pour déterminer le volume du trafic acheminé par ces compagnies aériennes sur les services convenus ainsi que les points d'origine et de destination de ce trafic.

Article 17. Application des lois et règlements nationaux

1) Les lois et règlements d'une Partie contractante régissant l'entrée, le séjour sur son territoire et la sortie de celui-ci d'un aéronef exploité dans les services aériens internationaux, l'exploitation ou la navigation de cet aéronef, ou ses vols au-dessus de ce territoire s'appliquent aux aéronefs de la compagnie aérienne désignée par l'autre Partie contractante.

2) Les lois et règlements d'une Partie contractante relatives à l'entrée et au séjour sur son territoire et au départ de son territoire de passagers, de membres d'équipage, de bagages, de

marchandises (y compris le courrier), telles que les formalités relatives à l'entrée, à la sortie, au dédouanement, à l'émigration et à l'immigration, à la sûreté de l'aviation, aux passeports, aux douanes, aux devises, aux mesures sanitaires et de quarantaine ainsi qu'au courrier, s'appliquent aux passagers, membres d'équipage, bagages, marchandises ou courrier transportés par les aéronefs des compagnies aériennes désignées de l'autre Partie contractante lorsqu'ils se trouvent sur ledit territoire.

3) Chaque Partie contractante, sur demande de l'autre Partie contractante, lui communique des copies des lois, réglementations et procédures pertinentes visées au présent Accord.

Article 18. Consultations et amendements

1) Dans un esprit d'étroite coopération, les autorités aéronautiques des Parties contractantes se consultent de temps à autre en vue de s'assurer de la mise en œuvre, de l'interprétation, de l'application ou de l'amendement du présent Accord et de ses annexes.

2) Si une Partie contractante demande des consultations dans le but de modifier le présent Accord ou ses annexes, ces consultations ont lieu le plus tôt possible, mais au plus tard 60 jours après la date de réception de la demande par l'autre Partie contractante, à moins que les Parties n'en soient convenues autrement. Ces consultations peuvent prendre la forme de discussions ou d'une correspondance. Chaque Partie contractante prépare, et présente lors de ces consultations, des arguments pertinents à l'appui de sa position afin de faciliter une prise de décisions rationnelle et rapide.

3) Si une Partie contractante juge souhaitable de modifier l'une quelconque des dispositions du présent Accord, cette modification entre en vigueur 30 jours après la date à laquelle les Parties contractantes se sont notifié l'accomplissement de toutes les procédures requises par leur droit interne pour son entrée en vigueur.

4) Les autorités aéronautiques des Parties contractantes peuvent convenir directement de modifications à l'annexe I. Ces modifications s'appliquent dès la date à laquelle elles ont été convenues et entrent en vigueur une fois confirmées par un échange de notes diplomatiques.

Article 19. Règlement des différends

1) En cas de différend portant sur l'interprétation ou l'application du présent Accord, les Parties contractantes s'efforcent, dans un premier temps, de le régler par voie de négociation entre leurs autorités aéronautiques.

2) Si lesdites autorités aéronautiques ne parviennent pas à un règlement par négociation, le différend est réglé par la voie diplomatique.

3) Si les Parties contractantes ne parviennent pas à régler le différend conformément aux paragraphes 1 et 2 ci-dessus, chaque Partie contractante peut, dans le respect de ses lois et règlements applicables, soumettre le différend à un tribunal d'arbitrage composé de trois arbitres choisis de la façon suivante : chaque Partie nomme un arbitre, et les deux arbitres ainsi choisis en nomment un troisième qui exercera la fonction de surarbitre, à condition de ne pas être un ressortissant des Parties contractantes, mais d'un pays entretenant des relations diplomatiques avec celles-ci au moment de sa nomination.

Chaque Partie contractante désigne son arbitre dans un délai de 60 jours à compter de la date de réception d'une notification d'arbitrage envoyée par lettre recommandée. Le surarbitre est nommé dans les 60 jours suivant la nomination des arbitres par les Parties contractantes.

Si une Partie contractante ne désigne pas son arbitre dans le délai prescrit, ou si les arbitres nommés ne parviennent pas à se mettre d'accord sur un surarbitre dans le délai imparti, chaque Partie contractante peut demander au Président du Conseil de l'OACI de nommer, selon le cas, l'arbitre manquant ou le surarbitre.

4) Le Vice-Président ou un haut fonctionnaire du Conseil de l'OACI, qui n'est un ressortissant d'aucune Partie contractante, procède à la nomination visée au paragraphe 3 du présent article à la place du Président de l'OACI, si ce dernier est absent ou incompétent pour le faire.

5) Le tribunal d'arbitrage détermine ses propres procédures et le lieu de l'arbitrage en tenant compte des dispositions convenues entre les Parties contractantes.

6) Les décisions du tribunal d'arbitrage sont définitives et contraignantes pour les Parties contractantes parties au différend.

7) Si une Partie contractante ou une compagnie aérienne désignée d'une Partie contractante ne se conforme pas à une décision rendue conformément au paragraphe 2 du présent article, l'autre Partie contractante peut limiter, suspendre ou révoquer les droits ou privilèges qu'elle a accordés en vertu du présent Accord à la Partie contractante défaillante.

8) Chaque Partie contractante supporte les frais de l'arbitre qu'elle a nommé. Les frais du surarbitre, y compris ses honoraires, ainsi que les dépenses exposées par l'OACI dans le cadre de la nomination du surarbitre et/ou de l'arbitre de la Partie contractante qui a omis de le désigner visée au paragraphe 3 du présent article, sont répartis de manière égale entre les Parties contractantes.

9) Pendant toute la période allant de la soumission du différend au tribunal d'arbitrage jusqu'à la publication de la sentence par ce dernier, les Parties contractantes continuent, sauf en cas de dénonciation, à honorer l'ensemble de leurs obligations en vertu du présent Accord, sans préjudice d'un ajustement final conformément à ladite sentence.

Article 20. Enregistrement

Le présent Accord, ses annexes et tout amendement qui leur est apporté sont enregistrés auprès de l'OACI.

Article 21. Accords multilatéraux

Si une convention ou un accord multilatéral relatif au transport aérien est conclu, auquel adhèrent les deux Parties contractantes, le présent Accord est modifié de manière à le rendre conforme aux dispositions de la convention ou de l'accord en question.

Article 22. Dénonciation

Le présent Accord est conclu pour une durée indéterminée.

Chaque Partie contractante peut, à tout moment, notifier à l'autre Partie contractante sa décision de dénoncer le présent Accord. Elle communique simultanément cette notification à l'OACI.

Dans ce cas, l'Accord prend fin 12 mois après la date de réception par l'autre Partie contractante de la notification de dénonciation, à moins que, d'un commun accord, la notification ne soit retirée avant l'expiration de ce délai. Si l'autre Partie contractante n'accuse pas réception de la notification, celle-ci est réputée avoir été reçue 14 jours après la date à laquelle l'OACI a reçu cette notification.

Article 23. Entrée en vigueur

Le présent Accord entre en vigueur 30 jours après que les Parties contractantes se sont notifié, par la voie diplomatique, l'accomplissement des formalités constitutionnelles nécessaires à cet effet.

EN FOI DE QUOI, les plénipotentiaires soussignés, à ce dûment autorisés par leurs Gouvernements respectifs, ont signé le présent Accord, constitué de 23 articles et de deux annexes.

FAIT à Ankara, le 17 décembre 2013, en double exemplaire, en langues espagnole, turque et anglaise. Tous les textes font également foi. En cas de divergence d'interprétation ou d'application du présent Accord, le texte anglais prévaut.

Pour le Gouvernement des États-Unis du Mexique :

JOSÉ ANTONIO MEADE KURIBREÑA
Ministre des affaires étrangères

Pour le Gouvernement de la République turque :

HAYATI YAZICI
Ministre des douanes et du commerce

ANNEXE I

TABLEAU DES ROUTES

1) Les compagnies aériennes désignées par les États-Unis du Mexique ont le droit d'assurer, dans les deux sens, les services aériens suivants :

Points de départ	Points intermédiaires	Points d'arrivée	Points au-delà
Points situés aux États-Unis du Mexique	Tous points	Points situés en Turquie	Tous points

2) Les compagnies aériennes désignées par la République turque ont le droit d'assurer, dans les deux sens, les services aériens suivants :

Points de départ	Points intermédiaires	Points d'arrivée	Points au-delà
Points situés en Turquie	Tous points	Points situés aux États-Unis du Mexique	Tous points

Remarques :

1) Les compagnies aériennes désignées peuvent omettre, à leur discrétion, les points intermédiaires et au-delà sur certains ou l'ensemble de leurs vols, à condition que le point de départ et le point d'arrivée de la route concernée se trouvent sur le territoire de la Partie contractante qui a désigné les compagnies aériennes en question.

2) Les compagnies aériennes désignées sont autorisées à exercer pleinement les troisième et quatrième libertés de l'air.

3) Les compagnies aériennes désignées ne peuvent exercer la cinquième liberté de l'air que si les autorités aéronautiques des deux Parties contractantes en sont convenues et ont donné leur autorisation préalable.

4) Les compagnies aériennes désignées d'une Partie contractante soumet à l'approbation des autorités aéronautiques de l'autre Partie contractante, au moins 30 jours avant de commencer à assurer ses services, les horaires prévus pour ceux-ci, en précisant la fréquence des vols, le type d'aéronef utilisé et la période de validité. Il est possible de demander, 48 heures à l'avance, une modification mineure et temporaire des horaires.

ANNEXE II

PARTAGE DE CODE

1) Les compagnies aériennes désignées d'une Partie contractante peuvent conclure des arrangements de commercialisation portant sur un contingent de sièges, un partage de code ou tout autre arrangement commercial avec :

a) Une compagnie aérienne de la même Partie contractante;

b) Une compagnie aérienne de l'autre Partie contractante;

c) Une compagnie aérienne d'un pays tiers;

À condition que toutes les compagnies aériennes impliquées dans les arrangements susmentionnés détiennent les droits nécessaires pour emprunter les routes et acheminer le trafic concernés et que, pour chaque billet vendu, l'acheteur soit informé au point de vente du nom de la compagnie aérienne qui assurera chaque partie du service.

2) Il est entendu par les deux Parties contractantes que les services de partage de code ne sont pas imputés sur les droits de fréquence du transporteur contractant.

3) Aucune compagnie aérienne d'une Partie contractante n'offre de service pour le transport de passagers locaux entre un point situé sur le territoire de l'autre Partie contractante et un point situé sur un territoire tiers, sauf si cette compagnie aérienne dispose des droits de trafic nécessaires pour proposer ce service entre ces deux points.

No. 52853

Germany
and
Mozambique

Agreement between the Government of the Federal Republic of Germany and the Government of the Republic of Mozambique concerning Financial Cooperation in 2014 - 2015. Maputo, 3 July 2015

Entry into force: *3 July 2015 by signature, in accordance with article 7*

Authentic texts: *German and Portuguese*

Registration with the Secretariat of the United Nations: *Germany, 12 August 2015*

Not published in print, in accordance with article 12(2) of the General Assembly regulations to give effect to Article 102 of the Charter of the United Nations, as amended, and the publication practice of the Secretariat.

Allemagne
et
Mozambique

Accord entre le Gouvernement de la République fédérale d'Allemagne et le Gouvernement de la République du Mozambique concernant la coopération financière en 2014 - 2015. Maputo, 3 juillet 2015

Entrée en vigueur : *3 juillet 2015 par signature, conformément à l'article 7*

Textes authentiques : *allemand et portugais*

Enregistrement auprès du Secrétariat de l'Organisation des Nations Unies : *Allemagne, 12 août 2015*

Non disponible en version imprimée, conformément au paragraphe 2 de l'article 12 du règlement de l'Assemblée générale destiné à mettre en application l'Article 102 de la Charte des Nations Unies, tel qu'amendé, et à la pratique du Secrétariat en matière de publication.

No. 52854

International Bank for Reconstruction and Development and Morocco

Guarantee Agreement (Noor-Ouarzazate Concentrated Solar Power Plant Project) between the Kingdom of Morocco and the International Bank for Reconstruction and Development (with International Bank for Reconstruction and Development General Conditions for Loans, dated 12 March 2012). Rabat, 19 December 2014

Entry into force: *5 May 2015 by notification*

Authentic text: *English*

Registration with the Secretariat of the United Nations: *International Bank for Reconstruction and Development, 13 August 2015*

Not published in print, in accordance with article 12(2) of the General Assembly regulations to give effect to Article 102 of the Charter of the United Nations, as amended, and the publication practice of the Secretariat.

Banque internationale pour la reconstruction et le développement et Maroc

Accord de garantie (Projet relatif à une centrale d'énergie solaire concentrée à Noor-Ouarzazate) entre le Royaume du Maroc et la Banque internationale pour la reconstruction et le développement (avec Conditions générales applicables aux prêts de la Banque internationale pour la reconstruction et le développement, en date du 12 mars 2012). Rabat, 19 décembre 2014

Entrée en vigueur : *5 mai 2015 par notification*

Texte authentique : *anglais*

Enregistrement auprès du Secrétariat de l'Organisation des Nations Unies : *Banque internationale pour la reconstruction et le développement, 13 août 2015*

Non disponible en version imprimée, conformément au paragraphe 2 de l'article 12 du règlement de l'Assemblée générale destiné à mettre en application l'Article 102 de la Charte des Nations Unies, tel qu'amendé, et à la pratique du Secrétariat en matière de publication.

No. 52855

Mexico
and
Turkey

Agreement between the Government of the United Mexican States and the Government of the Republic of Turkey for the avoidance of double taxation and the prevention of fiscal evasion with respect to taxes on income (with protocol). Ankara, 17 December 2013

Entry into force: *23 July 2015, in accordance with article 28*

Authentic texts: *English, Spanish and Turkish*

Registration with the Secretariat of the United Nations: *Mexico, 5 August 2015*

Mexique
et
Turquie

Accord entre le Gouvernement des États-Unis du Mexique et le Gouvernement de la République turque tendant à éviter les doubles impositions et à prévenir l'évasion fiscale en matière d'impôts sur le revenu (avec protocole). Ankara, 17 décembre 2013

Entrée en vigueur : *23 juillet 2015, conformément à l'article 28*

Textes authentiques : *anglais, espagnol et turc*

Enregistrement auprès du Secrétariat de l'Organisation des Nations Unies : *Mexique, 5 août 2015*

[ENGLISH TEXT – TEXTE ANGLAIS]

AGREEMENT BETWEEN THE GOVERNMENT OF THE UNITED MEXICAN STATES AND THE GOVERNMENT OF THE REPUBLIC OF TURKEY FOR THE AVOIDANCE OF DOUBLE TAXATION AND THE PREVENTION OF FISCAL EVASION WITH RESPECT TO TAXES ON INCOME

The Government of the United Mexican States and the Government of the Republic of Turkey

DESIRING to conclude an Agreement for the avoidance of double taxation and the prevention of fiscal evasion with respect to taxes on income,

HAVE AGREED as follows:

ARTICLE 1
Persons Covered

This Agreement shall apply to persons who are residents of one or both of the Contracting States.

ARTICLE 2
Taxes Covered

1. This Agreement shall apply to taxes on income imposed on behalf of Mexico and on behalf of Turkey, irrespective of the manner in which they are levied.

2. There shall be regarded as taxes on income all taxes imposed on total income or on elements of income, including taxes on gains from the alienation of movable or immovable property.

3. The existing taxes to which the Agreement shall apply are in particular:

a) in Mexico:

(i) the federal income tax;

(ii) the business flat rate tax;

(hereinafter referred to as "Mexican tax");

b) in Turkey:

(i) the income tax (Gelir Vergisi);

(ii) the corporation tax (Kurumlar Vergisi);

(hereinafter referred to as "Turkish tax").

4. The Agreement shall apply also to any identical or substantially similar taxes which are imposed after the date of signature of the Agreement in addition to, or in place of, the existing taxes. The competent authorities of the Contracting States shall notify each other of any significant changes which have been made in their respective taxation laws.

ARTICLE 3

General Definitions

1. For the purposes of this Agreement, unless the context otherwise requires:

a) the terms "Mexico" (the United Mexican States) and "Turkey" mean the territory of either Contracting State, including the land territory, internal waters, the territorial sea and air space above them, as well as any maritime area beyond the territorial sea, that in accordance with international law and its domestic law, either Contracting State exercises sovereign rights or jurisdiction with respect to the waters, seabed and subsoil and natural resources thereof,

b) the terms "a Contracting State" and "the other Contracting State" mean Mexico or Turkey, as the context requires;

c) the term "person" includes an individual, a company and any other body of persons;

d) the term "company" means any body corporate or any entity that is treated as a body corporate for tax purposes;

e) the term "legal head office" means the registered office registered under the Turkish Code of Commerce;

f) the terms "enterprise of a Contracting State" and "enterprise of the other Contracting State" mean respectively an enterprise carried on by a resident of a Contracting State and an enterprise carried on by a resident of the other Contracting State;

g) the term "international traffic" means any transport by a ship or aircraft operated by an enterprise of a Contracting State, except when the ship or aircraft is operated solely between places in the other Contracting State;

h) the term "competent authority" means:

(i) in Mexico, the Ministry of Finance and Public Credit; and

(ii) in Turkey, the Minister of Finance or his authorised representative;

i) the term "national" means:

(i) any individual possessing the nationality of a Contracting State;

(ii) any legal person, partnership or association deriving its status as such from the laws in force in a Contracting State.

2. As regards the application of the Agreement at any time by a Contracting State, any term not defined therein shall, unless the context otherwise requires, have the meaning that it has at that time under the law of that State for the purposes of the taxes to which the Agreement applies, any meaning under the applicable tax laws of that State prevailing over a meaning given to the term under other laws of that State.

ARTICLE 4
Resident

1. For the purposes of this Agreement, the term "resident of a Contracting State" means any person who, under the laws of that State, is liable to tax therein by reason of his domicile, residence, legal head office, place of management or any other criterion of a similar nature, and also includes that State and any political subdivision or local authority thereof. This term, however, does not include any person who is liable to tax in that State in respect only of income from sources in that State.

2. Where by reason of the provisions of paragraph 1 an individual is a resident of both Contracting States, then his status shall be determined as follows:

a) he shall be deemed to be a resident only of the State in which he has a permanent home available to him; if he has a permanent home available to him in both States, he shall be deemed to be a resident only of the State with which his personal and economic relations are closer (centre of vital interests);

b) if the State in which he has his centre of vital interests cannot be determined, or if he has not a permanent home available to him in either State, he shall be deemed to be a resident only of the State in which he has an habitual abode;

c) if he has an habitual abode in both States or in neither of them, he shall be deemed to be a resident only of the State of which he is a national;

d) if he is a national of both States or of neither of them, the competent authorities of the Contracting States shall settle the question by mutual agreement.

3. Where by reason of the provisions of paragraph 1, a person other than an individual is a resident of both Contracting States, when such person has its place of effective management in a Contracting State and its legal head office in the other Contracting State, then the competent authorities of the Contracting States shall determine by mutual agreement the State of which the person shall be deemed to be a resident for the purpose of the Agreement. In the absence of such agreement, such persons shall not be considered to be a resident of either Contracting State for the purpose of enjoying benefits under the Agreement.

ARTICLE 5

Permanent Establishment

1. For the purposes of this Agreement, the term "permanent establishment" means a fixed place of business through which the business of an enterprise is wholly or partly carried on.

2. The term "permanent establishment" includes especially:

a) a place of management;

b) a branch;

c) an office;

d) a factory;

e) a workshop, and

f) a mine, an oil or gas well, a quarry or any other place of extraction of natural resources.

3. A building site, construction, assembly or installation project or supervisory activities in connection therewith constitute a permanent establishment only if such site, project or activities continue for a period of more than six (6) months.

4. Notwithstanding the preceding provisions of this Article, the term "permanent establishment" shall be deemed not to include:

a) the use of facilities solely for the purpose of storage or display of goods or merchandise belonging to the enterprise;

b) the maintenance of a stock of goods or merchandise belonging to the enterprise solely for the purpose of storage or display;

c) the maintenance of a stock of goods or merchandise belonging to the enterprise solely for the purpose of processing by another enterprise;

d) the maintenance of a fixed place of business solely for the purpose of purchasing goods or merchandise or of collecting information, for the enterprise;

e) the maintenance of a fixed place of business solely for the purpose of carrying on, for the enterprise, any other activity of a preparatory or auxiliary character;

f) the maintenance of a fixed place of business solely for any combination of activities mentioned in sub-paragraphs a) to e), provided that the overall activity of the fixed place of business resulting from this combination is of a preparatory or auxiliary character.

5. Notwithstanding the provisions of paragraphs 1 and 2, where a person - other than an agent of an independent status to whom paragraph 7 applies - is acting on behalf of an enterprise and has, and habitually exercises, in a Contracting State an authority to conclude contracts in the name of the enterprise, that enterprise shall be deemed to have a permanent establishment in that State in respect of any activities which that person undertakes for the enterprise, unless the activities of such person are limited to those mentioned in paragraph 4 which, if exercised through a fixed place of business, would not make this fixed place of business a permanent establishment under the provisions of that paragraph.

6. Notwithstanding the foregoing provisions of this Article, an insurance enterprise of a Contracting State shall, except in regard to reinsurance, be deemed to have a permanent establishment in the other Contracting State if it collects premiums in the territory of that other State or insures risks situated therein through a person other than an agent of an independent status to whom paragraph 7 applies.

7. An enterprise shall not be deemed to have a permanent establishment in a Contracting State merely because it carries on business in that State through a broker, general commission agent or any other agent of an independent status, provided that such persons are acting in the ordinary course of their business.

8. The fact that a company which is a resident of a Contracting State controls or is controlled by a company which is a resident of the other Contracting State, or which carries on business in that other State (whether through a permanent establishment or otherwise), shall not of itself constitute either company a permanent establishment of the other.

ARTICLE 6

Income From Immovable Property

1. Income derived by a resident of a Contracting State from immovable property (including income from agriculture or forestry) situated in the other Contracting State may be taxed in that other State.

2. The term "immovable property" shall have the meaning which it has under the law of the Contracting State in which the property in question is situated. The term shall in any case include property accessory to immovable property, livestock and equipment used in agriculture and forestry, rights to which the provisions of general law respecting landed property apply, usufruct of immovable property and rights to variable or fixed payments as consideration for the working of, or the right to work, mineral deposits, sources and other natural resources; ships, boats and aircraft shall not be regarded as immovable property.

3. The provisions of paragraph 1 shall apply to income derived from the direct use, letting, or use in any other form of immovable property.

4. The provisions of paragraphs 1 and 3 shall also apply to the income from immovable property of an enterprise and to income from immovable property used for the performance of independent personal services.

ARTICLE 7
Business Profits

1. The profits of an enterprise of a Contracting State shall be taxable only in that State unless the enterprise carries on business in the other Contracting State through a permanent establishment situated therein. If the enterprise carries on business as aforesaid, the profits of the enterprise may be taxed in the other State but only so much of them as is attributable to that permanent establishment.

2. Subject to the provisions of paragraph 3, where an enterprise of a Contracting State carries on business in the other Contracting State through a permanent establishment situated therein, there shall in each Contracting State be attributed to that permanent establishment the profits which it might be expected to make if it were a distinct and separate enterprise engaged in the same or similar activities under the same or similar conditions and dealing wholly independently with the enterprise of which it is a permanent establishment.

3. In determining the profits of a permanent establishment, there shall be allowed as deductions expenses which are incurred for the purposes of the permanent establishment, including executive and general administrative expenses so incurred, whether in the State in which the permanent establishment is situated or elsewhere.

4. No profits shall be attributed to a permanent establishment by reason of the mere purchase by that permanent establishment of goods or merchandise for the enterprise.

5. Where profits include items of income which are dealt with separately in other Articles of this Agreement, then the provisions of those Articles shall not be affected by the provisions of this Article.

ARTICLE 8
Shipping and Air Transport

1. Profits derived by an enterprise of a Contracting State from the operation of ships or aircraft in international traffic shall be taxable only in that State.

2. The provisions of paragraph 1 shall also apply to profits from the participation in a pool, a joint business or an international operating agency.

ARTICLE 9
Associated Enterprises

1. Where

a) an enterprise of a Contracting State participates directly or indirectly in the management, control or capital of an enterprise of the other Contracting State, or

b) the same persons participate directly or indirectly in the management, control or capital of an enterprise of a Contracting State and an enterprise of the other Contracting State,

and in either case conditions are made or imposed between the two enterprises in their commercial or financial relations which differ from those which would be made between independent enterprises, then any profits which would, but for those conditions, have accrued to one of the enterprises, but, by reason of those conditions, have not so accrued, may be included in the profits of that enterprise and taxed accordingly.

2. Where a Contracting State includes in the profits of an enterprise of that State - and taxes accordingly - profits on which an enterprise of the other Contracting State has been charged to tax in that other State and the profits so included are by the first-mentioned State claimed to be profits which would have accrued to the enterprise of the first-mentioned State if the conditions made between the two enterprises had been those which would have been made between independent enterprises, then that other State shall make an appropriate adjustment to the amount of the tax charged therein on those profits, where that other State considers the adjustment justified. In determining such adjustment, due regard shall be had to the other provisions of this Agreement and the competent authorities of the Contracting States shall, if necessary, consult each other.

ARTICLE 10
Dividends

1. Dividends paid by a company which is a resident of a Contracting State to a resident of the other Contracting State may be taxed in that other State.

2. However, such dividends may also be taxed in the Contracting State of which the company paying the dividends is a resident and according to the laws of that State, but if the beneficial owner of the dividends is a resident of the other Contracting State, the tax so charged shall not exceed:

a) 5 per cent of the gross amount of the dividends if the beneficial owner is a company (other than a partnership) which holds directly at least 25 per cent of the capital of the company paying the dividends;

b) 15 per cent of the gross amount of the dividends in all other cases.

This paragraph shall not affect the taxation of the company in respect of the profits out of which the dividends are paid.

3. The term "dividends" as used in this Article means income from shares, "jouissance" shares or "jouissance" rights, mining shares, founders' shares or other rights, not being debt-claims, participating in profits, as well as income from other corporate rights and other income which is subjected to the same taxation treatment as income from shares by the laws of the State of which the company making the distribution is a resident, and income derived from an investment fund and investment trust.

4. Profits of a company of a Contracting State carrying on business in the other Contracting State through a permanent establishment situated therein may, after having been taxed under Article 7, be taxed on the remaining amount in the Contracting State in which the permanent establishment is situated and in accordance with paragraph 2 a) of this Article.

5. The provisions of paragraphs 1 and 2 shall not apply if the beneficial owner of the dividends, being a resident of a Contracting State, carries on business in the other Contracting State of which the company paying the dividends is a resident through a permanent establishment situated therein or performs in that other State independent personal services from a fixed base situated therein and the holding in respect of which the dividends are paid is effectively connected with such permanent establishment or fixed base. In such case the provisions of Article 7 or Article 14, as the case may be, shall apply.

6. Subject to the provisions of paragraph 4, where a company which is a resident of a Contracting State derives profits or income from the other Contracting State, that other State may not impose any tax on the dividends paid by the company, except insofar as such dividends are paid to a resident of that other State or insofar as the holding in respect of which the dividends are paid is effectively connected with a permanent establishment or a fixed base situated in that other State, nor subject the company's undistributed profits to a tax on the company's undistributed profits, even if the dividends paid or the undistributed profits consist wholly or partly of profits or income arising in such other State.

ARTICLE 11
Interest

1. Interest arising in a Contracting State and paid to a resident of the other Contracting State may be taxed in that other State.

2. However, such interest may also be taxed in the Contracting State in which it arises and according to the laws of that State; but if the beneficial owner of the interest is a resident of the other Contracting State, the tax so charged shall not exceed:

a) 10 per cent of the gross amount of the interest if it is paid to a bank.

b) 15 per cent of the gross amount of the interest in all other cases.

3. Notwithstanding the provisions of paragraph 2, interest referred to in paragraph 1 shall be taxable only in the Contracting State in which the beneficial owner is a resident if:

a) the beneficial owner is a Contracting State, a political subdivision or a local authority thereof, or the Central Bank of Mexico (Banco de México) or the Central Bank of Turkey (Türkiye Cumhuriyet Merkez Bankası);

b) the interest is paid by any of the entities mentioned in sub-paragraph a);

c) the interest arises in Turkey and is paid in respect of a loan for a period of not less than three (3) years granted by Banco Nacional de Comercio Exterior, S.N.C., Nacional Financiera, S.N.C. or Banco Nacional de Obras y Servicios Públicos, S.N.C.; or

d) the interest arises in Mexico and is paid in respect of a loan for a period of not less than three (3) years granted by the Eximbank of Turkey (Türkiye İhracat Kredi Bankası A.Ş.).

4. The term "interest" as used in this Article means income from debt-claims of every kind, whether or not secured by mortgage and whether or not carrying a right to participate in the debtor's profits, and in particular, income from government securities and income from bonds or debentures, including premiums and prizes attaching to such securities, bonds or debentures, as well as all other income that is treated as income from money lent by the laws of the Contracting State in which the income arises.

5. The provisions of paragraphs 1 and 2 shall not apply if the beneficial owner of the interest, being a resident of a Contracting State, carries on business in the other Contracting State in which the interest arises through a permanent establishment situated therein or performs in that other State independent personal services from a fixed base situated therein, and the debt-claim in respect of which the interest is paid is effectively connected with such permanent establishment or fixed base. In such case the provisions of Article 7 or Article 14, as the case may be, shall apply.

6. Interest shall be deemed to arise in a Contracting State when the payer is that State itself, a political subdivision, a local authority or a resident of that State. Where, however, the person paying the interest, whether he is a resident of a Contracting State or not, has in a Contracting State a permanent establishment or a fixed base and such interest is borne by such permanent establishment or fixed base, then such interest shall be deemed to arise in the State in which the permanent establishment or fixed base is situated.

7. Where, by reason of a special relationship between the payer and the beneficial owner or between both of them and some other person, the amount of the interest exceeds, for whatever reason, the amount which would have been agreed upon by the payer and the beneficial owner in the absence of such relationship, the provisions of this Article shall apply only to the last-mentioned amount. In such case, the excess part of the payments shall remain taxable according to the laws of each Contracting State, due regard being had to the other provisions of this Agreement.

ARTICLE 12
Royalties

1. Royalties arising in a Contracting State and paid to a resident of the other Contracting State may be taxed in that other State.

2. However, such royalties may also be taxed in the Contracting State in which they arise and according to the laws of that State, but if the beneficial owner of the royalties is a resident of the other Contracting State, the tax so charged shall not exceed 10 per cent of the gross amount of the royalties.

3. The term "royalties" as used in this Article means payments of any kind received as a consideration for:

a) the use of, or the right to use, any patent, trade mark, design or model, plan, secret formula or process;

b) the use of, or the right to use, any industrial, commercial or scientific equipment;

c) the supply of information concerning industrial, commercial or scientific experience;

d) the use of, or the right to use, any copyright of literary, artistic or scientific work, including cinematograph films and recordings or tapes for television or radio broadcasting;

4. The provisions of paragraphs 1 and 2 shall not apply if the beneficial owner of the royalties, being a resident of a Contracting State, carries on business in the other Contracting State in which the royalties arise through a permanent establishment situated therein or performs in that other State independent personal services from a fixed base situated therein and the right or property in respect of which the royalties are paid is effectively connected with such permanent establishment or fixed base, In such case the provisions of Article 7 or Article 14, as the case may be, shall apply.

5. Royalties shall be deemed to arise in a Contracting State when the payer is that State itself, a political subdivision, a local authority or a resident of that State. Where, however, the person paying the royalties, whether he is a resident of a Contracting State or not, has in a Contracting State a permanent establishment or fixed base and such royalties are borne by such permanent establishment or fixed base, then such royalties shall be deemed to arise in the State in which the permanent establishment or fixed base is situated.

6. Where, by reason of a special relationship between the payer and the beneficial owner or between both of them and some other person, the amount of the royalties exceeds, for whatever reason, the amount which would have been agreed upon by the payer and the beneficial owner in the absence of such relationship, the provisions of this Article shall apply only to the last-mentioned amount. In such case, the excess part of the payments shall remain taxable according to the laws of each Contracting State, due regard being had to the other provisions of this Agreement.

ARTICLE 13
Capital Gains

1. Gains derived by a resident of a Contracting State from the alienation of immovable property referred to in Article 6 and situated in the other Contracting State may be taxed in that other State.

2. Gains from the alienation of shares or other similar rights in a company the property of which consists directly or indirectly principally of immovable property situated in a Contracting State may be taxed in that State.

3. Gains derived by a resident of a Contracting State from the alienation of shares, participation or other rights in the capital of a company or other legal person that is a resident of the other Contracting State may be taxed in that other State.

4. Gains from the alienation of movable property forming part of the business property of a permanent establishment which an enterprise of a Contracting State has in the other Contracting State or of movable property pertaining to a fixed base available to a resident of a Contracting State in the other Contracting State for the purpose of performing independent personal services, including such gains from the alienation of such a permanent establishment (alone or with the whole enterprise) or of such fixed base, may be taxed in that other State.

5. Gains derived by a resident of a Contracting State from the alienation of ships or aircraft operated in international traffic, or of movable property pertaining to the operation of such ships or aircraft, shall be taxable only in that State.

6. Gains from the alienation of any property other than that referred to in the preceding paragraphs of this Article, shall be taxable only in the Contracting State of which the alienator is a resident. However, gains referred to in the previous sentence of this paragraph and derived from the other Contracting State, may be taxed in that other Contracting State, if the time elapsed between the date of acquisition and the date of alienation of such property does not exceed one (1) year.

ARTICLE 14

Independent Personal Services

1. Income derived by an individual who is a resident of a Contracting State in respect of professional services or other activities of an independent character shall be taxable only in that State. However, such income may also be taxed in the other Contracting State if such services or activities are performed in that other State and if:

a) he has a fixed base regularly available to him in the other State for the purpose of performing those services or activities; or

b) he is present in that other State for the purpose of performing those services or activities for a period or periods amounting in the aggregate to one hundred and eighty three (183) days or more in any continuous period of twelve (12) months.

In such circumstances, only so much of the income as is attributable to that fixed base or derived from the services or activities performed during his presence in that other State, as the case may be, may be taxed in that other State.

2. Income derived by an enterprise of a Contracting State in respect of professional services or other activities of an independent character shall be taxable only in that State. However, such income may also be taxed in the other Contracting State if such services or activities are performed in that other State and if:

a) the enterprise has a permanent establishment in that other State through which the services or activities are performed; or

b) the period or periods during which the services or activities are performed exceed in the aggregate one hundred and eighty three (183) days in any continuous period of twelve (12) months.

In such circumstances, only so much of the income as is attributable to that permanent establishment or to the services or activities performed in that other State, as the case may be, may be taxed in that other State.

3. The term "professional services" includes especially independent scientific, literary, artistic, educational or teaching activities as well as the independent activities of physicians, lawyers, engineers, architects, dentists and accountants.

ARTICLE 15

Dependent Personal Services

1. Subject to the provisions of Articles 16, 18, 19 and 20, salaries, wages and other similar remuneration derived by a resident of a Contracting State in respect of an employment shall be taxable only in that State unless the employment is exercised in the other Contracting State. If the employment is so exercised, such remuneration as is derived therefrom may be taxed in that other State.

2. Notwithstanding the provisions of paragraph 1, remuneration derived by a resident of a Contracting State in respect of an employment exercised in the other Contracting State shall be taxable only in the first-mentioned Contracting State if:

a) the recipient is present in the other State for a period or periods not exceeding in the aggregate one hundred and eighty three (183) days in any twelve (12) month period, and

b) the remuneration is paid by, or on behalf of, an employer who is not a resident of the other State, and

c) the remuneration is not borne by a permanent establishment or fixed base which the employer has in the other State.

3. Notwithstanding the preceding provisions of this Article, remuneration derived in respect of an employment exercised aboard a ship or aircraft operated by an enterprise of a Contracting State in international traffic, may be taxed in that Contracting State.

ARTICLE 16

Directors' Fees

Directors' fees and other similar payments derived by a resident of a Contracting State in his capacity as a member of the board of directors of a company which is a resident of the other Contracting State, may be taxed in that other State.

ARTICLE 17
Artistes and Sportspersons

1. Notwithstanding the provisions of Articles 14 and 15, income derived by a resident of a Contracting State as an entertainer, such as a theatre, motion picture, radio or television artiste, or a musician, or as a sportsperson, from his personal activities as such exercised in the other Contracting State, may be taxed in that other State.

2. Where income in respect of personal activities exercised by an entertainer or a sportsperson in his capacity as such accrues not to the entertainer or sportsperson himself but to another person, that income may, notwithstanding the provisions of Articles 7, 14 and 15, be taxed in the Contracting State in which the activities of the entertainer or sportsperson are exercised.

3. Income derived by an entertainer or a sportsperson from activities exercised in a Contracting State shall be exempt from tax in that State, if the visit to that State is supported wholly or mainly by public funds of the other Contracting State, a political subdivision or a local authority thereof.

ARTICLE 18
Pensions

1. Subject to the provisions of paragraph 2 of Article 19, pensions and other similar remuneration paid to a resident of a Contracting State in consideration of past employment shall be taxable only in that State. This provision shall also apply to life annuities paid to a resident of a Contracting State.

2. The term "life annuity" includes a stated sum payable periodically at stated times, during life or during a specified or ascertainable period of time, under an obligation to make the payments in return for adequate and full consideration in money or money's worth.

ARTICLE 19

Government Service

1. a) Salaries, wages and other similar remuneration, other than a pension, paid by a Contracting State or a political subdivision or a local authority thereof to an individual in respect of services rendered to that State or subdivision or authority shall be taxable only in that State.

   b) However, such salaries, wages and other similar remuneration shall be taxable only in the other Contracting State if the services are rendered in that State and the individual is a resident of that State who:

      (i) is a national of that State; or

      (ii) did not become a resident of that State solely for the purpose of rendering the services.

2. a) Notwithstanding the provisions of paragraph 1, any pension and other similar remuneration paid by, or out of funds created by, a Contracting State or a political subdivision or a local authority thereof to an individual in respect of services rendered to that State or subdivision or authority shall be taxable only in that State.

   b) However, such pension and other similar remuneration shall be taxable only in the other Contracting State if the individual is a resident of, and a national of, that State.

3. The provisions of Articles 15, 16, 17 and 18 shall apply to salaries, wages and other similar remuneration and pensions in respect of services rendered in connection with a business carried on by a Contracting State or a political subdivision or a local authority thereof.

ARTICLE 20

Teachers and Students

1. Payments which a student or business apprentice who is a national of a Contracting State and who is present in the other Contracting State solely for the purpose of his education or training receives for the purpose of his maintenance, education or training shall not be taxed in that other State, provided that such payments arise from sources outside that other State.

2. Likewise, remuneration received by a teacher or by an instructor who is a national of a Contracting State and who is present in the other Contracting State for the primary purpose of teaching or engaging in scientific research for a period or periods not exceeding two (2) years shall be exempt from tax in that other State on his remuneration from personal services for teaching or research, provided that such payments arise from sources outside that other State.

ARTICLE 21

Other Income

Items of income of a resident of a Contracting State not dealt with in the foregoing Articles of this Agreement and arising in the other Contracting State may be taxed in that other State.

ARTICLE 22

Elimination of Double Taxation

1. In accordance with the provisions and subject to the limitations of the laws of Mexico, as may be amended from time to time without changing the general principle hereof, Mexico shall allow its residents as a credit against the Mexican tax:

a) the Turkish tax paid on income arising in Turkey in an amount not exceeding the tax payable in Mexico on such income; and

b) in the case of a company owning at least 10 per cent of the capital of a company which is a resident of Turkey and from which the first-mentioned company receives dividends, the Turkish tax paid by the distributing company with respect to the profits out of which the dividends are paid.

2. Subject to the provisions of the laws of Turkey regarding the allowance as a credit against Turkish tax of tax payable in a territory outside Turkey (as they may be amended from time to time without changing the general principles hereof), Mexican tax payable under the laws of Mexico and in accordance with this Agreement in respect of income (including profits and chargeable gains) derived by a resident of Turkey from sources within Mexico shall be allowed as a deduction from the Turkish tax on such income. Such deduction, however, shall not exceed the amount of Turkish tax, as computed before the deduction is made, attributable to such income.

3. Where in accordance with any provision of the Agreement income derived by a resident of a Contracting State is exempt from tax in that State, such State may nevertheless, in calculating the amount of tax on the remaining income of such resident, take into account the exempted income.

ARTICLE 23

Non-Discrimination

1. Nationals of a Contracting State shall not be subjected in the other Contracting State to any taxation or any requirement connected therewith, which is other or more burdensome than the taxation and connected requirements to which nationals of that other State in the same circumstances, in particular with respect to residence, are or may be subjected. This provision shall, notwithstanding the provisions of Article 1, also apply to persons who are not residents of one or both of the Contracting States.

2. Subject to the provisions of paragraph 4 of Article 10, the taxation on a permanent establishment which an enterprise of a Contracting State has in the other Contracting State shall not be less favourably levied in that other State than the taxation levied on enterprises of that other State carrying on the same activities.

3. Except where the provisions of paragraph 1 of Article 9, paragraph 7 of Article 11, or paragraph 6 of Article 12, apply, interest, royalties and other disbursements paid by an enterprise of a Contracting State to a resident of the other Contracting State shall, for the purpose of determining the taxable profits of such enterprise, be deductible under the same conditions as if they had been paid to a resident of the first-mentioned State.

4. Enterprises of a Contracting State, the capital of which is wholly or partly owned or controlled, directly or indirectly, by one or more residents of the other Contracting State, shall not be subjected in the first-mentioned State to any taxation or any requirement connected therewith which is other or more burdensome than the taxation and connected requirements to which other similar enterprises of the first-mentioned State are or may be subjected.

5. These provisions shall not be construed as obliging a Contracting State to grant to residents of the other Contracting State any personal allowances, reliefs and reductions for taxation purposes on account of civil status or family responsibilities which it grants to its own residents.

6. The provisions of this Article shall, notwithstanding the provisions of Article 2, apply to taxes of every kind and description.

ARTICLE 24
Mutual Agreement Procedure

1. Where a person considers that the actions of one or both of the Contracting States result or will result for him in taxation not in accordance with the provisions of this Agreement, he may, irrespective of the remedies provided by the domestic law of those States, present his case to the competent authority of the Contracting State of which he is a resident or, if his case comes under paragraph 1 of Article 23, to that of the Contracting State of which he is a national. The case must be presented within three (3) years from the first notification of the action resulting in taxation not in accordance with the provisions of the Agreement.

2. The competent authority shall endeavour, if the objection appears to it to be justified and if it is not itself able to arrive at a satisfactory solution, to resolve the case by mutual agreement with the competent authority of the other Contracting State, with a view to the avoidance of taxation which is not in accordance with the Agreement.

3. The competent authorities of the Contracting States shall endeavour to resolve by mutual agreement any difficulties or doubts arising as to the interpretation or application of the Agreement. They may also consult together for the elimination of double taxation in cases not provided for in the Agreement.

4. The competent authorities of the Contracting States may communicate with each other directly for the purpose of reaching an agreement in the sense of the preceding paragraphs.

ARTICLE 25

Exchange of Information

1. The competent authorities of the Contracting States shall exchange such information as is foreseeably relevant for carrying out the provisions of this Agreement or to the administration or enforcement of the domestic laws concerning taxes of every kind and description imposed on behalf of the Contracting States, or of their political subdivisions or local authorities, insofar as the taxation thereunder is not contrary to the Agreement. The exchange of information is not restricted by Articles 1 and 2.

2. Any information received under paragraph 1 by a Contracting State shall be treated as secret in the same manner as information obtained under the domestic laws of that State and shall be disclosed only to persons or authorities (including courts and administrative bodies) concerned with the assessment or

collection of, the enforcement or prosecution in respect of, the determination of appeals in relation to the taxes referred to in paragraph 1, or the oversight of the above. Such persons or authorities shall use the information only for such purposes. They may disclose the information in public court proceedings or in judicial decisions.

3. In no case shall the provisions of paragraphs 1 and 2 be construed so as to impose on a Contracting State the obligation to:

a) carry out administrative measures at variance with the laws and administrative practice of that or of the other Contracting State;

b) supply information which is not obtainable under the laws or in the normal course of the administration of that or of the other Contracting State;

c) supply information which would disclose any trade, business, industrial, commercial or professional secret or trade process, or information the disclosure of which would be contrary to public policy *(ordre public)*.

4. If information is requested by a Contracting State in accordance with this Article, the other Contracting State shall use its information gathering measures to obtain the requested information, even though that other State may not need such information for its own tax purposes. The obligation contained in the preceding sentence is subject to the limitations of paragraph 3 but in no case shall such limitations be construed to permit a Contracting State to decline to supply information solely because it has no domestic interest in such information.

5. In no case shall the provisions of paragraph 3 be construed to permit a Contracting State to decline to supply information solely because the information is held by a bank, other financial institution, nominee or person acting in an agency or a fiduciary capacity or because it relates to ownership interests in a person.

ARTICLE 26

Assistance in the Collection of Taxes

1. The Contracting States shall lend assistance to each other in the collection of revenue claims. This assistance is not restricted by Articles 1 and 2. The competent authorities of the Contracting States may by mutual agreement settle the mode of application of this Article.

2. The term "revenue claim" as used in this Article means an amount owed in respect of taxes of every kind and description imposed on behalf of the Contracting States, or of their political subdivisions or local authorities, insofar as the taxation thereunder is not contrary to this Agreement or any other instrument to which the Contracting States are parties, as well as interest, administrative penalties and costs of collection or conservancy related to such amount.

3. When a revenue claim of a Contracting State is enforceable under the laws of that State and is owed by a person who, at that time, cannot, under the laws of that State, prevent its collection, that revenue claim shall, at the request of the competent authority of that State, be accepted for purposes of collection by the competent authority of the other Contracting State. That revenue claim shall be collected by that other State in accordance with the provisions of its laws applicable to the enforcement and collection of its own taxes as if the revenue claim were a revenue claim of that other State.

4. When a revenue claim of a Contracting State is a claim in respect of which that State may, under its law, take measures of conservancy with a view to ensure its collection, that revenue claim shall, at the request of the competent authority of that State, be accepted for purposes of taking measures of conservancy by the competent authority of the other Contracting State. That other State shall take measures of conservancy in respect of that revenue claim in accordance with the provisions of its laws as if the revenue claim were a revenue claim of that other State even if, at the time when such measures are applied, the revenue claim is not enforceable in the first-mentioned State or is owed by a person who has a right to prevent its collection.

5. Notwithstanding the provisions of paragraphs 3 and 4, a revenue claim accepted by a Contracting State for purposes of paragraph 3 or 4 shall not, in that State, be subject to the time limits or accorded any priority applicable to a revenue claim under the laws of that State by reason of its nature as such. In addition, a revenue claim accepted by a Contracting State for the purposes of paragraph 3 or 4 shall not, in that State, have any priority applicable to that revenue claim under the laws of the other Contracting State.

6. Proceedings with respect to the existence, validity or the amount of a revenue claim of a Contracting State shall not be brought before the courts or administrative bodies of the other Contracting State.

7. Where, at any time after a request has been made by a Contracting State under paragraph 3 or 4 and before the other Contracting State has collected and remitted the relevant revenue claim to the first-mentioned State, the relevant revenue claim ceases to be

a) in the case of a request under paragraph 3, a revenue claim of the first-mentioned State that is enforceable under the laws of that State and is owed by a person who, at that time, cannot, under the laws of that State, prevent its collection, or

b) in the case of a request under paragraph 4, a revenue claim of the first-mentioned State in respect of which that State may, under its laws, take measures of conservancy with a view to ensure its collection

the competent authority of the first-mentioned State shall promptly notify the competent authority of the other State of that fact and, at the option of the other State, the first-mentioned State shall either suspend or withdraw its request.

8. In no case shall the provisions of this Article be construed so as to impose on a Contracting State the obligation:

a) to carry out administrative measures at variance with the laws and administrative practice of that or of the other Contracting State;

b) to carry out measures which would be contrary to public policy *(ordre public)*;

c) to provide assistance if the other Contracting State has not pursued all reasonable measures of collection or conservancy, as the case may be, available under its laws or administrative practice;

d) to provide assistance in those cases where the administrative burden for that State is clearly disproportionate to the benefit to be derived by the other Contracting State.

ARTICLE 27

Members of Diplomatic Missions and Consular Posts

Nothing in this Agreement shall affect the fiscal privileges of members of diplomatic missions or consular posts under the general rules of international law or under the provisions of special agreements.

ARTICLE 28

Entry into Force

Each of the Contracting States shall notify each other, through the diplomatic channels, the completion of the procedures required by its domestic law for the bringing into force of this Agreement. This Agreement shall enter into force thirty (30) days after the date of the later of these notifications and its provisions shall have effect for taxes with respect to every taxable period beginning on or after the first day of January of the year following that of entry into force of this Agreement.

ARTICLE 29

Termination

This Agreement shall remain in force until terminated by a Contracting State. Either Contracting State may terminate the Agreement, through diplomatic channels, by giving notice of termination at least six (6) months before the end of any calendar year following after the period of five (5) years from the date on which the Agreement enters into force. In such event, the Agreement shall cease to have effect for taxes with respect to every taxable period beginning on or after the first day of January of the year following that in which the notice is given.

IN WITNESS whereof the undersigned, being duly authorised thereto, have signed this Agreement.

DONE in duplicate at Ankara on this seventeenth day of December of two thousand and thirteen, in the Spanish, Turkish and English languages, all texts being equally authentic. In the case of any divergence, the English text shall prevail.

FOR THE GOVERNMENT OF THE UNITED MEXICAN STATES	**FOR THE GOVERNMENT OF THE REPUBLIC OF TURKEY**
José Antonio Meade Kuribreña	**Mehmet ŞİMŞEK**
Minister of Foreign Affairs	**Minister of Finance**

PROTOCOL

At the signing of the Agreement between the Government of the United Mexican States and the Government of the Republic of Turkey for the Avoidance of Double Taxation and the Prevention of Fiscal Evasion with Respect to Taxes on Income, the undersigned have agreed that the following provisions shall form an integral part of the said Agreement:

1. With respect to Article 5

It is understood that for the purposes of paragraph 7 an enterprise shall not be deemed to have a permanent establishment in a Contracting State merely because it carries on business in that State through a broker, general commission agent or any other agent of an independent status, provided that such persons in their commercial or financial relations with the enterprise conditions are not made or imposed that differ from those generally agreed to by independent agents.

2. With respect to Article 6

It is understood that the term "immovable property" includes equipment used in the breeding and cultivation of fish.

3. With respect to paragraph 1 of Article 7

It is understood that if an enterprise of a Contracting State has a permanent establishment in the other Contracting State, where the enterprise carries on business, then, the profits of such enterprise may be taxed in that other Contracting State but only so much of them as is attributable to the sales in that other Contracting State of goods or merchandise of the same or similar kind as the goods or merchandise sold through that permanent establishment.

However, the profits derived from the sales described as aforesaid shall not be taxable in that other Contracting State if the enterprise demonstrates that such sales have been carried out for reasons other than obtaining a benefit under this Agreement.

4. With respect to paragraph 3 of Article 7

It is understood that no deduction shall be allowed in respect of amounts, if any, paid (otherwise than towards reimbursement of actual expenses) by the permanent establishment to the head office of the enterprise or any of its other offices, by way of royalties, fees or other similar payments in return for the use of patents or other rights, or by way of commission, for specific services performed or for management, or, except in the case of a banking enterprise, by way of interest on moneys lent to the permanent establishment. Likewise, no account shall be taken, in the determination of the profits of a permanent establishment, for amounts charged (otherwise than towards reimbursement of actual expenses) by the permanent establishment to the head office of the enterprise or any of its other offices, by way of royalties, fees or other similar payments in return for the use of patents or other rights, or by way of commission for specific services performed or for management, or, except in the case of a banking enterprise, by way of interest on moneys lent to the head office of the enterprise or any of its other offices.

5. With respect to Article 8

It is understood that profits referred to in paragraph 1 of Article 8 shall not include profits from the use of inland road transportation.

6. With respect to Article 11

It is understood that the term "interest" shall not include any item of income which is considered as a dividend under the provisions of paragraph 3 of Article 10.

It is understood that in case the institutions mentioned in subparagraphs c) and d) modify by way of merger, acquisition or any similar operation with the purpose of creating a new institution, the competent authorities will consult each other to determine the mode of application of the Agreement for the mentioned institutions to the extent that they keep being wholly owned by the Government.

7. With respect to Articles 10, 11, 12 and 13

It is understood that for the purposes of Articles 10, 11, 12 and 13 of the Agreement, each of the Contracting States shall keep the right of taxing in accordance with its domestic laws any income where double exemption results from a divergent classification of the income concerned.

8. With respect to Article 12

It is understood that notwithstanding the provisions of Article 13, the term "royalties" also includes payments derived from the alienation of any such right or property which are contingent on the productivity, use or disposition thereof.

9. With respect to Article 14

It is understood that where an individual or an enterprise of a Contracting State may be taxed in the other Contracting State according to paragraphs 1 or 2 of Article 14, that individual or enterprise may elect to be taxed in that other State in respect of such income in accordance with the provisions of Article 7 of this Agreement as if the income were attributable to a permanent establishment of the enterprise situated in that other State. This election shall not affect the right of that other State to impose a withholding tax on such income.

10. With respect to Article 24

It is understood that notwithstanding any other treaties of which the Contracting States are or may become parties, any dispute over a measure taken by a Contracting State involving a tax covered by Article 2 or, in the case of non-discrimination, any taxation measure taken by a Contracting State, including a dispute whether this Agreement applies, shall be settled only under the Agreement, unless the competent authorities of the Contracting States agree otherwise.

In the case of Turkey, it is understood that with respect to paragraph 2, the taxpayer must claim the refund resulting from such mutual agreement within a period of one (1) year after the tax administration has notified the taxpayer of the result of the mutual agreement.

11. In general

It is understood that the provisions of this Agreement shall not prevent a Contracting State from applying its provisions regarding thin capitalisation and controlled foreign corporation (in the case of Mexico, preferential tax regimes).

It is understood that for Mexican tax purposes, the fixed base will be treated in accordance with the principles that apply to permanent establishment.

IN WITNESS whereof the undersigned, being duly authorised thereto, have signed this Protocol.

DONE in duplicate at Ankara on this seventeenth day of December of two thousand and thirteen, in the Spanish, Turkish and English languages, all texts being equally authentic. In the case of any divergence, the English text shall prevail.

FOR THE GOVERNMENT OF THE UNITED MEXICAN STATES	FOR THE GOVERNMENT OF THE REPUBLIC OF TURKEY
José Antonio Meade Kuribreña **Minister of Foreign Affairs**	**Mehmet ŞİMŞEK** **Minister of Finance**

[SPANISH TEXT – TEXTE ESPAGNOL]

ACUERDO ENTRE EL GOBIERNO DE LOS ESTADOS UNIDOS MEXICANOS Y EL GOBIERNO DE LA REPÚBLICA DE TURQUÍA PARA EVITAR LA DOBLE IMPOSICIÓN Y PREVENIR LA EVASIÓN FISCAL EN MATERIA DE IMPUESTOS SOBRE LA RENTA

El Gobierno de los Estados Unidos Mexicanos y el Gobierno de la República de Turquía

DESEANDO concluir un Acuerdo para evitar la doble imposición y prevenir la evasión fiscal en materia de impuestos sobre la renta,

HAN ACORDADO lo siguiente:

ARTÍCULO 1
Personas Comprendidas

El presente Acuerdo se aplica a las personas residentes de uno o ambos Estados Contratantes.

ARTÍCULO 2
Impuestos Comprendidos

1. El presente Acuerdo se aplica a los impuestos sobre la renta exigibles por México y por Turquía, cualquiera que sea el sistema de su exacción.

2. Se considerarán impuestos sobre la renta todos los impuestos que graven la totalidad de la renta o elementos de la misma, incluidos los impuestos sobre las ganancias derivadas de la enajenación de bienes muebles o inmuebles.

3. Los impuestos existentes a los que se aplica el Acuerdo son en particular:

a) en México:

(i) el impuesto sobre la renta federal;

(ii) el impuesto empresarial a tasa única;

(en adelante denominados el "impuesto mexicano");

b) en Turquía:

(i) el impuesto sobre la renta (*Gelir Vergisi*);

(ii) el impuesto sobre sociedades (*Kurumlar Vergisi*);

(en adelante denominados el "impuesto turco").

4. El Acuerdo se aplicará igualmente a los impuestos de naturaleza idéntica o sustancialmente similares que se establezcan con posterioridad a la fecha de la firma del mismo y que se añadan a los actuales o los sustituyan. Las autoridades competentes de los Estados Contratantes se comunicarán mutuamente cualquier modificación significativa que se haya introducido en sus respectivas legislaciones fiscales.

ARTÍCULO 3

Definiciones Generales

1. Para los efectos del presente Acuerdo, a menos que de su contexto se infiera una interpretación diferente:

a) los términos "México" (los Estados Unidos Mexicanos) y "Turquía" significan el territorio de cualquier Estado Contratante, incluyendo el territorio terrestre, las aguas interiores, el mar territorial y el espacio aéreo sobre ellos, así como cualquier área marítima más allá del mar territorial, en los que, de conformidad con el derecho internacional y su derecho interno, cada Estado Contratante ejerce derechos soberanos o jurisdicción con respecto a las aguas, el fondo marino y el subsuelo y los recursos naturales de los mismos;

b) las expresiones "un Estado Contratante" y "el otro Estado Contratante" significan México o Turquía, según lo requiera el contexto;

c) el término "persona" incluye una persona física, una sociedad y cualquier otra agrupación de personas;

d) el término "sociedad" significa cualquier persona jurídica o cualquier entidad que se considere como persona jurídica para efectos impositivos;

e) la expresión "oficina central legal" significa la oficina registrada de acuerdo con el Código de Comercio Turco;

f) las expresiones "empresa de un Estado Contratante" y "empresa del otro Estado Contratante" significan, respectivamente, una empresa explotada por un residente de un Estado Contratante y una empresa explotada por un residente del otro Estado Contratante;

g) la expresión "tráfico internacional" significa todo transporte efectuado por un buque o aeronave explotado por una empresa de un Estado Contratante, salvo cuando el buque o aeronave se explote únicamente entre lugares situados en el otro Estado Contratante;

h) la expresión "autoridad competente" significa:

   (i) en México, la Secretaría de Hacienda y Crédito Público; y

   (ii) en Turquía, el Ministro de Finanzas o su representante autorizado;

i) el término "nacional" significa:

   (i) toda persona física que posea la nacionalidad de un Estado Contratante;

   (ii) toda persona jurídica, sociedad de personas o asociación constituida conforme a la legislación vigente en un Estado Contratante.

2. Para la aplicación del Acuerdo en cualquier momento por un Estado Contratante, cualquier término o expresión no definido en el mismo tendrá, a menos que de su contexto se infiera una interpretación diferente, el significado que en ese momento le atribuya la legislación de ese Estado para los efectos de los impuestos que son objeto del Acuerdo, prevaleciendo el significado atribuido por la legislación fiscal aplicable de ese Estado sobre el previsto para dicho término de conformidad con otras leyes de ese Estado.

ARTÍCULO 4
Residente

1. Para los efectos del presente Acuerdo, la expresión "residente de un Estado Contratante" significa toda persona que, en virtud de la legislación de ese Estado, esté sujeta a imposición en el mismo por razón de su domicilio, residencia, oficina central legal, sede de dirección o cualquier otro criterio de naturaleza análoga, y también incluye a ese Estado y cualquier subdivisión política o entidad local del mismo. Sin embargo, esta expresión no incluye a cualquier persona que esté sujeta a imposición en ese Estado exclusivamente por las rentas procedentes de fuentes en ese Estado.

2. Cuando en virtud de las disposiciones del párrafo 1, una persona física sea residente de ambos Estados Contratantes, su situación se determinará de conformidad con lo siguiente:

a) la persona será considerada residente solamente del Estado donde tenga una vivienda permanente a su disposición; si tuviera una vivienda permanente a su disposición en ambos Estados, se considerará residente solamente del Estado con el que mantenga relaciones personales y económicas más estrechas (centro de intereses vitales);

b) si no pudiera determinarse el Estado en el que dicha persona tiene el centro de sus intereses vitales o si no tuviera una vivienda permanente a su disposición en ninguno de los Estados, se considerará residente solamente del Estado donde viva habitualmente;

c) si viviera habitualmente en ambos Estados o no lo hiciera en ninguno de ellos, se considerará residente solamente del Estado del que sea nacional;

d) si es nacional de ambos Estados o de ninguno de ellos, las autoridades competentes de los Estados Contratantes resolverán el caso de común acuerdo.

3. Cuando en virtud de las disposiciones del párrafo 1, una persona que no sea una persona física sea residente de ambos Estados Contratantes y dicha persona tenga su sede de dirección efectiva en un Estado Contratante y su oficina central legal en el otro Estado Contratante, las autoridades competentes de los Estados Contratantes determinarán mediante acuerdo mutuo el Estado del que la persona será considerada residente para efectos del Acuerdo. En ausencia de dicho acuerdo, dichas personas no se considerarán residentes de ninguno de los Estados Contratantes para efectos de disfrutar de los beneficios de conformidad con el Acuerdo.

ARTÍCULO 5

Establecimiento Permanente

1. Para los efectos del presente Acuerdo, la expresión "establecimiento permanente" significa un lugar fijo de negocios mediante el cual una empresa realiza toda o parte de su actividad.

2. La expresión "establecimiento permanente" incluye, en especial:

a) una sede de dirección;

b) una sucursal;

c) una oficina;

d) una fábrica;

e) un taller, y

f) una mina, un pozo de petróleo o de gas, una cantera o cualquier otro lugar de extracción de recursos naturales.

3. Una obra, construcción, proyecto de montaje o instalación o las actividades de supervisión relacionadas con los mismos, constituyen un establecimiento permanente sólo si dicha obra, proyecto o actividades continúan por un periodo superior a seis (6) meses.

4. No obstante las disposiciones anteriores del presente Artículo, se considerará que la expresión "establecimiento permanente" no incluye:

a) la utilización de instalaciones con el único fin de almacenar o exponer bienes o mercancías pertenecientes a la empresa;

b) el mantenimiento de un depósito de bienes o mercancías pertenecientes a la empresa con el único fin de almacenarlas o exponerlas;

c) el mantenimiento de un depósito de bienes o mercancías pertenecientes a la empresa con el único fin de que sean transformadas por otra empresa;

d) el mantenimiento de un lugar fijo de negocios con el único fin de comprar bienes o mercancías o de recopilar información para la empresa;

e) el mantenimiento de un lugar fijo de negocios con el único fin de desarrollar para la empresa cualquier otra actividad que tenga carácter preparatorio o auxiliar;

f) el mantenimiento de un lugar fijo de negocios con el único fin de realizar cualquier combinación de las actividades mencionadas en los incisos a) al e), siempre que el conjunto de la actividad del lugar fijo de negocios, resultante de dicha combinación, conserve su carácter preparatorio o auxiliar.

5. No obstante lo dispuesto en los párrafos 1 y 2, cuando una persona - distinta de un agente que goce de un estatuto independiente, al cual se le aplica el párrafo 7 - actúe por cuenta de una empresa y ostente y ejerza habitualmente en un Estado Contratante poderes que la faculten para concluir contratos en nombre de la empresa, se considerará que dicha empresa tiene un establecimiento permanente en ese Estado con respecto a cualquiera de las actividades que dicha persona realice para la empresa, a menos que las actividades de dicha persona se limiten a las mencionadas en el párrafo 4 y que, de haber sido realizadas por medio de un lugar fijo de negocios, no se hubiera considerado este lugar fijo de negocios como un establecimiento permanente de acuerdo con las disposiciones de ese párrafo.

6. No obstante las disposiciones anteriores del presente Artículo, se considerará que una empresa aseguradora de un Estado Contratante tiene, salvo por lo que respecta a los reaseguros, un establecimiento permanente en el otro Estado Contratante si cobra primas en el territorio de ese otro Estado o si asegura contra riesgos situados en él por medio de una persona distinta de un agente que goce de un estatuto independiente al que se le aplique el párrafo 7.

7. No se considerará que una empresa tiene un establecimiento permanente en un Estado Contratante por el solo hecho de que realice sus actividades empresariales en ese Estado por medio de un corredor, comisionista general o cualquier otro agente que goce de un estatuto independiente, siempre que dichas personas actúen dentro del marco ordinario de su actividad.

8. El hecho de que una sociedad residente de un Estado Contratante controle o sea controlada por una sociedad residente del otro Estado Contratante, o que realice actividades empresariales en ese otro Estado (ya sea por medio de un establecimiento permanente o de otra manera), no convierte por sí solo a cualquiera de estas sociedades en establecimiento permanente de la otra.

ARTÍCULO 6
Rentas Inmobiliarias

1. Las rentas que un residente de un Estado Contratante obtenga de bienes inmuebles (incluidas las rentas de explotaciones agrícolas o silvícolas) situados en el otro Estado Contratante puede someterse a imposición en ese otro Estado.

2. La expresión "bienes inmuebles" tendrá el significado que le atribuya la legislación del Estado Contratante en el que los bienes en cuestión estén situados. Dicha expresión comprende, en todo caso, los accesorios de los bienes inmuebles, el ganado y el equipo utilizado en las explotaciones agrícolas y silvícolas, los derechos a los que se apliquen las disposiciones de derecho privado relativas a los bienes raíces, el usufructo de bienes inmuebles y los derechos a percibir pagos variables o fijos por la explotación o la concesión de la explotación de yacimientos minerales, fuentes y otros recursos naturales; los buques, embarcaciones y aeronaves no se considerarán bienes inmuebles.

3. Las disposiciones del párrafo 1 se aplicarán a las rentas derivadas de la utilización directa, del arrendamiento o uso en cualquier otra forma de los bienes inmuebles.

4. Las disposiciones de los párrafos 1 y 3 se aplicarán igualmente a las rentas derivadas de bienes inmuebles de una empresa y de bienes inmuebles utilizados para el ejercicio de servicios personales independientes.

ARTÍCULO 7
Beneficios Empresariales

1. Los beneficios de una empresa de un Estado Contratante solamente pueden someterse a imposición en ese Estado, a no ser que la empresa realice sus actividades empresariales en el otro Estado Contratante por medio de un establecimiento permanente situado en él. Si la empresa realiza su actividad empresarial de dicha manera, los beneficios de la empresa pueden someterse a imposición en el otro Estado, pero sólo en la medida en que puedan atribuirse a ese establecimiento permanente.

2. Sujeto a lo dispuesto en el párrafo 3, cuando una empresa de un Estado Contratante realice actividades empresariales en el otro Estado Contratante por medio de un establecimiento permanente situado en él, en cada Estado Contratante se atribuirán a dicho establecimiento permanente los beneficios que éste hubiera podido obtener de ser una empresa distinta y separada que realizase actividades idénticas o similares, en las mismas o similares condiciones, y tratase con total independencia con la empresa de la que es establecimiento permanente.

3. Para la determinación de los beneficios de un establecimiento permanente, se permitirá la deducción de los gastos incurridos para la realización de los fines del establecimiento permanente, incluyendo los gastos de dirección y generales de administración así incurridos, tanto si se efectúan en el Estado en el que se encuentre el establecimiento permanente como en otra parte.

4. No se atribuirá ningún beneficio a un establecimiento permanente por el solo hecho de que ese establecimiento permanente compre bienes o mercancías para la empresa.

5. Cuando los beneficios comprendan elementos de renta regulados separadamente en otros Artículos del presente Acuerdo, las disposiciones de dichos Artículos no se verán afectadas por las disposiciones de este Artículo.

ARTÍCULO 8

Transportación Marítima y Aérea

1. Los beneficios obtenidos por una empresa de un Estado Contratante procedentes de la explotación de buques o aeronaves en tráfico internacional sólo podrán someterse a imposición en ese Estado.

2. Las disposiciones del párrafo 1 son también aplicables a los beneficios procedentes de la participación en un consorcio, empresa conjunta o una agencia de explotación internacional.

ARTÍCULO 9

Empresas Asociadas

1. Cuando

a) una empresa de un Estado Contratante participe directa o indirectamente en la dirección, el control o el capital de una empresa del otro Estado Contratante, o

b) las mismas personas participen directa o indirectamente en la dirección, el control o el capital de una empresa de un Estado Contratante y de una empresa del otro Estado Contratante, y en cualquier caso las dos empresas estén, en sus relaciones comerciales o financieras, unidas por condiciones aceptadas o impuestas que difieran de las que serían acordadas por empresas independientes, entonces cualquier beneficio que hubiera sido obtenido por una de las empresas de no existir dichas condiciones, y que de hecho no se ha producido a causa de las mismas, puede ser incluido en los beneficios de esa empresa y, en consecuencia, ser sometido a imposición.

2. Cuando un Estado Contratante incluya en los beneficios de una empresa de ese Estado - y, en consecuencia, someta a imposición - los beneficios sobre los cuales una empresa del otro Estado Contratante ha sido sometida a imposición en ese otro Estado y los beneficios así incluidos son considerados por el Estado mencionado en primer lugar como beneficios que habrían sido obtenidos por la empresa del Estado mencionado en primer lugar si las condiciones convenidas entre las dos empresas hubieran sido las que se hubiesen convenido entre empresas independientes, entonces ese otro Estado procederá a efectuar el ajuste correspondiente al monto del impuesto cobrado sobre esos beneficios, cuando ese otro Estado considere que el ajuste está justificado. Para determinar dicho ajuste se tendrán en cuenta las demás disposiciones del presente Acuerdo y las autoridades competentes de los Estados Contratantes se consultarán mutuamente cuando sea necesario.

ARTÍCULO 10
Dividendos

1. Los dividendos pagados por una sociedad residente de un Estado Contratante a un residente del otro Estado Contratante pueden someterse a imposición en ese otro Estado.

2. Sin embargo, dichos dividendos también pueden someterse a imposición en el Estado Contratante en el que resida la sociedad que pague los dividendos y de conformidad con la legislación de ese Estado, pero si el beneficiario efectivo de los dividendos es un residente del otro Estado Contratante, el impuesto así exigido no podrá exceder del:

a) 5 por ciento del importe bruto de los dividendos si el beneficiario efectivo es una sociedad (distinta a una sociedad de personas) que tenga la propiedad directa de por lo menos el 25 por ciento del capital de la sociedad que paga los dividendos;

b) 15 por ciento del importe bruto de los dividendos en todos los demás casos.

El párrafo no afectará la imposición de la sociedad respecto de los beneficios con cargo a los cuales se pagan los dividendos.

3. El término "dividendos" empleado en el presente Artículo significa los rendimientos de las acciones, acciones o derechos de goce, partes de minas, partes de fundador u otros derechos, excepto los de crédito, que permitan participar en los beneficios, así como los rendimientos de otros derechos corporativos y otros ingresos que estén sujetos al mismo régimen fiscal que los rendimientos de las acciones, de conformidad con la legislación del Estado en que resida la sociedad que los distribuya y los rendimientos obtenidos de un fondo de inversión y de un fideicomiso de inversión.

4. Los beneficios de una sociedad de un Estado Contratante que realice actividades empresariales en el otro Estado Contratante a través de un establecimiento permanente situado en él, después de haber sido sometidos a imposición de conformidad con el Artículo 7, pueden someterse a imposición sobre el monto remanente en el Estado Contratante en el que esté situado el establecimiento permanente y de conformidad con el párrafo 2 a) del presente Artículo.

5. Las disposiciones de los párrafos 1 y 2 no se aplicarán si el beneficiario efectivo de los dividendos, residente de un Estado Contratante, realiza en el otro Estado Contratante, del que es residente la sociedad que paga los dividendos, actividades empresariales a través de un establecimiento permanente situado en él o presta en ese otro Estado servicios personales independientes por medio de una base fija situada en él y la participación con respecto a la cual se pagan los dividendos esté efectivamente vinculada con dicho establecimiento permanente o base fija. En este caso se aplicarán las disposiciones del Artículo 7 o del Artículo 14, según proceda.

6. Sin perjuicio de lo dispuesto en el párrafo 4, cuando una sociedad residente de un Estado Contratante obtenga beneficios o rentas procedentes del otro Estado Contratante, ese otro Estado no puede exigir ningún impuesto sobre los dividendos pagados por la sociedad, salvo en la medida en que estos dividendos sean pagados a un residente de ese otro Estado o la participación con respecto a la cual se pagan los dividendos esté efectivamente vinculada a un establecimiento permanente o a una base fija situados en ese otro Estado, ni someter los beneficios no distribuidos de la sociedad a un impuesto sobre los mismos, aún si los dividendos pagados o los beneficios no distribuidos consisten, total o parcialmente, en beneficios o rentas procedentes de ese otro Estado.

ARTÍCULO 11
Intereses

1. Los intereses procedentes de un Estado Contratante y pagados a un residente del otro Estado Contratante pueden someterse a imposición en ese otro Estado.

2. Sin embargo, dichos intereses también pueden someterse a imposición en el Estado Contratante del que procedan y de acuerdo con la legislación de ese Estado, pero si el beneficiario efectivo de los intereses es un residente del otro Estado Contratante, el impuesto así exigido no podrá exceder del:

a) 10 por ciento del importe bruto de los intereses cuando sean pagados a un banco.

b) 15 por ciento del importe bruto de los intereses en todos los demás casos.

3. No obstante las disposiciones del párrafo 2, los intereses a que se refiere el párrafo 1 sólo podrán someterse a imposición en el Estado Contratante en el que resida el beneficiario efectivo si:

a) el beneficiario efectivo es un Estado Contratante, una subdivisión política o una entidad local del mismo, o el Banco Central de México (Banco de México) o el Banco Central de Turquía (*Türkiye Cumhuriyet Merkez Bankası*);

b) los intereses son pagados por cualquiera de las entidades mencionadas en el inciso a);

c) los intereses procedan de Turquía y son pagados respecto de un préstamo a plazo no menor de tres (3) años otorgado por el Banco Nacional de Comercio Exterior, S.N.C., Nacional Financiera, S.N.C. o Banco Nacional de Obras y Servicios Públicos, S.N.C.; o

d) los intereses proceden de México y son pagados respecto de un préstamo a plazo no menor de tres (3) años otorgado por el Banco de Exportación-Importación de Turquía (*Türkiye İhracat Kredi Bankası A.Ş.*).

4. El término "intereses" empleado en el presente Artículo significa los rendimientos de los créditos de cualquier naturaleza, con o sin garantía hipotecaria o cláusula de participación en los beneficios del deudor y, en particular, las rentas de títulos de crédito gubernamentales y de bonos u obligaciones, incluidas las primas y premios unidos a dichos títulos, bonos u obligaciones, así como cualquier otra renta que la legislación del Estado Contratante de donde procedan los intereses, asimile a los rendimientos de las cantidades dadas en préstamo.

5. Las disposiciones de los párrafos 1 y 2 no se aplicarán si el beneficiario efectivo de los intereses, residente de un Estado Contratante, realiza actividades empresariales en el otro Estado Contratante, del que proceden los intereses, a través de un establecimiento permanente situado en él o presta servicios personales independientes por medio de una base fija situada en ese otro Estado, y el crédito con respecto al cual se pagan los intereses esté efectivamente vinculado con dicho establecimiento permanente o base fija. En dicho caso se aplicarán las disposiciones del Artículo 7 o el Artículo 14, según proceda.

6. Los intereses se considerarán procedentes de un Estado Contratante cuando el deudor sea el propio Estado, una subdivisión política, una entidad local o un residente de ese Estado. Sin embargo, cuando la persona que paga los intereses, sea o no residente de un Estado Contratante, tenga en un Estado Contratante un establecimiento permanente o una base fija y dichos intereses son soportados por dicho establecimiento permanente o base fija, entonces dichos intereses se considerarán procedentes del Estado donde esté situado el establecimiento permanente o base fija.

7. Cuando, en virtud de la relación especial existente entre el deudor y el beneficiario efectivo o de la que uno u otro mantengan con terceros, el importe de los intereses exceda, por cualquier motivo, del que hubieran convenido el deudor y el beneficiario efectivo en ausencia de tal relación, las disposiciones de este Artículo se aplicarán únicamente a este último importe. En tal caso, la cuantía en exceso de los pagos podrá someterse a imposición de acuerdo con la legislación de cada Estado Contratante, teniendo en cuenta la demás disposiciones del presente Acuerdo.

ARTÍCULO 12
Regalías

1. Las regalías procedentes de un Estado Contratante y pagadas a un residente del otro Estado Contratante pueden someterse a imposición en ese otro Estado.

2. Sin embargo, dichas regalías también pueden someterse a imposición en el Estado Contratante del que procedan y de acuerdo con la legislación de ese Estado, pero si el beneficiario efectivo de las regalías es un residente del otro Estado Contratante, el impuesto así exigido no podrá exceder del 10 por ciento del importe bruto de las regalías.

3. El término "regalías" empleado en este Artículo significa los pagos de cualquier clase recibidos en consideración por:

a) el uso o la concesión de uso, de cualquier patente, marca comercial, diseño o modelo, plano, fórmula o procedimiento secreto;

b) el uso o la concesión de uso, de cualquier equipo industrial, comercial o científico;

c) el suministro de información relativa a experiencias industriales, comerciales o científicas;

d) el uso o la concesión de uso, de cualquier derecho de autor sobre una obra literaria, artística o científica, incluidas las películas cinematográficas y las grabaciones o cintas para su difusión por televisión o radio;

4. Las disposiciones de los párrafos 1 y 2 no se aplicarán si el beneficiario efectivo de las regalías, residente de un Estado Contratante, realiza actividades empresariales en el otro Estado Contratante de donde procedan las regalías, a través de un establecimiento permanente situado en él o presta servicios personales independientes por medio de una base fija situada en ese otro Estado, y el derecho o bien con respecto al cual se pagan las regalías esté efectivamente vinculado con dicho establecimiento permanente o base fija. En este caso se aplicarán las disposiciones del Artículo 7 o del Artículo 14, según proceda.

5. Las regalías se considerarán procedentes de un Estado Contratante cuando el deudor sea el propio Estado, una subdivisión política, una entidad local o un residente de ese Estado. Sin embargo, cuando la persona que paga las regalías, sea o no residente de un Estado Contratante, tenga en un Estado Contratante un establecimiento permanente o una base fija, y dichas regalías sean soportadas por dicho establecimiento permanente o base fija, entonces dichas regalías se considerarán procedentes del Estado donde esté situado el establecimiento permanente o la base fija.

6. Cuando, en virtud de la relación especial existente entre el deudor y el beneficiario efectivo o de la que uno y otro mantengan con terceros, el importe de las regalías exceda, por cualquier motivo, del que hubieran convenido el deudor y el beneficiario efectivo en ausencia de tal relación, las disposiciones de este Artículo se aplicarán únicamente a este último importe. En dicho caso, la cuantía en exceso de los pagos podrá someterse a imposición de acuerdo con la legislación de cada Estado Contratante, teniendo en cuenta las demás disposiciones del presente Acuerdo.

ARTÍCULO 13
Ganancias de Capital

1. Las ganancias que un residente de un Estado Contratante obtenga de la enajenación de bienes inmuebles a los que se refiere el Artículo 6 y situados en el otro Estado Contratante pueden someterse a imposición en ese otro Estado.

2. Las ganancias derivadas de la enajenación de acciones u otros derechos similares en una sociedad, cuyos bienes consistan principalmente, directa o indirectamente, en bienes inmuebles situados en un Estado Contratante, pueden someterse a imposición en ese Estado.

3. Las ganancias obtenidas por un residente de un Estado Contratante derivadas de la enajenación de acciones, participaciones u otros derechos en el capital de una sociedad u otra persona jurídica residente del otro Estado Contratante pueden someterse a imposición en ese otro Estado.

4. Las ganancias derivadas de la enajenación de bienes muebles que formen parte del activo de un establecimiento permanente que una empresa de un Estado Contratante tenga en el otro Estado Contratante o de bienes muebles que pertenezcan a una base fija a disposición de un residente de un Estado Contratante en el otro Estado Contratante para la prestación de servicios personales independientes, incluyendo las ganancias derivadas de la enajenación de dicho establecimiento permanente (solo o con el conjunto de la empresa) o de dicha base fija pueden someterse a imposición en ese otro Estado.

5. Las ganancias obtenidas por un residente de un Estado Contratante derivadas de la enajenación de buques o aeronaves explotados en tráfico internacional o de bienes muebles afectos a la explotación de dichos buques o aeronaves, sólo pueden someterse a imposición en ese Estado.

6. Las ganancias derivadas de la enajenación de cualquier otro bien distinto a los mencionados en los párrafos anteriores del presente Artículo, sólo pueden someterse a imposición en el Estado Contratante en que resida el enajenante. Sin embargo, las ganancias a que se refiere el enunciado anterior de este párrafo y provenientes del otro Estado Contratante, pueden someterse a imposición en ese otro Estado Contratante si el tiempo transcurrido entre la fecha de adquisición y la fecha de enajenación de dicho bien no excede de un (1) año.

ARTÍCULO 14
Servicios Personales Independientes

1. Las rentas obtenidas por una persona física que sea residente de un Estado Contratante, por la prestación de servicios profesionales u otras actividades de naturaleza independiente, sólo podrán someterse a imposición en ese Estado. Sin embargo, dichas rentas también pueden someterse a imposición en el otro Estado Contratante si dichos servicios o actividades son prestados en ese otro Estado y si:

a) tiene una base fija disponible regularmente en el otro Estado con el propósito de prestar esos servicios o actividades; o

b) su estancia en ese otro Estado con el propósito de prestar esos servicios o actividades es por un periodo o periodos que sumen en su conjunto ciento ochenta y tres (183) días o más en cualquier periodo continuo de doce (12) meses.

En dichas circunstancias, sólo en la medida en que las rentas sean atribuibles a esa base fija o deriven de los servicios o actividades prestados durante su estancia en ese otro Estado pueden someterse a imposición en ese otro Estado, según proceda.

2. Las rentas obtenidas por una empresa de un Estado Contratante, por la prestación de servicios profesionales u otras actividades de una naturaleza independiente, sólo podrán someterse a imposición en ese Estado. Sin embargo, dichas rentas también pueden someterse a imposición en el otro Estado Contratante si dichos servicios o actividades son prestados en ese otro Estado y si:

a) la empresa tiene un establecimiento permanente en ese otro Estado a través del cual los servicios o actividades son prestados; o

b) el periodo o periodos durante los cuales los servicios o actividades son prestados exceden en su conjunto de ciento ochenta y tres (183) días en cualquier periodo continuo de doce (12) meses.

En dichas circunstancias, sólo en la medida en que las rentas sean atribuibles a ese establecimiento permanente o a los servicios o actividades prestados en ese otro Estado, pueden someterse a imposición en ese otro Estado, según proceda.

3. La expresión "servicios profesionales" comprende especialmente las actividades independientes de carácter científico, literario, artístico, educativo o pedagógico, así como las actividades independientes de médicos, abogados, ingenieros, arquitectos, dentistas y contadores.

ARTÍCULO 15

Servicios Personales Dependientes

1. Sujeto a lo dispuesto en los Artículos 16, 18, 19 y 20, los sueldos, salarios y otras remuneraciones similares obtenidos por un residente de un Estado Contratante en virtud de un empleo, sólo podrán someterse a imposición en ese Estado, a no ser que el empleo se ejerza en el otro Estado Contratante. Si el empleo se ejerce de esta forma, las remuneraciones percibidas por este concepto pueden someterse a imposición en ese otro Estado.

2. No obstante lo dispuesto en el párrafo 1, las remuneraciones obtenidas por un residente de un Estado Contratante por razón de un empleo ejercido en el otro Estado Contratante sólo pueden someterse a imposición en el Estado Contratante mencionado en primer lugar si:

a) el perceptor permanece en el otro Estado por un periodo o periodos que no excedan en conjunto de ciento ochenta y tres (183) días en cualquier periodo de doce (12) meses, y

b) las remuneraciones son pagadas por, o en nombre de, un empleador que no sea un residente del otro Estado, y

c) las remuneraciones no son soportadas por un establecimiento permanente o base fija que el empleador tenga en el otro Estado.

3. No obstante las disposiciones anteriores del presente Artículo, las remuneraciones obtenidas por razón de un empleo ejercido a bordo de un buque o aeronave explotados en tráfico internacional por una empresa de un Estado Contratante, pueden someterse a imposición en ese Estado Contratante.

ARTÍCULO 16

Participaciones de Consejeros

Las participaciones de consejeros y otras remuneraciones similares, que un residente de un Estado Contratante obtenga en su calidad como miembro del consejo de administración de una sociedad que sea residente del otro Estado Contratante, pueden someterse a imposición en ese otro Estado.

ARTÍCULO 17

Artistas y Deportistas

1. No obstante lo dispuesto en los Artículos 14 y 15, las rentas que un residente de un Estado Contratante obtenga del ejercicio de su actividad personal en el otro Estado Contratante, en calidad de artista del espectáculo, tal como actor de teatro, cine, radio o televisión, o músico, o como deportista, pueden someterse a imposición en ese otro Estado.

2. Cuando las rentas derivadas de las actividades personales ejercidas por un artista del espectáculo o un deportista, en su calidad de tal, se atribuyan no al propio artista del espectáculo o deportista, sino a otra persona, no obstante lo dispuesto en los Artículos 7, 14 y 15, esas rentas pueden someterse a imposición en el Estado Contratante en el que se realicen las actividades del artista del espectáculo o deportista.

3. Las rentas obtenidas por un artista del espectáculo o un deportista por actividades realizadas en un Estado Contratante estarán exentas de impuesto en ese Estado, si la visita a ese Estado se encuentra financiada total o principalmente por fondos públicos del otro Estado Contratante, una subdivisión política o una entidad local del mismo.

ARTÍCULO 18
Pensiones

1. Sujeto a lo dispuesto en el párrafo 2 del Artículo 19, las pensiones y otras remuneraciones similares pagadas a un residente de un Estado Contratante por razón de un empleo anterior, sólo podrán someterse a imposición en ese Estado. Esta disposición también se aplicará a las anualidades vitalicias pagadas a un residente de un Estado Contratante.

2. La expresión "anualidad vitalicia" comprende una suma determinada pagadera periódicamente en fechas determinadas, durante la vida o durante un periodo de tiempo determinado o determinable, de conformidad con una obligación de realizar pagos como contraprestación a una adecuada y total retribución en dinero o su equivalente.

ARTÍCULO 19

Funciones Públicas

1. a) Los sueldos, salarios y otras remuneraciones similares, distintas de una pensión, pagados por un Estado Contratante o una subdivisión política o una entidad local del mismo, a una persona física por razón de servicios prestados a ese Estado o subdivisión o entidad, sólo podrán someterse a imposición en ese Estado.

   b) Sin embargo, dichos sueldos, salarios y otras remuneraciones similares sólo podrán someterse a imposición en el otro Estado Contratante si los servicios se prestan en ese Estado y la persona física es un residente de ese Estado que:

      (i) es un nacional de ese Estado; o

      (ii) no ha adquirido la condición de residente de ese Estado solamente para prestar los servicios.

2. a) No obstante lo dispuesto en el párrafo 1, cualquier pensión u otras remuneraciones similares pagadas por, o con cargo a fondos constituidos por, un Estado Contratante o una subdivisión política o una entidad local del mismo, a una persona física por razón de servicios prestados a ese Estado o subdivisión o entidad, sólo serán sometidas a imposición en ese Estado.

   b) Sin embargo, dichas pensiones y otras remuneraciones similares sólo serán sometidas a imposición en el otro Estado Contratante si la persona física es un residente y un nacional de ese Estado.

3. Las disposiciones de los Artículos 15, 16, 17 y 18 se aplicarán a los sueldos, salarios y otras remuneraciones similares, así como pensiones, por razón de servicios prestados en relación con una actividad empresarial realizada por un Estado Contratante o una subdivisión política o una entidad local del mismo.

ARTÍCULO 20
Profesores y Estudiantes

1. Los pagos que reciba para cubrir sus gastos de manutención, estudios o formación, un estudiante o una persona en prácticas, que sea nacional de un Estado Contratante y que se encuentre en el otro Estado Contratante con el único fin de proseguir sus estudios o formación, no podrán someterse a imposición en ese otro Estado, siempre que dichos pagos procedan de fuentes situadas fuera de ese otro Estado.

2. De igual forma, las remuneraciones recibidas por un profesor o por un instructor que sea nacional de un Estado Contratante y que se encuentre en el otro Estado Contratante con el propósito principal de realizar actividades de enseñanza o de participar en una investigación científica, por un periodo o periodos que no excedan de dos (2) años, estarán exentas del impuesto en ese otro Estado sobre sus remuneraciones derivadas de servicios personales de enseñanza o investigación, siempre que dichos pagos procedan de fuentes situadas fuera de ese otro Estado.

ARTÍCULO 21
Otras Rentas

Los elementos de renta de un residente de un Estado Contratante, no mencionados en los Artículos anteriores del presente Acuerdo y procedentes del otro Estado Contratante, pueden someterse a imposición en ese otro Estado.

ARTÍCULO 22
Eliminación de la Doble Imposición

1. De conformidad con las disposiciones y sujeto a las limitaciones de la legislación de México, conforme a las modificaciones ocasionales de la misma que no afecten sus principios generales, México permitirá a sus residentes acreditar contra el impuesto mexicano:

a) el impuesto turco pagado sobre las rentas procedentes de Turquía en un monto que no exceda el impuesto exigible en México sobre dichas rentas; y

b) en el caso de una sociedad propietaria de por lo menos el 10 por ciento del capital de una sociedad que sea residente de Turquía, y de la cual la sociedad mencionada en primer lugar recibe dividendos, el impuesto turco pagado por la sociedad que distribuye los dividendos, respecto de los beneficios con cargo a los cuales se pagan los dividendos.

2. Sujeto a las disposiciones de la legislación de Turquía relativas a la posibilidad de acreditar contra el impuesto turco el impuesto exigible en un territorio fuera de Turquía (conforme a las modificaciones ocasionales de la misma que no afecten sus principios generales), el impuesto mexicano exigible conforme a la legislación de México y de conformidad con el presente Acuerdo, respecto de las rentas (incluidos los beneficios y las ganancias exigibles) obtenidas por un residente de Turquía de fuentes en México, podrá deducirse del impuesto turco sobre dichas rentas. Sin embargo, dicha deducción no excederá el monto del impuesto turco atribuible a dichas rentas, calculado antes de que la deducción sea realizada.

3. Cuando de conformidad con cualquier disposición del Acuerdo, las rentas obtenidas por un residente de un Estado Contratante estén exentas del impuesto en ese Estado, dicho Estado podrá, no obstante, tomar en cuenta las rentas exentas para calcular el monto del impuesto sobre el resto de las rentas de dicho residente.

ARTÍCULO 23
No Discriminación

1. Los nacionales de un Estado Contratante no serán sometidos en el otro Estado Contratante a ningún impuesto u obligación relativa al mismo, que no se exija o sea más gravoso que aquéllos a los que estén o puedan estar sometidos los nacionales de ese otro Estado que se encuentren en las mismas condiciones, en particular con respecto a la residencia. No obstante lo dispuesto por el Artículo 1, la presente disposición también se aplicará a las personas que no sean residentes de uno o de ambos Estados Contratantes.

2. Sin perjuicio de lo dispuesto en el párrafo 4 del Artículo 10, los establecimientos permanentes que una empresa de un Estado Contratante tenga en el otro Estado Contratante no serán sometidos a imposición en ese otro Estado de manera menos favorable que las empresas de ese otro Estado que realicen las mismas actividades.

3. A menos que se apliquen las disposiciones del párrafo 1 del Artículo 9, del párrafo 7 del Artículo 11 o del párrafo 6 del Artículo 12, los intereses, las regalías y otros gastos pagados por una empresa de un Estado Contratante a un residente del otro Estado Contratante serán deducibles para determinar los beneficios sujetos a imposición de dicha empresa, en las mismas condiciones que si hubieran sido pagados a un residente del Estado mencionado en primer lugar.

4. Las empresas de un Estado Contratante cuyo capital esté, total o parcialmente, detentado o controlado, directa o indirectamente, por uno o más residentes del otro Estado Contratante, no estarán sujetas en el Estado mencionado en primer lugar a ningún impuesto u obligación relativa al mismo que no se exija o que sea más gravoso que aquéllos a los que estén o puedan estar sometidas otras empresas similares del Estado mencionado en primer lugar.

5. Estas disposiciones no deberán interpretarse en el sentido de obligar a un Estado Contratante a conceder a los residentes del otro Estado Contratante las deducciones personales, desgravaciones y reducciones para efectos fiscales que otorgue a sus propios residentes, en consideración de su estado civil o cargas familiares.

6. No obstante los dispuesto por el Artículo 2, las disposiciones del presente Artículo se aplicarán a los impuestos de cualquier naturaleza y denominación.

ARTÍCULO 24
Procedimiento de Acuerdo Mutuo

1. Cuando una persona considere que las medidas adoptadas por uno o ambos Estados Contratantes implican o pueden implicar para ella una imposición que no esté conforme con las disposiciones del presente Acuerdo, con independencia de los recursos previstos por la legislación interna de esos Estados, podrá someter su caso a la autoridad competente del Estado Contratante del que sea residente o, si fuera aplicable el párrafo 1 del Artículo 23, a la del Estado Contratante del que sea nacional. El caso deberá ser presentado dentro de los tres (3) años siguientes a la primera notificación de la medida adoptada que implique una imposición no conforme a las disposiciones del Acuerdo.

2. La autoridad competente, si la reclamación le parece fundada y si no puede por sí misma llegar a una solución satisfactoria, hará lo posible por resolver la cuestión mediante acuerdo mutuo con la autoridad competente del otro Estado Contratante, a fin de evitar una imposición que no se ajuste al Acuerdo.

3. Las autoridades competentes de los Estados Contratantes harán lo posible por resolver, mediante acuerdo mutuo, cualesquiera dificultades o dudas que surjan de la interpretación o aplicación del Acuerdo. También podrán consultarse mutuamente para la eliminación de la doble imposición en los casos no previstos en el Acuerdo.

4. Las autoridades competentes de los Estados Contratantes podrán comunicarse directamente entre sí, a fin de llegar a un acuerdo en el sentido de los párrafos anteriores.

ARTÍCULO 25
Intercambio de Información

1. Las autoridades competentes de los Estados Contratantes intercambiarán la información que sea previsiblemente relevante para aplicar lo dispuesto en el presente Acuerdo o para la administración o cumplimiento de la legislación interna relativa a los impuestos de cualquier naturaleza y descripción exigidos por los Estados Contratantes, sus subdivisiones políticas o entidades locales, en la medida en que la imposición no sea contraria al Acuerdo. El intercambio de información no está limitado por los Artículos 1 y 2.

2. Cualquier información recibida de conformidad con el párrafo 1 por un Estado Contratante será mantenida secreta de igual forma que la información obtenida con base en la legislación interna de ese Estado y sólo se comunicará a las personas o autoridades (incluidos los tribunales y órganos administrativos) encargadas de la determinación o recaudación de los impuestos señalados en el párrafo 1, de los procedimientos declarativos o ejecutivos relativos a dichos impuestos, de la resolución de los recursos relativos a los mismos o encargadas de verificar el cumplimiento de lo anterior. Dichas personas o autoridades sólo utilizarán la información para estos fines. Podrán revelar la información en las audiencias públicas de los tribunales o en las sentencias judiciales.

3. En ningún caso las disposiciones de los párrafos 1 y 2 podrán interpretarse en el sentido de obligar a un Estado Contratante a:

a) adoptar medidas administrativas contrarias a su legislación y práctica administrativa, o a las del otro Estado Contratante;

b) suministrar información que no se pueda obtener de conformidad con su legislación o en el ejercicio normal de su práctica administrativa, o de las del otro Estado Contratante;

c) suministrar información que revele un secreto comercial, empresarial, industrial, mercantil o profesional o un procedimiento comercial, o información cuya comunicación sea contraria al orden público *(ordre public)*.

4. Si la información es solicitada por un Estado Contratante de conformidad con este Artículo, el otro Estado Contratante utilizará las medidas para recabar información de que disponga para obtener la información solicitada, aún cuando ese otro Estado pueda no necesitar dicha información para sus propios fines impositivos. La obligación contenida en la oración anterior está sujeta a las limitaciones del párrafo 3, pero en ningún caso dichas limitaciones deberán interpretarse en el sentido de permitir a un Estado Contratante negarse a otorgar la información únicamente porque no se tiene un interés interno en dicha información.

5. En ningún caso las disposiciones del párrafo 3 deberán interpretarse en el sentido de permitir a un Estado Contratante negarse a otorgar la información únicamente porque la misma sea detentada por un banco, otra institución financiera, un mandatario o una persona actuando en calidad de agente o fiduciario o porque se relaciona con participaciones en una persona.

ARTÍCULO 26

Asistencia en la Recaudación de Impuestos

1. Los Estados Contratantes se prestarán asistencia mutua en la recaudación de créditos fiscales. Esta asistencia no estará limitada por los Artículos 1 y 2. Las autoridades competentes de los Estados Contratantes podrán, mediante acuerdo mutuo, establecer la forma de aplicar este Artículo.

2. Para efectos de este Artículo, la expresión "crédito fiscal" significa un monto debido respecto de impuestos de cualquier naturaleza y descripción exigidos por los Estados Contratantes, o sus subdivisiones políticas o entidades locales, en la medida en que la imposición así exigida no sea contraria al presente Acuerdo o cualquier otro instrumento del que sean partes los Estados Contratantes, así como los intereses, multas administrativas y costos de recaudación o conservación relacionados con dicho monto.

3. Cuando un crédito fiscal de un Estado Contratante sea exigible de conformidad con la legislación de ese Estado y sea debido por una persona que, en ese momento y de conformidad con la legislación de ese Estado, no pueda impedir su cobro, dicho crédito fiscal, mediante solicitud de la autoridad competente de ese Estado, deberá ser aceptado para efectos de cobro por la autoridad competente del otro Estado Contratante. Dicho crédito fiscal deberá ser cobrado por ese otro Estado de conformidad con las disposiciones de su legislación aplicable a la ejecución y recaudación de sus propios impuestos como si el crédito fiscal fuera un crédito fiscal de ese otro Estado.

4. Cuando un crédito fiscal de un Estado Contratante sea un crédito respecto del cual ese Estado, de conformidad con su legislación, pueda adoptar medidas cautelares con el fin de garantizar su cobro, dicho crédito fiscal, mediante solicitud de la autoridad competente de ese Estado, deberá ser aceptado por la autoridad competente del otro Estado Contratante con el fin de adoptar las medidas cautelares. Ese otro Estado tomará medidas cautelares respecto de ese crédito fiscal, de conformidad con las disposiciones de su legislación, como si el crédito fiscal fuera de ese otro Estado, aún si, en el momento en el que dichas medidas sean aplicadas, el crédito fiscal no fuera exigible en el Estado mencionado en primer lugar o sea debido por una persona que tiene derecho a impedir su cobro.

5. No obstante lo dispuesto por los párrafos 3 y 4, un crédito fiscal aceptado por un Estado Contratante para efectos del párrafo 3 ó 4 no estará sujeto en ese Estado a la prescripción o prelación aplicables a los créditos fiscales bajo la legislación de ese Estado, por virtud de su naturaleza como tal. Asimismo, un crédito fiscal aceptado por un Estado Contratante para efectos de los párrafos 3 ó 4 no deberá tener en ese Estado ninguna prelación aplicable a dicho crédito fiscal de conformidad con la legislación del otro Estado Contratante.

6. Los procesos respecto a la existencia, validez o monto de un crédito fiscal de un Estado Contratante no deberán presentarse ante los tribunales u órganos administrativos del otro Estado Contratante.

7. Cuando, en cualquier momento posterior a la formulación de una solicitud por parte de un Estado Contratante de conformidad con los párrafos 3 ó 4 y antes de que el otro Estado Contratante haya cobrado y remitido el crédito fiscal correspondiente al Estado mencionado en primer lugar, dicho crédito fiscal dejará de ser

a) en el caso de una solicitud de conformidad con el párrafo 3, un crédito fiscal del Estado mencionado en primer lugar que sea exigible de conformidad con la legislación de ese Estado y que sea debido por una persona que, en ese momento, conforme a la legislación de ese Estado, no pueda impedir su cobro, o

b) en el caso de una solicitud de conformidad con el párrafo 4, un crédito fiscal del Estado mencionado en primer lugar respecto del cual dicho Estado, de conformidad con su legislación, pueda tomar medidas cautelares con miras a garantizar su cobro

la autoridad competente del Estado mencionado en primer lugar deberá notificar inmediatamente ese hecho a la autoridad competente del otro Estado y, a elección del otro Estado, el Estado mencionado en primer lugar suspenderá o retirará su solicitud.

8. En ningún caso, las disposiciones del presente Artículo deberán interpretarse en el sentido de obligar a un Estado Contratante a:

a) adoptar medidas administrativas contrarias a la legislación y práctica administrativa de ese o del otro Estado Contratante;

b) adoptar medidas que serían contrarias al orden público *(ordre public)*;

c) prestar asistencia si el otro Estado Contratante no ha adoptado todas las medidas razonables de cobro o cautelares, según sea el caso, disponibles conforme a su legislación o práctica administrativa;

d) prestar asistencia en aquellos casos en los que la carga administrativa para ese Estado sea claramente desproporcionada respecto del beneficio que obtendrá el otro Estado Contratante.

ARTÍCULO 27

Miembros de Misiones Diplomáticas y de Oficinas Consulares

Las disposiciones del presente Acuerdo no afectarán los privilegios fiscales de los miembros de misiones diplomáticas o de las oficinas consulares, de acuerdo con los principios generales del derecho internacional o en virtud de las disposiciones de acuerdos especiales.

ARTÍCULO 28

Entrada en Vigor

Cada uno de los Estados Contratantes notificará al otro, a través de la vía diplomática, el cumplimiento de los procedimientos requeridos por su legislación interna para la entrada en vigor del presente Acuerdo. El presente Acuerdo entrará en vigor treinta (30) días después de la fecha de la última de estas notificaciones y sus disposiciones surtirán efectos para los impuestos respecto de cada ejercicio fiscal que inicie el o a partir del primer día de enero del año siguiente a aquél en que el presente Acuerdo entre en vigor.

ARTÍCULO 29
Terminación

El presente Acuerdo permanecerá en vigor hasta que se dé por terminado por un Estado Contratante. Cualquiera de los Estados Contratantes puede dar por terminado el Acuerdo, a través de la vía diplomática, dando aviso de la terminación al menos seis (6) meses antes de que termine cualquier año de calendario posterior a un periodo de cinco (5) años a partir de la fecha en que el Acuerdo entre en vigor. En dicho caso, el Acuerdo dejará de surtir efectos para los impuestos respecto a cada ejercicio fiscal que inicie el o a partir del primer día de enero del año siguiente a aquél en que se realice la notificación.

EN FE de lo cual los suscritos, debidamente autorizados para tal efecto, han firmado el presente Acuerdo.

HECHO en duplicado en Ankara el diecisiete de diciembre de dos mil trece, en los idiomas español, turco e inglés, siendo todos los textos igualmente auténticos. En el caso de cualquier divergencia, el texto en inglés prevalecerá.

POR EL GOBIERNO DE LOS ESTADOS UNIDOS MEXICANOS

José Antonio Meade Kuribreña
Secretario de Relaciones Exteriores

POR EL GOBIERNO DE LA REPÚBLICA DE TURQUÍA

Mehmet ŞİMŞEK
Ministro de Finanzas

PROTOCOLO

Al momento de proceder a la firma del Acuerdo entre el Gobierno de los Estados Unidos Mexicanos y el Gobierno de la República de Turquía para Evitar la Doble Imposición y Prevenir la Evasión Fiscal en Materia de Impuestos sobre la Renta, los suscritos han acordado que las siguientes disposiciones formarán parte integrante del referido Acuerdo:

1. En relación con el Artículo 5

Se entiende que para los fines del párrafo 7 no se considerará que una empresa tiene un establecimiento permanente en un Estado Contratante simplemente porque realiza actividades empresariales en ese Estado por medio de un corredor, comisionista general o cualquier otro agente que goce de un estatuto independiente, siempre que dichas personas, en sus relaciones comerciales o financieras con la empresa, no establezcan o impongan condiciones que difieran de aquéllas que generalmente serían acordadas por agentes independientes.

2. En relación con el Artículo 6

Se entiende que la expresión "bienes inmuebles" incluye el equipo utilizado en la cría y cultivo de peces.

3. En relación con el párrafo 1 del Artículo 7

Se entiende que si una empresa de un Estado Contratante tiene un establecimiento permanente en el otro Estado Contratante, donde la empresa realiza actividades empresariales, los beneficios de dicha empresa pueden someterse a imposición en ese otro Estado Contratante pero solamente en la medida en que sean atribuibles a las ventas en ese otro Estado Contratante de bienes o mercancías de la misma o similar naturaleza que los bienes o mercancías vendidos a través de ese establecimiento permanente.

Sin embargo, los beneficios derivados de las ventas descritas anteriormente no se someterán a imposición en ese otro Estado Contratante si la empresa demuestra que dichas ventas han sido realizadas por razones distintas a la obtención de un beneficio conforme al presente Acuerdo.

4. En relación con el párrafo 3 del Artículo 7

Se entiende que no serán deducibles los montos pagados que efectúe, en su caso, el establecimiento permanente (que no sean los hechos por concepto de reembolso de gastos efectivos) a la oficina central de la empresa o a cualquiera de sus otras oficinas, a título de regalías, honorarios u otros pagos similares a cambio del derecho a utilizar patentes u otros derechos, o a título de comisión, por servicios específicos prestados o por gestiones hechas o, salvo en el caso de un banco, a título de intereses sobre dinero prestado al establecimiento permanente. Asimismo, no se tomarán en cuenta para la determinación de los beneficios de un establecimiento permanente las cantidades cobradas por el establecimiento permanente (que no sean por concepto de reembolso de gastos efectivos) a la oficina central de la empresa o a cualquiera de sus otras oficinas, a título de regalías, honorarios u otros pagos similares a cambio del derecho a utilizar patentes u otros derechos, o a título de comisión por servicios específicos prestados o por gestiones hechas o, salvo en el caso de un banco, a título de intereses sobre dinero prestado a la oficina central de la empresa o a cualquiera de sus otras oficinas.

5. En relación con el Artículo 8

Se entiende que los beneficios a que se refiere el párrafo 1 del Artículo 8 no comprenderán los beneficios provenientes de la utilización de transporte interior por carretera.

6. En relación con el Artículo 11

Se entiende que el término "intereses" no incluirá cualquier elemento de renta que sea considerado como un dividendo de conformidad con las disposiciones del párrafo 3 del Artículo 10.

Se entiende que en el caso de que las instituciones mencionadas en los incisos c) y d) se modifiquen mediante fusión, adquisición o cualquier operación similar con el propósito de crear una nueva institución, las autoridades competentes se consultarán mutuamente para determinar el modo de aplicación del Acuerdo para las instituciones mencionadas en la medida en que continúen siendo totalmente propiedad del Gobierno.

7. En relación con los Artículos 10, 11, 12 y 13

Se entiende que para los fines de los Artículos 10, 11, 12 y 13 del Acuerdo, cuando resulte una doble exención derivada de una clasificación divergente de cualquier renta, cada uno de los Estados Contratantes mantendrá el derecho de someter a imposición, de acuerdo con su legislación interna, la renta en cuestión.

8. En relación con el Artículo 12

Se entiende que, no obstante las disposiciones del Artículo 13, el término "regalías" también incluye los pagos derivados de la enajenación de cualquier derecho o propiedad que estén condicionados a la productividad, uso o disposición del mismo.

9. **En relación con el Artículo 14**

Se entiende que cuando una persona física o una empresa de un Estado Contratante pueda someterse a imposición en el otro Estado Contratante de acuerdo con los párrafos 1 ó 2 del Artículo 14, esa persona física o empresa puede elegir ser sometida a imposición en ese otro Estado respecto de dicha renta de acuerdo con las disposiciones del Artículo 7 del presente Acuerdo como si la renta fuera atribuible a un establecimiento permanente de la empresa situada en ese otro Estado. Esta elección no afectará el derecho de ese otro Estado a imponer una retención del impuesto sobre dicha renta.

10. **En relación con el Artículo 24**

Se entiende que, no obstante cualquier otro tratado del que los Estados Contratantes sean o puedan ser partes, cualquier controversia sobre una medida adoptada por un Estado Contratante que se relacione con un impuesto comprendido en el Artículo 2 o, en el caso de no discriminación, cualquier medida fiscal adoptada por un Estado Contratante, incluyendo una controversia sobre la aplicación del presente Acuerdo, será resuelta únicamente de conformidad con el Acuerdo, a no ser que las autoridades competentes de los Estados Contratantes acuerden lo contrario.

En el caso de Turquía, se entiende que en relación con el párrafo 2, el contribuyente debe solicitar la devolución que resulte de dicho acuerdo mutuo dentro de un periodo de un (1) año posterior a que la administración fiscal haya notificado al contribuyente el resultado del acuerdo mutuo.

11. **En general**

Se entiende que las disposiciones del presente Acuerdo no impedirán a un Estado Contratante aplicar sus disposiciones relacionadas con capitalización delgada y sociedades extranjeras controladas (en el caso de México, regímenes fiscales preferentes).

Se entiende que para los efectos fiscales mexicanos, la base fija será tratada de conformidad con los principios que aplican al establecimiento permanente.

EN FE de lo cual los suscritos, debidamente autorizados para tal efecto, han firmado el presente Protocolo.

HECHO en duplicado en Ankara el diecisiete de diciembre de dos mil trece, en los idiomas español, turco e inglés, siendo todos los textos igualmente auténticos. En el caso de cualquier divergencia, el texto en inglés prevalecerá.

POR EL GOBIERNO DE LOS ESTADOS UNIDOS MEXICANOS	POR EL GOBIERNO DE LA REPÚBLICA DE TURQUÍA
José Antonio Meade Kuribreña Secretario de Relaciones Exteriores	Mehmet ŞİMŞEK Ministro de Finanzas

[TURKISH TEXT – TEXTE TURC]

BİRLEŞİK MEKSİKA DEVLETLERİ HÜKÜMETİ İLE TÜRKİYE CUMHURİYETİ HÜKÜMETİ ARASINDA GELİR ÜZERİNDEN ALINAN VERGİLERDE ÇİFTE VERGİLENDİRMEYİ ÖNLEME VE VERGİ KAÇAKÇILIĞINA ENGEL OLMA ANLAŞMASI

BİRLEŞİK MEKSİKA DEVLETLERİ HÜKÜMETİ ve TÜRKİYE CUMHURİYETİ HÜKÜMETİ

Gelir üzerinden alınan vergilerde çifte vergilendirmeyi önleyen ve vergi kaçakçılığına engel olan bir Anlaşma yapmak isteğiyle,

AŞAĞIDAKİ ANLAŞMAYA VARMIŞLARDIR:

MADDE 1
KAPSANAN KİŞİLER

Bu Anlaşma, Akit Devletlerden birinin veya her ikisinin mukimi olan kişilere uygulanacaktır.

MADDE 2
KAPSANAN VERGİLER

1. Bu Anlaşma, ne şekilde alındığına bakılmaksızın, Meksika adına ve Türkiye adına gelir üzerinden alınan vergilere uygulanacaktır.

2. Menkul veya gayrimenkul varlıkların devrinden doğan kazançlara uygulanan vergiler de dahil olmak üzere, toplam gelir veya gelir unsurları üzerinden alınan tüm vergiler, gelir üzerinden alınan vergiler olarak kabul edilecektir.

3. Anlaşmanın uygulanacağı mevcut vergiler özellikle:

a) Meksika'da:

(i) federal gelir vergisi;

(ii) düz oranlı işletme vergisi;

(bundan böyle "Meksika vergisi" olarak bahsedilecektir);

b) Türkiye'de:

(i) gelir vergisi;

(ii) kurumlar vergisi;

(bundan böyle "Türk vergisi" olarak bahsedilecektir).

4. Anlaşma aynı zamanda, Anlaşmanın imza tarihinden sonra mevcut vergilere ilave olarak veya onların yerine alınan ve mevcut vergilerle aynı nitelikte olan veya onlara önemli ölçüde benzeyen vergilere de uygulanacaktır. Akit Devletlerin yetkili makamları, ilgili vergi mevzuatlarında yapılan önemli değişiklikleri birbirlerine bildireceklerdir.

MADDE 3

GENEL TANIMLAR

1. Bu Anlaşmanın amaçları yönünden, metin aksini gerektirmedikçe:

a) "Meksika" (Birleşik Meksika Devletleri) ve "Türkiye" terimleri, kara sahası, iç suları, karasuları ve bunların üzerinde bulunan hava sahası dahil olmak üzere her iki Akit Devletin egemenlik alanını, bunun yanı sıra, uluslararası hukuka ve iç mevzuatlarına uygun olarak her iki Akit Devletin sular, deniz yatağı ve deniz altı ve buralardaki doğal kaynaklar bakımından üzerinde egemen hak veya yetkilerini kullanabileceği karasularının ötesindeki deniz alanını ifade eder.

b) "bir Akit Devlet" ve "diğer Akit Devlet" terimleri metnin gereğine göre, Meksika veya Türkiye anlamına gelir;

c) "kişi" terimi, bir gerçek kişiyi, bir şirketi ve kişilerin oluşturduğu diğer herhangi bir kuruluşu kapsamına alır;

d) "şirket" terimi, herhangi bir kurum veya vergileme yönünden kurum olarak muamele gören herhangi bir kuruluş anlamına gelir;

e) "kanuni merkez" terimi Türk Ticaret Kanunu'na göre tescil edilmiş olan kayıtlı merkezi ifade eder;

f) "bir Akit Devlet teşebbüsü" ve "diğer Akit Devlet teşebbüsü" terimleri sırasıyla, bir Akit Devletin mukimi tarafından işletilen bir teşebbüs ve diğer Akit Devletin mukimi tarafından işletilen bir teşebbüs anlamına gelir;

g) "uluslararası trafik" terimi, yalnızca diğer Akit Devletin sınırları içinde bulunan yerler arasında yapılan gemi veya uçak işletmeciliği hariç olmak üzere, bir Akit Devlet teşebbüsü tarafından gemi veya uçak işletilerek yapılan her türlü taşımacılığı ifade eder;

h) "yetkili makam" terimi:

(i) Meksika'da, Maliye ve Kamu Kredisi Bakanlığını; ve

(ii) Türkiye'de, Maliye Bakanını veya onun yetkili temsilcisini

ifade eder;

i) "vatandaş" terimi:

(i) bir Akit Devletin vatandaşlığına sahip herhangi bir gerçek kişiyi;

(ii) bir Akit Devlette yürürlükte olan mevzuata göre statü kazanan herhangi bir tüzel kişiyi, ortaklığı veya birliği

ifade eder.

2. Anlaşmanın bir Akit Devlet tarafından herhangi bir tarihte uygulanması bakımından, Anlaşmada tanımlanmamış herhangi bir terim, metin aksini gerektirmedikçe, bu Anlaşmanın uygulandığı vergilerin amaçları bakımından, o tarihte bu Devletin mevzuatında sahip olduğu anlamı taşıyacak ve bu Devletin yürürlükteki vergi mevzuatında yer alan herhangi bir anlam, bu Devletin diğer mevzuatında bu terime verilen anlama göre üstünlük taşıyacaktır.

MADDE 4
MUKİM

1. Bu Anlaşmanın amaçları bakımından, "bir Akit Devletin mukimi" terimi, bu Devlet, herhangi bir politik alt bölümü veya mahalli idaresi de dahil olmak üzere, o Devletin mevzuatı gereğince ev, ikametgah, kanuni merkez, yönetim yeri veya benzer yapıda diğer herhangi bir kriter nedeniyle burada vergiye tabi olan herhangi bir kişi anlamına gelir. Ancak bu terim, yalnızca o Devletteki kaynaklardan elde edilen gelir nedeniyle o Devlette vergiye tabi tutulan herhangi bir kişiyi kapsamaz.

2. 1 inci fıkra hükümleri dolayısıyla bir gerçek kişi her iki Akit Devletin de mukimi olduğunda, bu kişinin durumu aşağıdaki şekilde belirlenecektir:

a) bu kişi, yalnızca daimi olarak kalabileceği bir evin bulunduğu Devletin mukimi kabul edilecektir; eğer bu kişinin her iki Devlette de daimi olarak kalabileceği bir evi varsa, bu kişi yalnızca kişisel ve ekonomik ilişkilerinin daha yakın olduğu (hayati menfaatlerin merkezi olan) Devletin mukimi kabul edilecektir;

b) eğer kişinin hayati menfaatlerinin merkezinin yer aldığı Devlet saptanamazsa veya her iki Devlette de daimi olarak kalabileceği bir evi yoksa, bu kişi yalnızca kalmayı adet edindiği evin bulunduğu Devletin mukimi kabul edilecektir;

c) eğer kişinin her iki Devlette de kalmayı adet edindiği bir ev varsa veya her iki Devlette de böyle bir ev söz konusu değilse, bu kişi yalnızca vatandaşı olduğu Devletin mukimi kabul edilecektir;

d) eğer kişi her iki Devletin de vatandaşıysa veya her iki Devletin de vatandaşı değilse, Akit Devletlerin yetkili makamları sorunu karşılıklı anlaşmayla çözeceklerdir.

3. Gerçek kişi dışındaki bir kişinin 1 inci fıkra hükümleri dolayısıyla her iki Akit Devletin de mukimi olduğu durumda, bu kişi bir Akit Devlette etkin yönetim merkezine ve diğer Akit Devlette kanuni merkeze sahip ise, bu kişinin Anlaşmanın amaçları bakımından hangi Devletin mukimi kabul edileceğini, Akit Devletlerin yetkili makamları karşılıklı anlaşma ile belirleyeceklerdir. Böyle bir anlaşmaya varılamadığı takdirde, bu kişiler, Anlaşmanın sağlayacağı avantajlar bakımından her iki Akit Devletin de mukimi olarak kabul edilmeyeceklerdir.

MADDE 5

İŞ YERİ

1. Bu Anlaşmanın amaçları bakımından "iş yeri" terimi, bir teşebbüsün işinin tamamen veya kısmen yürütüldüğü işe ilişkin sabit bir yer anlamına gelir.

2. "İş yeri" terimi özellikle şunları kapsamına alır:

a) yönetim yeri;

b) şube;

c) büro;

d) fabrika;

e) atölye, ve

f) maden ocağı, petrol veya doğal gaz kuyusu, taş ocağı veya doğal kaynakların çıkarıldığı diğer herhangi bir yer.

3. Bir inşaat şantiyesi, yapım, montaj veya kurma projesi veya bunlarla ilgili gözetim faaliyetleri, yalnızca altı (6) ayı aşan bir süre devam etmesi durumunda bir iş yeri oluşturur.

4. Bu maddenin daha önceki hükümleri ile bağlı kalınmaksızın, "iş yeri" teriminin aşağıdaki hususları kapsamadığı kabul edilecektir:

a) Tesislerin, teşebbüse ait malların veya ticari eşyanın yalnızca depolanması veya teşhiri amacıyla kullanılması;

b) Teşebbüse ait mal veya ticari eşya stoklarının, yalnızca depolama veya teşhir amacıyla elde tutulması;

c) Teşebbüse ait mal veya ticari eşya stoklarının, yalnızca bir başka teşebbüse işlettirilmesi amacıyla elde tutulması;

d) İşe ilişkin sabit bir yerin, yalnızca teşebbüse mal veya ticari eşya satın alma veya bilgi toplama amacıyla elde tutulması;

e) İşe ilişkin sabit bir yerin, teşebbüs için yalnızca hazırlayıcı veya yardımcı nitelik taşıyan diğer herhangi bir işin yürütülmesi amacıyla elde tutulması;

f) İşe ilişkin sabit bir yerin yalnızca, a) ile e) bentleri arasında bahsedilen faaliyetlerin bir ya da birkaçını bir arada icra etmek için elde tutulması; ancak söz konusu faaliyetlerin bir arada yürütülmesi sonucunda işe ilişkin sabit yerde oluşan bütün bu faaliyetlerin hazırlayıcı veya yardımcı nitelikte olması şarttır.

5. 1 inci ve 2 nci fıkra hükümleriyle bağlı kalınmaksızın, bir kişi - 7 nci fıkranın uygulanacağı bağımsız nitelikteki bir acente dışında- bir Akit Devlette, bir teşebbüs adına hareket eder ve o teşebbüs adına sözleşme akdetme yetkisine sahip olup, bu yetkisini mutaden kullanırsa, bu kişinin faaliyetleri, 4 üncü fıkrada bahsedilen ve anılan fıkra hükümlerine göre işe ilişkin sabit bir yer aracılığıyla yürütüldüğünde, bu sabit yere iş yeri mahiyeti kazandırmayan faaliyetler ile sınırlı olmadıkça, bu teşebbüs, bu Devlette, söz konusu kişinin teşebbüs için gerçekleştirdiği her türlü faaliyet dolayısıyla bir iş yerine sahip kabul edilecektir.

6. Bu maddenin daha önceki hükümleri ile bağlı kalınmaksızın, bir Akit Devletin sigortacılık teşebbüsü, reasüransa ilişkin olanlar hariç, diğer Akit Devlette, 7 nci fıkranın uygulanacağı bağımsız nitelikteki bir acenta dışındaki bir kişi vasıtasıyla prim tahsil eder veya risk sigortası yaparsa, bu diğer Devlette bir iş yerine sahip kabul edilecektir.

7. Bir teşebbüs, bir Akit Devlette, işlerini yalnızca kendi işlerine olağan şekilde devam eden bir simsar, genel komisyon acentesi veya bağımsız statüde diğer herhangi bir acente vasıtasıyla yürüttüğü için bu Devlette bir iş yerine sahip kabul olunmayacaktır.

8. Bir Akit Devletin mukimi olan bir şirket, diğer Akit Devletin mukimi olan veya bu diğer Devlette ticari faaliyette bulunan (bir iş yeri vasıtasıyla veya diğer bir şekilde) bir şirketi kontrol eder ya da onun tarafından kontrol edilirse, bu şirketlerden herhangi biri diğeri için bir iş yeri oluşturmayacaktır.

MADDE 6

GAYRİMENKUL VARLIKLARDAN ELDE EDİLEN GELİR

1. Bir Akit Devlet mukiminin diğer Akit Devlette bulunan gayrimenkul varlıklardan elde ettiği gelir (tarım veya ormancılıktan elde edilen gelir dahil), bu diğer Devlette vergilendirilebilir.

2. "Gayrimenkul varlık" terimi, söz konusu varlığın bulunduğu Akit Devletin mevzuatına göre tanımlanacaktır. Bu terim her halükarda, gayrimenkul varlığa müteferri varlıkları, tarım ve ormancılıkta kullanılan hayvanları ve araçları, özel hukuk hükümlerinin uygulanacağı gayrimenkul mülkiyetine ilişkin hakları, gayrimenkul intifa haklarını ve maden ocaklarının, kaynakların ve diğer doğal kaynakların işletilmesi veya işletme hakkı karşılığında doğan sabit ya da değişken ödemeler üzerindeki hakları kapsayacak; gemiler, vapurlar ve uçaklar gayrimenkul varlık olarak değerlendirilmeyecektir.

3. 1 inci fıkra hükümleri, gayrimenkul varlığın doğrudan kullanımından, kiralanmasından veya diğer herhangi bir şekilde kullanımından elde edilen gelire uygulanacaktır.

4. 1 inci ve 3 üncü fıkraların hükümleri aynı zamanda, bir teşebbüsün gayrimenkul varlıklarından elde edilen gelir ile serbest meslek faaliyetlerinin icrasında kullanılan gayrimenkul varlıklardan elde edilen gelire de uygulanacaktır.

MADDE 7
TİCARİ KAZANÇLAR

1. Bir Akit Devlet teşebbüsüne ait kazanç, söz konusu teşebbüs diğer Akit Devlette yer alan bir iş yeri vasıtasıyla ticari faaliyette bulunmadıkça, yalnızca bu Devlette vergilendirilecektir. Eğer teşebbüs yukarıda bahsedilen şekilde ticari faaliyette bulunursa, teşebbüsün kazançları, yalnızca bu iş yerine atfedilebilen miktarla sınırlı olmak üzere bu diğer Devlette vergilendirilebilir.

2. 3 üncü fıkra hükümleri saklı kalmak üzere, bir Akit Devlet teşebbüsü diğer Akit Devlette yer alan bir iş yeri vasıtasıyla ticari faaliyette bulunduğunda, her iki Akit Devlette de bu iş yerine atfedilecek kazanç, bu iş yeri aynı veya benzer koşullar altında, aynı veya benzer faaliyetlerde bulunan ayrı ve bağımsız bir teşebbüs olsaydı ve iş yerini oluşturduğu teşebbüsten tamamen bağımsız bir nitelik kazansaydı ne kazanç elde edecek ise aynı miktarda bir kazanç olacaktır.

3. Bir iş yerinin kazancı belirlenirken, iş yerinin bulunduğu Devlette veya başka yerde yapılan, yönetim ve genel idare giderleri de dahil olmak üzere, iş yerinin amaçlarına uygun olan giderlerin indirilmesine müsaade edilecektir.

4. Bir iş yerine, bu iş yeri tarafından teşebbüs adına yalnızca mal veya ticari eşya satın alınması dolayısıyla hiç bir kazanç atfedilmeyecektir.

5. Kazanç, bu Anlaşmanın diğer maddelerinde ayrı olarak düzenlenen gelir unsurlarını da kapsamına aldığında, o maddelerin hükümleri bu madde hükümlerinden etkilenmeyecektir.

MADDE 8

DENİZ VE HAVA TAŞIMACILIĞI

1. Bir Akit Devlet teşebbüsünün uluslararası trafikte gemi veya uçak işletmeciliğinden elde ettiği kazanç, yalnızca bu Devlette vergilendirilecektir.

2. 1 inci fıkra hükümleri aynı zamanda, bir ortaklığa (pool), bir ortak girişime veya uluslararası işletilen bir acenteye iştirak dolayısıyla elde edilen kazançlara da uygulanacaktır.

MADDE 9

BAĞIMLI TEŞEBBÜSLER

1. a) Bir Akit Devlet teşebbüsü doğrudan veya dolaylı olarak diğer Akit Devlet teşebbüsünün yönetim, kontrol veya sermayesine katıldığında veya

   b) Aynı kişiler doğrudan veya dolaylı olarak bir Akit Devlet teşebbüsünün ve diğer Akit Devlet teşebbüsünün yönetim, kontrol veya sermayesine katıldığında,

ve her iki halde de, iki teşebbüs arasındaki ticari veya mali ilişkilerde oluşan veya oluşturulan koşullar, bağımsız teşebbüsler arasında oluşması gereken koşullardan farklılaştığında, bu şartlar altında, teşebbüslerden birisinde olması gereken, fakat bu koşullar nedeniyle kendini göstermeyen kazanç, o teşebbüsün kazancına eklenir ve buna göre vergilendirilebilir.

2. Bir Akit Devletin kendi teşebbüsünün kazancına dahil edip vergilendirdiği kazancın, diğer Akit Devlette vergilendirilen diğer Devletin bir teşebbüsünün kazancını içermesi ve aynı zamanda, ilk bahsedilen Devletin kavradığı bu kazancın, iki bağımsız teşebbüs arasında olması gereken koşullar göz önünde tutularak, bu ilk Devlet tarafından, kendi teşebbüsünde kendisini göstermesi gereken kazanç olduğunun iddia edilmesi durumunda, diğer Devlet bu belirlemenin yerinde olduğu kanaatine varırsa, söz konusu kazanç üzerinden alınan verginin miktarında gerekli düzeltmeleri yapacaktır. Bu düzeltme yapılırken, bu Anlaşmanın diğer hükümleri göz önünde tutulacak ve gerektiğinde Akit Devletlerin yetkili makamları birbirlerine danışacaklardır.

MADDE 10

TEMETTÜLER

1. Bir Akit Devletin mukimi olan bir şirket tarafından diğer Akit Devletin bir mukimine ödenen temettüler, bu diğer Devlette vergilendirilebilir.

2. Bununla beraber söz konusu temettüler, temettüyü ödeyen şirketin mukim olduğu Akit Devlette ve bu Devletin mevzuatına göre de vergilendirilebilir; ancak, temettünün gerçek lehtarı diğer Akit Devletin bir mukimi ise bu şekilde alınacak vergi:

a) gerçek lehtar, temettü ödeyen şirketin sermayesinin doğrudan doğruya en az yüzde 25 ini elinde tutan bir şirket (ortaklık hariç) ise, gayrisafi temettü tutarının yüzde 5 ini;

b) diğer tüm durumlarda gayrisafi temettü tutarının yüzde 15 ini aşmayacaktır.

Bu fıkra, içinden temettü ödemesi yapılan kazançlar yönünden şirketin vergilendirilmesini etkilemeyecektir.

3. Bu maddede kullanılan "temettü" terimi, hisse senetlerinden, intifa senetlerinden veya intifa haklarından, madencilik hisselerinden, kurucu hisse senetlerinden veya alacak niteliğinde olmayıp kazanca katılmayı sağlayan diğer haklardan elde edilen gelirleri, bunun yanı sıra diğer şirket haklarından elde edilen gelir ve dağıtımı yapan şirketin mukim olduğu Devletin mevzuatına göre, vergileme yönünden hisse senetlerinden elde edilen gelirle aynı muameleyi gören diğer gelirler ile yatırım fonu ve yatırım ortaklığından elde edilen gelirleri ifade eder.

4. Diğer Akit Devlette yer alan bir iş yeri vasıtasıyla ticari faaliyette bulunan bir Akit Devlet şirketinin kazancı 7 nci maddeye göre vergilendirildikten sonra, kalan kısım üzerinden bu maddenin 2 nci fıkrasının a) bendine uygun olarak, iş yerinin bulunduğu Akit Devlette vergilendirilebilir.

5. Bir Akit Devlet mukimi olan temettünün gerçek lehtarı, temettüyü ödeyen şirketin mukim olduğu diğer Akit Devlette yer alan bir iş yeri vasıtasıyla ticari faaliyette bulunursa veya bu diğer Devlette yer alan sabit bir yer vasıtasıyla serbest meslek faaliyeti icra ederse ve söz konusu temettülerin elde edilmesi ile bu iş yeri veya sabit yer arasında etkin bir bağ bulunmaktaysa, 1 inci ve 2 nci fıkra hükümleri uygulanmayacaktır. Bu durumda, olayına göre 7 nci veya 14 üncü madde hükümleri uygulanacaktır.

6. 4 üncü fıkra hükümleri saklı kalmak üzere, bir Akit Devlet mukimi olan bir şirket, diğer Akit Devletten kazanç veya gelir elde ettiğinde, bu diğer Devlet, temettülerin kendi mukimlerinden birisine ödenmesi veya temettü elde edilmesi ile bu diğer Devlette bulunan iş yeri veya sabit yer arasında etkin bir bağ bulunması durumları hariç olmak üzere, bu şirket tarafından ödenen temettüler üzerinden herhangi bir vergi alamayacağı gibi, ödenen temettülerin veya dağıtılmamış kazancın tamamen veya kısmen bu diğer Devlette elde edilen kazanç veya gelirden oluşması durumunda bile, bu şirketin dağıtılmayan kazançları üzerinden dağıtılmayan kazançlara uygulanan bir vergi alamaz.

MADDE 11
FAİZ

1. Bir Akit Devlette doğan ve diğer Akit Devletin bir mukimine ödenen faiz, bu diğer Devlette vergilendirilebilir.

2. Bununla beraber söz konusu faiz, elde edildiği Akit Devlette ve o Devletin mevzuatına göre de vergilendirilebilir; ancak, faizin gerçek lehtarı diğer Akit Devletin bir mukimi ise, bu şekilde alınacak vergi:

a) faizin bir bankaya ödenmesi halinde, faizin gayrisafi tutarının yüzde 10 unu;

b) tüm diğer durumlarda faizin gayrisafi tutarının yüzde 15 ini aşmayacaktır.

3. 2 nci fıkra hükümlerine bakılmaksızın, eğer:

a) gerçek lehtar bir Akit Devletin kendisi, politik alt bölümü veya mahalli idaresi ya da Meksika Merkez Bankası (Banco de México) veya Türkiye Merkez Bankası (Türkiye Cumhuriyet Merkez Bankası) ise;

b) faiz, a) bendinde belirtilen herhangi bir kuruluş tarafından ödeniyor ise;

c) Türkiye'de doğan ve Banco Nacional de Comercio Exterior, S.N.C., Nacional Financiera, S.N.C. veya Banco Nacional de Obras y Servicios Publicos, S.N.C. tarafından üç (3) yıldan kısa süreli olmamak üzere verilen krediler için ödenen faiz ise; veya

d) Meksika'da doğan ve Türk Eximbank (Türkiye İhracat Kredi Bankası A.Ş.) tarafından üç (3) yıldan kısa süreli olmamak üzere verilen krediler için ödenen faiz ise;

1 inci fıkrada belirtilen faiz, yalnızca gerçek lehtarın mukim olduğu Akit Devlette vergilendirilecektir.

4. Bu maddede kullanılan "faiz" terimi, ipotek garantisine bağlı olsun olmasın ve borçlunun kazancına katılma hakkı tanısın tanımasın, her nevi alacaktan doğan gelirleri ve özellikle kamu menkul kıymetleri ile tahvil veya borç senetlerine ilişkin prim ve ikramiyeler dahil olmak üzere, söz konusu menkul kıymet, tahvil veya borç senetlerinden elde edilen gelirler ile gelirin elde edildiği Akit Devletin mevzuatına göre ikrazat geliri sayılan diğer bütün gelirleri ifade eder.

5. Bir Akit Devlet mukimi olan faizin gerçek lehtarı, faizin elde edildiği diğer Akit Devlette bulunan bir iş yeri vasıtasıyla ticari faaliyette bulunursa veya bu diğer Devlette yer alan sabit bir yer vasıtasıyla serbest meslek faaliyeti icra ederse ve söz konusu faizin ödendiği alacak ile bu iş yeri veya sabit yer arasında etkin bir bağ bulunmaktaysa, 1 inci ve 2 nci fıkra hükümleri uygulanmayacaktır. Bu durumda, olayına göre, 7 nci veya 14 üncü madde hükümleri uygulanacaktır.

6. Bir Akit Devletin kendisi, politik alt bölümü, mahalli idaresi veya bu Devletin bir mukimi tarafından ödenen faizin, o Devlette elde edildiği kabul olunacaktır. Bununla beraber, faiz ödeyen kişi, bir Akit Devletin mukimi olsun veya olmasın, bir Akit Devlette bir iş yerine veya sabit yere sahip olduğunda ve faiz bu iş yeri veya sabit yerden kaynaklandığında, söz konusu faizin iş yerinin veya sabit yerin bulunduğu Devlette elde edildiği kabul olunacaktır.

7. Faizin miktarı, ödeyici ile gerçek lehtar arasında veya her ikisi ile bir başka kişi arasında var olan özel ilişki nedeniyle, böyle bir ilişkinin olmadığı durumda ödeyici ve gerçek lehtar arasında kararlaştırılacak miktarı herhangi bir nedenle aştığında, bu madde hükümleri yalnızca en son bahsedilen miktara uygulanacaktır. Bu durumda ödemelerin aşan kısmı, bu Anlaşmanın diğer hükümleri de dikkate alınarak, her bir Akit Devletin mevzuatına göre vergilendirilecektir.

MADDE 12

GAYRİMADDİ HAK BEDELLERİ

1. Bir Akit Devlette doğan ve diğer Akit Devletin bir mukimine ödenen gayrimaddi hak bedelleri, bu diğer Devlette vergilendirilebilir.

2. Bununla beraber, söz konusu gayrimaddi hak bedelleri elde edildikleri Akit Devlette ve o Devletin mevzuatına göre de vergilendirilebilir; ancak gayrimaddi hak bedelinin gerçek lehtarı diğer Akit Devletin bir mukimi ise, bu şekilde alınacak vergi gayrimaddi hak bedelinin gayrisafi tutarının yüzde 10 unu aşmayacaktır.

3. Bu maddede kullanılan "gayrimaddi hak bedelleri" terimi:

a) her nevi patentin, ticari markanın, desen veya modelin, planın, gizli formül veya üretim yönteminin kullanımı ya da kullanım hakkı;

b) her nevi sınai, ticari veya bilimsel teçhizatın kullanımı ya da kullanım hakkı;

c) sınai, ticari veya bilimsel tecrübeye dayalı bilginin sağlanması;

d) sinema filmleri ile televizyon veya radyo yayınlarında kullanılan kayıtlar veya bantlar dahil olmak üzere, edebi, sanatsal veya bilimsel her nevi telif hakkının kullanımı ya da kullanım hakkı karşılığında yapılan her türlü ödemeyi ifade eder.

4. Bir Akit Devlet mukimi olan gayrimaddi hak bedelinin gerçek lehtarı, gayrimaddi hak bedelinin elde edildiği diğer Akit Devlette yer alan bir iş yeri vasıtasıyla ticari faaliyette bulunursa veya bu diğer Devlette yer alan sabit bir yer vasıtasıyla serbest meslek faaliyeti icra ederse ve söz konusu bedelin ödendiği hak veya varlık ile bu iş yeri veya sabit yer arasında etkin bir bağ bulunmaktaysa, 1 inci ve 2 nci fıkra hükümleri uygulanmayacaktır. Bu durumda, olayına göre, 7 nci veya 14 üncü madde hükümleri uygulanacaktır.

5. Bir Akit Devletin kendisi, politik alt bölümü, mahalli idaresi veya bu Devletin bir mukimi tarafından ödenen gayrimaddi hak bedelinin o Akit Devlette elde edildiği kabul olunacaktır. Bununla beraber, gayrimaddi hak bedelini ödeyen kişi bir Akit Devletin mukimi olsun veya olmasın, bir Akit Devlette bir iş yerine veya sabit yere sahip olduğunda ve gayrimaddi hak bedeli bu iş yerinden veya sabit yerden kaynaklandığında, söz konusu gayrimaddi hak bedelinin iş yerinin veya sabit yerin bulunduğu Devlette elde edildiği kabul olunacaktır.

6. Gayrimaddi hak bedelinin miktarı, ödeyici ile gerçek lehtar arasında veya her ikisi ile bir başka kişi arasında var olan özel ilişki nedeniyle, böyle bir ilişkinin olmadığı durumda ödeyici ile gerçek lehtar arasında kararlaştırılacak miktarı herhangi bir nedenle aştığında, bu madde hükümleri yalnızca en son bahsedilen miktara uygulanacaktır. Bu durumda ödemelerin aşan kısmı, bu Anlaşmanın diğer hükümleri de dikkate alınarak, her bir Akit Devletin mevzuatına göre vergilendirilecektir.

MADDE 13
SERMAYE DEĞER ARTIŞ KAZANÇLARI

1. Bir Akit Devlet mukimince, diğer Akit Devlette yer alan ve 6 ncı maddede belirtilen gayrimenkul varlıkların elden çıkarılmasından sağlanan kazançlar, bu diğer Devlette vergilendirilebilir.

2. Varlıkları doğrudan ya da dolaylı olarak esas itibarıyla bir Akit Devlette bulunan gayrimenkul varlıklardan oluşan bir şirketin hisselerinin veya diğer benzeri haklarının elden çıkarılmasından doğan kazançlar, bu Devlette vergilendirilebilir.

3. Bir Akit Devlet mukimi tarafından diğer Akit Devlet mukimi bir şirket ya da diğer bir tüzel kişiliğin sermayesindeki hisselerin, iştiraklerin ya da diğer hakların elden çıkarılmasından elde edilen kazançlar bu diğer Devlette vergilendirilebilir.

4. Bir Akit Devlet teşebbüsünün diğer Akit Devlette sahip olduğu bir iş yerinin ticari varlığına dahil menkul varlıkların veya bir Akit Devlet mukiminin diğer Akit Devlette serbest meslek faaliyeti icra etmek üzere kullandığı sabit bir yere ait menkul varlıkların elden çıkarılmasından doğan kazançlar, bu iş yerinin (yalnız veya tüm teşebbüsle birlikte) veya sabit yerin elden çıkarılmasından doğan kazanç da dahil olmak üzere, bu diğer Devlette vergilendirilebilir.

5. Bir Akit Devlet mukiminin uluslararası trafikte işletilen gemi ya da uçakların veya söz konusu gemi ve uçakların işletilmesiyle ilgili menkul varlıkların elden çıkarılmasından sağladığı kazançlar, yalnızca bu Devlette vergilendirilecektir.

6. Bu maddenin bundan önceki fıkralarında belirtilenlerin dışında kalan varlıkların elden çıkarılmasından doğan kazançlar, yalnızca elden çıkaranın mukim olduğu Akit Devlette vergilendirilecektir. Bununla beraber, diğer Akit Devlette elde edilen ve bu fıkrada bir önceki cümlede bahsedilen kazançlar, iktisap tarihi ve elden çıkarma tarihi arasında geçen sürenin bir (1) yılı aşmaması halinde, bu diğer Akit Devlette vergilendirilebilir.

MADDE 14

SERBEST MESLEK FAALİYETLERİ

1. Bir Akit Devletin mukimi olan bir gerçek kişinin serbest meslek hizmetleri veya bağımsız nitelikteki diğer faaliyetleri dolayısıyla elde edilen gelir, yalnızca bu Devlette vergilendirilecektir. Bununla beraber, bu hizmet veya faaliyetler diğer Devlette icra edilirse ve eğer:

a) bu kişi, bu diğer Devlette, söz konusu hizmet veya faaliyetleri icra etmek amacıyla sürekli kullanabileceği sabit bir yere sahip ise; veya

b) bu kişi, bu diğer Devlette, söz konusu hizmet veya faaliyetleri icra etmek amacıyla, on iki (12) aylık herhangi bir kesintisiz dönemde, bir veya birkaç seferde toplam yüz seksen üç (183) gün veya daha uzun bir süre kalırsa,

söz konusu gelir aynı zamanda bu diğer Akit Devlette de vergilendirilebilir.

Böyle bir durumda, olayına göre, yalnızca söz konusu sabit yere atfedilebilen gelir ya da yalnızca bu diğer Devlette bulunulan süre içinde icra edilen hizmet veya faaliyetlerden elde edilen gelir, bu diğer Devlette vergilendirilebilir.

2. Bir Akit Devlet teşebbüsünün serbest meslek hizmetleri veya bağımsız nitelikteki diğer faaliyetleri dolayısıyla elde ettiği gelir, yalnızca bu Devlette vergilendirilecektir. Bununla beraber, eğer bu hizmet veya faaliyetler diğer Devlette icra edilirse ve eğer:

a) teşebbüs, söz konusu hizmet veya faaliyetleri icra etmek üzere bu diğer Devlette bir iş yerine sahip olursa; veya

b) hizmet veya faaliyetlerin icra edildiği süre veya süreler, on iki (12) aylık herhangi bir kesintisiz dönemde toplam yüz seksen üç (183) günü aşarsa,

söz konusu gelir aynı zamanda bu diğer Akit Devlette de vergilendirilebilir.

Böyle bir durumda, olayına göre, yalnızca söz konusu iş yerine veya bu diğer Devlette icra edilen hizmet ya da faaliyetlere atfedilebilen gelir bu diğer Devlette vergilendirilebilir.

3. "Serbest meslek faaliyetleri" terimi, özellikle bağımsız olarak yürütülen bilimsel, edebi, sanatsal, eğitici veya öğretici faaliyetleri, bunun yanı sıra doktorların, avukatların, mühendislerin, mimarların, dişçilerin ve muhasebecilerin bağımsız faaliyetlerini kapsamına alır.

MADDE 15

BAĞIMLI FAALİYETLER

1. 16, 18, 19 ve 20 nci maddelerin hükümleri saklı kalmak üzere, bir Akit Devlet mukiminin bir hizmet dolayısıyla elde ettiği maaş, ücret ve diğer benzeri gelirler, bu hizmet diğer Akit Devlette ifa edilmedikçe, yalnızca bu Devlette vergilendirilecektir. Hizmet diğer Devlette ifa edilirse, buradan elde edilen söz konusu gelir bu diğer Devlette vergilendirilebilir.

2. 1 inci fıkra hükümlerine bakılmaksızın, bir Akit Devlet mukiminin diğer Akit Devlette ifa ettiği bir hizmet dolayısıyla elde ettiği gelir, eğer:

a) gelir elde eden kişi, diğer Devlette herhangi bir on iki (12) aylık dönemde bir veya bir kaç seferde toplam yüz seksen üç (183) günü aşmayan bir süre kalırsa, ve

b) ödeme, diğer Devletin mukimi olmayan bir işveren tarafından veya bu işveren adına yapılırsa, ve

c) ödeme, işverenin diğer Devlette sahip olduğu bir iş yerinden veya sabit yerden yapılmazsa yalnızca ilk bahsedilen Devlette vergilendirilecektir.

3. Bu maddenin önceki hükümlerine bakılmaksızın, bir Akit Devlet teşebbüsü tarafından, uluslararası trafikte işletilen bir gemi veya uçakta ifa edilen bir hizmet dolayısıyla elde edilen gelir, bu Akit Devlette vergilendirilebilir.

MADDE 16
YÖNETİCİLERE YAPILAN ÖDEMELER

Bir Akit Devlet mukiminin, diğer Akit Devletin mukimi olan bir şirketin yönetim kurulu üyesi olması dolayısıyla elde ettiği ücret ve diğer benzeri ödemeler, bu diğer Devlette vergilendirilebilir.

MADDE 17
SANATÇI VE SPORCULAR

1. 14 ve 15 inci maddelerin hükümlerine bakılmaksızın, bir Akit Devlet mukimi olan tiyatro, sinema, radyo veya televizyon sanatçısı gibi bir sanatçının, bir müzisyenin veya bir sporcunun diğer Akit Devlette bu sıfatla icra ettiği şahsi faaliyetleri dolayısıyla elde ettiği gelir, bu diğer Devlette vergilendirilebilir.

2. Bir sanatçının ya da sporcunun bu sıfatla icra ettiği şahsi faaliyetlerden doğan gelir, sanatçının veya sporcunun kendisi adına değil de bir başkası adına tahakkuk ederse, bu gelir 7, 14 ve 15 inci maddelerin hükümlerine bakılmaksızın, sanatçı ya da sporcunun faaliyetlerinin icra edildiği Akit Devlette vergilendirilebilir.

3. Bir sanatçı veya sporcunun bir Akit Devlette icra ettiği faaliyetlerden elde ettiği gelir, bu Devlete yapılan ziyaretin tamamen veya önemli ölçüde diğer Akit Devletin, politik alt bölümünün veya mahalli idaresinin kamusal fonlarından karşılanması halinde, bu Devlette vergiden istisna edilecektir.

MADDE 18
EMEKLİ MAAŞLARI

1. 19 uncu maddenin 2 nci fıkrası hükümleri saklı kalmak üzere, bir Akit Devlet mukimine geçmiş çalışmaları karşılığında ödenen emekli maaşları ve diğer benzeri ödemeler yalnızca bu Devlette vergilendirilecektir. Bu hüküm, aynı zamanda, bir Akit Devlet mukimine yapılan düzenli ödemelere de uygulanacaktır.

2. "Düzenli ödeme" terimi, para veya para ile ölçülebilir bir menfaat karşılığında, tam ve yeterli ödemelerde bulunma yükümlülüğüne bağlı olarak, ömür boyu veya belirli ya da belirlenebilir bir süre, belirli zamanlarda, düzenli olarak ödenecek belli bir meblağı kapsamına alır.

MADDE 19

KAMU HİZMETİ

1. a) Bir Akit Devlete, politik alt bölümüne veya mahalli idaresine bir gerçek kişi tarafından verilen hizmetler karşılığında, bu Devlet, alt bölüm veya idare tarafından yapılan ve emekli maaşı dışında kalan maaş, ücret ve diğer benzeri ödemeler, yalnızca bu Devlette vergilendirilecektir.

b) Bununla birlikte, hizmet diğer Akit Devlette ifa edilirse ve gerçek kişi bu diğer Devletin bir mukimi ise, söz konusu maaş, ücret ve diğer benzeri ödemeler yalnızca bu diğer Devlette vergilendirilecektir.

Ancak bu kişinin:

(i) bu Devletin bir vatandaşı olması; veya

(ii) yalnızca bu hizmeti ifa etmek için bu Devletin bir mukimi durumuna geçmemiş olması zorunludur.

2. a) 1 inci fıkra hükümlerine bakılmaksızın, bir Akit Devlete, politik alt bölümüne veya mahalli idaresine bir gerçek kişi tarafından verilen hizmetler karşılığında, bu Devlet, alt bölüm veya idare tarafından veya bunlarca oluşturulan fonlardan ödenen emekli maaşları ve diğer benzeri ödemeler, yalnızca bu Devlette vergilendirilecektir.

b) Bununla birlikte, gerçek kişinin diğer Akit Devletin bir mukimi ve vatandaşı olması halinde, söz konusu emekli maaşları ve diğer benzeri ödemeler yalnızca bu diğer Devlette vergilendirilecektir.

3. Bir Akit Devlet, politik alt bölümü veya mahalli idaresi tarafından yürütülen ticari faaliyetlerle bağlantılı olarak verilen hizmetler karşılığında yapılan maaş, ücret ve diğer benzeri ödemeler ile emekli maaşlarına 15, 16, 17 ve 18 inci maddelerin hükümleri uygulanacaktır.

MADDE 20

ÖĞRETMENLER VE ÖĞRENCİLER

1. Bir Akit Devletin vatandaşı olan ve diğer Akit Devlette yalnızca öğrenim veya mesleki eğitim amacıyla bulunan bir öğrenci veya stajyere geçimini, öğrenimini veya mesleki eğitimini sağlayabilmesi için bu diğer Devletin dışındaki kaynaklardan yapılan ödemeler, bu diğer Devlette vergilendirilmeyecektir.

2. Benzer şekilde, bir Akit Devletin vatandaşı olan ve diğer Akit Devlette esas itibarıyla öğretim veya bilimsel araştırma yapmak amacıyla iki (2) yılı aşmayan bir süre veya süreler için bulunan bir öğretmen veya öğretim üyesinin söz konusu öğretim veya araştırmaya ilişkin kişisel hizmetleri karşılığında diğer Devletin dışındaki kaynaklardan elde ettiği gelirler, bu diğer Devlette vergiden istisna edilecektir.

MADDE 21

DİĞER GELİRLER

Bir Akit Devlet mukiminin, bu Anlaşmanın daha önceki maddelerinde ele alınmayan ve diğer Akit Devlette doğan gelir unsurları, bu diğer Devlette vergilendirilebilir.

MADDE 22

ÇİFTE VERGİLENDİRMENİN ÖNLENMESİ

1. Meksika, buradaki genel prensibi değiştirmeksizin, zaman zaman değiştirilebilen Meksika kanunları hükümleri uyarınca ve bu kanunlardaki sınırlamalar saklı kalmak üzere, kendi mukimlerinin ödeyeceği Meksika vergisinden, aşağıdaki vergilerin mahsubuna müsaade edecektir:

a) Türkiye'de doğan gelir üzerinden ödenen Türk vergisinin, Meksika'da bu gelir üzerinden ödenecek vergiyi aşmayan tutarı; ve

b) Bir şirketin, Türkiye mukimi bir şirketin sermayesinin en az yüzde 10'una sahip olması ve bu şirketten temettü geliri elde etmesi halinde, içinden temettünün ödendiği kazanç üzerinden temettü dağıtan şirket tarafından ödenen Türk vergisi.

2. Türkiye dışındaki bir ülkede ödenen verginin Türk vergisinden mahsubunu düzenleyen Türk mevzuatı hükümleri saklı kalmak üzere, (bu hükümler, buradaki genel prensipleri değiştirmeksizin zaman zaman tadil edilebilir) bir Türkiye mukiminin Meksika'daki kaynaklardan elde ettiği gelir (kazançlar ve vergiye tabi gelirler dahil) üzerinden Meksika mevzuatı gereğince ve bu Anlaşmaya uygun olarak ödenen Meksika vergisinin, söz konusu gelir üzerinden alınacak Türk vergisinden mahsubuna müsaade edilecektir. Bununla beraber bu mahsup, söz konusu gelire atfedilebilen, mahsuptan önce hesaplanan Türk vergisi miktarını aşmayacaktır.

3. Anlaşmanın herhangi bir hükmü uyarınca, bir Akit Devlet mukimi tarafından elde edilen gelir bu Devlette vergiden istisna edilirse, bu Devlet, bu mukimin geriye kalan geliri üzerinden alınacak vergi miktarını hesaplarken, istisna edilmiş olan geliri de dikkate alabilir.

MADDE 23
AYRIM YAPILMAMASI

1. Bir Akit Devletin vatandaşları, diğer Akit Devlette, bu diğer Devletin vatandaşlarının aynı koşullarda, özellikle mukimlik yönünden, karşı karşıya kaldıkları veya kalabilecekleri vergilemeden ve buna bağlı mükellefiyetlerden değişik veya daha ağır bir vergilemeye ve buna bağlı mükellefiyetlere tabi tutulmayacaklardır. Bu hüküm,1 inci madde hükümlerine bakılmaksızın, Akit Devletlerin birinin veya her ikisinin mukimi olmayan kişilere de uygulanacaktır.

2. 10 uncu maddenin 4 üncü fıkrası hükümleri saklı kalmak üzere, bir Akit Devlet teşebbüsünün diğer Akit Devlette sahip olduğu bir iş yeri, diğer Devlette, bu diğer Devletin aynı faaliyetleri yürüten teşebbüslerine göre daha az lehe bir vergileme ile karşı karşıya kalmayacaktır.

3. 9 uncu maddenin 1 inci fıkrası, 11 inci maddenin 7 nci fıkrası veya 12 nci maddenin 6 ncı fıkrası hükümlerinin uygulanacağı durumlar hariç olmak üzere, bir Akit Devlet teşebbüsünün diğer Akit Devletin bir mukimine ödediği faiz, gayrimaddi hak bedeli ve diğer ödemeler, söz konusu teşebbüsün vergilendirilebilir kazancının belirlenmesi amacıyla, bu ödemeler ilk bahsedilen Devletin bir mukimine yapılmış gibi, aynı koşullarda indirilebilecektir.

4. Bir Akit Devletin, diğer Akit Devletin bir veya bir kaç mukimi tarafından, doğrudan veya dolaylı olarak, kısmen veya tamamen sermayesine sahip olunan veya kontrol edilen teşebbüsleri, ilk bahsedilen Devlette, bu Devletin diğer benzeri teşebbüslerinin tabi oldukları veya olabilecekleri vergilemeden ve buna bağlı mükellefiyetlerden değişik veya daha ağır vergilemeye ya da buna bağlı mükellefiyetlere tabi tutulmayacaklardır.

5. Bu hükümler, bir Akit Devletin kendi mukimlerine şahsi veya ailevi durumları dolayısıyla uyguladığı şahsi indirimleri, vergi ve matrah indirimlerini diğer Akit Devletin mukimlerine de uygulamak zorunda olduğu yönünde anlaşılmayacaktır.

6. Bu maddenin hükümleri, 2 nci maddenin hükümlerine bakılmaksızın, her tür ve tanımdaki vergilere uygulanacaktır.

MADDE 24

KARŞILIKLI ANLAŞMA USULÜ

1. Bir kişi, Akit Devletlerden birinin veya her ikisinin işlemlerinin kendisi için bu Anlaşma hükümlerine uygun düşmeyen bir vergileme yarattığı veya yaratacağı kanaatine vardığında, bu Devletlerin iç mevzuatlarında öngörülen müracaat usulleriyle bağlı kalmaksızın, durumu mukimi olduğu Akit Devletin yetkili makamına veya durumu 23 üncü maddenin 1 inci fıkrasına uygun düşerse, vatandaşı olduğu Akit Devletin yetkili makamına arz edebilir. Söz konusu müracaat, Anlaşma hükümlerine aykırı düşen bir vergilemeyle sonuçlanan eylemin ilk bildiriminden itibaren üç (3) yıl içerisinde yapılmalıdır.

2. Söz konusu yetkili makam, itirazı haklı bulur ve kendisi tatminkâr bir çözüme ulaşamaz ise, Anlaşmaya ters düşen vergilemeyi önlemek amacıyla, diğer Akit Devletin yetkili makamıyla karşılıklı anlaşma yoluyla sorunu çözmeye gayret sarf edecektir.

3. Akit Devletlerin yetkili makamları, Anlaşmanın yorumundan veya uygulanmasından kaynaklanan her türlü güçlüğü veya tereddüdü karşılıklı anlaşma yoluyla çözmek için gayret göstereceklerdir. Yetkili makamlar aynı zamanda, Anlaşmada ele alınmayan durumlardan kaynaklanan çifte vergilendirmenin ortadan kaldırılması için de birbirlerine danışabilirler.

4. Akit Devletlerin yetkili makamları, bundan önceki fıkralarda belirtilen hususlarda anlaşmaya varabilmek için birbirleriyle doğrudan haberleşebilirler.

MADDE 25

BİLGİ DEĞİŞİMİ

1. Akit Devletlerin yetkili makamları, bu Anlaşma hükümlerinin uygulanmasıyla ilgili bilgileri veya Anlaşma ile uyumsuzluk göstermediği sürece Akit Devletler, politik alt bölümleri veya mahalli idareleri adına alınan her tür ve tanımdaki vergilerle ilgili iç mevzuat hükümlerinin idaresi veya uygulanması ile ilgili olduğu öngörülen bilgileri değişime tabi tutacaklardır. Bilgi değişimi 1 inci ve 2 nci maddelerle sınırlı değildir.

2. Bir Akit Devlet tarafından 1 inci fıkra kapsamında alınan her türlü bilgi, o Devletin kendi iç mevzuatı çerçevesinde elde ettiği bilgiler gibi gizli tutulacak ve yalnızca 1 inci fıkrada bahsedilen vergilerin tahakkuk veya tahsilleri veya cebri icra ya da kovuşturmasıyla veya bu hususlardaki itirazlara bakmakla görevli kişi veya makamlara (adli makamlar ve idari kuruluşlar dahil) veya bunları denetlemekle görevli olan kişilere verilebilecektir. Bu kişi veya makamlar söz konusu bilgileri yalnızca bu amaçlar doğrultusunda kullanacaklardır. Bu kişi veya makamlar, söz konusu bilgileri mahkeme duruşmalarında veya adli kararlar alınırken açıklayabilirler.

3. 1 inci ve 2 nci fıkra hükümleri hiçbir surette bir Akit Devleti:

a) kendisinin veya diğer Akit Devletin mevzuatına ve idari uygulamalarına aykırı idari önlemler alma;

b) kendisinin veya diğer Akit Devletin mevzuatı veya normal idari işlemleri çerçevesinde elde edilemeyen bilgileri sunma;

c) herhangi bir ticari, sınai, mesleki sırrı veya ticari işlemi aleni hale getiren bilgileri veya aleniyeti kamu düzenine *(ordre public)* aykırı düşen bilgileri verme yükümlülüğü altına sokacak şekilde yorumlanamaz.

4. Bir Akit Devlet tarafından bu madde uyarınca bilgi talep edilmesi durumunda, diğer Akit Devlet, kendi vergi amaçları yönünden bu bilgilere ihtiyacı olmasa bile, talep edilen bilgiyi sağlamak için kendi bilgi toplama yöntemlerini kullanacaktır. Önceki cümlede yer alan yükümlülük, 3 üncü fıkradaki sınırlamalara tabi olmakla birlikte, bu sınırlamalar hiçbir surette bir Akit Devlete, sadece ulusal menfaati olmadığı gerekçesiyle bilgi sağlamayı reddetme hakkı verecek şekilde yorumlanmayacaktır.

5. 3 üncü fıkra hükümleri hiçbir surette bir Akit Devlete, bilginin bir banka, diğer finansal kurum, temsilci veya bir acente ya da yediemin gibi hareket eden bir kişide bulunması veya bir kişinin sermaye payları ile ilgili olması nedeniyle bu bilgiyi sağlamayı reddetme hakkı verecek şekilde yorumlanmayacaktır.

MADDE 26
VERGİLERİN TAHSİLATINDA YARDIMLAŞMA

1. Akit Devletler, alacaklarının tahsilatında birbirlerine yardım edeceklerdir. Bu yardım 1 inci ve 2 nci maddelerle sınırlı değildir. Akit Devletlerin yetkili makamları, bu maddenin uygulama biçimini karşılıklı anlaşma yoluyla belirleyebilirler.

2. Bu maddede kullanılan "alacak" terimi, bu Anlaşmaya veya Akit Devletlerin taraf olduğu diğer herhangi bir hukuki belgeye aykırı olmadığı sürece, Akit Devletler, politik alt bölümleri ya da mahalli idareleri adına alınan her tür ve tanımdaki vergiler dolayısıyla borçlanılan bir tutarı, bunun yanı sıra faiz, idari cezalar ve bu tutara ilişkin tahsilat veya koruma masraflarını ifade eder.

3. Bir Akit Devletin alacağının, bu Devletin mevzuatı uyarınca icra yoluyla istenebildiği ve borçlunun, o esnada bu Devletin mevzuatı uyarınca alacağın tahsilatını engelleyemediği durumda, söz konusu alacak, bu Devletin yetkili makamının talebi üzerine diğer Akit Devletin yetkili makamınca tahsil edilmek amacıyla kabul edilecektir. Bu alacak, bu diğer Devlet tarafından, kendi alacağıymış gibi, kendi vergilerinin icrası ve tahsilatına uyguladığı mevzuat hükümlerine göre tahsil edilecektir.

4. Bir Akit Devlet alacağının, bu Devletin kendi mevzuatı uyarınca tahsilatını sağlamak için koruma tedbirleri alabileceği bir alacak olması durumunda, söz konusu alacak, bu Devletin yetkili makamının talebi üzerine, koruma önlemleri almak amacıyla diğer Akit Devletin yetkili makamınca kabul edilecektir. Bu diğer Devlet, bu tür tedbirlerin uygulandığı sırada, alacağın ilk bahsedilen Devlette icra yoluyla alınamayacağı veya borçlunun tahsilatı önleme hakkının bulunduğu durumlarda bile, kendi mevzuatı hükümleri uyarınca, bu alacak kendi alacağıymış gibi koruma tedbirleri alacaktır.

5. 3 üncü ve 4 üncü fıkra hükümlerine bakılmaksızın, 3 üncü veya 4 üncü fıkranın amaçları yönünden bir Akit Devlet tarafından kabul edilen bir alacak, bu Devlette zaman aşımına tabi olmayacak veya niteliği gereği, bu Devletin mevzuatı uyarınca bir alacağa tanınan herhangi bir öncelik, bu alacağa tanınmayacaktır. Bunun yanı sıra, 3 üncü veya 4 üncü fıkranın amaçları bakımından, bir Akit Devlet tarafından kabul edilen bir alacak, bu Devlette, diğer Akit Devletin mevzuatı uyarınca bu alacağa tanınan herhangi bir önceliğe sahip olmayacaktır.

6. Bir Akit Devlet alacağının varlığı, geçerliliği veya tutarıyla ilgili davalar, diğer Akit Devletin mahkemeleri veya idari kuruluşlarına getirilemez.

7. Bir Akit Devletin, 3 üncü veya 4 üncü fıkra uyarınca bir talepte bulunmasından sonra ve diğer Akit Devletin alacağı tahsil ederek ilk bahsedilen Devlete göndermesinden önceki herhangi bir zamanda, ilgili alacağın,

a) 3 üncü fıkraya göre talepte bulunulması durumunda, ilk bahsedilen Devletin alacağının, bu Devletin mevzuatı uyarınca icra yoluyla istenebilen ve borçlusunun o esnada bu Devletin mevzuatı uyarınca tahsilatını engelleyemediği, veya

b) 4 üncü fıkraya göre talepte bulunulması durumunda, ilk bahsedilen Devletin alacağının, alacağın tahsilatını sağlamak amacıyla kendi mevzuatı uyarınca koruma tedbirleri alabileceği bir alacak olmaktan çıkması durumunda, ilk bahsedilen Devletin yetkili makamı, diğer Devletin yetkili makamını derhal durumdan haberdar edecek ve ilk bahsedilen Devlet, diğer Devletin tercihi doğrultusunda talebini ya askıya alacak ya da geri çekecektir.

8. Bu madde hükümleri hiçbir şekilde bir Akit Devleti:

a) kendisinin veya diğer Akit Devletin mevzuatına ve idari uygulamalarına aykırı idari önlemler alma;

b) kamu düzenine *(ordre public)* aykırı önlemler alma;

c) diğer Akit Devletin, olayına göre, kendi mevzuatı ve idari uygulamaları gereğince tahsilat ve korumaya ilişkin gerekli önlemlerin tümünü almaması durumunda, yardım sağlama;

d) bu Devletin idari külfetinin, diğer Akit Devletin elde edeceği faydadan açık bir şekilde fazla olduğu durumlarda, yardım sağlama yükümlülüğü altına sokacak şekilde yorumlanamaz.

MADDE 27

DİPLOMATİK TEMSİLCİLER VE KONSOLOSLUK MEMURLARI

Bu Anlaşma hükümleri, diplomatik temsilciler veya konsolosluk memurlarının uluslararası hukukun genel kuralları veya özel anlaşma hükümleri uyarınca yararlandıkları mali ayrıcalıkları etkilemeyecektir.

MADDE 28

YÜRÜRLÜĞE GİRME

Her bir Akit Devlet, bu Anlaşmanın yürürlüğe girmesi için kendi iç mevzuatında öngörülen işlemlerin tamamlandığını diplomatik yollardan birbirine bildirecektir. Bu Anlaşma, bu bildirimlerden sonuncusunun yapıldığı tarihten otuz (30) gün sonra yürürlüğe girecek ve hükümleri Anlaşmanın yürürlüğe girmesini izleyen yılın Ocak ayının birinci günü veya daha sonra başlayan her vergilendirme dönemine ilişkin vergiler için hüküm ifade edecektir.

MADDE 29

YÜRÜRLÜKTEN KALKMA

Bu Anlaşma, bir Akit Devlet tarafından feshedilinceye kadar yürürlükte kalacaktır. Her bir Akit Devlet, Anlaşmanın yürürlüğe girdiği tarihten itibaren beş (5) yıllık sürenin bitimini izleyen herhangi bir takvim yılının bitiminden en az altı (6) ay önce, diplomatik yollardan fesih ihbarnamesi vermek suretiyle Anlaşmayı feshedebilir. Bu durumda Anlaşma, fesih ihbarnamesinin verilmesini izleyen yılın Ocak ayının birinci günü veya daha sonra başlayan her vergilendirme dönemine ilişkin vergiler için hüküm ifade etmeyecektir.

BU HUSUSLARI TEYİDEN, aşağıda imzaları bulunan tam yetkili temsilciler, bu Anlaşmayı imzaladılar.

İspanyolca, Türkçe ve İngilizce dillerinde, ikişer nüsha halinde, her üç metin de aynı derecede geçerli olmak üzere, 17 Aralık 2013 tarihinde, Ankara'da düzenlenmiştir. Metinler arasında farklılık olması halinde, İngilizce metin geçerli olacaktır.

BİRLEŞİK MEKSİKA DEVLETLERİ HÜKÜMETİ ADINA	**TÜRKİYE CUMHURİYETİ HÜKÜMETİ ADINA**
José Antonio Meade KURIBREÑA **Dışişleri Bakanı**	**Mehmet ŞİMŞEK** **Maliye Bakanı**

PROTOKOL

Birleşik Meksika Devletleri Hükümeti ve Türkiye Cumhuriyeti Hükümeti Arasında Gelir Üzerinden Alınan Vergilerde Çifte Vergilendirmeyi Önleme ve Vergi Kaçakçılığına Engel Olma Anlaşmasının imzalanması sırasında, imzalayan taraflar, aşağıdaki hükümlerin Anlaşmanın ayrılmaz bir parçasını oluşturduğu hususunda anlaşmaya varmışlardır.

1. 5 inci madde ile ilgili olarak:

7 nci fıkranın amaçları bakımından bir teşebbüsün, bir Akit Devlette, işlerini yalnızca bir simsar, genel komisyon acentesi veya bağımsız statüde diğer herhangi bir acente vasıtasıyla yürüttüğü için, bu kişilerin teşebbüsle olan ticari veya mali ilişkilerinde oluşan veya oluşturulan koşulların, genel olarak bağımsız acenteler tarafından kararlaştırılan koşullardan farklı olmaması şartıyla, bu Devlette bir iş yerine sahip kabul edilmeyeceği anlaşılmaktadır.

2. 6 ncı madde ile ilgili olarak:

"Gayrimenkul varlık" teriminin balık üretimi ve yetiştiriciliğinde kullanılan teçhizatı da kapsadığı anlaşılmaktadır.

3. 7 nci maddenin 1 inci fıkrası ile ilgili olarak:

Bir Akit Devlet teşebbüsünün diğer Akit Devlette yer alan bir iş yeri vasıtasıyla ticari faaliyette bulunması halinde, söz konusu teşebbüse ait kazançların yalnızca diğer Akit Devlette, bu işyeri vasıtasıyla satılan mal veya emtia ile aynı veya benzer nitelikteki mal veya emtia satışlarına atfedilebilen miktarla sınırlı olmak üzere, bu diğer Akit Devlette vergilendirilebileceği anlaşılmaktadır.

Bununla birlikte, teşebbüs, bu satışların bu Anlaşma uyarınca bir fayda sağlamak dışında nedenlerle yapıldığını ispatlarsa yukarıda bahsedilen türde satışlardan elde edilen kazançlar, bu diğer Akit Devlette vergilendirilmeyecektir.

4. 7 nci maddenin 3 üncü fıkrası ile ilgili olarak

İş yeri tarafından teşebbüsün ana merkezine ya da diğer herhangi bir bürosuna, patent veya diğer hakların kullanılması karşılığında, gayrimaddi hak bedeli, ücret veya diğer benzeri ödemelerin yapılması veya verilen özel hizmetler veya yönetim karşılığında komisyon ödenmesi veya bankacılık teşebbüsleri hariç olmak üzere, iş yerine borç olarak verilen paralar karşılığında faiz ödenmesi halinde, söz konusu ödemelerin gider olarak indirilmesine (gerçekten yapılan giderlerin geri ödenmesi hariç) müsaade edilmeyeceği anlaşılmaktadır. Aynı şekilde, iş yeri tarafından, teşebbüsün ana merkezine ya da diğer herhangi bir bürosuna yüklenen patent veya diğer hakların kullanılması karşılığındaki gayrimaddi hak bedeli, ücret veya diğer benzeri ödemeler veya verilen özel hizmetler veya yönetim karşılığındaki komisyonlar veya bankacılık teşebbüsleri hariç olmak üzere, teşebbüsün ana merkezine ya da diğer herhangi bir bürosuna borç olarak verilen paralar karşılığındaki faizler, iş yerinin kazancının tespitinde (gerçekten yapılan giderlerin geri ödenmesi hariç) dikkate alınmayacaktır.

5. 8 inci madde ile ilgili olarak

8 inci maddenin 1 inci fıkrasında belirtilen kazançların iç kara taşımacılığının kullanılmasından elde edilen kazançları kapsamadığı anlaşılmaktadır.

6. 11 inci madde ile ilgili olarak

"Faiz" teriminin, 10 uncu maddenin 3 üncü fıkrasının hükümleri uyarınca temettü olarak değerlendirilen herhangi bir gelir unsurunu kapsamadığı anlaşılmaktadır.

c) ve d) bentlerinde bahsedilen kurumların, yeni bir kurum oluşturmak amacı ile birleşme, devir veya benzeri herhangi bir işlemle değişime uğramaları durumunda, bu kurumlar tamamen Devlete ait olarak kaldıkları sürece, Anlaşmanın söz konusu kurumlar bakımından uygulama şeklini belirlemek için yetkili makamların birbirlerine danışacakları anlaşılmaktadır.

7. **10, 11, 12 ve 13 üncü maddelerle ilgili olarak**

Anlaşmanın 10, 11, 12 ve 13 üncü maddelerinin amaçları bakımından, Akit Devletlerden her birinin, gelirin farklı sınıflandırılmasından kaynaklanan çifte istisna durumunda, söz konusu geliri kendi iç mevzuatları gereğince vergileme hakkını elinde tutacağı anlaşılmaktadır.

8. **12 nci madde ile ilgili olarak**

13 üncü madde hükümleriyle bağlı kalınmaksızın, "gayrimaddi hak bedelleri" teriminin aynı zamanda, verimliliğe, kullanıma veya tasarrufa bağlı herhangi bir hak veya varlığın elden çıkarılmasından elde edilen bedelleri de kapsadığı anlaşılmaktadır.

9. **14 üncü madde ile ilgili olarak**

Bir Akit Devlet gerçek kişisi ya da teşebbüsü 14 üncü maddenin 1 inci veya 2 nci fıkraları uyarınca diğer Akit Devlette vergilendirilebildiğinde, bu gerçek kişi ya da teşebbüsün söz konusu gelirinin, teşebbüsün bu diğer Devlette bulunan iş yerine atfedilebilen bir gelirmiş gibi, Anlaşmanın 7 nci maddesi hükümlerine göre bu diğer Devlette, vergilendirilmeyi tercih edebileceği anlaşılmaktadır. Bu tercih, bu diğer Devletin, söz konusu gelir üzerinden tevkifat suretiyle vergi alma hakkını etkilemeyecektir.

10. **24 üncü madde ile ilgili olarak**

Akit Devletlerin taraf oldukları ya da olabilecekleri diğer Anlaşmalarla bağlı kalınmaksızın, bu Anlaşmanın uygulanıp uygulanmamasına ilişkin ihtilaf da dahil olmak üzere, bir Akit Devlet tarafından 2 nci maddede kavranan bir vergiye ilişkin olarak alınan bir önlem hakkındaki her türlü ihtilafın veya ayrım yapılmaması söz konusu olduğunda bir Akit Devlet tarafından alınan herhangi bir vergileme önlemi hakkındaki her türlü ihtilafın, Akit Devletlerin yetkili makamları aksini kararlaştırmadıkça, yalnızca bu Anlaşma uyarınca çözümleneceği anlaşılmaktadır.

Türkiye yönünden, 2 nci fıkra ile ilgili olarak; mükellefin, karşılıklı anlaşmadan kaynaklanan iadeyi, vergi idaresinin karşılıklı anlaşma sonucunu kendisine tebliğ etmesinden sonraki bir (1) yıllık süre içerisinde talep etmek zorunda olduğu anlaşılmaktadır.

11. Genel olarak

Bu Anlaşma hükümlerinin, bir Akit Devleti, örtülü sermaye ve kontrol edilen yabancı kurumlara (Meksika yönünden tercihli vergi rejimlerini) ilişkin kendi iç mevzuat hükümlerini uygulamaktan alıkoymayacağı anlaşılmaktadır.

Meksika'nın vergi amaçları bakımından, sabit yerin, iş yerine uygulanan ilkelere göre ele alınacağı anlaşılmaktadır.

BU HUSUSLARI TEYİDEN, aşağıda imzaları bulunan tam yetkili temsilciler, bu Protokolü imzaladılar.

İspanyolca, Türkçe ve İngilizce dillerinde, ikişer nüsha halinde, tüm metinler aynı derecede geçerli olmak üzere, 17 Aralık 2013 tarihinde, Ankara'da düzenlenmiştir. Metinler arasında farklılık olması halinde, İngilizce metin geçerli olacaktır.

BİRLEŞİK MEKSİKA DEVLETLERİ HÜKÜMETİ ADINA	**TÜRKİYE CUMHURİYETİ HÜKÜMETİ ADINA**
José Antonio Meade KURIBREÑA **Dışişleri Bakanı**	**Mehmet ŞİMŞEK** **Maliye Bakanı**

[TRANSLATION – TRADUCTION]

ACCORD ENTRE LE GOUVERNEMENT DES ÉTATS-UNIS DU MEXIQUE ET LE GOUVERNEMENT DE LA RÉPUBLIQUE TURQUE TENDANT À ÉVITER LES DOUBLES IMPOSITIONS ET À PRÉVENIR L'ÉVASION FISCALE EN MATIÈRE D'IMPÔTS SUR LE REVENU

Le Gouvernement des États-Unis du Mexique et le Gouvernement de la République turque,

Désireux de conclure un Accord en vue d'éviter les doubles impositions et de prévenir l'évasion fiscale en matière d'impôts sur le revenu,

Sont convenus de ce qui suit :

Article premier. Personnes visées

Le présent Accord s'applique aux personnes qui sont des résidents d'un État contractant ou des deux États contractants.

Article 2. Impôts visés

1. Le présent Accord s'applique aux impôts sur le revenu prélevés pour le compte du Mexique et de la Turquie, quel que soit le système de perception.

2. Sont considérés comme des impôts sur le revenu tous les impôts prélevés sur le revenu total ou sur des éléments de revenu, y compris les impôts sur les gains provenant de l'aliénation de biens mobiliers ou immobiliers.

3. Les impôts actuels auxquels s'applique le présent Accord sont notamment :

a) Au Mexique :

i) L'impôt fédéral sur le revenu;

ii) L'impôt forfaitaire sur les sociétés;

(ci-après dénommés « impôt mexicain »);

b) En Turquie :

i) L'impôt sur le revenu (Gelir Vergisi);

ii) L'impôt sur les sociétés (Kurumlar Vergisi);

(ci-après dénommés « impôt turc »).

4. L'Accord s'applique également aux impôts de nature identique ou analogue qui seraient établis après la signature de l'Accord et qui s'ajouteraient aux impôts actuels ou qui les remplaceraient. Les autorités compétentes des États contractants se communiquent les modifications significatives apportées à leur législation fiscale.

Article 3. Définitions générales

1. Aux fins du présent Accord, à moins que le contexte n'exige une interprétation différente :

a) Les termes « Mexique » (États-Unis du Mexique) et « Turquie » désignent le territoire de l'un ou l'autre État contractant, y compris son territoire terrestre, ses eaux intérieures, sa mer territoriale et l'espace aérien surjacent, ainsi que toute zone maritime située au-delà de la mer territoriale où l'un ou l'autre État contractant exerce, conformément au droit international et à son droit interne, ses droits souverains ou sa compétence à l'égard des eaux, des fonds marins, des sous-sols et de leurs ressources naturelles;

b) Les expressions « un État contractant » et « l'autre État contractant » désignent, selon le contexte, le Mexique ou la Turquie;

c) Le terme « personne » comprend les personnes physiques, les sociétés et autres groupements de personnes;

d) Le terme « société » désigne toute personne morale ou toute entité qui est considérée comme une personne morale aux fins d'imposition;

e) L'expression « siège social » désigne le siège social enregistré conformément au Code du commerce turc;

f) Les expressions « entreprise d'un État contractant » et « entreprise de l'autre État contractant » désignent, respectivement, une entreprise exploitée par un résident d'un État contractant et une entreprise exploitée par un résident de l'autre État contractant;

g) L'expression « trafic international » désigne tout transport effectué par un navire ou un aéronef exploité par une entreprise d'un État contractant, sauf lorsque ce navire ou cet aéronef n'est exploité qu'entre des points situés dans l'autre État contractant;

h) L'expression « autorité compétente » désigne :

   i) Au Mexique, le Ministère des finances et du crédit public; et

   ii) En Turquie, le Ministre des finances ou son représentant autorisé;

i) Le terme « ressortissant » désigne, en ce qui concerne un État contractant :

   i) Toute personne physique qui possède la nationalité d'un État contractant;

   ii) Toute personne morale, société de personnes ou association constituée conformément à la législation en vigueur dans l'État contractant concerné.

2. Pour l'application du présent Accord à un moment donné par un État contractant, tout terme ou expression qui n'y est pas défini a, sauf si le contexte exige une interprétation différente, le sens que lui attribue le droit de cet État concernant les impôts auxquels le présent Accord s'applique, le sens attribué à ce terme ou à cette expression par le droit fiscal de cet État prévalant sur le sens que lui attribuent les autres branches du droit de cet État.

Article 4. Résidence

1. Au sens du présent Accord, l'expression « résident d'un État contractant » désigne toute personne qui, en vertu de la législation de cet État, est assujettie à l'impôt dans cet État en raison de son domicile, de sa résidence, de son siège social, de son siège de direction ou de tout autre

critère de nature semblable, et s'applique aussi à cet État ainsi qu'à toutes ses subdivisions politiques ou à ses collectivités locales. Toutefois, cette expression ne comprend pas les personnes qui ne sont assujetties à l'impôt dans cet État que pour les revenus de sources qui sont situées dans cet État.

2. Lorsque, selon les dispositions du paragraphe 1, une personne physique est un résident des deux États contractants, sa situation est réglée de la manière suivante :

a) Cette personne est considérée comme un résident seulement de l'État dans lequel elle dispose d'un foyer d'habitation permanent; si elle dispose d'un foyer d'habitation permanent dans les deux États, elle est considérée comme un résident de l'État avec lequel ses liens personnels et économiques sont les plus étroits (centre des intérêts vitaux);

b) Si l'État dans lequel elle a ses intérêts vitaux ne peut pas être déterminé ou si elle ne dispose d'un foyer d'habitation permanent dans aucun des États, elle est considérée comme un résident de l'État où elle séjourne de façon habituelle;

c) Si elle séjourne de façon habituelle dans les deux États ou si elle ne séjourne de façon habituelle dans aucun d'eux, elle est considérée comme un résident seulement de l'État dont elle possède la nationalité;

d) Si elle possède la nationalité des deux États ou si elle ne possède la nationalité d'aucun d'eux, les autorités compétentes des États contractants tranchent la question d'un commun accord.

3. Lorsque, selon les dispositions du paragraphe 1, une personne autre qu'une personne physique est un résident des deux États contractants et que cette personne a son siège de direction effective dans un État contractant et son siège social dans l'autre État contractant, les autorités compétentes des États contractants déterminent d'un commun accord de quel État la personne est considérée comme un résident aux fins du présent Accord. À défaut d'un tel accord, cette personne n'est considérée comme un résident d'aucun des États contractants pour bénéficier des avantages prévus au présent Accord.

Article 5. Établissement stable

1. Au sens du présent Accord, l'expression « établissement stable » désigne toute installation fixe d'affaires par l'intermédiaire de laquelle une entreprise exerce tout ou partie de son activité.

2. L'expression « établissement stable » désigne notamment :

a) Un siège de direction;

b) Une succursale;

c) Un bureau;

d) Une usine;

e) Un atelier; et

f) Une mine, un puits de pétrole ou de gaz, une carrière ou tout autre lieu d'extraction de ressources naturelles.

3. Un chantier de construction, un projet de montage ou d'installation ou des activités de supervision liées à ce projet peuvent constituer un établissement stable, mais uniquement si ce chantier, ce projet ou ces activités durent plus de six mois.

4. Nonobstant les dispositions précédentes du présent article, il est considéré que l'expression « établissement stable » ne comprend pas :

a) L'utilisation d'installations pour le stockage ou l'exposition de biens ou de marchandises appartenant à l'entreprise;

b) L'exploitation d'un stock de biens ou de marchandises appartenant à l'entreprise aux seules fins de stockage ou d'exposition;

c) L'exploitation d'un stock de biens ou de marchandises appartenant à l'entreprise aux seules fins de transformation par une autre entreprise;

d) L'exploitation d'une installation fixe d'affaires aux seules fins d'acheter des biens ou des marchandises ou de réunir des informations pour l'entreprise;

e) L'exploitation d'une installation fixe d'affaires aux seules fins d'exercer, pour l'entreprise, toute autre activité de caractère préparatoire ou auxiliaire;

f) L'exploitation d'une installation fixe d'affaires aux seules fins d'exercice cumulé d'activités visées aux alinéas a) à e), à condition que l'activité d'ensemble de l'installation fixe d'affaires résultant de ce cumul garde un caractère préparatoire ou auxiliaire.

5. Nonobstant les dispositions des paragraphes 1 et 2, lorsqu'une personne, autre qu'un agent jouissant d'un statut indépendant auquel s'applique le paragraphe 7, agit dans un État contractant pour le compte d'une entreprise et dispose de pouvoirs qu'elle y exerce habituellement lui permettant de conclure des contrats au nom de l'entreprise, cette entreprise est considérée comme ayant un établissement stable dans cet État pour toutes les activités que cette personne entreprend pour l'entreprise, à moins que les activités de cette personne ne soient limitées à celles qui sont mentionnées au paragraphe 4 et qui, si elles étaient exercées au moyen d'une installation fixe d'affaires, ne permettraient pas de considérer cette installation fixe d'affaires comme un établissement stable au sens de ce paragraphe.

6. Nonobstant les dispositions précédentes du présent article, une société d'assurances d'un État contractant est, sauf en matière de réassurance, considérée comme ayant un établissement stable dans l'autre État contractant si elle perçoit des primes sur le territoire de cet autre État ou si elle y assure contre des risques par l'intermédiaire d'une personne autre qu'un agent jouissant d'un statut indépendant auquel s'applique le paragraphe 7.

7. Une entreprise n'est pas considérée comme ayant un établissement stable dans un État contractant du seul fait qu'elle y exerce son activité par l'entremise d'un courtier, d'un

commissionnaire général ou de tout autre agent jouissant d'un statut indépendant, à condition que ces personnes agissent dans le cadre ordinaire de leurs activités.

8. Le fait qu'une société qui est un résident d'un État contractant contrôle ou est contrôlée par une société qui est un résident de l'autre État contractant ou qui y exerce son activité (que ce soit par l'intermédiaire d'un établissement stable ou non) ne suffit pas, en lui-même, à faire de l'une quelconque de ces sociétés un établissement stable de l'autre.

Article 6. Revenus immobiliers

1. Les revenus qu'un résident d'un État contractant tire de biens immobiliers (y compris les revenus des exploitations agricoles ou forestières) situés dans l'autre État contractant sont imposables dans cet autre État.

2. L'expression « biens immobiliers » a le sens que lui attribue le droit de l'État contractant où les biens considérés sont situés. Cette expression englobe dans tous les cas les accessoires, le cheptel et l'équipement utilisé dans les exploitations agricoles et forestières, les droits auxquels s'appliquent les dispositions du droit privé concernant la propriété foncière, l'usufruit des biens immobiliers et les droits à des paiements variables ou fixes pour l'exploitation ou la concession de l'exploitation de gisements minéraux, sources et autres ressources naturelles; les navires, bateaux et aéronefs ne sont pas considérés comme des biens immobiliers.

3. Les dispositions du paragraphe 1 s'appliquent aux revenus provenant de l'exploitation directe, de la location ainsi que de toute autre forme d'exploitation de biens immobiliers.

4. Les dispositions des paragraphes 1 et 3 s'appliquent également aux revenus provenant des biens immobiliers des entreprises ainsi qu'aux revenus des biens immobiliers servant à l'exercice d'une profession indépendante.

Article 7. Bénéfices des entreprises

1. Les bénéfices d'une entreprise d'un État contractant ne sont imposables que dans cet État, à moins qu'elle n'exerce son activité dans l'autre État contractant par l'intermédiaire d'un établissement stable qui y est situé. Si l'entreprise exerce son activité d'une telle façon, les bénéfices de l'entreprise sont imposables dans cet autre État, mais uniquement dans la mesure où ils sont imputables à cet établissement stable.

2. Sous réserve des dispositions du paragraphe 3, lorsqu'une entreprise d'un État contractant exerce son activité dans l'autre État contractant par l'intermédiaire d'un établissement stable qui y est situé, il est imputé à cet établissement stable, dans chaque État contractant, les bénéfices qu'il aurait pu réaliser s'il avait constitué une entreprise distincte exerçant des activités identiques ou analogues dans des conditions identiques ou analogues et traitant en toute indépendance avec l'entreprise dont il constitue un établissement stable.

3. Pour déterminer les bénéfices d'un établissement stable, sont admises en déduction les dépenses relatives aux fins poursuivies par cet établissement stable, y compris les dépenses de direction et les frais généraux d'administration ainsi exposés, soit dans l'État où est situé cet établissement stable, soit ailleurs.

4. Aucun bénéfice n'est attribué à un établissement stable du seul fait que celui-ci a acheté des biens ou marchandises pour l'entreprise.

5. Lorsque les bénéfices comprennent des éléments de revenu traités séparément dans d'autres articles du présent Accord, les dispositions de ces articles ne sont pas affectées par les dispositions du présent article.

Article 8. Transport maritime et aérien

1. Les bénéfices qu'une entreprise d'un État contractant tire de l'exploitation de navires ou d'aéronefs exploités en trafic international ne sont imposables que dans cet État.

2. Les dispositions du paragraphe 1 s'appliquent également aux bénéfices provenant de la participation à un consortium, à une coentreprise ou à un organisme international d'exploitation.

Article 9. Entreprises associées

1. Lorsque :

a) Une entreprise d'un État contractant participe directement ou indirectement à la direction, au contrôle ou au capital d'une entreprise de l'autre État contractant; ou que

b) Les mêmes personnes participent directement ou indirectement à la direction, au contrôle ou au capital d'une entreprise d'un État contractant et d'une entreprise de l'autre État contractant;

et que, dans l'un ou l'autre cas, les deux entreprises sont, dans leurs relations commerciales ou financières, liées par des conditions convenues ou imposées qui diffèrent de celles qui seraient convenues entre des entreprises indépendantes, les bénéfices qui, sans ces conditions, auraient été réalisés par l'une des entreprises, mais n'ont pu l'être en fait à cause de ces conditions, peuvent être inclus dans les bénéfices de cette entreprise et imposés en conséquence.

2. Lorsqu'un État contractant inclut dans les bénéfices d'une entreprise de cet État et impose en conséquence des bénéfices sur lesquels une entreprise de l'autre État contractant a été imposée dans cet autre État, et que les bénéfices ainsi inclus sont des bénéfices qui auraient été réalisés par l'entreprise du premier État si les conditions convenues entre les deux entreprises avaient été celles qui auraient été convenues entre des entreprises indépendantes, alors cet autre État procède à un ajustement approprié du montant de l'impôt qui y a été perçu sur ces bénéfices, lorsque cet autre État estime qu'un tel ajustement est justifié. Pour déterminer cet ajustement, il est tenu compte des autres dispositions du présent Accord et, si c'est nécessaire, les autorités compétentes des États contractants se consultent.

Article 10. Dividendes

1. Les dividendes payés par une société qui est un résident d'un État contractant à un résident de l'autre État contractant sont imposables dans cet autre État.

2. Toutefois, ces dividendes sont également imposables dans l'État contractant dont la société qui paie les dividendes est un résident et selon la législation de cet État, mais si le bénéficiaire effectif des dividendes est un résident de l'autre État contractant, l'impôt ainsi établi ne peut excéder :

a) 5 % du montant brut des dividendes si le bénéficiaire effectif est une société (autre qu'une société de personnes) qui détient directement au moins 25 % du capital de la société qui paie les dividendes;

b) 15 % du montant brut des dividendes dans tous les autres cas.

Le présent paragraphe n'affecte pas l'imposition de la société au titre des bénéfices qui servent au paiement des dividendes.

3. Le terme « dividendes » employé dans le présent article désigne les revenus d'actions, actions ou bons de jouissance, parts de mine, parts de fondateur ou autres parts bénéficiaires à l'exception des créances, ainsi que les revenus d'autres parts sociales et les autres revenus soumis au même régime fiscal que les revenus d'actions par la législation de l'État dont la société distributrice est un résident, ainsi que les revenus provenant de fonds d'investissement et de sociétés de placement.

4. Les bénéfices d'une société d'un État contractant qui exerce des activités dans l'autre État contractant par l'intermédiaire d'un établissement stable qui y est situé sont, après avoir été imposé en vertu de l'article 7, imposables sur le montant résiduel dans l'État contractant où l'établissement stable est situé et conformément à l'alinéa a) du paragraphe 2 du présent article.

5. Les dispositions des paragraphes 1 et 2 ne s'appliquent pas lorsque le bénéficiaire effectif des dividendes, résident d'un État contractant, exerce, dans l'autre État contractant dont la société qui paie les dividendes est un résident, soit une activité par l'intermédiaire d'un établissement stable qui y est situé, soit une profession indépendante au moyen d'une base fixe qui y est située et que la participation génératrice des dividendes s'y rattache effectivement. Dans ce cas, les dispositions de l'article 7 ou de l'article 14, selon le cas, s'appliquent.

6. Sous réserve des dispositions du paragraphe 4, lorsqu'une société qui est un résident d'un État contractant tire des bénéfices ou des revenus de l'autre État contractant, cet autre État ne peut percevoir aucun impôt sur les dividendes payés par la société, sauf dans la mesure où ces dividendes sont payés à un résident de cet autre État ou dans la mesure où la participation génératrice des dividendes se rattache effectivement à un établissement stable ou à une base fixe qui y est située, ni prélever aucun impôt au titre de l'imposition des bénéfices non distribués, sur les bénéfices non distribués de la société, même si les dividendes payés ou les bénéfices non distribués consistent, en tout ou en partie, en bénéfices ou revenus provenant de cet autre État.

Article 11. Intérêts

1. Les intérêts provenant d'un État contractant et payés à un résident de l'autre État contractant sont imposables dans cet autre État.

2. Toutefois, ces intérêts sont également imposables dans l'État contractant d'où ils proviennent et selon la législation de cet État, mais si le bénéficiaire effectif des intérêts est un résident de l'autre État contractant, l'impôt ainsi établi ne peut excéder :

a) 10 % du montant brut des intérêts s'ils sont payés à une banque;

b) 15 % du montant brut des intérêts dans tous les autres cas.

3. Nonobstant les dispositions du paragraphe 2, les intérêts visés au paragraphe 1 ne sont imposables que dans l'État contractant dont le bénéficiaire effectif est un résident si :

a) Le bénéficiaire effectif est un État contractant ou une de ses subdivisions politiques ou collectivités locales, ou la Banque centrale du Mexique (Banco de México) ou la Banque centrale de la Turquie (Türkiye Cumhuriyet Merkez Bankası);

b) Les intérêts sont payés par l'une des entités mentionnées à l'alinéa a);

c) Les intérêts proviennent de Turquie et sont payés à l'égard d'un prêt d'une durée d'au moins trois ans accordé par la Banco Nacional de Comercio Exterior, S.N.C., la Nacional Financiera, S.N.C. ou la Banco Nacional de Obras y Servicios Públicos, S.N.C.; ou

d) Les intérêts proviennent du Mexique et sont payés à l'égard d'un prêt d'une durée d'au moins trois ans accordé par la Eximbank de Turquie (Türkiye İhracat Kredi Bankası A.Ş.).

4. Le terme « intérêts » employé dans le présent article désigne les revenus des créances de toute nature, assorties ou non de garanties hypothécaires ou d'une clause de participation aux bénéfices du débiteur, et notamment les revenus des fonds publics et des obligations d'emprunts, y compris les primes et lots attachés à ces titres, ainsi que tous autres revenus considérés comme des revenus de sommes prêtées par la législation de l'État contractant d'où les revenus proviennent.

5. Les dispositions des paragraphes 1 et 2 ne s'appliquent pas lorsque le bénéficiaire effectif des intérêts, résident d'un État contractant, exerce, dans l'autre État contractant d'où proviennent les intérêts, soit une activité industrielle ou commerciale par l'intermédiaire d'un établissement stable qui y est situé, soit une profession indépendante au moyen d'une base fixe qui y est située, et que la créance génératrice des intérêts se rattache effectivement à cet établissement stable ou à cette base fixe. Dans ce cas, les dispositions de l'article 7 ou de l'article 14, selon le cas, s'appliquent.

6. Les intérêts sont considérés comme provenant d'un État contractant lorsque le débiteur est cet État lui-même ou une de ses subdivisions politiques ou collectivités locales ou un résident de cet État. Toutefois, lorsque le débiteur des intérêts, qu'il soit ou non un résident d'un État contractant, a dans un État contractant un établissement stable ou une base fixe qui supportent la charge de ces intérêts, ceux-ci sont considérés comme provenant de l'État où l'établissement stable, ou la base fixe, est situé.

7. Lorsque, en raison de relations spéciales entre le débiteur et le bénéficiaire effectif ou entre l'un et l'autre et quelque autre personne, le montant des intérêts excède, pour quelque raison que ce soit, celui dont seraient convenus le débiteur et le bénéficiaire effectif en l'absence de pareilles relations, les dispositions du présent article ne s'appliquent qu'à ce dernier montant. Dans ce cas, la partie excédentaire reste imposable selon la législation de chaque État contractant et compte tenu des autres dispositions du présent Accord.

Article 12. Redevances

1. Les redevances générées dans un État contractant et payées à un résident de l'autre État contractant sont imposables dans cet autre État.

2. Toutefois, ces redevances sont également imposables dans l'État contractant de la source et selon la législation de cet État, mais si le bénéficiaire effectif de ces redevances est un résident de l'autre État contractant, l'impôt ainsi établi ne peut excéder 10 % du montant brut des redevances.

3. Le terme « redevances » employé dans le présent article désigne les rémunérations de toute nature payées pour :

a) L'usage ou la concession de l'usage d'un brevet, d'une marque de commerce, d'un dessin ou modèle, d'un plan, d'une formule ou d'un procédé secrets;

b) L'usage ou la concession de l'usage d'un équipement industriel, commercial ou scientifique;

c) La fourniture d'informations ayant trait à une expérience acquise dans le domaine industriel, commercial ou scientifique;

d) L'usage ou la concession de l'usage d'un droit d'auteur sur une œuvre littéraire, artistique ou scientifique, y compris les films cinématographiques, et les enregistrements ou bandes utilisés pour les émissions radiophoniques ou télévisées.

4. Les dispositions des paragraphes 1 et 2 ne s'appliquent pas lorsque le bénéficiaire effectif des redevances, résident d'un État contractant, exerce, dans l'autre État contractant source des redevances, soit une activité industrielle ou commerciale par l'intermédiaire d'un établissement stable qui y est situé, soit une profession indépendante au moyen d'une base fixe qui y est située, et que le droit ou le bien générateur des redevances se rattache effectivement à cet établissement stable ou à cette base fixe. Dans ce cas, les dispositions de l'article 7 ou de l'article 14, selon le cas, s'appliquent.

5. Les redevances sont considérées comme provenant d'un État contractant lorsque le débiteur est cet État lui-même, une de ses subdivisions politiques ou de ses collectivités locales ou un résident de cet État. Toutefois, lorsque le débiteur des redevances, qu'il soit ou non un résident d'un État contractant, a dans un État contractant un établissement stable ou une base fixe qui supportent la charge de ces redevances, celles-ci sont considérées comme provenant de l'État où l'établissement stable, ou la base fixe, est situé.

6. Lorsque, en raison de relations spéciales qui existent entre le débiteur et le bénéficiaire effectif ou que l'un et l'autre entretiennent avec des tierces personnes, le montant des redevances excède, pour quelque raison que ce soit, celui dont seraient convenus le débiteur et le bénéficiaire effectif en l'absence de pareilles relations, les dispositions du présent article ne s'appliquent qu'à ce dernier montant. Dans ce cas, la partie excédentaire reste imposable selon la législation de chaque État contractant et compte tenu des autres dispositions du présent Accord.

Article 13. Gain en capital

1. Les gains qu'un résident d'un État contractant tire de l'aliénation de biens immobiliers visés à l'article 6 et situés dans l'autre État contractant sont imposable dans cet autre État.

2. Les gains issus de l'aliénation d'actions ou autres titres similaires dans une société dont les biens consistent à titre principal, directement ou indirectement, en des biens immobiliers situés dans un État contractant sont imposables dans cet État.

3. Les gains qu'un résident d'un État contractant tire de l'aliénation d'actions, de parts ou d'autres participations au capital d'une société ou autre personne morale qui est un résident de l'autre État contractant sont imposables dans cet autre État.

4. Les gains provenant de l'aliénation de biens meubles qui font partie de l'actif d'un établissement stable qu'une entreprise d'un État contractant a dans l'autre État contractant ou de biens meubles qui appartiennent à une base fixe dont un résident d'un État contractant dispose dans l'autre État contractant pour l'exercice d'une profession indépendante, y compris l'aliénation de cet établissement stable (seul ou avec l'ensemble de l'entreprise) ou de cette base fixe, sont imposables dans cet autre État.

5. Les gains qu'un résident d'un État contractant tire de l'aliénation de navires ou d'aéronefs exploités en trafic international, ou de biens meubles affectés à l'exploitation de ces navires ou aéronefs, ne sont imposables que dans cet État.

6. Les gains provenant de l'aliénation de tous biens autres que ceux visés aux paragraphes précédents du présent article ne sont imposables que dans l'État contractant dont le cédant est un résident. Toutefois, lorsque les gains visés à la phrase précédente proviennent de l'autre État contractant, ils sont imposables dans cet autre État contractant si le temps écoulé entre la date d'acquisition et la date d'aliénation des biens ne dépasse pas un an.

Article 14. Professions indépendantes

1. Les revenus qu'une personne physique qui est un résident d'un État contractant tire d'une profession libérale ou d'autres activités de caractère indépendant ne sont imposables que dans cet État. Toutefois, ces revenus sont également imposables dans l'autre État contractant si cette profession ou ces activités sont exercées dans cet autre État et si :

a) Cette personne physique dispose de façon habituelle, dans l'autre État contractant, d'une base fixe pour l'exercice de cette profession ou de ces activités; ou

b) Cette personne physique séjourne dans cet autre État pour l'exercice de cette profession ou de ces activités pendant une période ou des périodes d'une durée totale égale ou supérieure à 183 jours au cours de toute période ininterrompue de 12 mois.

Dans ces cas, seule la fraction des revenus imputable à ladite base fixe ou tirée de cette profession ou de ces activités lorsque la personne physique séjourne dans cet autre État, selon le cas, est imposable dans cet autre État.

2. Les revenus qu'une entreprise d'un État contractant tire d'une profession libérale ou d'autres activités de caractère indépendant ne sont imposables que dans cet État. Toutefois, ces revenus sont également imposables dans l'autre État contractant si cette profession ou ces activités sont exercées dans cet autre État et si :

a) L'entreprise dispose d'un établissement stable dans cet autre État par l'intermédiaire duquel elle exerce cette profession ou ces activités; ou

b) Cette profession ou ces activités sont exercées pendant une période ou des périodes qui s'étendent sur une durée totale supérieure à 183 jours au cours de toute période ininterrompue de 12 mois.

Dans ces cas, seule la fraction des revenus imputable à cet établissement stable ou tirée de l'exercice de ladite profession ou desdites activités dans l'autre État, selon le cas, est imposable dans cet autre État.

3. L'expression « profession indépendante » se rapporte notamment aux activités indépendantes d'ordre scientifique, littéraire, artistique, éducatif ou pédagogique, ainsi qu'aux activités indépendantes des médecins, avocats, ingénieurs, architectes, dentistes et comptables.

Article 15. Professions dépendantes

1. Sous réserve des dispositions des articles 16, 18, 19 et 20, les salaires, traitements ou autres rémunérations similaires qu'un résident d'un État contractant reçoit au titre d'un emploi salarié ne sont imposables que dans cet État, à moins que l'emploi ne soit exercé dans l'autre État contractant. Si l'emploi y est exercé, les rémunérations reçues à ce titre sont imposables dans cet autre État.

2. Nonobstant les dispositions du paragraphe 1, les rémunérations qu'un résident d'un État contractant reçoit au titre d'un emploi salarié exercé dans l'autre État contractant ne sont imposables que dans le premier État contractant si :

a) Le bénéficiaire séjourne dans l'autre État pendant une période ou des périodes n'excédant pas au total 183 jours au cours de toute période de 12 mois; et

b) Les rémunérations sont payées par un employeur ou pour le compte d'un employeur qui n'est pas un résident de l'autre État; et

c) La charge des rémunérations n'est pas supportée par un établissement stable ou une base fixe que l'employeur a dans l'autre État.

3. Nonobstant les dispositions précédentes du présent article, les rémunérations reçues au titre d'un emploi salarié exercé à bord d'un navire ou aéronef exploité par une entreprise d'un État contractant en trafic international sont imposables dans cet État contractant.

Article 16. Tantièmes

Les tantièmes, jetons de présence et autres rémunérations similaires qu'un résident d'un État contractant reçoit en sa qualité de membre du conseil d'administration d'une société qui est un résident de l'autre État contractant sont imposables dans cet autre État.

Article 17. Artistes du spectacle et sportifs

1. Nonobstant les dispositions des articles 14 et 15, les revenus qu'un résident d'un État contractant tire de ses activités personnelles exercées dans l'autre État contractant en tant qu'artiste du spectacle - artiste de théâtre, de cinéma, de radio ou de télévision ou musicien - ou en tant que sportif, sont imposables dans cet autre État.

2. Lorsque les revenus d'activités qu'un artiste du spectacle ou un sportif exerce personnellement et en cette qualité sont attribués non pas à l'artiste du spectacle ou au sportif lui-même, mais à une tierce personne, ces revenus sont, nonobstant les dispositions des articles 7, 14 et 15, imposables dans l'État contractant où les activités de l'artiste du spectacle ou du sportif sont exercées.

3. Les revenus qu'un artiste du spectacle ou un sportif tire d'activités exercées dans un État contractant sont exonérés d'impôt dans cet État si son séjour est entièrement ou principalement financé par des fonds publics de l'autre État contractant ou de l'une de ses subdivisions politiques ou collectivités locales.

Article 18. Pensions

1. Sous réserve des dispositions du paragraphe 2 de l'article 19, les pensions et autres émoluments similaires versés à un résident d'un État contractant au titre d'un emploi antérieur ne sont imposables que dans cet État. La présente disposition s'applique également aux rentes viagères versées à un résident d'un État contractant.

2. L'expression « rente viagère » désigne une somme déterminée payable périodiquement à des dates déterminées, la vie durant ou pendant une période définie ou définissable, en exécution d'une obligation d'effectuer des versements en contrepartie d'un capital suffisant et intégralement versé en espèces ou en valeurs appréciables en espèces.

Article 19. Fonction publique

1. a) Les traitements, salaires ou autres rémunérations similaires, autres que les pensions, payés par un État contractant ou l'une de ses subdivisions politiques ou collectivités locales à une personne physique, au titre de services qui ont été fournis à cet État, cette subdivision ou collectivité, ne sont imposables que dans cet État;

   b) Toutefois, ces traitements, salaires ou rémunérations similaires ne sont imposables que dans l'autre État contractant si les services sont exécutés dans cet État et si la personne physique est un résident de cet État qui :

      i) Possède la nationalité de cet État;

      ii) N'est pas devenu un résident à seule fin de fournir les services en question.

2. a) Nonobstant les dispositions du paragraphe 1, les pensions et autres rémunérations similaires payées par un État contractant ou l'une de ses subdivisions politiques ou collectivités locales, soit directement soit par prélèvement sur des fonds qu'ils ont constitués, à une personne physique au titre de services fournis à cet État ou à cette subdivision ou collectivité ne sont imposables que dans cet État;

   b) Toutefois, ces pensions et autres rémunérations similaires ne sont imposables que dans l'autre État contractant si la personne physique est un résident de cet État et en possède la nationalité.

3. Les dispositions des articles 15, 16, 17 et 18 s'appliquent aux traitements, salaires et autres rémunérations et pensions analogues payés au titre de services fournis dans le cadre d'une activité industrielle ou commerciale exercée par un État contractant ou l'une de ses subdivisions politiques ou collectivités locales.

Article 20. Enseignants et étudiants

1. Les sommes qu'un étudiant ou un stagiaire qui est un ressortissant d'un État contractant et qui séjourne dans l'autre État contractant à seule fin d'y poursuivre ses études ou sa formation reçoit pour couvrir ses frais d'entretien, d'études ou de formation ne sont pas imposables dans cet autre État, à condition qu'elles proviennent de sources situées en dehors de cet autre État.

2. De même, les rémunérations perçues par un enseignant ou un chargé de cours qui est un ressortissant d'un État contractant et qui séjourne dans l'autre État contractant principalement pour y mener des activités d'enseignement ou de recherche scientifique pour une période ou des périodes dont la durée totale n'excède pas deux ans, sont exonérées dans cet autre État de tout impôt sur les revenus provenant de ces activités d'enseignement ou de recherche, pour autant que ces rémunérations proviennent de sources situées en dehors de cet autre État.

Article 21. Autres revenus

Les éléments du revenu d'un résident d'un État contractant qui ne sont pas visés aux articles précédents du présent Accord et qui proviennent de l'autre État contractant sont imposables dans cet autre État.

Article 22. Élimination des doubles impositions

1. Conformément aux dispositions et sous réserve des limitations de la législation du Mexique, telle qu'elle peut être amendée de temps à autre sans que ses principes généraux ne s'en trouvent modifiés, le Mexique permet à ses résidents de déduire de l'impôt mexicain :

a) L'impôt turc payé sur les revenus provenant de Turquie, à concurrence d'un montant ne dépassant pas l'impôt dû au Mexique sur ces revenus; et

b) Dans le cas d'une société détenant au moins 10 % du capital d'une société qui est un résident de la Turquie et qui verse des dividendes à la première, l'impôt turc payé par la société distributrice sur les bénéfices qui servent au paiement des dividendes.

2. Sous réserve des dispositions de la législation de la Turquie concernant la possibilité de déduire de l'impôt turc l'impôt dû dans un territoire situé en dehors de la Turquie (telle qu'elle peut être amendée de temps à autre sans que ses principes généraux ne s'en trouvent modifiés), l'impôt mexicain payable en vertu de la législation du Mexique et conformément au présent Accord sur les revenus (y compris les bénéfices et gains en capital) qu'un résident de la Turquie tire de sources situées au Mexique peut être déduit de l'impôt turc prélevé sur ces revenus. Cette déduction ne peut toutefois excéder le montant de l'impôt turc, calculé avant déduction, imputable à ces revenus.

3. Lorsque, conformément à une disposition quelconque du présent Accord, les revenus qu'un résident d'un État contractant reçoit sont exonérés d'impôt dans cet État, cet État peut cependant, pour calculer le montant de l'impôt sur le reste des revenus de ce résident, tenir compte des revenus exemptés.

Article 23. Non-discrimination

1. Les ressortissants d'un État contractant ne sont soumis dans l'autre État contractant à aucune imposition ou obligation correspondante qui est autre ou plus lourde que celles auxquelles sont ou peuvent être assujettis les ressortissants de cet autre État qui se trouvent dans la même situation, notamment au regard de la résidence. La présente disposition s'applique aussi, nonobstant les dispositions de l'article premier, aux personnes qui ne sont pas des résidents d'un État contractant ou des deux États contractants.

2. Sous réserve des dispositions du paragraphe 4 de l'article 10, l'imposition d'un établissement stable qu'une entreprise d'un État contractant a dans l'autre État contractant n'est pas établie d'une façon moins favorable que l'imposition des entreprises de cet autre État qui exercent la même activité.

3. À moins que les dispositions du paragraphe 1 de l'article 9, du paragraphe 7 de l'article 11 ou du paragraphe 6 de l'article 12 ne s'appliquent, les intérêts, redevances et autres montants payés par une entreprise d'un État contractant à un résident de l'autre État contractant sont déductibles, pour le calcul des bénéfices imposables de cette entreprise, dans les mêmes conditions que s'ils avaient été payés à un résident du premier État.

4. Les entreprises d'un État contractant dont le capital est, en tout ou en partie, directement ou indirectement, détenu ou contrôlé par un ou plusieurs résidents de l'autre État contractant ne sont soumises dans le premier État à aucune imposition ou obligation correspondante qui est autre ou plus lourde que celles auxquelles sont ou peuvent être assujetties les autres entreprises similaires du premier État.

5. Ces dispositions ne peuvent être interprétées comme obligeant un État contractant à accorder aux résidents de l'autre État contractant les déductions personnelles, abattements et réductions d'impôt en fonction de la situation ou des charges de famille qu'il accorde à ses propres résidents.

6. Les dispositions du présent article s'appliquent, nonobstant les dispositions de l'article 2, aux impôts de toute nature ou dénomination.

Article 24. Procédure amiable

1. Lorsqu'une personne estime que les mesures prises par l'un des États contractants ou par les deux entraînent ou entraîneront pour elle une imposition non conforme aux dispositions du présent Accord, elle peut, indépendamment des recours prévus par le droit interne de ces États, soumettre son cas à l'autorité compétente de l'État contractant dont elle est un résident ou, si son cas relève du paragraphe 1 de l'article 23, à celle de l'État contractant dont elle possède la nationalité. Le cas doit être soumis dans les trois ans à partir de la première notification de la mesure qui entraîne une imposition non conforme aux dispositions de l'Accord.

2. L'autorité compétente s'efforce, si la réclamation lui paraît fondée et si elle n'est pas elle-même en mesure d'y apporter une solution satisfaisante, de résoudre le cas par voie amiable avec l'autorité compétente de l'autre État contractant, en vue d'éviter une imposition non conforme au présent Accord.

3. Les autorités compétentes des États contractants s'efforcent, par voie d'accord amiable, de résoudre les difficultés ou de dissiper les doutes auxquels peuvent donner lieu l'interprétation

ou l'application du présent Accord. Elles peuvent aussi se concerter en vue d'éliminer les doubles impositions dans les cas non prévus par l'Accord.

4. Les autorités compétentes des États contractants peuvent communiquer directement entre elles en vue de parvenir à un règlement au sens des paragraphes précédents.

Article 25. Échange de renseignements

1. Les autorités compétentes des États contractants échangent les renseignements vraisemblablement pertinents pour appliquer les dispositions du présent Accord ou celles de la législation interne relative aux impôts de toute nature ou dénomination prélevés pour le compte des États contractants, de leurs subdivisions politiques ou de leurs collectivités locales, à condition que l'imposition qu'elle prévoit ne soit pas contraire au présent Accord. L'échange de renseignements n'est pas restreint par les articles premier et 2.

2. Les renseignements reçus en vertu du paragraphe 1 par un État contractant sont tenus secrets de la même manière que les renseignements obtenus en application de la législation interne de cet État et ne sont communiqués qu'aux personnes ou autorités (y compris les tribunaux et organes administratifs) concernées par l'établissement ou le recouvrement des impôts mentionnés au paragraphe 1, par les procédures ou poursuites concernant ces impôts, par les décisions sur les recours relatifs à ces impôts ou par la supervision de ce qui précède. Ces personnes ou autorités ne peuvent utiliser ces renseignements qu'à ces fins, mais peuvent faire état de ces renseignements au cours d'audiences publiques de tribunaux ou dans des jugements.

3. Les dispositions des paragraphes 1 et 2 ne peuvent en aucun cas être interprétées comme imposant à un État contractant l'obligation :

a) De prendre des mesures administratives dérogeant à sa législation et à sa pratique administrative ou à celles de l'autre État contractant;

b) De fournir des renseignements qui ne pourraient être obtenus sur la base de sa législation ou dans le cadre de sa pratique administrative normale ou de celles de l'autre État contractant;

c) De fournir des renseignements qui révéleraient un secret commercial, industriel ou professionnel, un procédé commercial ou des renseignements dont la communication serait contraire à l'ordre public.

4. Si des renseignements sont demandés par un État contractant conformément au présent article, l'autre État contractant utilise ses mesures de collecte de renseignements pour obtenir les renseignements demandés quand bien même il n'en aurait pas besoin à ses propres fins fiscales. L'obligation contenue dans la phrase précédente est subordonnée aux limites prévues au paragraphe 3, mais en aucun cas ces limitations ne doivent être interprétées comme autorisant un État contractant à refuser de communiquer des renseignements pour la seule raison qu'il ne détient aucun intérêt national dans de tels renseignements.

5. Les dispositions du paragraphe 3 ne peuvent en aucun cas être interprétées comme autorisant un État contractant à refuser de communiquer des renseignements pour la seule raison que ceux-ci sont détenus par une banque, une autre institution financière, un mandataire ou une personne agissant en qualité d'agent ou à titre fiduciaire, ou parce que cela concerne les intérêts fonciers d'une personne.

Article 26. Assistance en matière de recouvrement des impôts

1. Les États contractants se prêtent mutuellement assistance pour le recouvrement de leurs créances fiscales. Cette assistance n'est pas limitée par les articles premier et 2. Les autorités compétentes des États contractants peuvent régler d'un commun accord les modalités d'application du présent article.

2. L'expression « créance fiscale » employée dans le présent article désigne une somme due au titre des impôts de toute nature ou dénomination perçus pour le compte des États contractants, de leurs subdivisions politiques ou de leurs collectivités locales, dans la mesure où l'imposition ainsi prévue n'est pas contraire au présent Accord ou à tout autre instrument auquel les États contractants sont parties, ainsi que les intérêts, pénalités administratives et frais de recouvrement ou de gestion afférents à ce montant.

3. Lorsqu'une créance fiscale d'un État contractant qui est recouvrable en vertu des lois de cet État est due par une personne qui, à cette date, ne peut, en vertu de ces lois, empêcher son recouvrement, cette créance fiscale est, à la demande des autorités compétentes de cet État, acceptée en vue de son recouvrement par les autorités compétentes de l'autre État contractant. Cette créance fiscale est recouvrée par cet autre État conformément aux dispositions de sa législation applicable en matière de recouvrement de ses propres impôts comme si la créance en question était une créance fiscale de cet autre État.

4. Lorsqu'une créance fiscale d'un État contractant est une créance à l'égard de laquelle cet État peut, en vertu de sa législation, prendre des mesures conservatoires pour assurer son recouvrement, cette créance doit, à la demande des autorités compétentes de cet État, être acceptée aux fins d'adoption de mesures conservatoires par les autorités compétentes de l'autre État contractant. Cet autre État doit prendre des mesures conservatoires à l'égard de cette créance fiscale conformément aux dispositions de sa législation comme s'il s'agissait d'une créance fiscale de cet autre État même si, au moment où ces mesures sont appliquées, la créance fiscale n'est pas recouvrable dans le premier État ou est due par une personne qui a le droit d'empêcher son recouvrement.

5. Nonobstant les dispositions des paragraphes 3 et 4, les délais de prescription et l'ordre de priorité applicables, en vertu de la législation d'un État contractant, à une créance fiscale en raison de sa nature en tant que telle ne s'appliquent pas à une créance fiscale acceptée par cet État aux fins du paragraphe 3 ou 4. En outre, une créance fiscale acceptée par un État contractant aux fins du paragraphe 3 ou 4 ne peut se voir appliquer aucune priorité dans cet État en vertu de la législation de l'autre État contractant.

6. Les procédures concernant l'existence, la validité ou le montant d'une créance fiscale d'un État contractant ne sont pas soumises aux tribunaux ou organismes administratifs de l'autre État contractant.

7. Quand, à tout moment après qu'une demande a été formulée par un État contractant en vertu du paragraphe 3 ou 4 et avant que l'autre État contractant ait recouvré et transmis le montant de la créance fiscale en question au premier État, cette créance fiscale cesse d'être :

a) Dans le cas d'une demande présentée en vertu du paragraphe 3, une créance fiscale du premier État qui est recouvrable en vertu des lois de cet État et est due par une personne qui, à ce moment, ne peut, en vertu des lois de cet État, empêcher son recouvrement; ou

b) Dans le cas d'une demande présentée en vertu du paragraphe 4, une créance fiscale du premier État à l'égard de laquelle cet État peut, en vertu de sa législation, prendre des mesures conservatoires pour assurer son recouvrement;

Les autorités compétentes du premier État notifient promptement ce fait aux autorités compétentes de l'autre État et le premier État, au choix de l'autre État, suspend ou retire sa demande.

8. Les dispositions du présent article ne peuvent en aucun cas être interprétées comme imposant à un État contractant l'obligation :

a) De prendre des mesures administratives dérogeant à sa législation et à sa pratique administrative ou à celles de l'autre État contractant;

b) De prendre des mesures qui seraient contraires à l'ordre public;

c) De prêter assistance si l'autre État contractant n'a pas pris toutes les mesures raisonnables de recouvrement ou de conservation, selon le cas, qui sont disponibles en vertu de sa législation ou de sa pratique administrative;

d) De prêter assistance dans les cas où la charge administrative qui en résulte pour cet État est nettement disproportionnée par rapport aux avantages que peut en tirer l'autre État contractant.

Article 27. Membres de missions diplomatiques et de postes consulaires

Aucune disposition du présent Accord ne porte atteinte aux privilèges fiscaux dont bénéficient les membres des missions diplomatiques ou des postes consulaires en vertu soit des règles générales du droit international soit des dispositions d'accords particuliers.

Article 28. Entrée en vigueur

Les États contractants se notifient mutuellement, par la voie diplomatique, l'accomplissement des procédures requises par leur législation pour l'entrée en vigueur du présent Accord. Le présent Accord entre en vigueur 30 jours après la date de la dernière de ces notifications, et ses dispositions s'appliquent aux impôts afférents à tout exercice fiscal commençant le 1er janvier, ou après le 1er janvier, de l'année suivant celle de l'entrée en vigueur du présent Accord.

Article 29. Dénonciation

Le présent Accord demeure en vigueur jusqu'à ce qu'il soit dénoncé par un État contractant. Chaque État contractant peut le dénoncer moyennant un préavis de dénonciation adressé par la voie diplomatique au moins six mois avant la fin de toute année civile, et au moins cinq ans après la date d'entrée en vigueur de l'Accord. Dans ce cas, le présent Accord cesse de produire ses effets sur les impôts relatifs à tout exercice fiscal commençant le 1er janvier, ou après le 1er janvier, de l'année suivant celle au cours de laquelle le préavis est donné.

EN FOI DE QUOI, les soussignés, à ce dûment autorisés, ont signé le présent Accord.

FAIT à Ankara, le 17 décembre 2013, en double exemplaire, en langues espagnole, turque et anglaise, les trois textes faisant également foi. En cas de divergence, le texte anglais prévaut.

Pour le Gouvernement des États-Unis du Mexique :
JOSÉ ANTONIO MEADE KURIBREÑA
Ministre des affaires étrangères

Pour le Gouvernement de la République Turque :
MEHMET ŞIMSEK
Ministre des finances

PROTOCOLE

À la signature de l'Accord entre le Gouvernement des États-Unis du Mexique et le Gouvernement de la République turque tendant à éviter les doubles impositions et à prévenir l'évasion fiscale en matière d'impôts sur le revenu, les soussignés sont convenus des dispositions ci-après, lesquelles font partie intégrante de l'Accord :

1. En ce qui concerne l'article 5

Il est entendu que, aux fins du paragraphe 7, une entreprise n'est pas considérée comme ayant un établissement stable dans un État contractant du seul fait qu'elle y exerce une activité par l'entremise d'un courtier, d'un commissionnaire général ou de tout autre agent indépendant, pour autant que ces personnes ne soient pas, dans leurs relations commerciales ou financières avec l'entreprise, liées par des conditions convenues ou imposées qui diffèrent de celles qui seraient généralement convenues par des agents indépendants.

2. En ce qui concerne l'article 6

Il est entendu que l'expression « biens immobiliers » désigne également le matériel de pisciculture.

3. En ce qui concerne le paragraphe 1 de l'article 7

Il est entendu que si une entreprise d'un État contractant a un établissement stable dans l'autre État contractant, où elle exerce des activités, ses bénéfices sont imposables dans cet autre État contractant, mais uniquement la fraction de ces bénéfices qui est imputable à la vente, dans cet autre État contractant, de biens ou marchandises de nature identique ou similaire à des biens ou marchandises vendus par l'intermédiaire de cet établissement stable.

Toutefois, les bénéfices tirés des ventes décrites ci-dessus ne sont pas imposables dans cet autre État contractant si l'entreprise démontre que ces ventes ont été effectuées pour des raisons autres que l'obtention d'un avantage au titre du présent Accord.

4. En ce qui concerne le paragraphe 3 de l'article 7

Il est entendu qu'il ne peut être déduit aucune somme versée, le cas échéant (à d'autres titres que le remboursement de frais réels), par l'établissement stable au siège social de l'entreprise ou à l'un quelconque de ses bureaux, à titre de redevances, honoraires ou autres paiements similaires, pour l'utilisation de brevets ou d'autres droits, ou à titre de commission, pour tout service fourni ou toute activité de gestion ou, sauf dans le cas d'une entreprise bancaire, à titre d'intérêt sur des sommes prêtées à l'établissement stable. De même, il n'est pas tenu compte dans le calcul des bénéfices d'un établissement stable des sommes (autres que le remboursement de frais réels) portées par l'établissement stable au débit du siège social de l'entreprise ou de l'un quelconque de ses autres bureaux, à titre de redevances, honoraires ou autres paiements similaires, pour l'utilisation de brevets ou d'autres droits, ou à titre de commission pour tout service fourni ou toute activité de gestion ou, sauf dans le cas d'une entreprise bancaire, à titre d'intérêts sur des sommes prêtées au siège social de l'entreprise ou à l'un quelconque de ses autres bureaux.

5. En ce qui concerne l'article 8

Il est entendu que les bénéfices visés au paragraphe 1 de l'article 8 n'incluent pas les bénéfices provenant de l'utilisation de moyens de transport routiers intérieurs.

6. En ce qui concerne l'article 11

Il est entendu que le terme « intérêts » ne désigne pas les éléments du revenu considérés comme des dividendes au sens des dispositions du paragraphe 3 de l'article 10.

Il est entendu qu'en cas de modification des institutions mentionnées aux alinéas c) et d), par voie de fusion, d'acquisition ou de toute opération similaire visant à créer une nouvelle institution, les autorités compétentes se consulteront pour définir les modalités d'application de l'Accord aux institutions mentionnées, dans la mesure où elles restent exclusivement détenues par le Gouvernement.

7. En ce qui concerne les articles 10, 11, 12 et 13

Il est entendu qu'aux fins des articles 10, 11, 12 et 13 de l'Accord, chacun des États contractants conserve le droit d'imposer, conformément à sa législation interne, tous revenus lorsqu'une double exonération découle d'une classification divergente des revenus en question.

8. En ce qui concerne l'article 12

Il est entendu que, nonobstant les dispositions de l'article 13, le terme « redevances » désigne également les paiements provenant de l'aliénation de droits ou biens dépendant de la productivité, de l'utilisation ou de la cession desdits droits ou biens.

9. En ce qui concerne l'article 14

Il est entendu que lorsqu'une personne physique ou une entreprise d'un État contractant est imposable dans l'autre État contractant en application du paragraphe 1 ou 2 de l'article 14, cette personne physique ou cette entreprise peut choisir d'être imposée dans cet autre État pour les revenus en question, conformément aux dispositions de l'article 7 du présent Accord, comme si ces revenus étaient imputables à un établissement stable de l'entreprise situé dans cet autre État. Ce choix est sans incidence sur le droit de cet autre État de retenir à la source un impôt sur ces revenus.

10. En ce qui concerne l'article 24

Il est entendu que nonobstant tout autre traité auquel les États contractants sont ou peuvent devenir parties, tout différend relatif à une mesure prise par un État contractant concernant un impôt visé à l'article 2 ou, en cas de non-discrimination, toute mesure fiscale prise par un État contractant, y compris tout différend quant à savoir si le présent Accord s'applique, est réglé exclusivement en vertu du présent, sauf si les autorités compétentes des États contractants en conviennent autrement.

Dans le cas de la Turquie, il est entendu qu'en ce qui concerne le paragraphe 2, le contribuable doit demander le remboursement résultant d'un tel accord amiable dans un délai d'un an à compter de la notification du résultat de l'accord amiable par l'administration fiscale.

11. En général

Il est entendu que les dispositions du présent Accord n'empêchent pas un État contractant d'appliquer ses dispositions relatives aux sous-capitalisations et aux sociétés étrangères contrôlées (dans le cas du Mexique, les régimes fiscaux préférentiels).

Il est entendu qu'aux fins de la fiscalité mexicaine, la base fixe sera traitée conformément aux principes qui s'appliquent aux établissements stables.

EN FOI DE QUOI, les soussignés, à ce dûment autorisés, ont signé le présent Protocole.

FAIT à Ankara, le 17 décembre 2013, en double exemplaire en langues espagnole, turque et anglaise, les trois textes faisant également foi. En cas de divergence, le texte anglais prévaut.

Pour le Gouvernement des États-Unis du Mexique :

JOSÉ ANTONIO MEADE KURIBREÑA
Ministre des affaires étrangères

Pour le Gouvernement de la République turque :

MEHMET ŞIMSEK
Ministre des finances